CW01238078

Dear Suzanne,
Merry Christmas 2019
Lots of Love,
Abi, Adi' & Hattie
xxx

Something for Everyone

LOUISE FULTON KEATS

Something for Everyone

FAMILY MEALS FOR BABY, TODDLER AND BEYOND

hardie grant books
MELBOURNE · LONDON

ACKNOWLEDGEMENTS

This book would never have come to life without the many helping hands of my wonderful family and friends.

Thank you from the bottom of my heart to Suzanne Gibbs and Steve Lewis, who have both been by my side throughout this project, helping at photo shoots and providing unwavering support. I'd have been lost without you.

To Claire and Hughie Dunne and their perfect baby, Davin, who appears throughout this book. Thank you so much for your boundless patience and generosity; your Davin is a total joy.

To Ruth Maddigan and Bob Dwyer for the use of their stunning Highlands home for our location shoot and for their extraordinary warmth and care. We feel very blessed to have you as neighbours.

To the bunny A-team and the best in the business: Ben Dearnley, Michelle Noerianto and Kerrie Ray. Thank you for yet again delivering the most exceptionally beautiful photographs while keeping it such fun. Time with the three of you is always a treasure.

My heartfelt thanks to all the team at Hardie Grant for this wonderful opportunity: Paul McNally, Lucy Heaver, Jacqueline Blanchard and Megan Ellis, as well as the stunning book design from Arielle Gamble. I'm ever-so grateful for all of your varied and extraordinary talents and your unwavering dedication to this project. Paul and Lucy, your ongoing support means the world.

Finally to the best family a girl could have: John, Harry, Mum, Dad, Grandma, Kate and Ben. A million thank yous for your patience and encouragement. I love you to bits.

Contents

Introduction **7**
Using this book **10**
Cooking for your family **12**
Breakfast **34**
Snacks and lunch **76**
Dinner **120**
Desserts and baking **182**

Index **228**

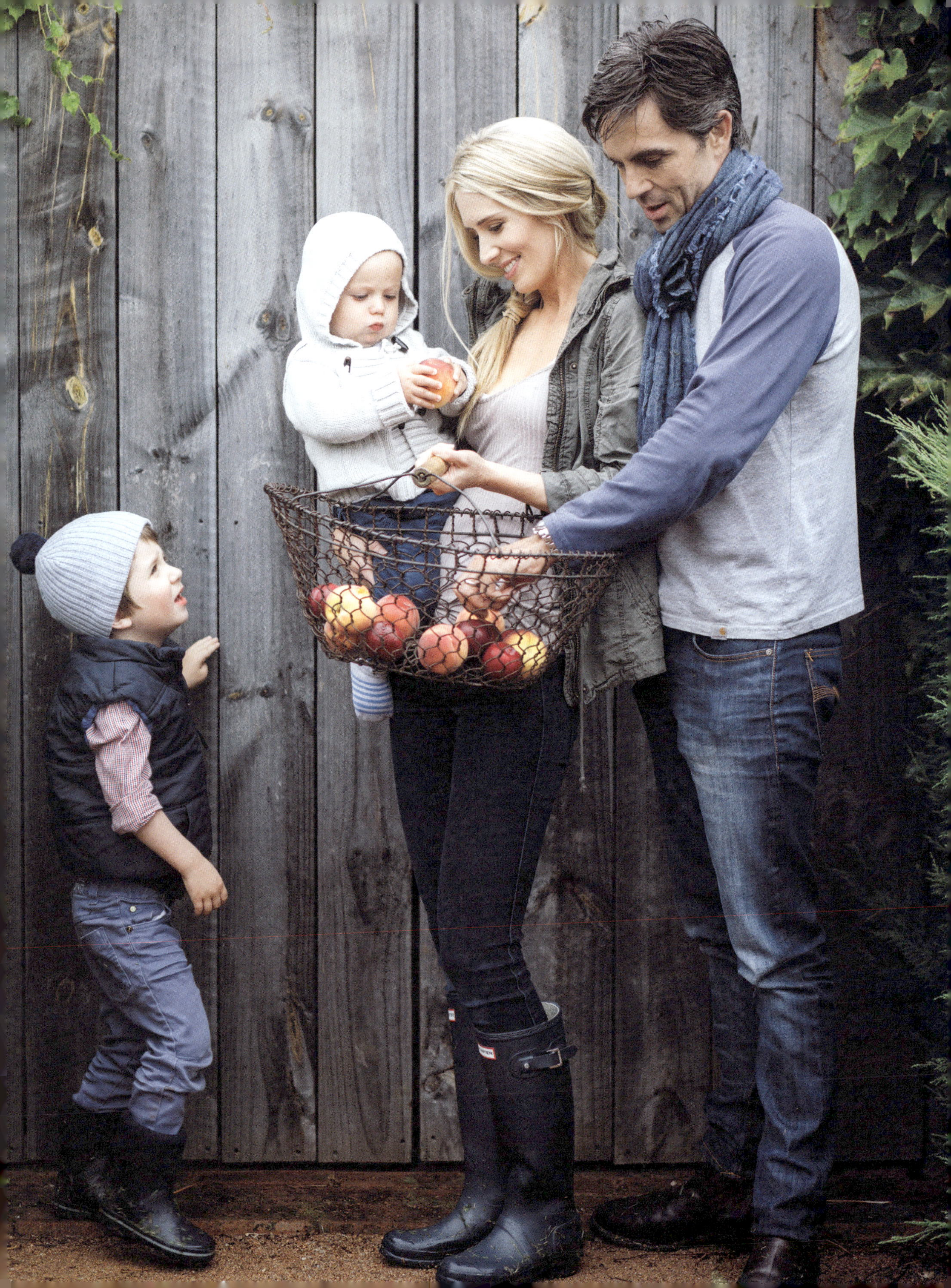

Introduction

When I was a child, my parents were pretty firm about sticking to a routine where as a family we would sit down together each night, share a meal and chat about our day. I remember occasionally thinking how boring that was, at least compared with some other children I knew who were lucky enough to have dinner in front of the television, often eating at a different time from their parents. Yet, fundamentally, I also knew that it was a good thing to do, that it was valuable for all of us, that I was fortunate to come from a family who set the table and made the effort; I just didn't know why.

As a food and nutrition writer, understanding the 'why' is now part of my work. The subject of family meals comes up time and again across a range of research subjects – from baby's taste preferences to teenage alcohol abuse – and, repeatedly, the same conclusion is reached: family meals produce extraordinary outcomes for kids. Not only do children who sit down with their parents eat more nutritious foods, they're also more likely to perform well at school, and are less likely to end up with an eating disorder or a drug or alcohol problem. Best of all, as teenagers, they're more likely to say that their parents really know what's going on in their lives.

There are huge benefits to be gained from including your child in family mealtimes from the outset, as soon as she begins eating solids. For a start, she'll be seeing food in its whole form, instead of just as a purée. This will help build her familiarity with different ingredients and reduce her chances of being a fussy eater down the track. It will also help her develop a taste for your home cooking. Plus, it spares you from the bane of every busy parent's life – having to prepare two different dinners each night.

My great hope is that this book might help more families sit down together for a meal and share the same foods. When I think of how this simple act can profoundly affect the health and happiness of an entire generation, it seems to me that it's a goal worth prioritising.

Having said that, I'm also conscious of the food we provide our children being yet another source of comparison in the super-competitive world of parenting, where so many of us feel like we're always falling short. I confess I often feel the pressure of trying to recreate the near-perfect home environment that I grew up in. I can now see just how hard my parents had to work to provide it. So, although there are unquestionable benefits arising from giving your children nourishing, home-cooked meals, and sitting down at the table with them to eat, I don't believe it should come at the cost of your enjoyment of parenthood. So if what gets you through the week is your Saturday movie night with a pizza and a glass of wine, keep it up!

My overarching philosophy is that cooking for your children should be simple and relaxed. As a working mum, I certainly don't have time to make complex dishes. I hope this book gives you the confidence to navigate those early years of feeding your children, without feeling like you have to cook special, individual meals for every member of the family. Thankfully, the best thing for them is also the best for you – sharing one meal.

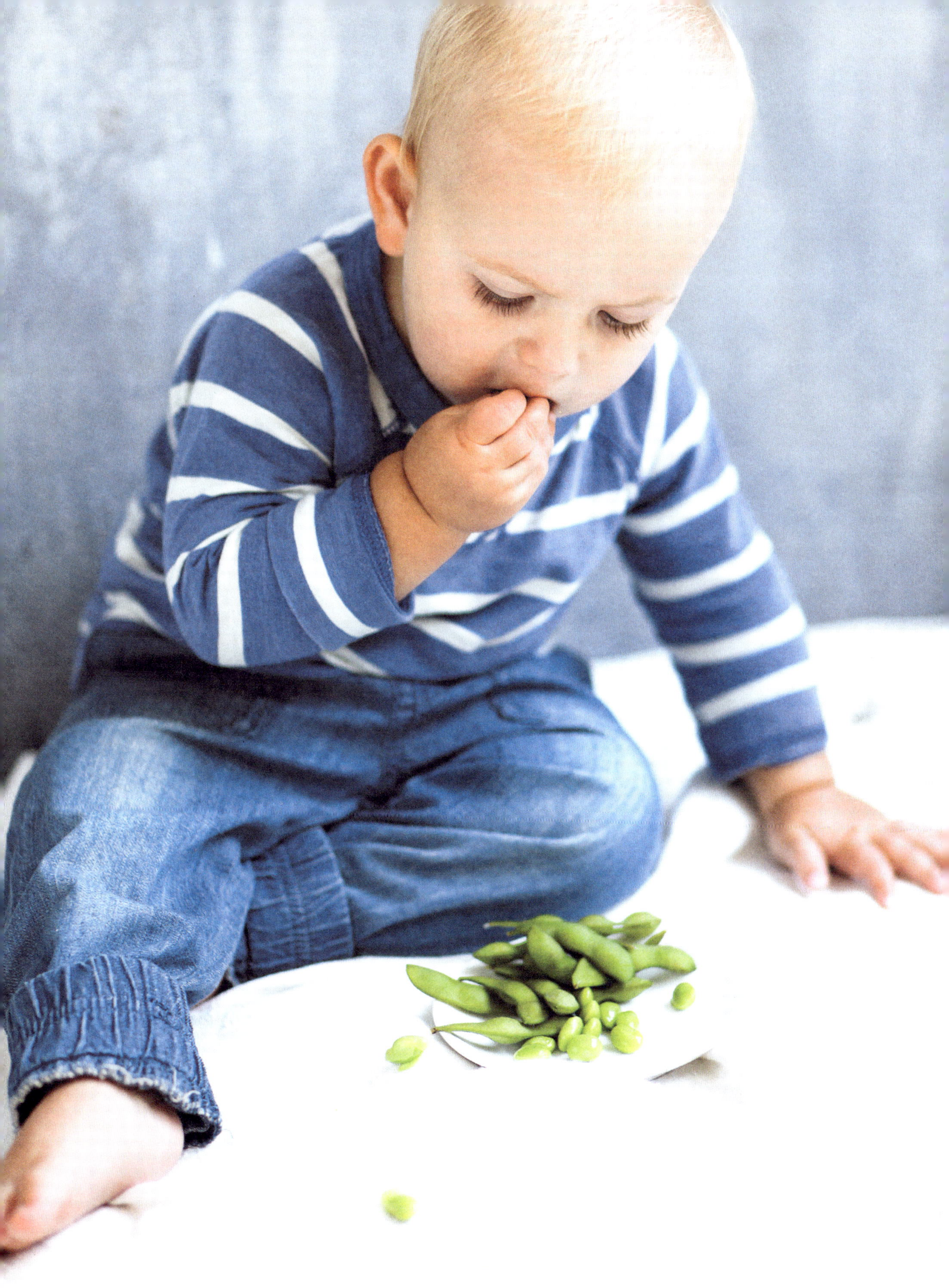

Using this book

BABY AND TODDLER RECIPE ADAPTATIONS

Unless otherwise noted, all of the recipes in this book are suitable for babies aged 6 months and older. Each recipe provides adaptations for both younger babies (6–9 months as a guide) and older babies (10–12 months as a guide), as well as toddlers (1–4 years as a guide).

Where a recipe adaptation refers to 'your baby's milk', you may use either expressed breast milk or formula milk. It is fine to use a little cow's milk in cooking from time to time, however it is not as nutrient-dense as your baby's drinking milk, and it definitely shouldn't be served as a drink in your baby's first year.

The key thing to remember when cooking for babies is to take care not to use any ingredients that aren't suitable for them, such as honey, raw eggs, salt and any choking hazards. There is a full list of 'Food and Drinks to Avoid' on page 18, which you should read carefully if you are preparing food for a young child.

For a guide to starting your baby on solids and adapting family meals, see pages 16–24.

SERVING SIZES

Because babies, toddlers and older children eat such widely varying amounts, the serving sizes given in this book are for adults. In the case of baby purées, it's quite useful to have an adult-sized serving for your baby, because you can set aside one portion and then freeze the remainder in separate portions for later meals. In the case of your toddler or older child, you may like to adjust the quantities according to her usual appetite.

SEASONINGS

As a general rule, the recipes in this book don't include salt and pepper. Added salt is bad news for younger children in particular – their less mature kidneys can't cope. Furthermore, too much can give them a taste preference for salty foods, which can have long-term health implications. Pepper is great nutritionally, but many children find it too spicy. However, you might wish to add a little, gradually increasing the amount, to help your child develop a liking for it. After setting aside your child's serving, by all means season your food as you normally would (although most adults would benefit from a lower-salt diet too).

RECIPE SYMBOLS KEY

- nut free (may contain sesame)
- gluten free
- dairy free
- egg free
- sesame free (may contain nuts)
- suitable for freezing

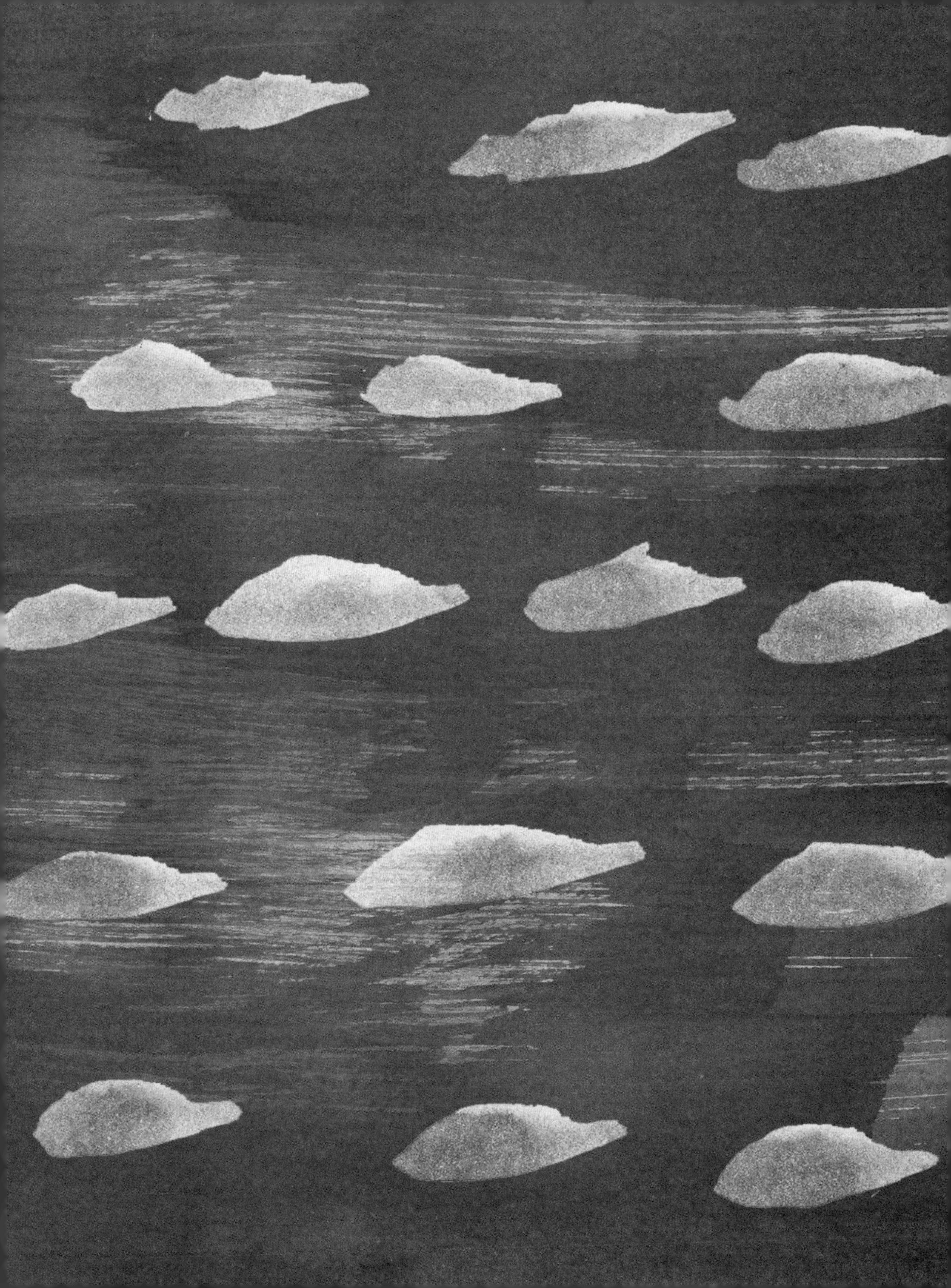

Cooking for your Family

FAMILY MEALS: WHY THEY MATTER

You've probably heard before that it's a good idea to sit down as a family each evening and eat dinner together, sharing the same foods. But why is that?

As a starting point, there's the obvious benefit of not having to shop for and cook two separate meals each night. After all, the average mum with school-age children, including those who work full-time, spends over an hour a day on family meals – and that doesn't even include the grocery shopping! For the average dad, the figure is closer to half an hour a day.

Beyond the fact that it takes up a huge proportion of our time, there are a whole range of benefits for your child that have considerable implications for her physical and emotional wellbeing. Let's take a look at them.

A more nutritious diet

Quite simply, kids who eat the same food as their parents eat better than kids who don't. Studies from around the world have found that children who eat more frequent family meals consume more key nutrients, vegetables, fruit, fibre and protein, and eat fewer processed foods, sweets and soft drinks. What's more, there's evidence that the meal patterns and food choices set in childhood persist into the adult years, so the effect continues for years to come. There's also evidence that children who eat frequent family meals are less likely to be overweight or obese, which is not surprising given their healthier diet.

Interestingly, a recent UK study found that it was this particular aspect of family meals – children eating the same foods as their parents – that was the most strongly associated with better diets. While sitting together and talking brings a range of social benefits (discussed below), nutritionally what matters is that children are eating adult food, not a different 'kids meal'. The problem with meals designed specifically for children is that they're usually of inferior nutritional value. So, on those nights – and we all have them – that sitting down together isn't feasible, it's useful to know that preparing one meal is still worthwhile, even when it's served at different times.

Of course, many parents face a constant struggle with getting their children to eat the same foods as they're eating. It's one reason the best approach is to start as young as possible. If children have only ever known one meal shared by the family, they're less likely to resist it later on. As discussed on pages 24–30, when you do get into the trying toddler years and beyond, the key is consistency and persistence – calmly persevere with offering varied foods even when they've been rejected before, and keep less-healthy options out of your house.

Developing taste preferences

Children are born with innate taste preferences – such as an innate preference for sweet and an innate dislike for bitter. But despite these early preferences, children develop in vastly different ways according to their food environment, which is largely shaped by their parents. To start, a baby's taste preferences form according to what she tastes in the womb and in breastmilk, which makes her mum's diet a crucial influence on her own likes and dislikes. But once a child starts solids, her taste preferences develop according to the food that's put on her plate.

Interestingly, scientists have done quite a bit of research into children's food preferences and they believe that children's early taste experiences – during their first year of life – can shape their taste preferences for years to come. For example, one study found that children who were given a sour-tasting hydrolysate formula milk in their first year were significantly more likely to prefer sour-flavoured apple juice at 4–5 years old. Although the theory is yet to be tested extensively, it appears that the first months of life may constitute a critical 'sensitive window' for flavour learning, potentially with lifelong consequences.

With this in mind, introducing solids as part of family meals provides the perfect opportunity to expose your child to as many different flavours as possible. By bringing your baby to the family table and simply letting her share your home-cooked meal – whether in puréed form, or as finger foods (see pages 21–22 for a general guide on how to adapt family meals for babies) – you'll help her to develop a liking for a wide range of ingredients and a taste for your home cooking. Plus, she'll also have all the fun that comes with getting stuck into a proper meal – squishing some avocado, diving into some noodles – undoubtedly more wondrous than any toy you could buy. Compare that with a baby who only experiences packaged baby food in her first year, with such limited flavour and texture experiences, it's no wonder that approach seems so often to produce the pickiest of eaters.

Mental health and academic performance
Once children are a bit older, and particularly during their pre-teen and teenage years, clear evidence emerges of the positive impact of family meals on their psychological wellbeing. A number of studies have found that family meals are associated with fewer depressive symptoms, fewer suicidal thoughts or attempts, better emotional wellbeing, greater life satisfaction and higher academic performance. Interestingly, this link has been found even after adjusting for demographic factors, such as wealth and education. In other words, family meals seem to offer protection against mental health problems in their own right, despite the characteristics of the particular family.

In one US study, girls who had more than seven family meals per week were almost half as likely to have attempted suicide as girls who ate no family meals. In another US study, teens who had frequent family meals were twice as likely to report having high self-esteem, a commitment to learning, being engaged at school and resisting negative peer pressure than those eating few or no family dinners.

While the psychological impact of family meals is clearest in older children, which is where most of the research has been focused to date, a recent US study found that being involved in family dinners was linked with better social-emotional health even in pre-school aged children.

Eating disorders

Numerous studies have also found that family meals help to protect children against developing an eating disorder, particularly where the atmosphere at mealtimes is positive. For example, one US study found that girls who had only one to two family meals per week were more than twice as likely to engage in extreme weight control behaviour as girls who had three to four family meals per week. Another US study similarly found that teens who had frequent family meals were half as likely to engage in binge or purge eating as those who had few or no family meals each week.

Drug and alcohol use

Family meals have been a major research focus of the US National Center on Addiction and Substance Abuse. According to the Center, over their years of examining how to prevent drug and alcohol abuse, parental engagement at the dinner table has emerged as 'one of the most potent tools to help parents raise healthy, drug-free children'. In a recent study, they found that, compared to teens who have dinner with their parents five to seven times a week, teens who have fewer than three family dinners per week are three-and-a-half times more likely to say it's okay for teens their age to get drunk and almost three times more likely to say it's okay for teens their age to use marijuana. Similar links have been found elsewhere, with another US study finding that teens who had frequent family meals were half as likely to report using alcohol, tobacco and illicit drugs as those who had few or no family meals each week.

Family cohesion

Not surprisingly, the research into family meals has also revealed that families who regularly eat together are more likely to be a cohesive, supportive unit. For example, the US National Center on Addiction and Substance Abuse has found that, compared with teenagers who eat few family dinners per week, teens who have frequent family meals are five times less likely to say their parents know 'very little or nothing at all' about what's really going on in their lives. Another US study has revealed that teenagers who eat frequent family dinners are three times more likely to report having family support, positive family communication and parental involvement in school, than those who eat one or fewer family dinners per week.

Aside from all these statistics, family meals are a precious time to step away from the computer, put down the phone, turn off the television and talk to one another. It can be really hard to put that into practice in the everyday craziness of our lives (don't I know it!). But for those nights you can manage it, rest assured that over the years the investment will pay off.

BABY AND FAMILY MEALS

Making the transition from milk feeds to solid foods can be a daunting time for many parents. There seem to be so many rules! If you would like a comprehensive guide to feeding your baby – including meal planners and recipes for different stages – you can find it in my book *Cooking For Your Baby and Toddler*. Below is an overview of the key points you need to know.

Best age to start solids

The best age to start solids is a controversial subject and official advice has changed over the years. However, based on the latest research, 'around 6 months' is now widely recommended as the ideal age, including in Australia, New Zealand, the UK and the US.

Although the phrase 'around 6 months' is typically not defined, it's often interpreted in practice to mean between 22 and 26 weeks, which equates to between 5 and 6 months.

You sometimes hear certain groups, including allergy associations, argue that solids should ideally be introduced before this time – as early as 4 months – but there are good reasons not to be in a rush to begin. For a start, breastmilk is the ultimate food for your baby, and starting solids too early can interfere with her milk supply. Furthermore, young babies have immature kidneys and digestive systems that simply can't cope with much solid food. By around 6 months, their bodies are more developed for processing solids.

Conversely, introducing solids much later than 6 months is also problematic. Babies' iron levels start to deplete at this time and they need iron-rich foods to restore them. Furthermore, there is some evidence that delaying solids may increase the risk of food allergy. Solids are also needed at around 6 months for the optimal development of certain motor skills, such as chewing.

When to introduce certain foods

The old rules that stated you should introduce solids in a particular order – such as rice cereal on Day One, pumpkin purée on Day Two, avocado on Day Three and so on – are no longer based on current science. Thank goodness for that, because they certainly made starting solids a high-maintenance, anxiety-inducing task!

The latest thinking is:

- When you start your baby on solids at around 6 months, you don't need to delay introducing any food. In fact, delaying common allergens, such as egg, appears to increase the chances of your baby being allergic.
- With the important exception of certain contraband items – listed on page 18 – you can give your baby any food you like from the beginning, preferably plenty of iron-rich foods.
- You don't need to worry about introducing foods in a particular order. It doesn't matter if you give rice cereal first, then sweet potato, then apple. The idea that you have to follow a strict order is nonsense.
- You don't need to wait 3–5 days before introducing a new food. Although this will help you identify the cause if your child has an allergic reaction, the majority of children won't have a reaction and the waiting game is a nuisance. Giving new foods in quick succession does not increase your child's allergy risk.

Food and drinks to avoid

Although the rules around introducing potential allergens have relaxed, there are still some foods you shouldn't give your baby, as set out in the table on page 18. The main culprits are cow's milk as a drink

Something for everyone

Food and drinks to avoid

Food / Drink to avoid	Until which age?	Reason
Honey	12 months	Small risk of infant botulism.
Foods high in added sugar	12 months, but preferably as long as possible	Can displace nutrient-dense foods, cause dental damage and create a stronger taste preference for sweet foods.
Foods high in added salt/sodium	12 months, but preferably as long as possible	Places too much strain on babies' developing kidneys, and can create a stronger taste preference for salty foods.
Cow's milk as a drink	12 months	Can be a major contributor to iron deficiency anaemia. Small amounts used in cooking are fine.
Goat's milk, sheep's milk and almond milk as drinks	2 years	Nutritionally incomplete, can be a contributor to iron deficiency anaemia. Breastmilk, formula milk or – after baby's first birthday – pasteurised cow's milk are preferred milk drinks. Soy, rice and oat milk can be given after your baby's first birthday, so long as they are full-fat, fortified varieties.
Sweet drinks, including soft drinks and juices	12 months, but preferably as long as possible	Displaces nutrient-dense foods and milk, plus they create a risk of dental damage and obesity.
Raw/under-cooked eggs (including raw egg products like homemade mayonnaise)	2 years	Risk of salmonella poisoning. You should cook eggs until the whites have completely set and the yolks have started to thicken.
Reduced-fat or skim dairy foods	2 years or older	Dietary fat derived from full-fat dairy foods is an important source of energy for growing infants, plus full-fat products sometimes contain more nutrients than skim products.
Hard, small/round foods (such as whole grapes, popcorn and whole nuts)	around 4 years	Risk of choking.
Uncooked fermented meats (such as salami)	5 years	Higher risk of food poisoning ('heat-treated' or 'cooked' products are safe – check the label).
Raw sprouts (such as alfalfa, radish and mung bean sprouts)	5 years	Higher risk of food poisoning.
Artificial sweeteners	for as long as possible	There is very little data about the safety or risk of artificial sweeteners when consumed by infants and toddlers.
Tea, coffee and caffeinated soft drinks	for as long as possible	High caffeine content overstimulates a child's nervous system and the tannins in tea bind with iron and other minerals, reducing absorption and contributing to iron deficiency.

(babies should be having breastmilk or formula milk instead) and foods or drinks with added salt or sugar.

As a general rule, if you're giving your baby home-cooked foods made from fresh ingredients without sugar or salt, you're probably doing the right thing. But, it's definitely worth being familiar with this list to make sure you're aware of the potential risks.

Getting the texture right

To help your baby develop proper chewing skills, it's important to adjust the texture of her food over the passing months. When your baby first starts solids, you will need to keep her purées very smooth, with a semi-liquid consistency similar to runny custard. Mix as much liquid (water or your baby's milk – you can use expressed breastmilk or formula) through your purées as you need to achieve this texture. You should also avoid any big lumps as they're a bit much for a young baby to cope with.

As your baby gets the hang of eating, start to move to lumpier purées and mashes, which are very important for learning to chew. If she kicks up a fuss, you can make the transition more gradual, but make sure you're also giving her plenty of finger food for her chewing practice. Also, you may find your baby is more comfortable with a thicker, overall lumpier purée, than a thin purée with the occasional big lump. For those of you trying 'baby-led weaning' (see page 24) you will skip purées and begin with finger foods from the time of starting solids.

Finger foods

If your baby can sit upright with little or no support, there's no reason you can't start offering her finger foods from the age of 6 months, and certainly by 8 or 9 months.

Don't expect her to start munching and swallowing finger foods from the start. To begin with, they're just a fantastic plaything, undoubtedly more amazing than any toy you could give her. But as the weeks progress, you will notice your baby start to get a good handle on them, get them to her own mouth, have a little gummy chew and – finally – swallow.

When choosing finger foods, go for larger shapes that your baby is able to grasp, and avoid any choking hazards, such as nuts, whole grapes, popcorn and carrot sticks. Make sure that your baby is sitting

---

> **Watching out for food allergies**
>
> *Monitor your baby closely when you introduce the following nine foods, which cause over 90 per cent of food allergies: **cow's milk**, **egg**, **fish**, **shellfish**, **peanuts**, **sesame**, **wheat**, **soy** and **tree nuts** (such as almonds, cashews and walnuts). If your baby has an allergy to one of these, you'll probably know about it within a few hours of her eating it, possibly even a few minutes.*
>
> *Getting through the first taste of a food doesn't mean she's not allergic – she may not have any reaction until the second or subsequent taste.*
>
> *If you have a family history of allergies, you should have a chat with your doctor, who may have particular, individual advice for your baby.*

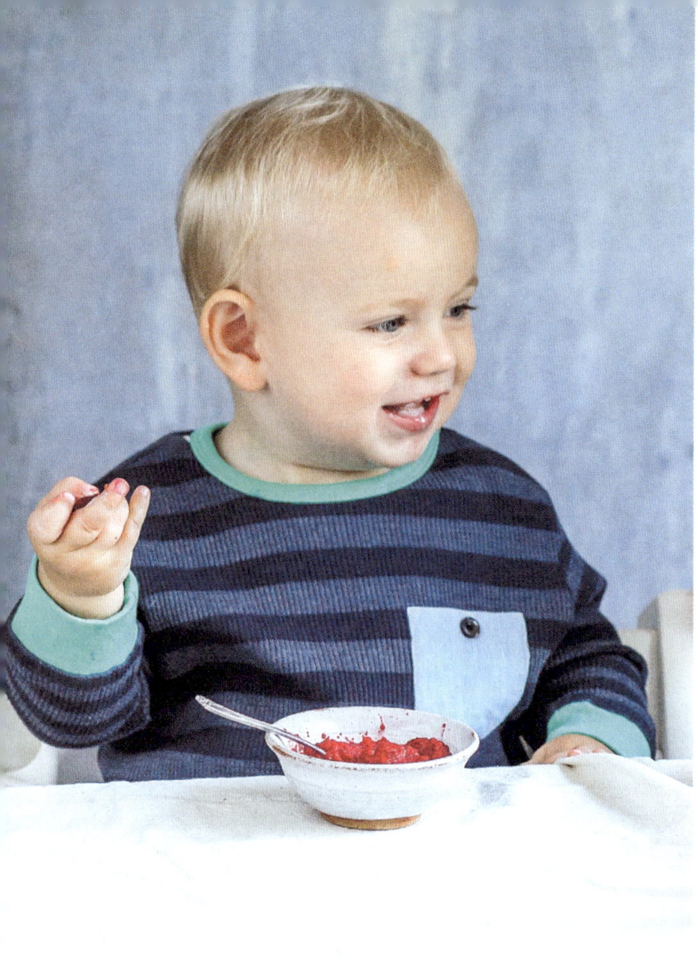
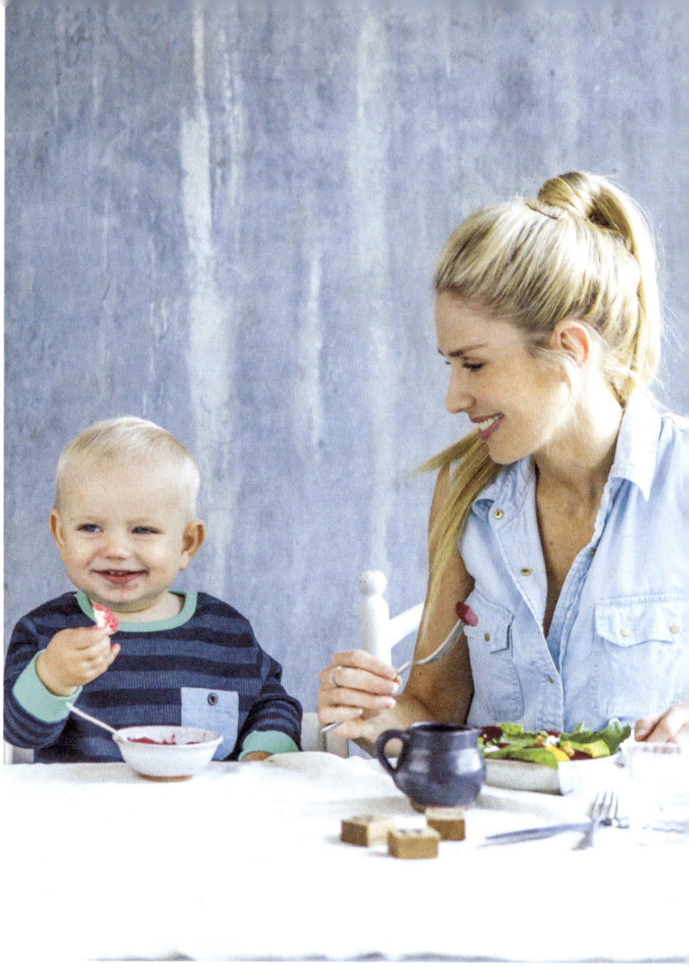
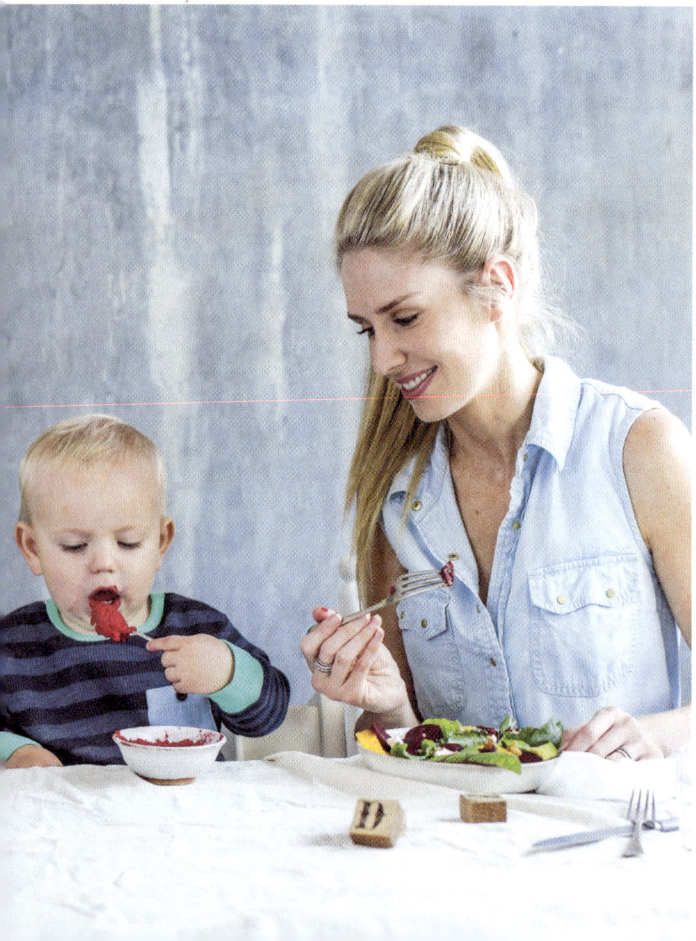
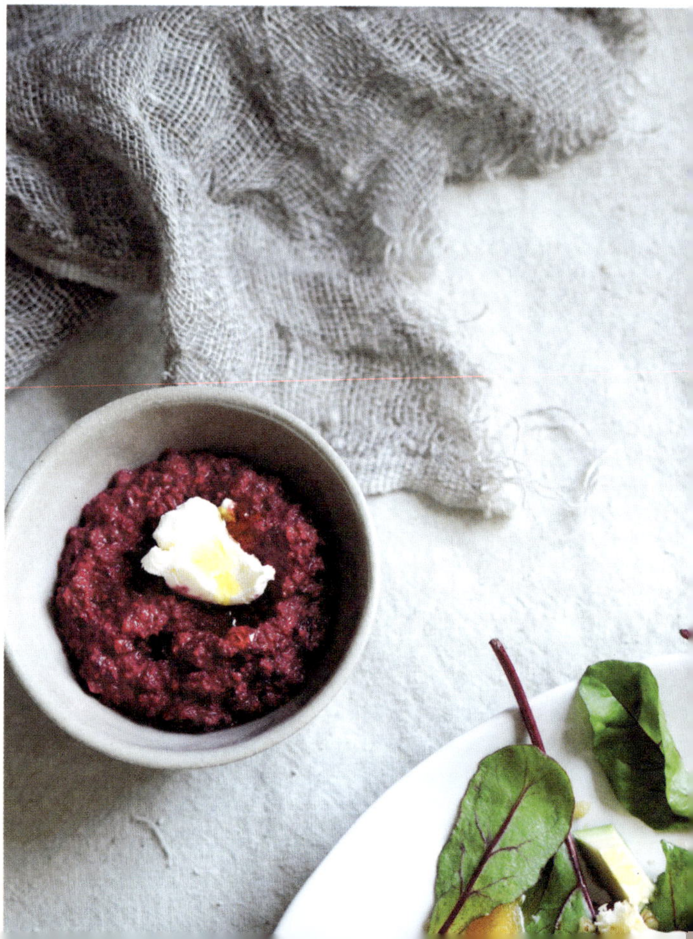

upright, and never give her food if she's not closely supervised. Also make sure you know what first-aid steps to follow in the event she does start choking.

To begin, finger foods should be soft so that your baby is able to mouth them. One exception is rusks, which should be hard enough that your baby can't bite pieces off and choke on them.

Adapting family meals for babies

When your baby first starts solids, you might like to have a week or two where you give her quite simple purées, such as chicken and pumpkin, or apple and rice cereal. Once she's accepting these and you're not detecting any food allergies, you can start to be more adventurous. All you need to do is prepare her the same food that the rest of the family is eating, puréeing and mashing it in the early months and then transitioning to finger foods as she gets older.

Unless otherwise noted, all of the recipes in this book are suitable for babies aged 6 months and older and each recipe provides adaptations both for younger babies (6–9 months as a general guide) and older babies (10–12 months). Remember not to add sugar or salt or other ingredients that aren't appropriate for babies, such as honey, raw eggs and any choking hazards (see the full list on page 18).

Preparing purées

There aren't many foods that can't be puréed although some foods – such as fruit, vegetables and meats – will obviously work better than others, such as salad or crispy foods.

The first step for preparing a purée is to choose an appropriate blending appliance. Your options include:

- a hand-held stick blender for smaller quantities – they're also good for putting straight into a saucepan;
- a blender for medium quantities and foods that blend easily;
- a food processor or a high-powered appliance, such as a Thermomix, for larger quantities or foods that blend less easily.

The next step is to add as much liquid as you need to achieve the appropriate consistency for your baby. In some cases, such as a casserole, you may not need to add any, as the cooking liquids may be adequate.

Where some liquid is required you can use water or your baby's milk – expressed breast milk or formula milk. A little cow's milk from time to time is also fine, it's just not as nutrient-dense as your baby's drinking milk, and it definitely shouldn't be served as a drink.

It is generally recommended to give babies under 12 months cooled, boiled tap water, rather than water straight from the tap. However, if you're confident that your water is of a high-quality drinking standard, you may feel comfortable serving it to your baby from 6 months. Most purified water is also fine, although it may not contain fluoride, which is important for dental health. Avoid sparkling water as it can have added minerals, including salt, which aren't always suitable for babies.

Plain (unsweetened) yoghurt can also be mixed through a purée to achieve the right consistency.

Where a purée is too runny – such as a soup – you can use a number of different ingredients to thicken it including rice cereal, quinoa, couscous and pasta stars.

Storing purées

Once you've prepared a batch of purée, you can set aside one serving and then put the remainder in individual storage containers to use later. Pop them immediately into the fridge or freezer. Purées will typically last up to 3 days in the fridge and several months in the freezer.

Don't freeze foods more than once. The exception to this is frozen raw ingredients which you then cook. For example, it's fine to put frozen peas in a beef casserole and then freeze the casserole.

If you want to avoid a case of food poisoning, it's useful to know that the 'temperature danger zone' at which maximum bacterial growth occurs is 5°C–60°C (41°F–140°F). To keep out of this zone, you need to keep cold foods below this range and hot foods above it.

Eating together

In the early months of starting solids, it can be virtually impossible to time dinner so that it fits in with your baby, so you might prefer to leave it to weekends to include her at the family table. As your baby gets older and her routines change, you might be able to bring dinnertime forward. However, ultimately, your sanity is more important than having your baby at the table. So if a relaxed late dinner with your partner is the highlight of your day, then don't change a thing. Once your baby reaches the toddler and pre-schooler years, eating together becomes far more feasible, so it will happen all in good time.

Developing taste preferences

While it may often feel like the reverse is true, as a parent, you have an extraordinary amount of control over your child's taste preferences. Babies first experience taste in the womb, via the amniotic fluid, and then as a newborn, via breastmilk. There have been studies showing that breastfed babies are more accepting of fruit and vegetables than formula-fed babies if their mothers regularly ate these foods themselves. Mums can expose their babies to different flavours by eating a varied diet during pregnancy and breastfeeding.

Between the time your baby starts solids and the age of 2 or 3 years, when 'food neophobia' (a fear of new foods) often starts to really kick in, there is a lot you can do to expand your child's palate as much as possible.

The most important thing is to keep introducing new and different foods, even if your child is not keen. Familiarity is one of the key factors dictating whether a child will eat a particular food. The best way to build familiarity is to give your child plenty of opportunities to taste, see and touch different foods – both raw and cooked, in a variety of different forms – from the time she starts solids.

So, don't just give her kiwi fruit purée, let her see and touch the whole fruit, point out its fuzzy skin, let her watch you eating some, give her a wedge to squish and try to bite.

Going hand-in-hand with familiarity, repeated taste exposure is another key

Baby nutrition – key points

- **Food groups** Once your baby is well established on solids, she should be eating some food from each of the major food groups every day – grains and cereals, vegetables and legumes, fruit, meat and eggs, and dairy.
- **Fat** Make sure she's also getting some fat in her diet, for proper growth and development. Go for healthy sources of fat, such as avocado, olive oil, nuts, seeds and oily fish. In moderation, the saturated fats found in meat and dairy are fine for babies, although as your child gets older, it's generally advised to keep a closer eye on her saturated fat intake.
- **Milk** Until she is over 12 months, breastmilk or formula is your child's most important food source. From 6–12 months, she needs about 600 ml (20½ fl oz) a day. After her first birthday, gradually reduce her milk intake in favour of other foods, although she'll still need at least 250 ml (8½ fl oz/1 cup) a day (more if she's not eating other dairy foods).
- **Water** Once your baby starts solids, you should also be offering her water regularly, although she may not take much interest at first. Don't serve her juice as it's been linked to tooth decay and excess weight – milk and water are the only two drinks she needs.
- **Wholegrains and high-fibre foods** Don't overload your baby on wholegrains and other high-fibre foods. They're fantastic in moderation, and as she gets older you can increase her intake, but too much fibre can interfere with a baby's nutrient uptake.
- **Iron** One nutrient to be conscious of is iron, as many babies don't get enough. From about 6 months, your baby's natural iron stores will deplete (this may happen sooner in premature babies), so make sure she's getting plenty of iron-rich foods – such as red meat, cooked chicken liver and eggs – from this age onward. It's worth knowing that chicken thigh meat has twice as much iron as chicken breast, so I always prefer it for young children.
- **Vitamin D** This is another nutrient to watch out for. Breastmilk contains vitamin D but the precise amount is highly variable, depending on Mum's own vitamin D levels. Although it's not a good idea for babies to be exposed to too much sun, because of the skin cancer risks, a few minutes of early morning and later afternoon sunlight is generally acceptable and can help protect against vitamin D deficiency.
- **Preserving nutrients** Certain nutrients are easily destroyed by heat, including vitamin B1 (thiamine), vitamin B6, vitamin C, folate, vitamin E and omega-3 fats. Take care when cooking and heating your child's food not to overdo it, as more of these precious nutrients will be destroyed.

factor in building acceptance of a food. It may take up to 10, even 15, tastes of a food before your child will accept it, so definitely don't give up after a few rejections.

What is baby-led weaning?

'Baby-led weaning' is an infant feeding philosophy that rejects the idea of feeding babies puréed food from a spoon. Instead, it says that babies should be given finger food and encouraged to feed themselves from the time of starting solids at 6 months (no earlier). One important feature of baby-led weaning is that the baby decides how much she eats – her parents do not put food in her mouth or try to encourage her to have more.

Supporters of baby-led weaning say that it is preferable to conventional spoon-feeding because it helps teach children to enjoy food and reduces the likelihood of fussy eating.

Baby-led weaning can be a bit nerve-wracking for parents because of the concern that a baby may choke on her finger food. It's one reason to ensure a baby can sit upright properly and never to leave her eating unattended. It's also very messy, something some parents find difficult to cope with.

While baby-led weaning really suits some babies, it's not appropriate for all – particularly those who can't sit well by 6 months or who aren't adept at getting food into their mouths. One concern I have is that if children aren't managing to eat much, they're at risk of iron deficiency, as their natural iron stores start to deplete at around 6 months.

I believe the best approach for most children is a hybrid approach, drawing a happy balance between the baby-led and conventional spoon-feeding methods. Ultimately, taking a flexible, relaxed approach will produce the best outcome.

TODDLERS AND FAMILY MEALS

The toddler years – typically described as between 1 and 4 years – are some of the most joyful and some of the most trying for parents when it comes to feeding children. Although toddlers are generally much easier to have at the table than babies, many of them develop very strong opinions about every aspect of their meal, down to what bowl their meal is served in and what spoon they use. As a mum of a particularly opinionated four year old, I know all too well how exasperating this can be!

If you would like a comprehensive guide to feeding children during these early years – including meal planners and toddler-specific recipes – you can find it in my book *Cooking For Your Baby and Toddler*. Below is an overview of the key points you need to know.

Food refusal and mealtime tension

The term 'fussy eating' is usually used to describe the behaviour of children who will eat only a small variety of food. In more serious cases, it may be just a few ingredients. Fussy eaters are typically unwilling to try new foods (this is called 'food neophobia') and are also usually unwilling to eat many of the foods that they have seen, perhaps even eaten, before.

Often fussy eaters won't eat anything from an entire food group, such as dairy, vegetables or meat.

Thankfully, there are a whole lot of concrete steps you can take to minimise fussy eating in the first place, and to stop things from getting worse if it does occur.

A common problem

The most important starting point for any discussion on fussy eating is this: *fussy eating is very common*. A number of studies estimate its prevalence at 25–40 per cent. In a US survey of over 3000 children, the figure was even higher, with 50 per cent of parents reporting that their 19- to 24-month-old toddler was a picky eater.

It is rare to have a child who doesn't experience some food fussiness at least once during her childhood. Even children who usually eat well will often experience phases of picky eating. These phases will come, and hopefully go, and it is a matter of getting through them as calmly as possible. As discussed below, staying relaxed is a key part of not making matters worse.

Minimising fussy eating

The easiest way of dealing with fussy eating is to try to reduce the likelihood of it occurring in the first place. Particularly before your child's first and even second birthday, you have a golden opportunity to set the stage for healthy eating behaviours. By repeatedly exposing your baby to a wide range of different flavours, building her familiarity with different ingredients and helping her to manage different textures – see pages 19–21 – you will be well on the way to reducing fussy eating down the track.

Having said that, there are no guarantees as a parent, and despite your best efforts you may end up with the world's trickiest eater. Hard as it is, you should definitely not see this as a reflection of your parenting. Undiagnosed medical conditions might be at play, such as tonsil or adenoid problems, or food intolerances. Other times, for no apparent reason, your child is simply one of those who just isn't interested in food. If this happens, don't give up. There is still plenty you can do to stop your child's eating from getting worse over time.

Handling a fussy toddler

Having a child who is a seriously fussy eater can make life difficult. Instead of sitting down and enjoying a lovely

> **Coping with waste**
>
> *If, like me, you're concerned about food waste – both the expense and the environmental impact – it's really hard to keep serving up food you're pretty sure won't get eaten. Here is something to remember:* **if a child has seen food on her plate, it has served a purpose***.*
>
> *You might think that strawberry was wasted if it wasn't eaten, but I can assure you it played an important role. Seeing a range of different ingredients on her plate is a crucial tool in combating fussiness, even if your child doesn't always eat them.*
>
> *Give your child ample opportunity to try a particular food and if she rejects it, then eat it yourself, so it doesn't end up in the bin. So long as your own meal portions remain controlled, you can watch your own waist while avoiding excess food waste.*

Something for everyone

home-cooked dinner each night, you feel like you're going into battle.

Interestingly, we now know that most of the tactics our parents used on us – 'You can't leave the table until you finish what's on your plate', 'No dessert unless you eat your vegetables', 'If you don't eat those brussels sprouts, you'll be getting them for breakfast' – are counter-productive and actually tend to make matters worse.

In a nutshell, the research findings tell us that the best approach for minimising fussy eating is simply to keep serving up healthy varied foods, avoid all coercive behaviours and be a good role model by eating well yourself. Here are the key strategies arising from the research:

- **Just keep offering it** One of the key predictors of whether or not a child will eat a certain food is familiarity. Children eat what they like and they like what they know. Unfortunately, many parents give up on an ingredient after just a few rejections from their child. Persistence is the key. If your child has a meltdown because the peas are touching her other food, put them in a separate bowl. Just don't stop serving them.

- **Let your child choose how much she eats** A useful guiding motto is this: *you as the parent choose the quality (of what food is served) and your child chooses the quantity.* What if your child has only eaten two mouthfuls of a meal? That's fine. You wouldn't want that happening every meal, but from time to time children won't eat much and forcing them to have more will make matters worse. Ultimately, children of the same age and gender have wildly different appetites. That's why, when you're assessing whether your child is eating enough, it's better to be guided by her growth (checking it against a growth standards chart) than her serving sizes. Having said that, if the sparrow-style eating persists, you may have to investigate any possible medical problems.

- **Make sure she's hungry** This sounds so obvious, but in my experience it's one of the biggest mistakes parents (including myself) make. Before you have your own toddler meltdown when your child won't eat her meal, stop and think about her day. How many snacks has she had? How much milk? Any juice? What time? If your child has had a muffin at 4.30 p.m. it should come as no surprise that she's not going to have much of an appetite for dinner. I find it extraordinary the extent to which snacking affects my four-year-old's fussiness. If he's hungry, he'll eat just about anything. But if he's had a big afternoon snack or a glass of milk – forget about it; only pasta, bread and cheese will do.

- **Don't pressure your child to eat** This is a really hard one and requires mountains of patience. It means not saying, 'You can't watch TV until you eat all your peas.' It means not saying, 'You can't leave the table unless you clear your plate.' The biggest problem with these kinds of strategies is that they backfire. In the short term, your child may finish his plate of fish, but, in the long term, she's less likely to enjoy fish and more likely to try to manipulate you at mealtimes. Unfortunately, lots of children soon learn that by being difficult eaters they get lots of attention and some pretty cool rewards. Keeping the pressure off means that mealtimes are far less likely to become a battleground.

- **Encouraging a 'try' is fine** While pressuring your child to eat is counter-productive, calmly suggesting that they have a little try or a taste of a food is fine. Just watch that you don't cross the line into coercion. There's a big difference between suggesting your child has a try and insisting that she finishes the whole bowl. If she refuses to have a try, don't flip out. Otherwise, she'll soon learn it's a great way to get you worked up. Just offer the same food again another day.

- **Be a good role model** Don't underestimate the power of your actions on your child. A number of studies have found the number of vegetables liked by a child's parent to be a reliable predictor of the vegetable variety consumed by the child. This is one reason it's great if your child can eat with you as a family – the more she sees you eating up your vegetables, the more likely she will be to do the same. What's more, if you don't like a food, try not to share that sentiment with your child. Give her the opportunity to form a liking for it, even if you don't.

- **Don't offer food rewards** 'If you eat your peas, you can have some chocolate cake!' Sounds like a good deal. What's more, it will probably work. Peas eaten, mission accomplished. If only it were that simple. Unfortunately, we now know that this strategy is likely to make your child like peas even less, and chocolate cake even more. And it's not hard to see why. From your child's perspective, peas are suddenly a chore, a task, a dreaded thing you have to get through, and cake is a special treat, a deluxe reward. If you want your child to eat peas, serve them to her regularly, make mealtimes a positive experience and eat peas yourself. Just don't offer her any cake for her efforts.

- **Be strict on your shopping, not on your child** The more restrictions you put on your child's consumption of a particular food, the more likely she is to want that food. However, it's important to distinguish between two types of restriction. The kind of restriction that backfires is when you tell your child that she's not allowed any of the chocolates that are sitting in full view on the kitchen shelf. This is known as 'overt restriction', because your child knows about the thing she's not allowed to have and she'll end up wanting it more. However, 'covert restriction' – which involves keeping unhealthy foods out of the house or walking home a different way so you avoid the cupcake shop – does work. The key is to be strict on your shopping list and keep unhealthy foods to a minimum. However, when treat foods are in your house (and your child knows about them), don't overly restrict her access to them or she'll just want them more.

- **Positive mealtimes** A child's emotional associations with a particular food can profoundly affect her liking for it. For example, I have a friend who won't eat apples because, as a child, he was physically bullied by some older children into eating one. He now feels physically ill at the thought of eating them. The same is true in reverse. If your child's experience of mealtimes is positive and conflict-free, according to the research, she's more likely to form a liking for the foods you serve her.

Adapting family meals for toddlers

By the time your baby has her first birthday, she's covered a lot of ground when it comes to food and eating. From this time onwards, involving her in family meals gets easier and easier.

After your child turns one, you may still like to purée or mash the occasional meal, but just make sure you keep the consistency quite textured. As before, you still need to keep an eye on how much sugar and salt she's eating, and there are certain foods she's still not allowed, such as raw eggs and choking hazards (for example, popcorn – see page 18). Finger foods should become the norm now that she's a toddler.

Toddler adaptations are offered for each of the recipes in Chapters 2–5 of this book, but you're the best person to know how your child likes to eat. Some children prefer to eat entirely with their hands, picking up larger pieces they can bite off, others like using a spoon, in which case smaller pieces will work better. Be guided by your child and she'll enjoy mealtimes more.

Encouraging self-feeding

As your child enters her toddler years, she'll probably be well on the way to learning to feed herself, even if she's still messy. As well as using her hands, it's a good idea to let her have her own shorter-handled spoon (you can even do this as early as the time she starts solids). As frustrating as it can be to watch a child miss her mouth and drop her food in her lap, it is important to let her have a go. As with anything, if you always do it for her, she'll never learn.

If your child is showing no interest in feeding herself, it may be that she needs more guidance in what to do. The best way to teach her is to involve her in family mealtimes so that she can observe exactly how this whole business of eating works. Make sure you're also giving her a wide variety of finger foods that she can hold with ease.

She may also be feeling some performance anxiety. Lots of children like to have some time and space to enjoy their food, without a parent hovering over them. Although you shouldn't leave your child unattended because of the choking risk, giving her an opportunity to have a good play with her lunch without any interference may create the pressure-free environment she needs to have a go.

Toddler nutrition – key points

- **Variety** As hard as it can be when fussy eating kicks in, the best thing your toddler can be eating is a wide variety of ingredients from all the major food groups – grains and cereals, vegetables and legumes, fruit, meat and eggs, and dairy. It's wonderful if she eats an apple a day, but it's even better if she eats an apple one day, an orange the next, an apricot the following day, then some papaya, kiwi fruit and strawberry. The more varied your child's diet is, the more likely it is that she'll be eating all the nutrients and phytochemicals she needs for optimal growth and health.

- **Watch the sugar** Even after your child's first birthday, you need to keep a close eye on added sugar. Not only do sugary foods cause dental damage, they also displace nutrient-dense foods, particularly when eaten before mealtimes. The best approach is to keep them as occasional treats and make them as nutritious as possible, such as an oat biscuit (cookie).

- **Iron** Many toddlers don't get enough iron, so this is one nutrient to be particularly mindful of. An iron deficiency can affect your child's immune system and her cognitive abilities, making it harder for her to concentrate and learn. Make sure your toddler is getting plenty of iron-rich foods, such as red meat, chicken (the thigh meat has twice as much as the breast meat) and eggs.

- **Snacks** Most toddlers' tummies are too small to consume all the kilojoules they need in three meals a day. What's more, a child's brain metabolises glucose about twice as fast as an adult's, so they need a more constant source of energy. The trick is to keep your toddler's snacks just as healthy as the rest of her meals – fresh fruit, steamed vegetables, a mixed nut butter with celery stalks – and time them so that she still has an appetite at mealtimes.

- **Not too much milk** Milk is a really important source of calcium, but too much can cause iron deficiency. Children who are 'milkoholics' tend to fill up on milk, which is low in iron, and then they have no appetite for iron-rich foods. So, definitely no big glasses of milk or smoothies before mealtimes.

- **Watch the juice** Juice should be a treat, not a staple. Drinking too much juice can cause diarrhoea, tooth decay and iron deficiency (because your child eats less at mealtimes). When you do offer juice, go for a freshly squeezed option with plenty of fibre and perhaps some carrot or beetroot mixed in.

- **Vitamin supplements** I'm a firm believer that food is the best way of meeting daily mineral and vitamin requirements. However, in the case of serious fussy eaters, a multivitamin can offer some protection against nutritional deficiencies. So long as it's not used as a substitute for proper meals, and healthy foods continue to be served, it can be a helpful way of meeting recommended daily intakes.

Ultimately, the best tools for her learning are a range of foods of different sizes and shapes and plenty of patience from you.

SCHOOL YEARS AND BEYOND

As your child starts school and eventually enters her teenage years, she will begin making many more food choices for herself. Soon enough, she will be the one choosing what goes in her lunchbox and what she orders from a restaurant menu. What's more, her food influences will increasingly come from outside sources – particularly her friends and the media – and less from your kitchen.

Social pressures will also begin to play a role and your child will eventually start taking a greater interest in how nutrition affects her life – whether it's choosing low-calorie foods so she can fit into those new jeans or, in the case of many boys, opting for high-protein diets to increase their muscle mass.

Having said that, as a parent, your role in your child's food choices continues to be pivotal. Offering varied, healthy ingredients remains just as important as it was during the baby and toddler years, and including her at the family dinner table is perhaps more crucial than ever before.

If your child or teenager is resisting family meals and rejecting the food you're serving, all the advice on pages 24–28 regarding fussy eating applies. Ultimately, the best approach is to just keep serving healthy meals, keep eating them yourself and don't make a big deal of it. As hard as it is, staying calm and not engaging in food-related battles is your best bet for overcoming them. As your child gets older, you may also step up the amount of nutrition information you give her. If you explain to your teenager how a low-GI diet with minimal processed foods will improve her acne, it might be the first time she actually follows your food advice!

Vegetarian diets

Switching to a vegetarian diet is not uncommon during the teenage years. From a health perspective, it's not necessarily a bad thing. For a start, studies show vegetarians have a lower incidence of obesity, diabetes, cardiovascular disease and certain cancers. What's more, eating plenty of fruit, vegetables, wholegrains and legumes has been linked with overall good health.

Nevertheless, a vegetarian diet does have its pitfalls and there's no question that it requires careful planning to avoid nutrient deficiencies. Here are the main concerns:

- **Iron** Iron is crucial for good immune function and energy levels and it's one nutrient many vegetarians don't get enough of. The recommended daily intake (RDI) for boys aged 14–18 years is 8 mg per day, while for girls it's 11 mg per day. To put that in perspective, an egg contains around 2 mg, while 100 g (3½ oz) tinned red kidney beans also contains 2 mg. Iron-fortified breakfast cereals and other fortified foods can help your child reach her RDI, and eating vitamin C-rich foods/drinks at the same meal will help with iron absorption.

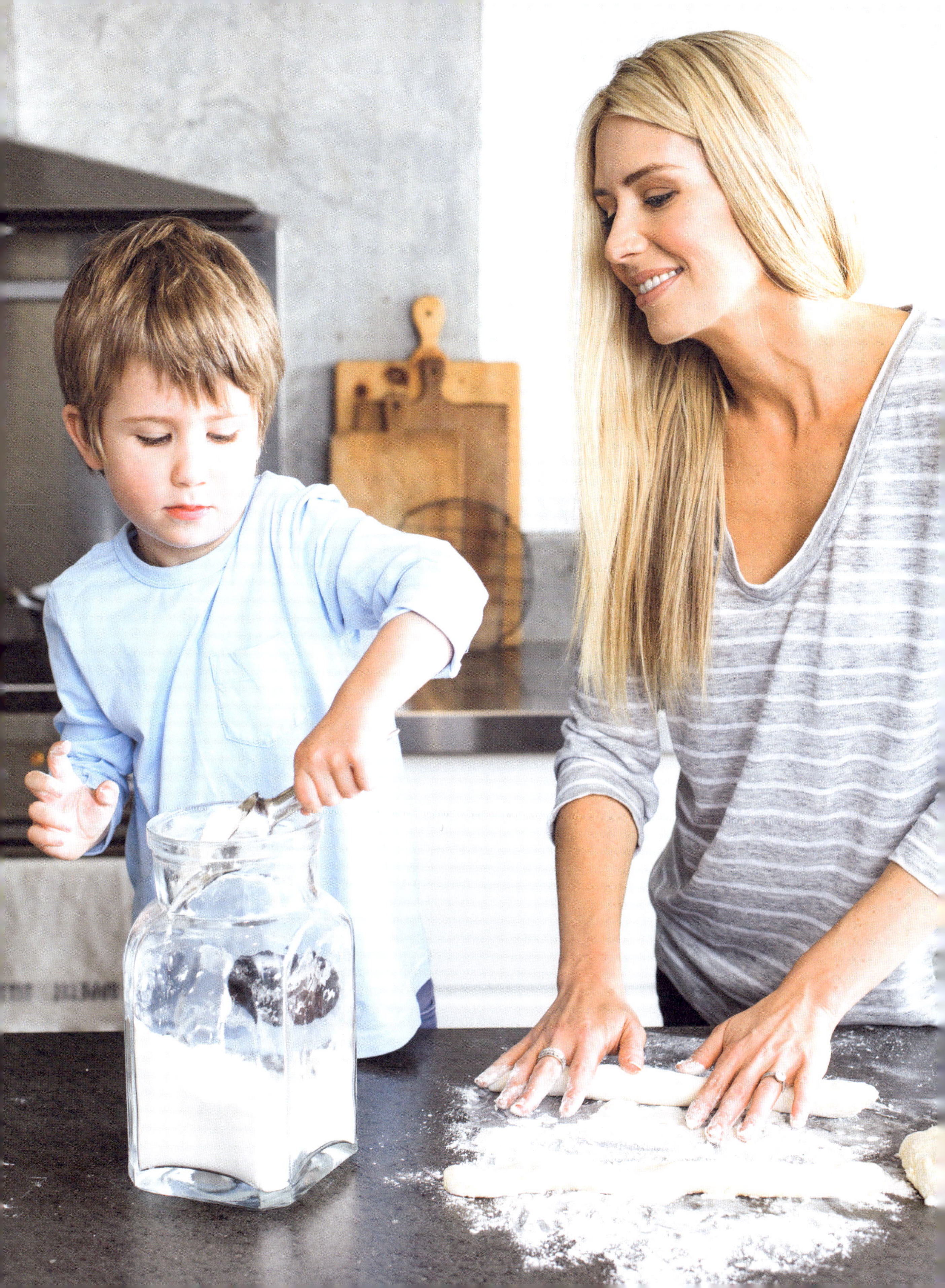

- **Zinc** Like iron, zinc also affects immunity. Dairy foods are a reasonable source and vegetarians can also find zinc in wholegrains and some seeds and nuts, such as pepitas (pumpkin seeds), sunflower seeds, pine nuts and cashews (each of these contains iron, too). If your child eats the occasional piece of seafood, then oysters, crab and prawns (shrimp) are also great sources.
- **Vitamin B12** Needed for healthy red blood cells and nerve function, vitamin B12 is only found in animal-derived and fortified foods, so it's another one vegetarians need to be really mindful of. Your child should be fine if she eats eggs and dairy products, as these are good sources. Another option is fortified soy milk. Even though seaweed and fermented soy products, such as tempeh, include vitamin B12, they're in an inactive, unavailable form and so they're not reliable sources.
- **Omega-3 fats** Important for your child's brain function and heart health. Because oily fish, which are a rich source of omega-3 fats, are off the menu, you'll need to include plant-based sources in your child's diet such as linseeds (flax seeds), chia seeds and walnuts. Omega-3-enriched eggs are another good source.
- **Protein** There are many plant-based sources of protein, such as wholegrains, legumes, seeds, nuts and vegetables. So long as your child eats a wide variety of these foods, she'll probably meet her daily protein requirements. If she eats eggs and dairy products, the task is much easier because these are excellent 'high-quality proteins' – meaning they contain all the essential amino acids that the human body requires. Quinoa is another good protein source.
- **Vitamin D** As long as your child is getting sufficient exposure to sunlight, vitamin D is unlikely to be a problem. It's also found in fatty fish and eggs, as well as fortified milk and margarine. However, diet alone rarely provides enough, which is why some time in the sun is important.

In addition to these nutritional concerns, it's worth being aware that a vegetarian diet can signal the start of – or be used to disguise – an eating disorder. Although vegetarian diets certainly don't cause eating disorders, there is evidence of a very high incidence of vegetarianism among people with eating disorders. Particularly for teenage girls, vegetarianism might be the first step in more extreme attempts to control food intake.

If your child adopts a vegan diet, the risk of nutrient deficiency is much greater. In addition to the concerns above, calcium deficiency can be a real problem, because dairy foods are off the menu. You should consult a nutritionist or dietician to help you plan a suitable diet for your child.

Nutrition during the school years – key points

- **Calcium** Your child will reach what's known as her 'peak bone mass' (her maximum bone density) in her twenties. From this time onwards, her bones will only get weaker, not stronger. In order to maximise her peak bone mass, which will give her the strongest protection against osteoporosis later in life, it's absolutely crucial that she gets plenty of calcium in her childhood and teenage years. From the age of 9 years onwards, boys and girls need 3 or 4 cups (750 ml–1 litre/25½–34 fl oz) of milk a day – or the equivalent amount of calcium from other sources – to meet the recommended daily intakes. Dairy foods are the best source, along with tinned salmon and sardines (so long as the soft bones are eaten) and, to a lesser extent, plant foods such as tofu, bok choy (pak choy), broccoli and almonds.

- **Iron** Once girls start menstruating, their iron requirements nearly double. Boys also need plenty of iron to support their rapid growth. Iron is crucial for good immune function and energy levels, and it also helps with cognitive development. If your child doesn't get enough iron, she may have difficulties concentrating at school. Eating plenty of iron-rich foods, such as red meat, liver pâté, chicken (thigh and leg meat) and eggs will help minimise the risk of an iron deficiency.

- **Breakfast** It really is the most important meal of the day. Numerous studies have shown that children who eat breakfast have better concentration and attention spans and perform better at school. On the other hand, those who miss their morning meal are more likely to be irritable, tired, restless and easily distracted. They're also more likely to be overweight. Take the time in the morning to get your child into the habit of eating a proper breakfast – you'll be rewarded for your efforts when you read her next report card.

- **Soft drinks** Around the world, soft drinks are a major contributor to obesity and dental problems. There is simply no good reason to have them in your house. They are loaded with sugar and offer virtually no nutritional benefits. Cordials are in the same boat. The longer you can keep them out of your child's life, the better. If she wants a drink other than water then milk or a freshly squeezed juice (preferably with some vegetables) are both streets ahead nutritionally.

- **Food independence** Once children and teens have the independence to make and buy their own food, their diets may suffer as sugary, fatty, low-nutrient snacks often become their preferred options. You can help your child make healthy food choices by stocking your house with the foods you're happy for her to eat. By keeping unhealthy foods out of the house, and loading your fridge and pantry with fruit, vegetables, unsweetened dairy foods, wholegrains and nutritious snacks, she's more likely to end up eating these foods. Teaching your child how to prepare a healthy meal for herself – how to cook pasta, boil an egg, cook a piece of fish and prepare a salad – will also help her make better food choices.

Breakfast

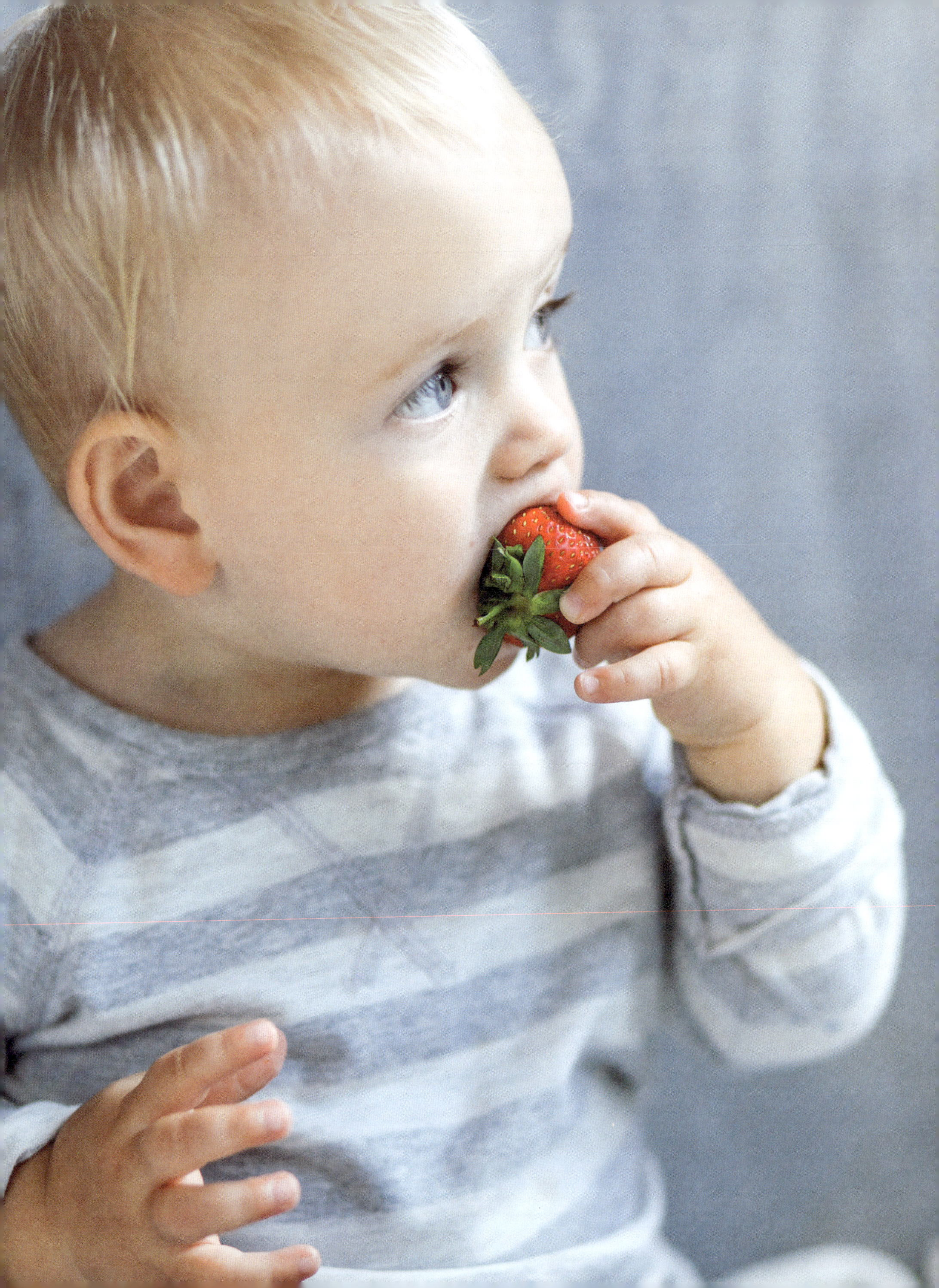

It's something we've all heard before, but breakfast really is the most important meal of the day. The research tells us that children who eat breakfast have longer attention spans and do better at school, whereas those who don't are more likely to be easily distracted and fatigued.

Choosing a nutritious breakfast – such as any of the recipes in this chapter – is best, as the slow release of energy will give your child a more steady flow of fuel, making it easier for him to learn new things.

Aside from the research, breakfast is a great time to start the day on the right foot and perhaps to spend time with the parent who may not be around so much in the evenings. When I was a kid, my dad was always my breakfast companion because he sometimes worked late. He used to share a little life lesson with me each morning over my boiled egg and I still fondly remember his words of wisdom.

Fresh fruit with cinnamon ricotta yoghurt

Serves 4

This cinnamon ricotta yoghurt turns a plate of fruit into a delicious, balanced breakfast. Feel free to use whichever local fruits are in season.

If you have a baby, offering him smaller pieces of fruit, such as blueberries and pomegranate, is a great way to help develop his 'pincer grasp'. This involves picking up an object between his thumb and forefinger and happens when he is about 9 months old.

250 g (9 oz/1 cup) Greek-style yoghurt
250 g (9 oz/1 cup) fresh ricotta (see note)
1 tablespoon wheatgerm
1 tablespoon LSA (see note, page 44)
1–2 tablespoons maple syrup, plus extra to serve (optional – omit for baby's serve)
1 teaspoon ground cinnamon
½ pomegranate
2 fresh figs, quartered
2 plums, quartered and stones removed
125 g (4½ oz/heaped ¾ cup) fresh blueberries
125 g (4½ oz/1 cup) fresh raspberries

Place the yoghurt, ricotta, wheatgerm, LSA, maple syrup (if using) and cinnamon in a food processor and process until fluffy and smooth.

Remove the seeds from the pomegranate, discarding the skin. Arrange the fruit on a serving plate and serve with the ricotta yoghurt. Drizzle a little extra maple syrup over the top, if liked.

Baby's serve: for a **younger baby**, blend the ricotta yoghurt, blueberries and raspberries to a smooth purée. If using plums and figs, you may prefer to peel the skins first (see note, page 50). Omit the pomegranates as their seeds can be difficult to blend. For an **older baby**, serve as is, chopping fruit into smaller pieces to eat as finger food.

Toddler's serve: serve as is.

Soft cheeses Ricotta and other soft cheeses, such as feta, are considered a high-risk food in terms of contamination with listeria bacteria. As such, pregnant women are advised not to eat them. You can give soft cheeses to healthy babies over 6 months of age, however, you should be careful when purchasing and storing them. Make sure they're very fresh, packaged hygienically (in a sealed packet) and stored in the refrigerator. Don't re-serve any unfinished portions.

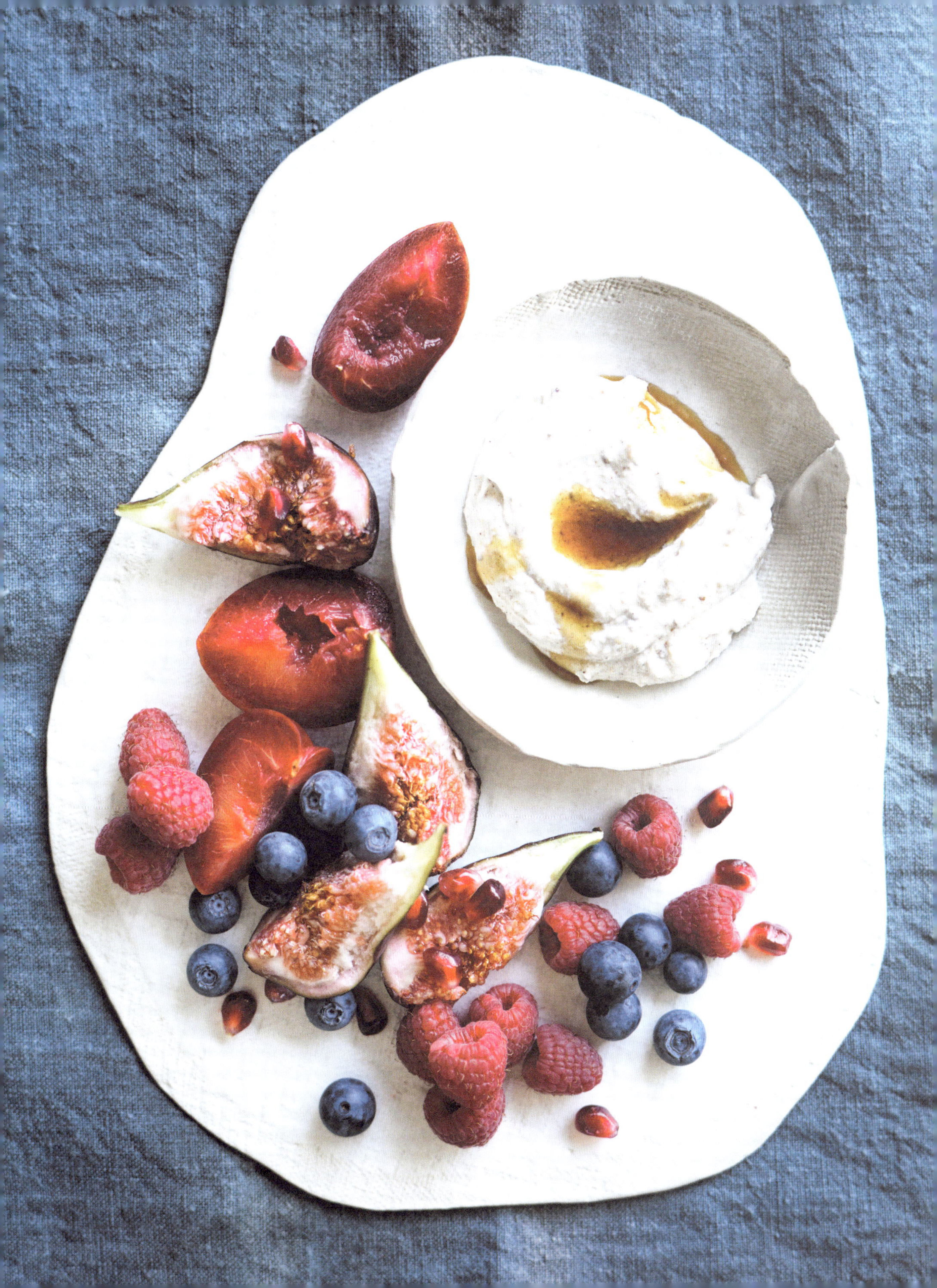

Raspberry and pear quinoa porridge

Serves 3

Quinoa is a small seed that packs a big nutritional punch. It's a rich source of iron, folate, fibre and protein, amongst other goodness. One reason it outperforms other cereals is that it's not a true grain. Botanically, it comes from the same family as beetroot and spinach, which means it has quite a different nutritional profile from grains such as wheat and oats.

100 g (3½ oz/½ cup) quinoa, washed and drained
1 pear, cored and chopped
60 g (2 oz/½ cup) fresh raspberries, plus extra to serve
¼ teaspoon ground cinnamon
milk, to serve (optional)

Tip *After setting aside one serving for your baby, you can freeze any remaining quinoa porridge in individual portions for later use.*

Place the quinoa and 500 ml (17 fl oz/2 cups) water in a saucepan over low heat. Bring to a simmer and stir occasionally, for 15–20 minutes, or until tender – there should still be some liquid remaining.

Add the pear to the quinoa and continue to simmer, stirring occasionally, for a further 5 minutes until the pear has softened (if the pear is very ripe it may not require cooking). You can simply add the raspberries and cinnamon and serve stirred through the quinoa or transfer to a blender and blend until smooth.

Divide between serving bowls and top with fresh raspberries and a little milk, if liked.

Baby's serve: for a **younger baby**, blend until smooth. If the puréed consistency of this porridge is too thick for your baby, simply add a little extra liquid – either some water or your baby's milk. Younger babies in particular need a thinner consistency until they're more established on solids. For an **older baby**, keep the puréed consistency lumpier so that he experiences more texture.

Toddler's serve: serve as is.

Breakfast

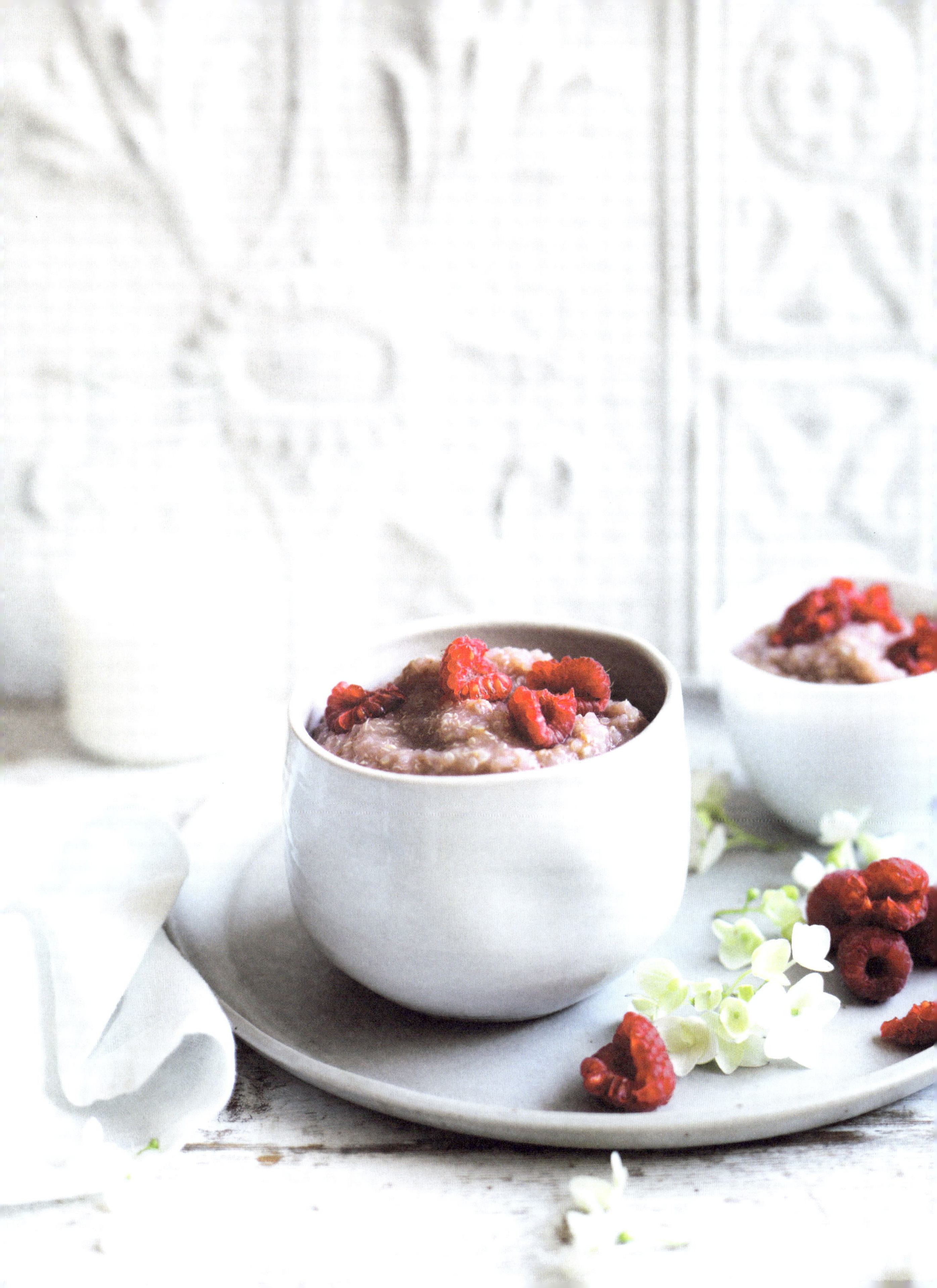

Three-grain blueberry and apricot porridge

Serves 2–3

One of the most important things at mealtimes for you and your family is variety. Oats are a wonderful food, but adding some diversity by combining different grains will ensure your breakfast porridge covers an even greater nutritional base.

You can now buy three-grain (and five-grain) porridge mixes, but feel free to make up your own blend using rolled oats, millet and barley – you might also like to try spelt or whichever other grains you can source.

100 g (3½ oz/1 cup) three-grain porridge mix
160 ml (5½ fl oz) milk, plus extra to serve
60 g (2 oz/¼ cup) diced dried apricots
1–2 teaspoons maple syrup (optional – omit for baby's serve)
1 tablespoon wheatgerm or LSA (see note, page 44)
¼ teaspoon ground cinnamon
125 g (4½ oz/heaped ¾ cup) fresh blueberries
2 apricots, quartered and stones removed

Place the porridge mix in a saucepan with the milk and 190 ml (6½ fl oz/¾ cup) water. Cook over medium heat, stirring, for 10 minutes. Stir through the dried apricot and cook for a further 1 minute, or until the porridge has reached the desired consistency – you can add a little more liquid if required.

Stir through the maple syrup (if using). Add the wheatgerm, cinnamon and half of the blueberries and stir through. Divide the porridge among serving bowls and top with the remaining blueberries and fresh apricots. Serve with a little milk, if liked.

Tip *Dried apricots are a good source of beta-carotene and iron. If you want a preservative-free option, look for a brand with no added sulphites. Sulphites have been associated with a range of food intolerance symptoms and can particularly affect asthmatics.*

Baby's serve: for a **younger baby**, blend until smooth. For an **older baby**, keep the puréed consistency lumpier – or don't purée at all – so that he experiences more texture.

Toddler's serve: serve as is.

Breakfast

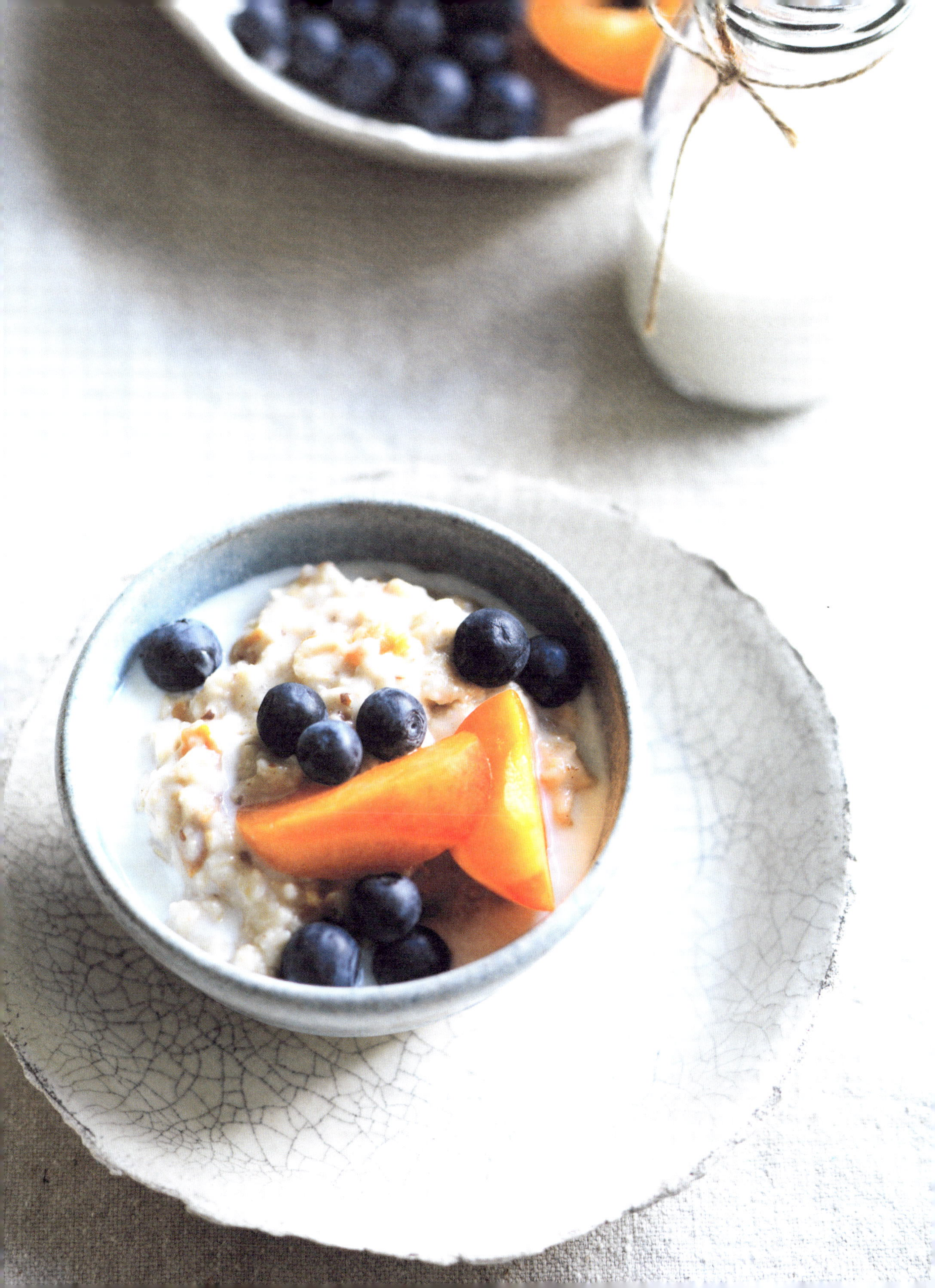

Fig bircher muesli

Serves 2–3

Bircher muesli is one of my favourite breakfasts during the warmer months. It can be prepared the night before to avoid the dreaded weekday morning rush.

Dried figs are a good source of potassium and calcium – gram-for-gram they have about twice as much calcium as milk.

100 g (3½ oz/1 cup) rolled oats
2 tablespoons chopped dried figs
   (or use dried apricots)
200 ml (7 fl oz) milk, plus extra to serve
1 pink or red apple, grated with skin on
1 teaspoon ground cinnamon
2 tablespoons LSA (see note)
   or ground almonds
90 g (3 oz/⅓ cup) plain yoghurt
2–3 fresh figs, quartered

Combine the oats, dried figs and milk in a bowl. Cover with plastic wrap (cling film) and refrigerate for at least 1 hour, or preferably overnight, to allow the milk to soak in.

Stir in the grated apple, cinnamon and half of the LSA. Divide the bircher muesli among serving bowls and top each bowl with a dollop of yoghurt, the fresh figs and the remaining LSA. Serve with a little extra milk, if liked.

LSA *Made up of ground linseeds, sunflower seeds and almonds, LSA is high in essential fats and other nutrients. It is best not to cook LSA as heat destroys the omega-3 fats. Instead, add to meals at the last minute or sprinkle on top before serving.*

Baby's serve: for a **younger baby**, blend the bircher muesli, LSA, yoghurt and fresh fig until smooth. For an **older baby**, keep the puréed consistency lumpier – or don't purée at all – so that he experiences more texture. You can chop up the fresh fig and stir it through the muesli or serve as finger food on the side.

Toddler's serve: serve as is.

Breakfast

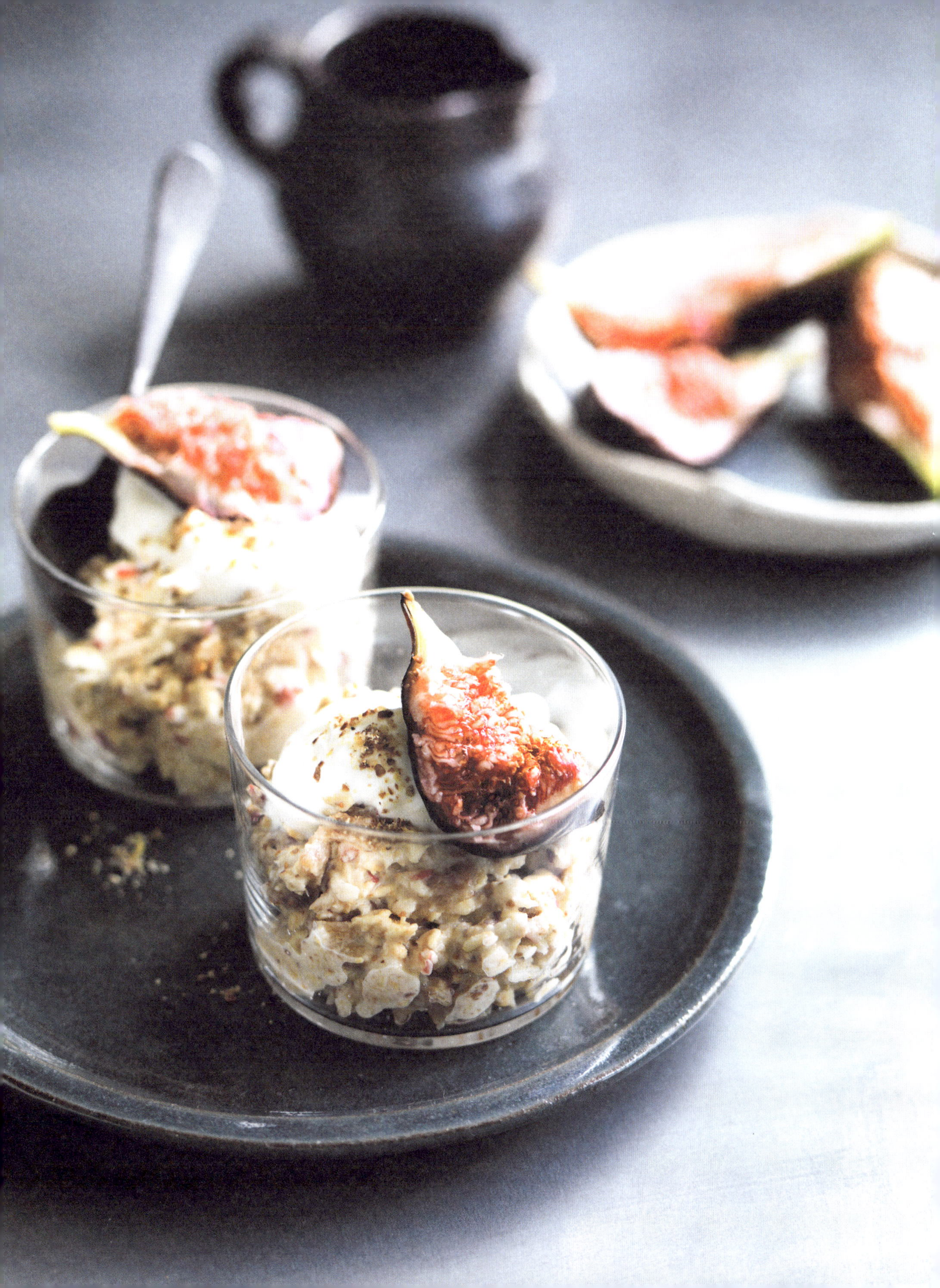

Strawberry coconut porridge

Serves 2–3

I love my morning porridge, but it can sometimes get a little monotonous, particularly by late winter. To keep things interesting I use coconut milk from time to time – it adds a delicious creaminess, which is balanced by the fresh strawberries. Feel free to substitute the strawberries with whichever seasonal fruits are available.

If you'd like a dairy-free version of this porridge, you can use dairy-free coconut yoghurt instead of the plain yoghurt.

100 g (3½ oz/1 cup) rolled oats
125 ml (4 fl oz/½ cup) light coconut milk
1 tablespoon chia seeds, wheatgerm or LSA (see note, page 44)
1–2 teaspoons maple syrup (optional – omit for baby's serve)
115 g (4 oz/⅔ cup) chopped strawberries, plus extra strawberries to serve
2 tablespoons plain yoghurt
toasted almonds or coconut chips (see note), to serve

Place the rolled oats in a saucepan with the coconut milk and 250 ml (8½ fl oz/1 cup) water. Cook over medium heat, stirring, for about 5 minutes or until the porridge has reached the desired consistency – you can add a little more water if required.

Stir through the chia seeds and maple syrup (if using). Gently stir through the strawberries. Divide among serving bowls and top with the yoghurt, toasted almonds or coconut chips and the extra strawberries.

Coconut chips *When buying coconut chips, look for a brand with no added preservatives and for babies under 12 months, no added honey.*

Baby's serve: for a **younger baby**, blend together the porridge and yoghurt (omit the almonds/coconut chips) until smooth. For an **older baby**, keep the puréed consistency lumpier – or don't purée at all – so that he experiences more texture. If you like you can serve some of the strawberries as finger food on the side.

Toddler's serve: serve as is.

Breakfast

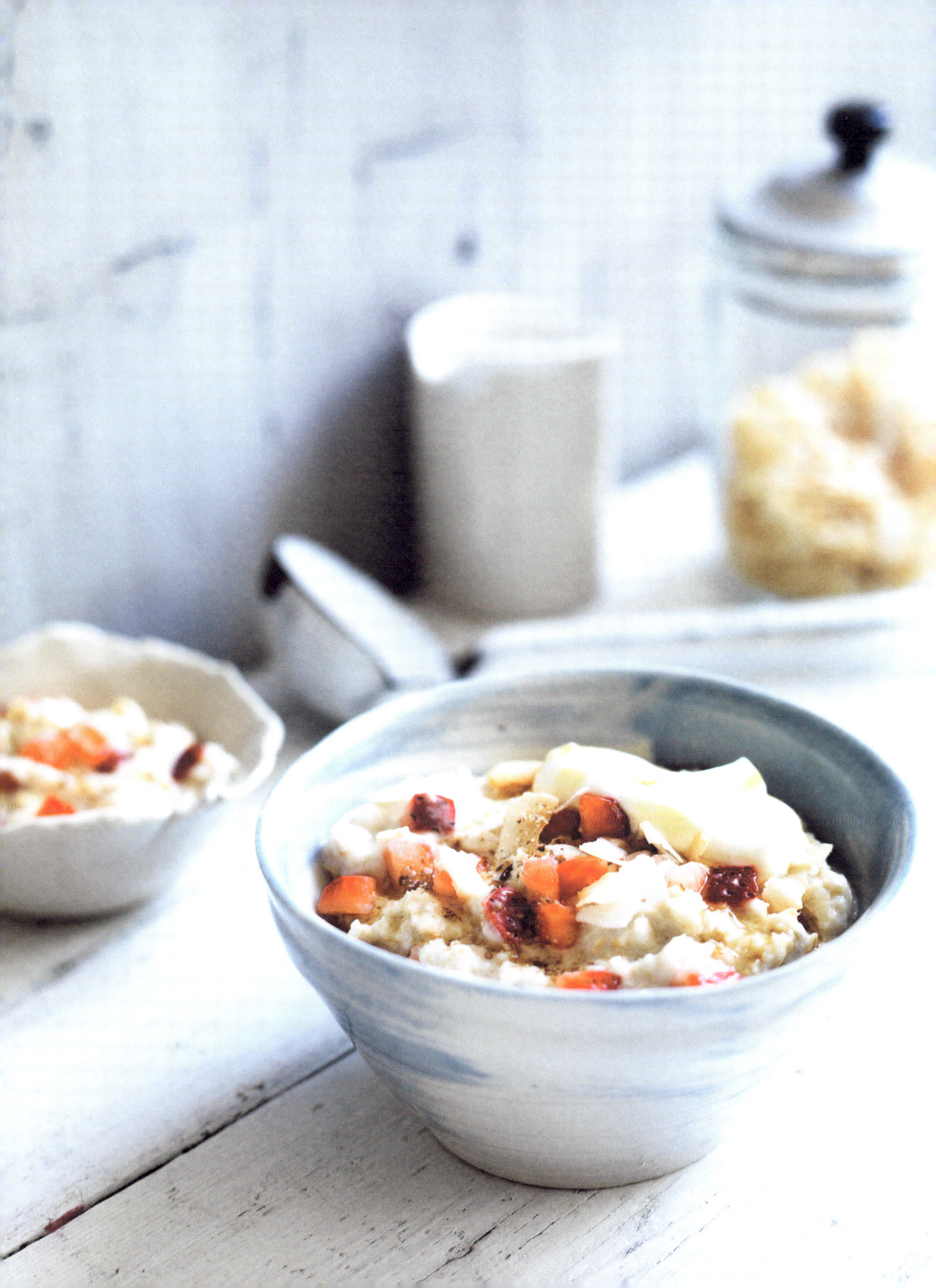

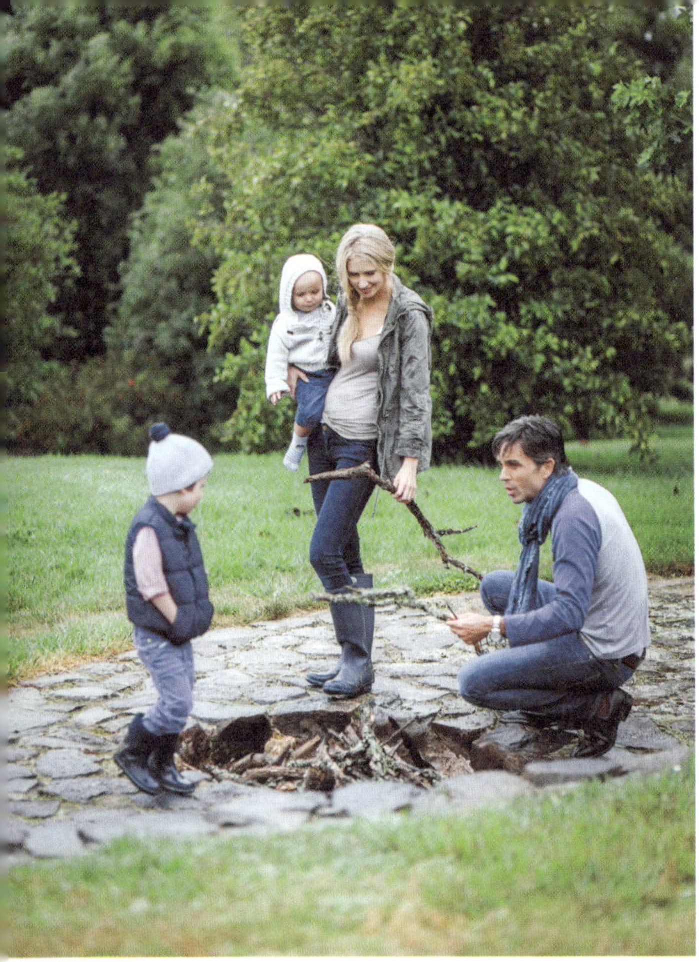
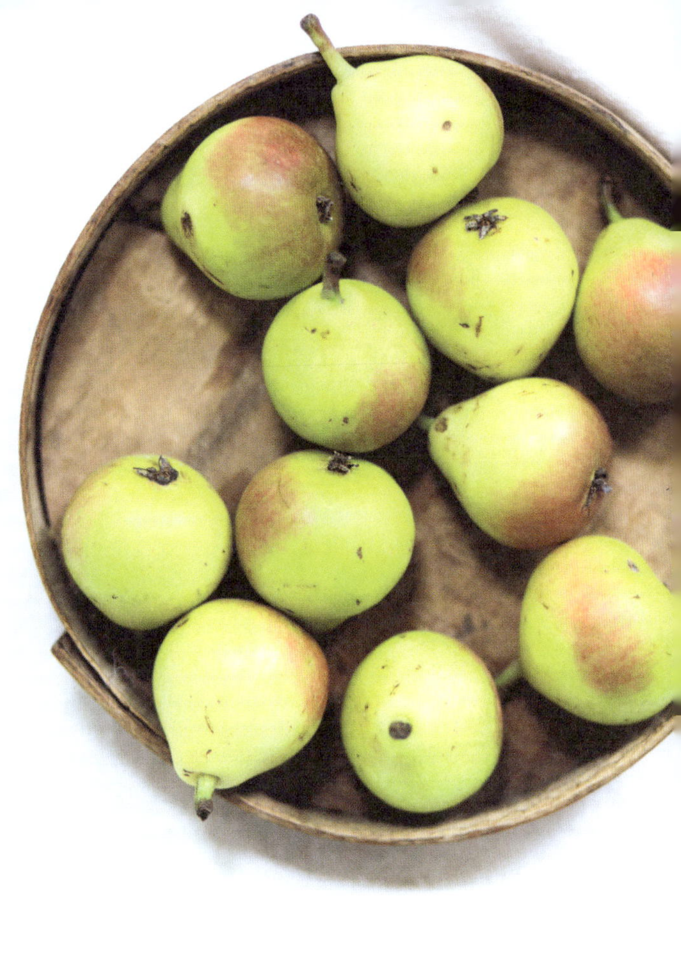
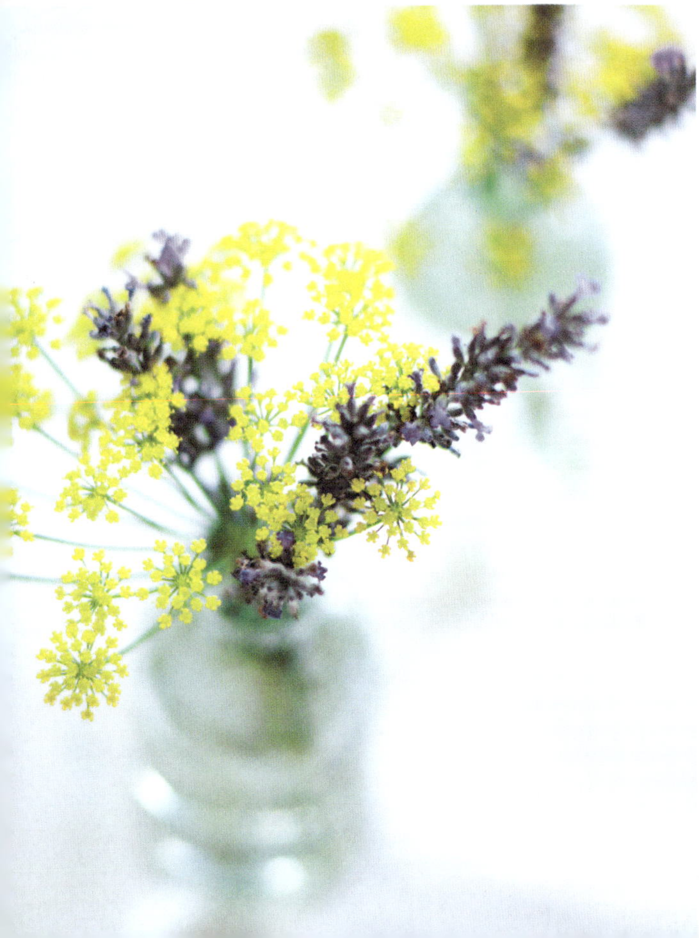
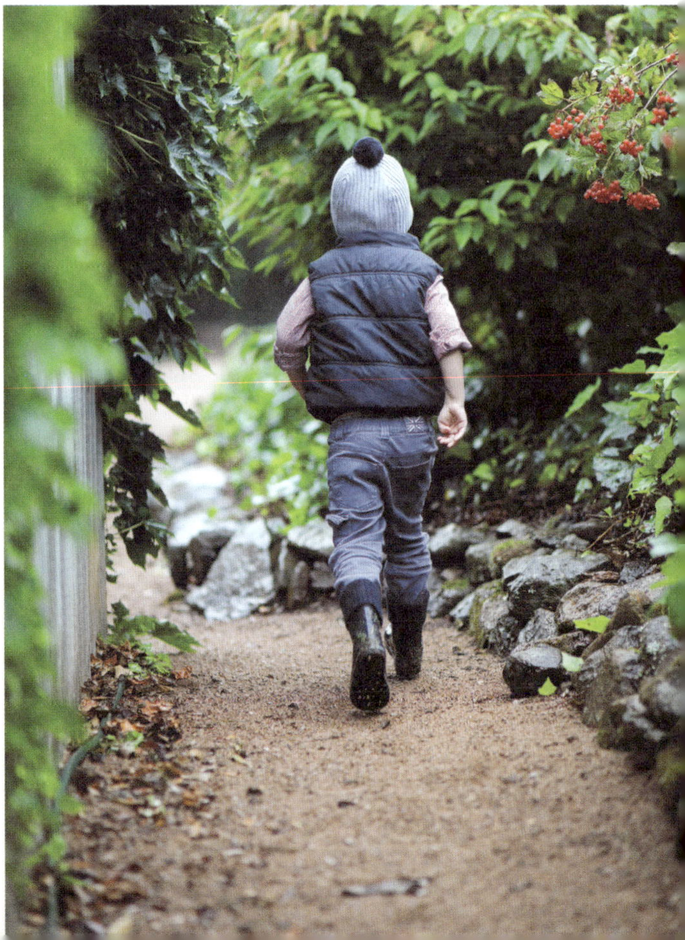

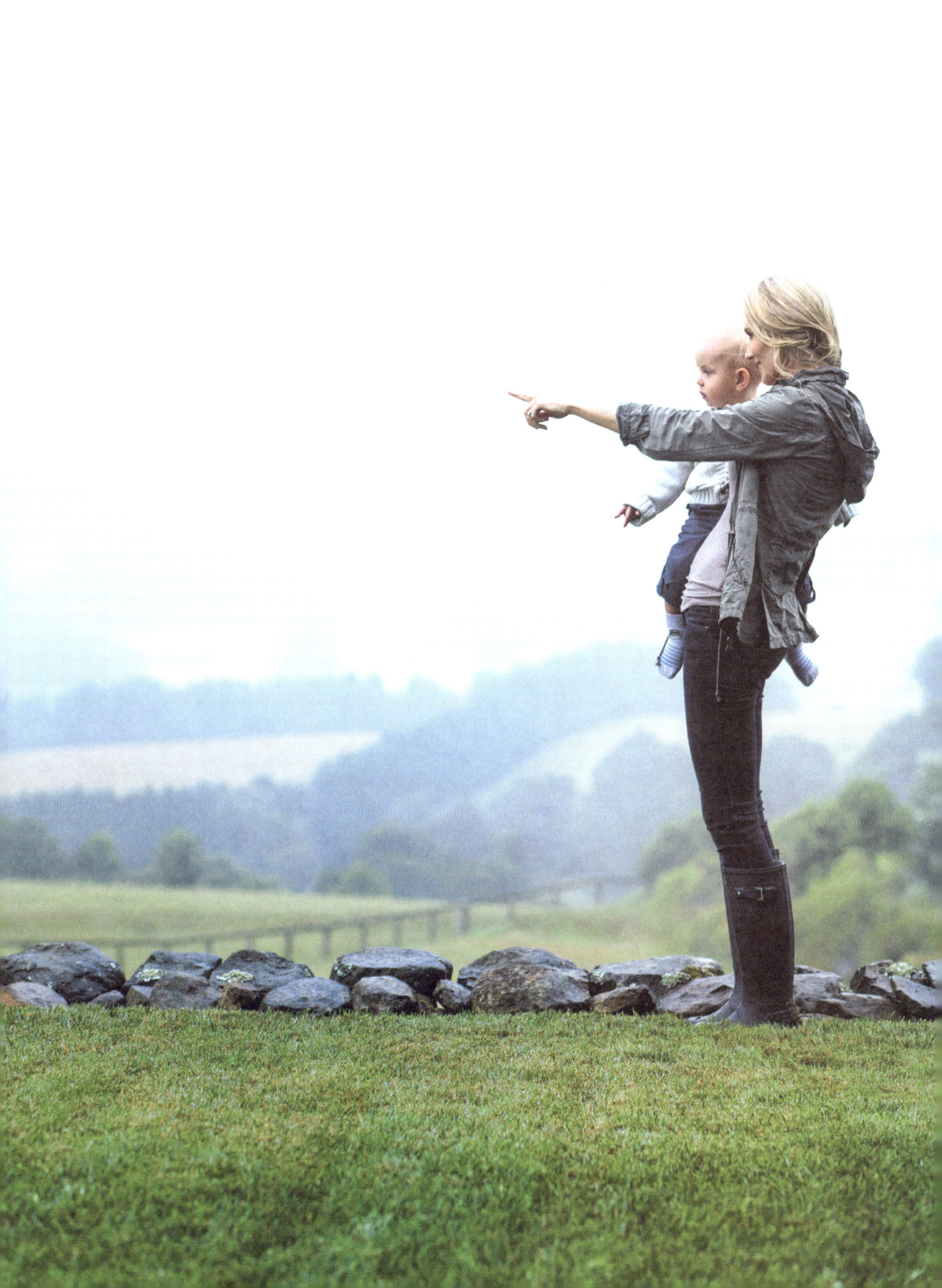

Spiced fruit compote

Serves 2–3

If star anise and cardamom are not spices you usually cook with, you're in for a treat. I love adding flavours like this to children's food as it exposes them to a more interesting world of taste than the fruit alone and helps cultivate their rapidly developing palates.

3 plums, halved and stones removed
3 apricots, halved and stones removed
2 white nectarines, halved and stones removed
250 ml (8½ fl oz/1 cup) pure (100%) apple juice or water
3 cardamom pods, crushed
1 whole star anise
plain yoghurt, to serve (optional – omit for dairy-free)

Place the fruit and apple juice or water in a saucepan with the cardamom and star anise. Bring to the boil, then reduce the heat to low, cover, and simmer for 6–8 minutes or until the fruit is tender. Divide the spiced fruit compote between serving bowls and serve with yoghurt, if liked.

Fruit skins *The benefit of keeping the skins on your fruit is that your baby is getting more fibre and nutrients. However, for younger babies in particular, giving them lots of fibre is not always desirable as it can affect their nutrient absorption. Also, if fruit isn't organic, removing the skins can be one way of getting rid of some of the pesticide residue. If the skins are easy to remove, you might like to do so until your baby is older and handling more texture in his meals.*

Baby's serve: for a **younger baby**, remove and discard the cardamom and star anise from the poached fruit and blend until smooth. For an **older baby**, keep the puréed consistency lumpier – or you can mash or chop the fruit instead of blending – so that he experiences more texture. (Wait until serving to stir in the yoghurt, as it's better to eat yoghurt fresh, particularly because freezing and reheating can destroy some of the precious probiotics.)

Toddler's serve: serve as is, chopping the fruit into smaller pieces for your child.

Breakfast

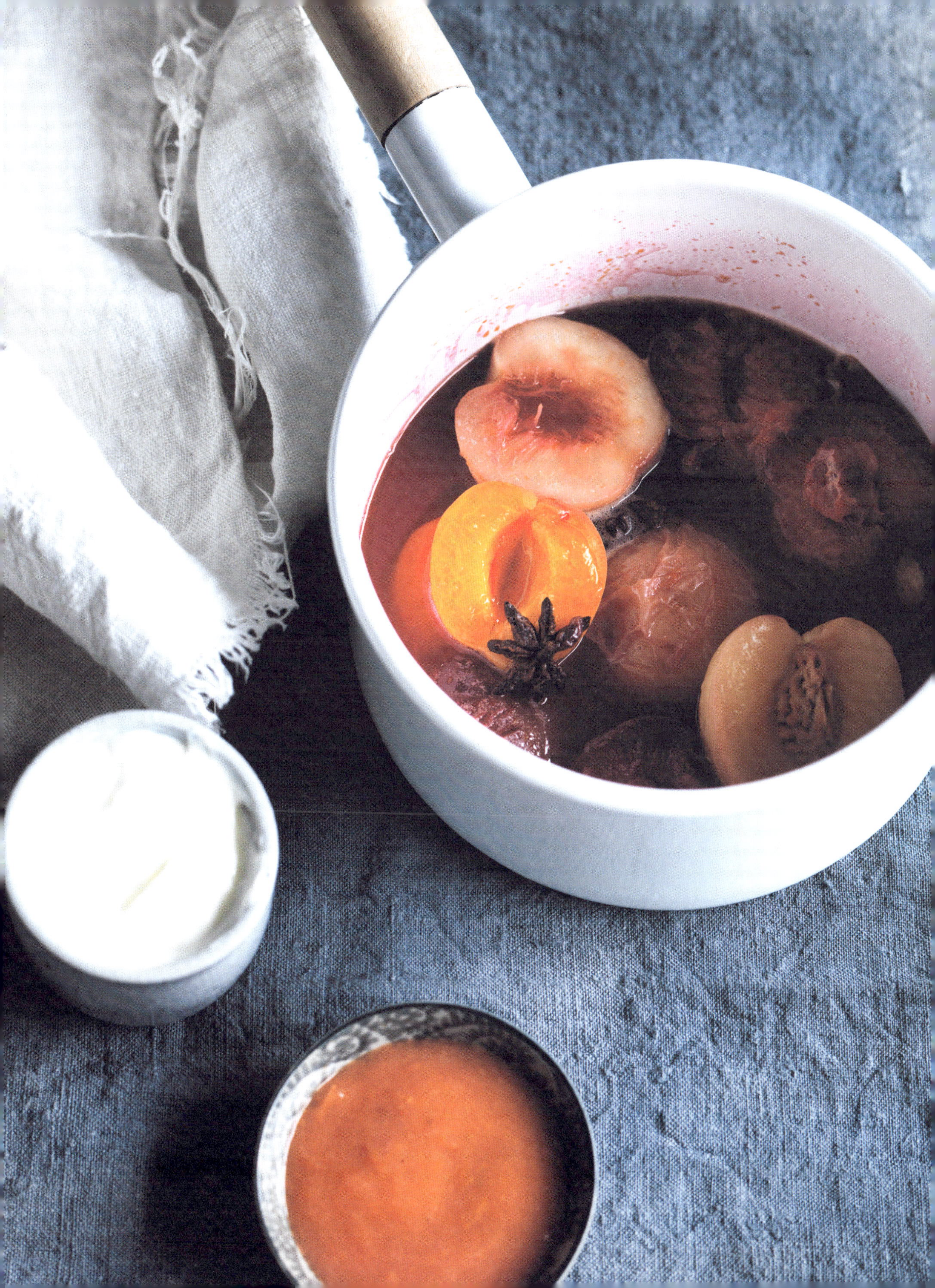

Homemade baked beans

Serves 2–3

Baked beans are a wonderfully nutritious food – homemade are definitely better than anything you'll find in a tin. For a start, tinned baked beans tend to have extra additives, such as thickeners and salt, which are best to avoid where possible. Secondly, making the beans yourself means you can include a lovely serve of vegetables at breakfast time. The end result is so much healthier (and tastier) than even the best store-bought options.

Although not essential, adding tomato sauce may come in handy for children who are used to tinned beans, as it makes the flavour more like what they're used to. Eventually, with a bit of luck, you can wean them off it altogether.

400 g (14 oz) tin cannellini (lima) beans, rinsed and drained
250 ml (8½ fl oz/1 cup) Five-vegetable pasta sauce (page 142)
1 tablespoon tomato sauce (ketchup) (optional)
wholegrain (whole-wheat) toast, to serve (choose gluten-free brand if needed)

Place the beans, pasta sauce and tomato sauce in a saucepan over low–medium heat. Cook the beans, stirring occasionally, for about 5 minutes, or until warmed through. Serve the warm beans with toast.

Baby's serve: for a **younger baby**, blend the baked beans until smooth, adding a little extra liquid if needed. For an **older baby**, keep the puréed consistency lumpier – or you can mash or chop the beans instead of blending – so that he experiences more texture. You can serve toast fingers on the side as finger food.

Toddler's serve: serve as is, with toast fingers on the side.

Cooking dried beans If you have dried cannellini beans on hand, soak them in plenty of cold water for 5 hours or overnight. Drain, rinse and transfer them to a large saucepan. Cover with cold water and bring to the boil. Scoop any foam off the top, reduce to a simmer and cook, partially covered, for about 2 hours or until tender. Keep an eye on the water level, topping it up if needed.

Breakfast

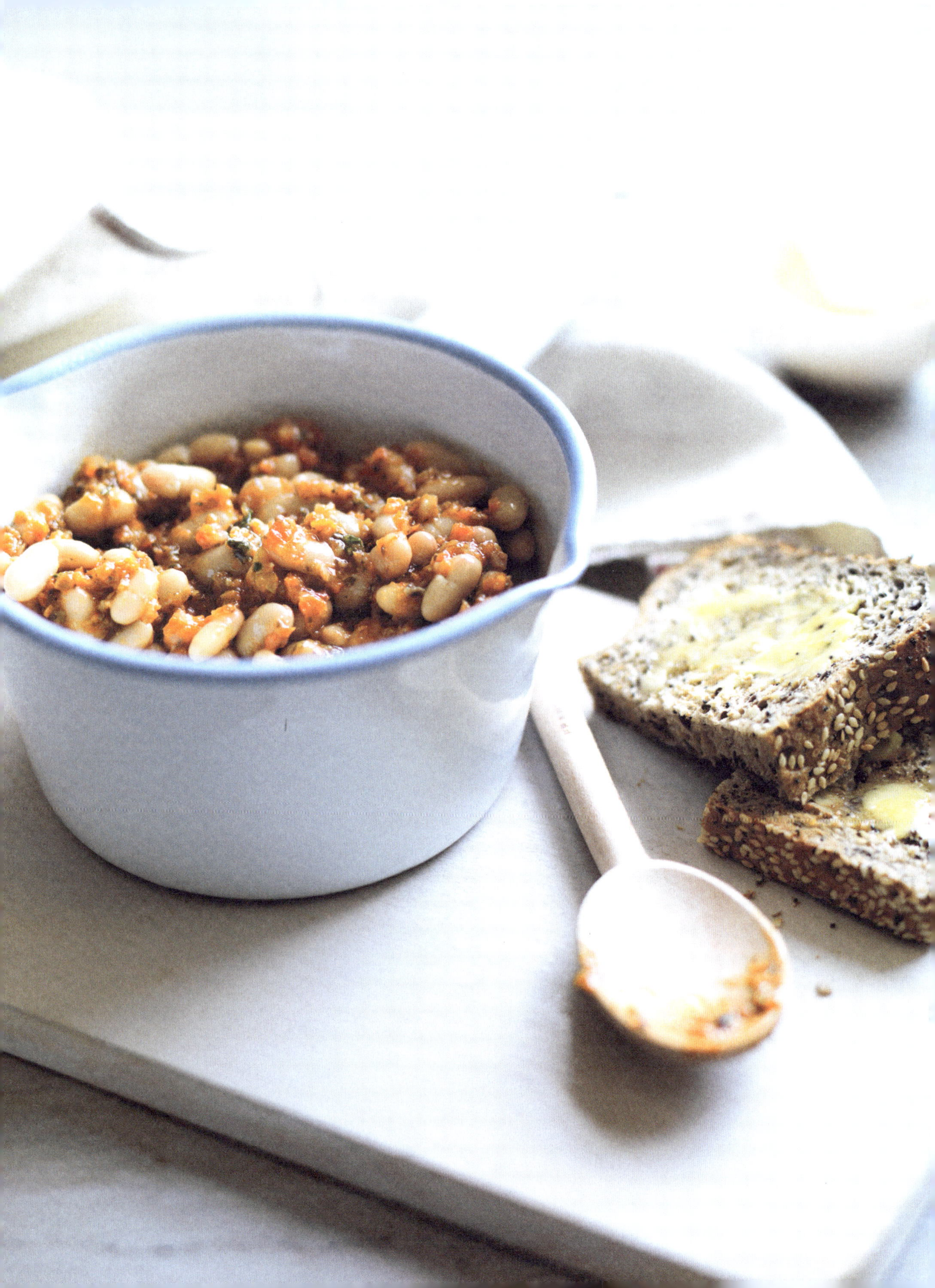

Sweetcorn fritters with smoked salmon

Makes 10–12 fritters

If your child wants to join you in the kitchen, there are plenty of steps in this breakfast he can get involved in. While it may make things slower and messier for you now, one day he might reward your patience by making it all by himself and bringing you breakfast in bed. We parents have to dream, right?

400 g (14 oz/2 cups) fresh sweet corn kernels (about 2 corn cobs)
3 spring onions (scallions), roughly chopped
2 eggs
1 small handful coriander (cilantro) or flat-leaf (Italian) parsley leaves
150 g (5½ oz/1 cup) self-raising flour
1 zucchini (courgette), finely grated
light olive oil or rice bran oil for shallow frying
smoked salmon (optional, see note)
lemon wedges, to serve

AVOCADO SALSA
1 avocado, stone removed and flesh diced
1 tomato, finely diced
1 spring onion (scallion), finely chopped
2 tablespoons chopped coriander (cilantro) leaves
1 tablespoon lemon juice

Note *Smoked salmon is a great source of omega-3 fats, however, as with other smoked foods, you might prefer to have it in moderation due to the possible links between the smoking process and adverse health outcomes. For your baby and toddler, keep it for a more occasional treat.*

To make the avocado salsa, gently stir all of the ingredients together. Set aside.

To make the fritters, place half of the corn kernels in a food processor with the spring onion, eggs, coriander and flour and process until combined. Transfer to a large bowl.

Using your hands, squeeze the zucchini to remove the excess moisture. Add to the fritter batter with the remaining corn. Stir to combine.

Heat the oil in a non-stick frying pan over medium heat. Working in batches, drop large spoonfuls of the mixture into the pan and cook for 2–3 minutes on each side, or until golden and cooked through. Drain on paper towels. Serve the warm fritters with the avocado salsa, smoked salmon (if using) and lemon wedges.

Baby's serve: for a **younger baby**, wait until your baby is managing some finger foods (which may not happen until 8–9 months or older) before offering him these fritters. Spread the fritters with avocado and cut into strips. For an **older baby**, serve as for a younger baby.

Toddler's serve: serve as is.

Breakfast

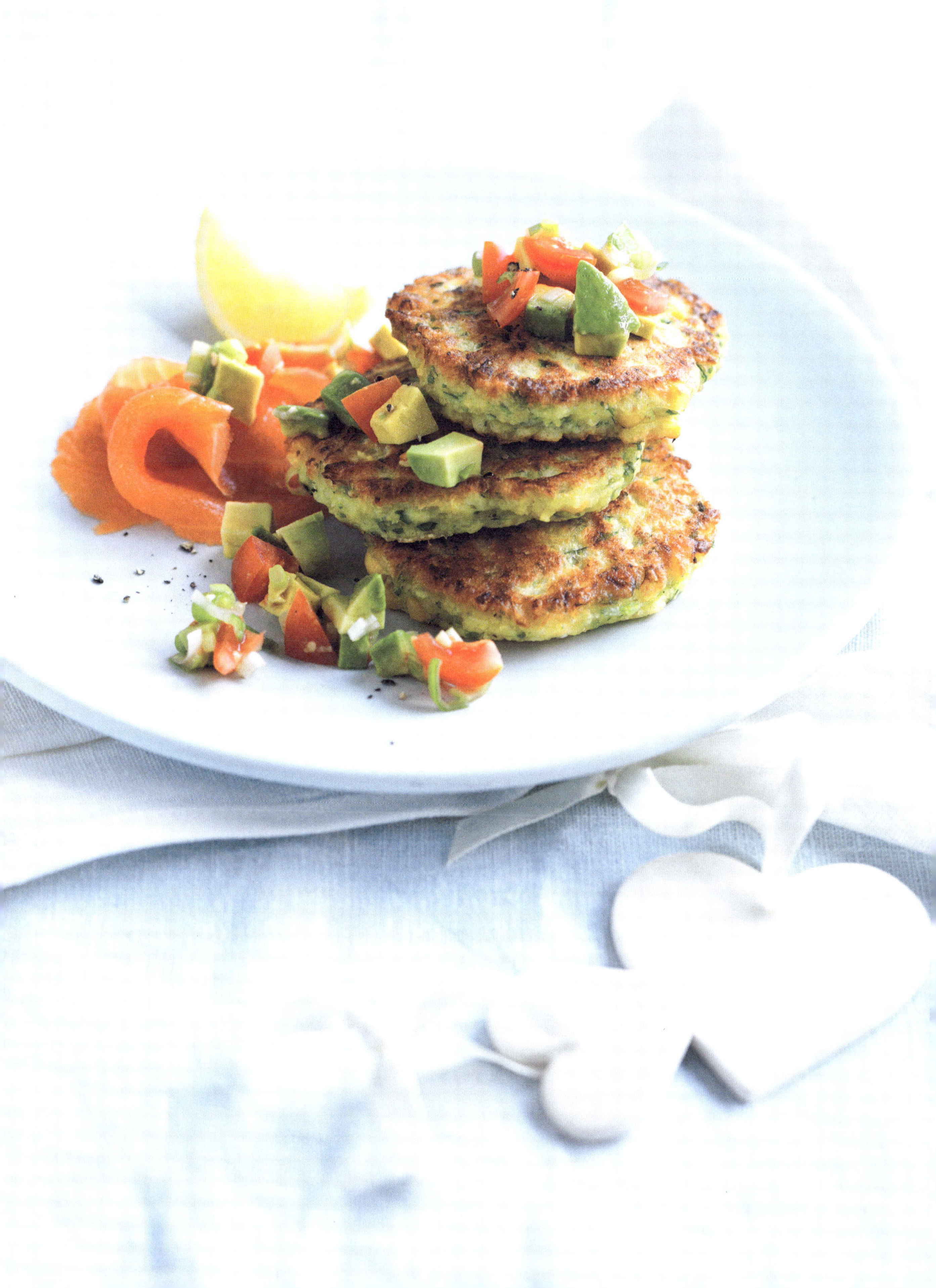

Boiled eggs with two green dippers

Serves 4

Sometimes foods that are not so well liked can become popular when there's dipping involved. Serving eggs with asparagus dippers might just help your child develop a liking for this super-nutritious vegetable. If he's a toast lover, spreading his toast with this lovely broad (fava) bean dip makes for a seriously tasty and healthy breakfast.

1 bunch asparagus, woody ends trimmed
4 eggs
wholemeal (whole-wheat) toast soldiers, to serve (choose a gluten-free brand if needed)

BROAD BEAN DIP
230 g (8 oz) frozen or fresh broad (fava) beans
½ garlic clove
50 g (1¾ oz/⅓ cup) cashews (raw or dry-roasted)
40 g (1½ oz) salt-reduced feta cheese (see note, page 38)
1 teaspoon extra-virgin olive oil
2 teaspoons lemon juice

Baby's serve: for a **younger baby**, blend together some egg, asparagus and a little of the broad bean dip until smooth. You may need to add some liquid (water or your baby's milk) to achieve the desired consistency. For an **older baby**, keep the puréed consistency lumpier or serve as finger food. Gently remove the shell before putting the egg in an egg cup and slicing off the top of the egg.

Toddler's serve: serve as for an older baby or as is.

To make the broad bean dip, steam or microwave the broad beans until tender. Refresh under cold running water. Peel and set aside.

Place the garlic and cashews in a food processor and process until roughly chopped. Add the shelled broad beans, feta, olive oil and lemon juice and process until combined but still a little chunky. Set aside.

Cook the asparagus in a shallow saucepan of boiling water for 1–2 minutes, or until bright green and tender (or you can steam it if preferred). Drain and cut in half crossways.

Place the eggs in a saucepan and add enough cold water to cover. Bring to the boil, then reduce the heat to low–medium and simmer for 3 minutes for soft-boiled, or until cooked to your liking. (Avoid giving under-cooked eggs to children under 2 years – see page 18 – cook until the whites have completely set and the yolks have started to thicken.)

Serve the boiled eggs in egg cups with the asparagus on the side and the broad bean dip spread over the toast soldiers.

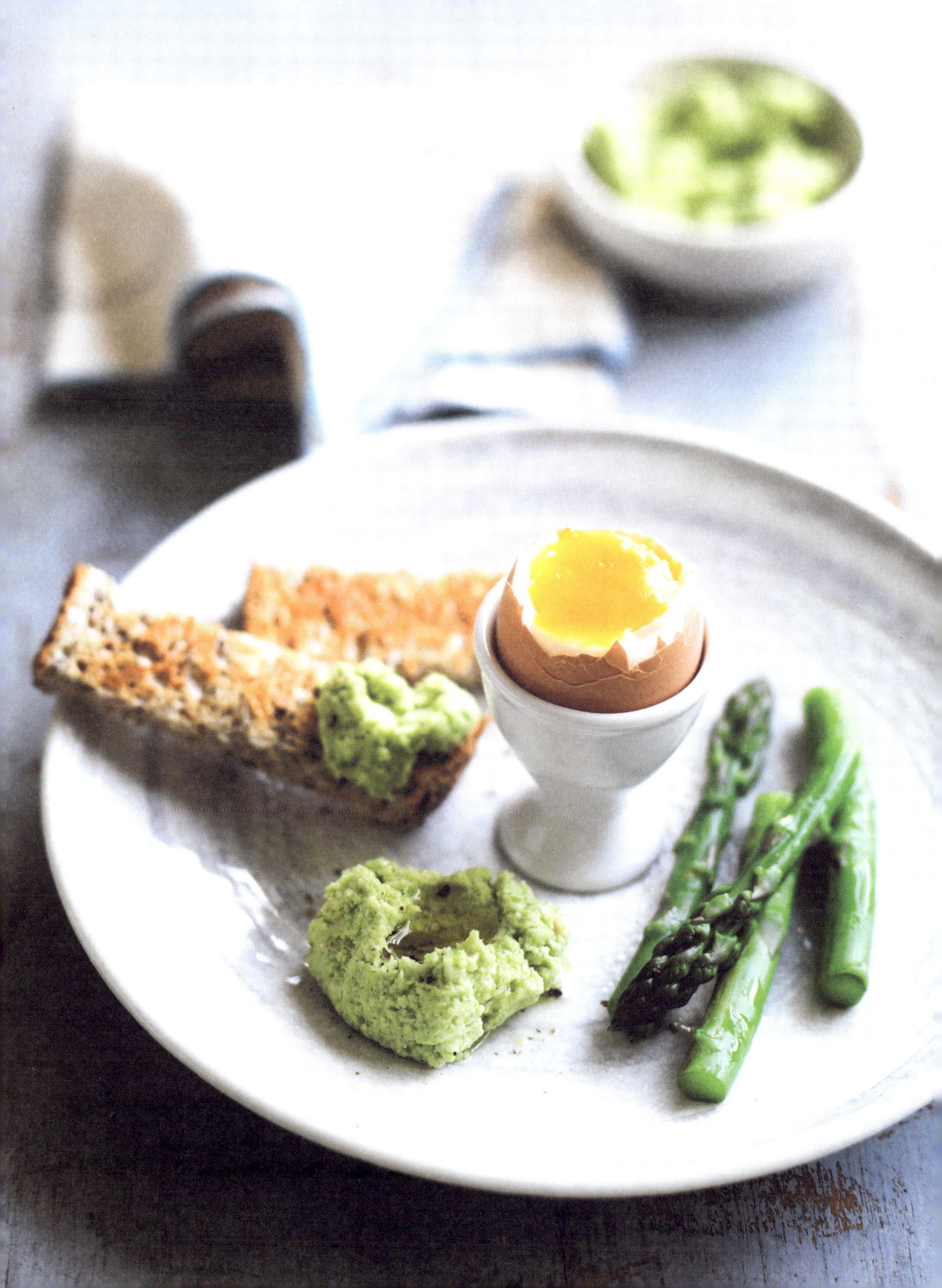

Sweet potato rösti with herbed ricotta and poached egg

Serves 4

If you have a child who doesn't like whole eggs, you can just serve him the sweet potato rösti, which has one egg mixed through it. The rösti also make a great side for lunch or dinner.

185 g (6½ oz/¾ cup) fresh ricotta (see note, page 38)
1 teaspoon finely grated lemon zest (optional – omit for baby's serve)
1 tablespoon finely chopped flat-leaf (Italian) parsley
1 tablespoon finely snipped chives, plus extra for garnish
300 g (10½ oz/2 cups) peeled, grated sweet potato
2 tablespoons plain (all-purpose) flour
5 eggs
1–2 tablespoons olive oil

Baby's serve: for a **younger baby**, blend together the egg and ricotta mixture with some cooked rösti until smooth (try to use a softer, not-too-crispy rösti for this). Add as much liquid (water or your baby's milk) as you need to achieve the desired consistency. For an **older baby**, keep the consistency lumpier or serve as finger food – spread the ricotta mixture over the rösti, cut up the rösti and the poached egg and let him eat with his hands.

Toddler's serve: serve as is, cutting into pieces he can pick up with his hands or with cutlery.

Place the ricotta, lemon zest (if using) and herbs in a bowl and mix until well combined. Refrigerate until needed.

Place the sweet potato, flour and 1 of the eggs in a bowl and stir until well combined.

Heat 2 teaspoons of the oil in a frying pan over low–medium heat. Working in batches, drop large spoonfuls of the sweet potato mixture into the pan. Lightly press and shape each one into a circular shape. Cover and cook for 3–4 minutes on each side, or until golden and cooked through. Transfer to a plate and keep warm.

Fill a deep frying pan with 3 cm (1¼ inches) water. Bring to a simmer over low–medium heat and gently crack in the remaining eggs. Cook for about 4 minutes, or until cooked to your liking. (Avoid giving under-cooked eggs to children under 2 years – see page 18 – cook until the whites have completely set and the yolks have started to thicken.)

To serve, place 2 rösti on each plate, then top each with a dollop of the ricotta mixture and a poached egg. Garnish with the extra chives.

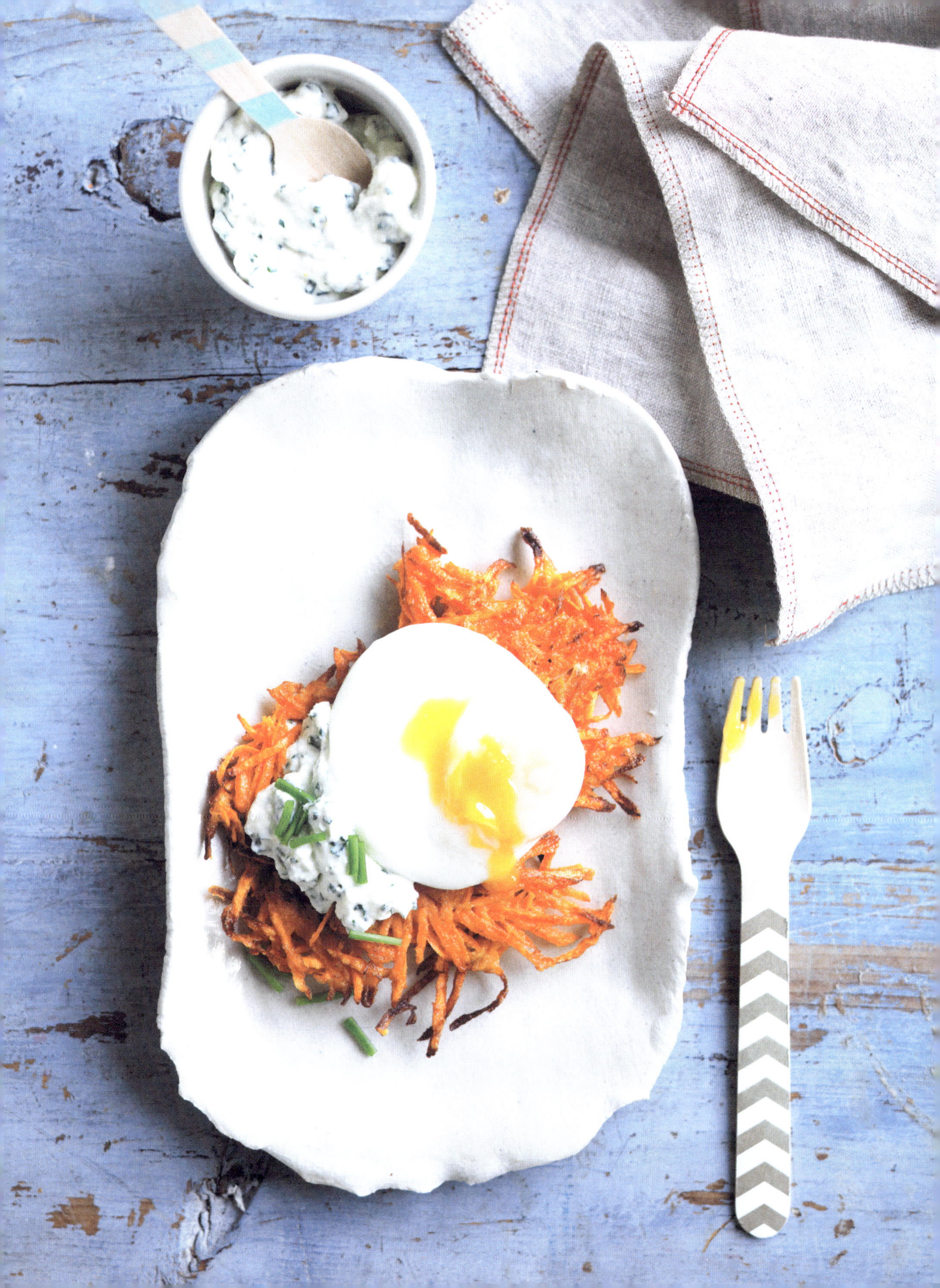

Mediterranean baked eggs

Serves 4

These Mediterranean-style baked eggs make a delicious alternative to poached eggs. They're sophisticated enough that adults love them, but also a hit with younger members of the family. If you have dried beans on hand, you can soak and cook them instead of using tinned (see note, page 52).

2 tablespoons olive oil
1 onion, finely chopped
1 large red capsicum (pepper), seeded and cut into thin strips
3 tomatoes, diced
400 g (14 oz) tin cannellini (lima), borlotti (cranberry) or red kidney beans, rinsed and drained
4 eggs
100 g (3½ oz/⅔ cup) crumbled reduced-salt feta cheese (see note, page 38)
toast, to serve (choose a gluten-free brand if needed)

Preheat the oven to 190°C (375°F). Heat the oil in a frying pan over medium heat and cook the onion for 5 minutes, or until softened. Add the capsicum and cook for a further 3 minutes or until softened. Add the diced tomato, cover, and cook for about 5 minutes, or until the vegetables are tender. Stir in the beans.

Divide the mixture among four small shallow baking dishes. Make a well in the centre of each and break an egg into each dish. Scatter the feta over the vegetables and beans, then cover each dish loosely with foil. Bake in the oven for 15 minutes, or until the eggs are cooked to your liking. (Avoid giving under-cooked eggs to children under 2 years – see page 18 – cook until the whites have completely set and the yolks have started to thicken.)

Serve the Mediterranean baked eggs in their dishes with toast on the side.

Baby's serve: for a **younger baby**, blend together some of the egg and the cooked vegetable mixture until smooth. You may need to add some liquid (water or your baby's milk) to achieve the desired consistency. For an **older baby**, keep the consistency lumpier or just chop into small pieces.

Toddler's serve: serve as is, cutting into pieces he can pick up with his hands or cutlery.

Breakfast

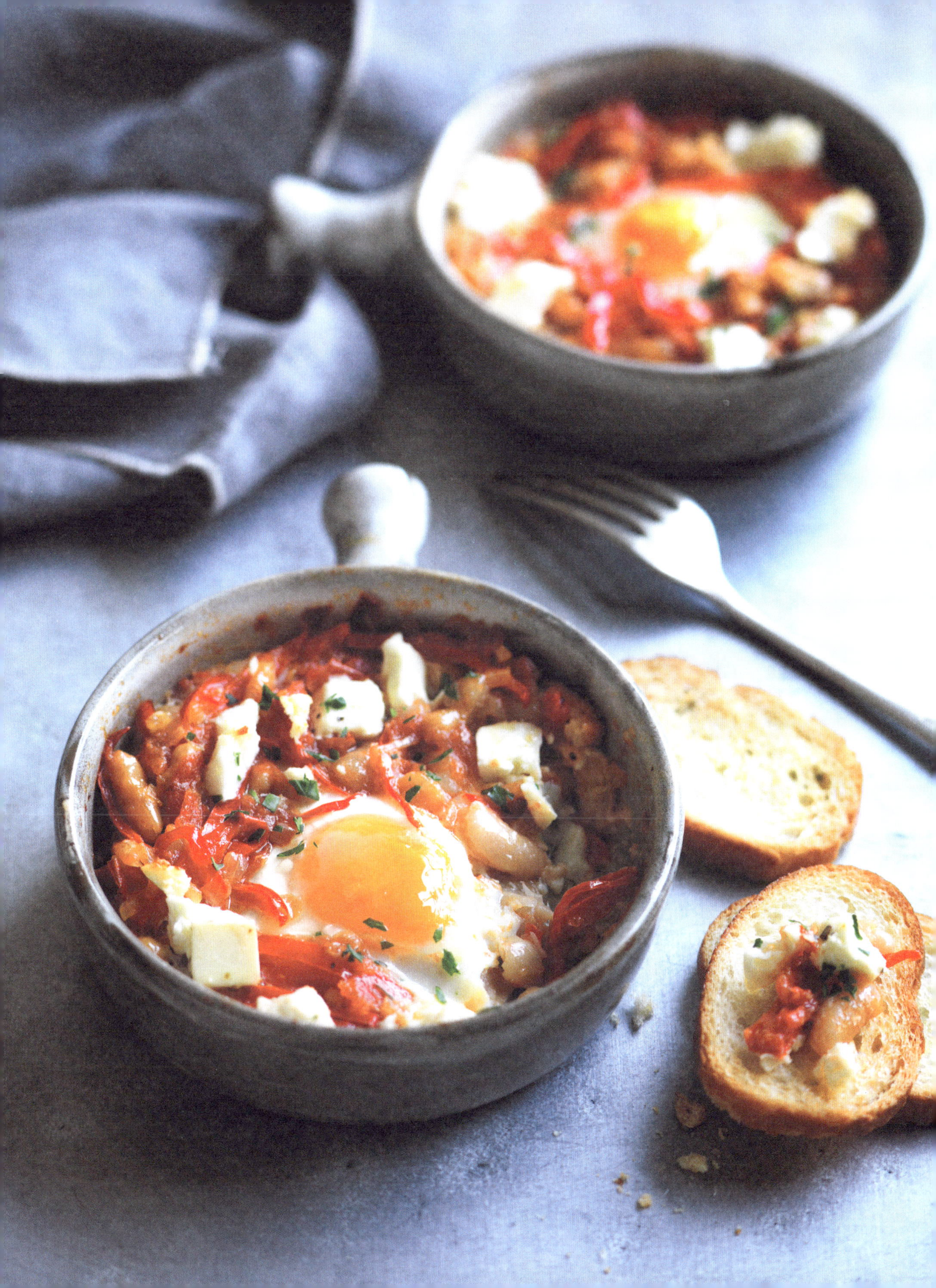

Wholemeal almond berry pikelets

Makes about 15

This is a favourite breakfast in my house. This recipe is healthier than traditional pikelets because it uses wholemeal flour and includes nutrient-rich berries and ground almonds, without any added sugar. For a delicious variation, replace the mixed berries with one mashed banana. For an extra nutrient boost, stir one tablespoon of chia seeds through the mixture.

- 150 g (5½ oz/1 cup) wholemeal (whole-wheat) self-raising flour
- ¼ teaspoon baking powder (baking soda)
- 25 g (1 oz/¼ cup) ground almonds
- 2 eggs
- 170 ml (5½ fl oz/⅔ cup) milk
- 40 g (1½ oz) butter, melted (or use a nut oil, see note)
- 100 g (3½ oz) fresh or frozen mixed raspberries and blueberries
- maple syrup (optional), to serve
- fresh fruit, to serve

Nut oils *I love using walnut or hazelnut oil in my pikelets instead of butter – both add a beautiful flavour. If you have either on hand, replace the butter with 2 tablespoons of oil. Store nut oils in the refrigerator to maximise their shelf life and preserve nutrients.*

Combine the flour, baking powder and ground almonds in a large bowl. Make a well in the centre and add the egg, milk and melted butter. Start stirring the wet ingredients, gradually drawing in the dry ingredients until just combined – do not overmix. Gently stir through the berries.

Heat a non-stick frying pan over medium heat. Working in batches, drop spoonfuls of batter into the pan and cook for 2–3 minutes on each side, or until golden and cooked through. Transfer to a plate and keep warm while cooking the remainder.

Serve the warm pikelets topped with maple syrup (if using) and fresh fruit of your liking.

Baby's serve: for a **younger baby**, wait until your baby is managing some finger foods (which may not happen until 8–9 months or older) before offering him these pikelets. Omit the maple syrup and cut into strips that he can easily hold. For an **older baby**, serve as for a younger baby.

Toddler's serve: serve as is with just a little or no maple syrup.

Breakfast

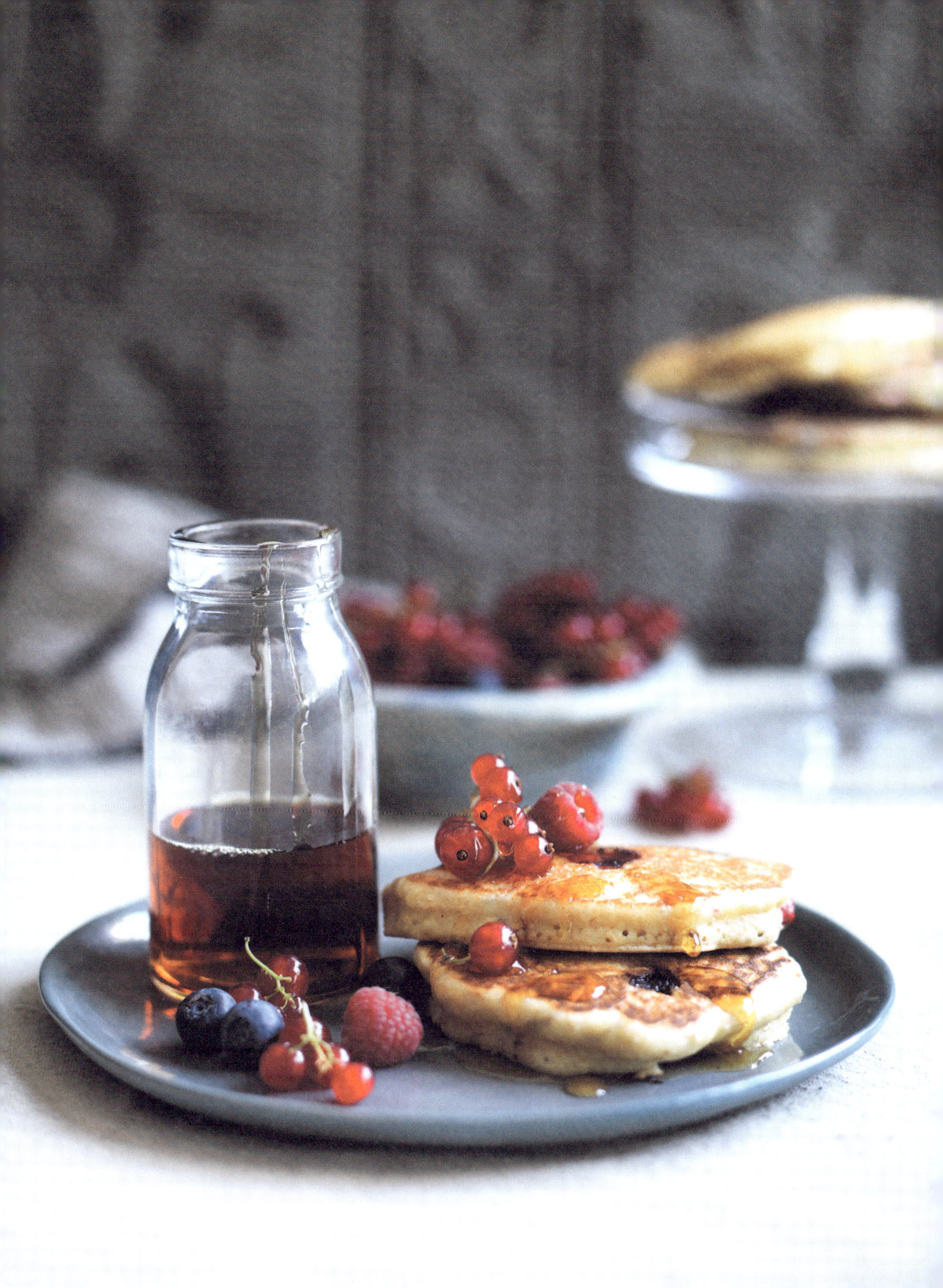

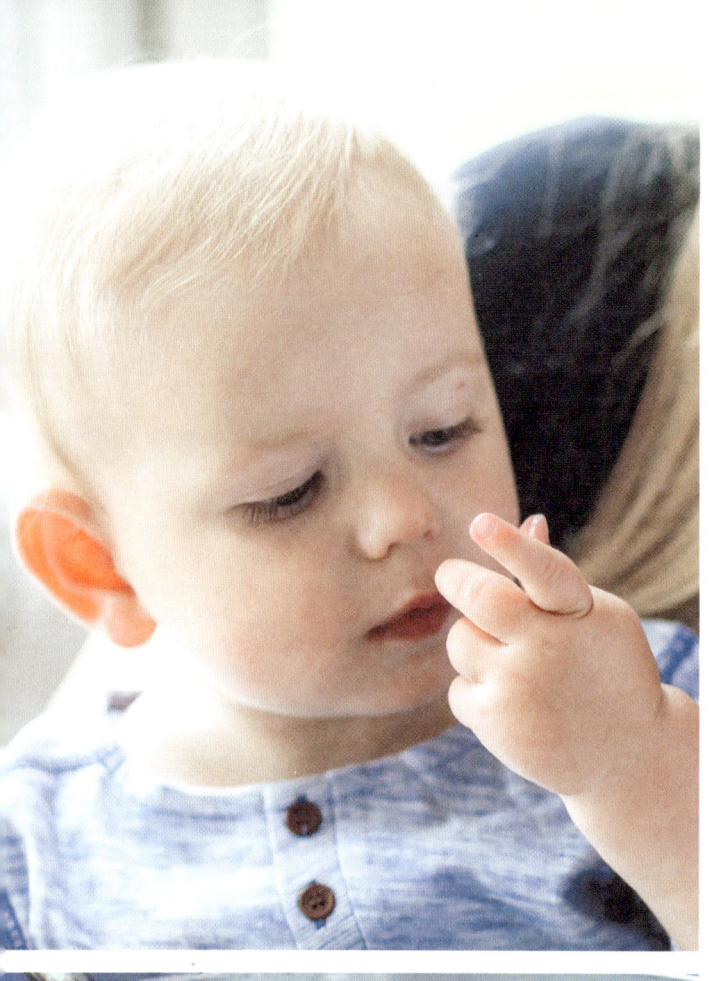

You can encourage your children to have a love of good food by offering them a wide range of ingredients, giving them plenty of time to enjoy their wondrous sight, taste and feel, and being patient as they learn to feed themselves.

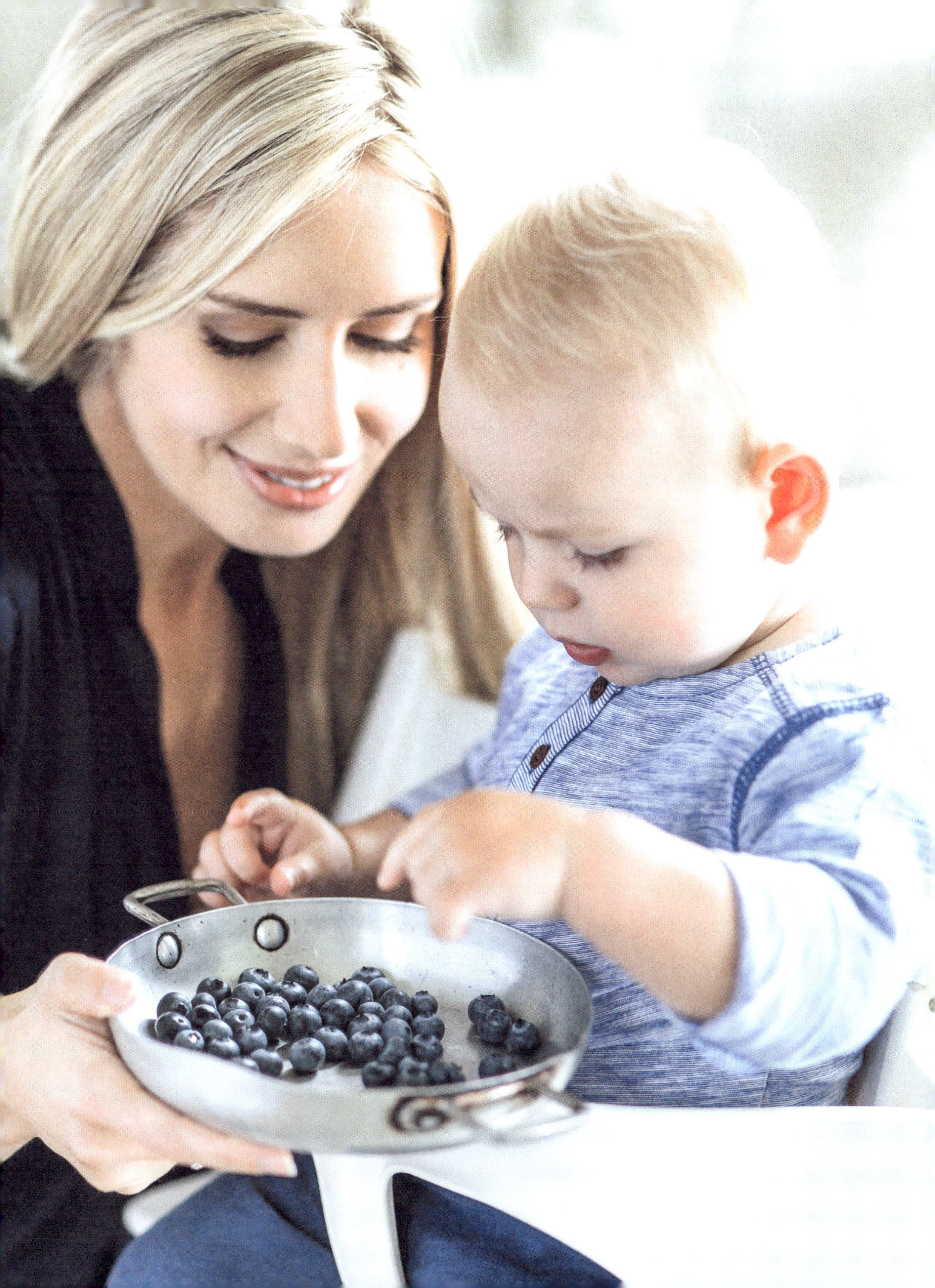

Crêpes with warm maple oranges

Serves 4

Everyone loves crêpes and this recipe, which uses eggs, wholemeal flour and no sugar makes for a guilt-free breakfast treat. If you'd like a little more zing, add a teaspoon of finely grated orange zest to the maple sauce.

200 g (7 oz/1⅓ cups) wholemeal (whole-wheat) plain (all-purpose) flour
3 eggs
375 ml (12½ fl oz/1½ cups) milk, plus extra for thinning
10 g (⅓ oz) butter, melted, plus extra for cooking

MAPLE ORANGES
20 g (¾ oz) butter
2 tablespoons maple syrup
juice of 1 orange (about 3 tablespoons)
2 oranges, peeled and cut into segments

Baby's serve: for a **younger baby**, wait until your baby is managing some finger foods (which may not happen until 8–9 months or older), before offering him these crêpes. Cut into strips that he can easily hold and serve with fresh fruit (it's best not to serve the maple oranges because babies under 12 months shouldn't be having any added sugar, but fresh orange segments are fine). For an **older baby**, serve as for a younger baby.

Toddler's serve: serve as is, cut into small pieces.

To make the maple oranges, heat a large non-stick frying pan over medium heat. Add the butter, maple syrup and orange juice. Cook, stirring occasionally, for 6 minutes, or until the sauce has thickened and is a syrupy consistency. Stir through the orange segments. Remove from the heat and keep warm.

To make the crêpes, place the flour in a large bowl. Make a well in the centre and add the eggs and milk. Start whisking the wet ingredients, gradually drawing in the flour until combined. Stir in the melted butter. If you have time, let the mixture stand for 1–2 hours or overnight. (If the mixture thickens while standing, add a little more milk before cooking for a thinner consistency.)

Melt a little butter in a small or medium non-stick frying pan over medium heat. When the butter is bubbling, pour in enough batter to cover the base of the pan, and swirl to spread evenly. Cook the crêpes for about 1 minute on each side, or until golden and cooked through. Transfer to a plate and keep warm while cooking the remainder.

Serve the crêpes with the maple oranges and sauce.

Breakfast

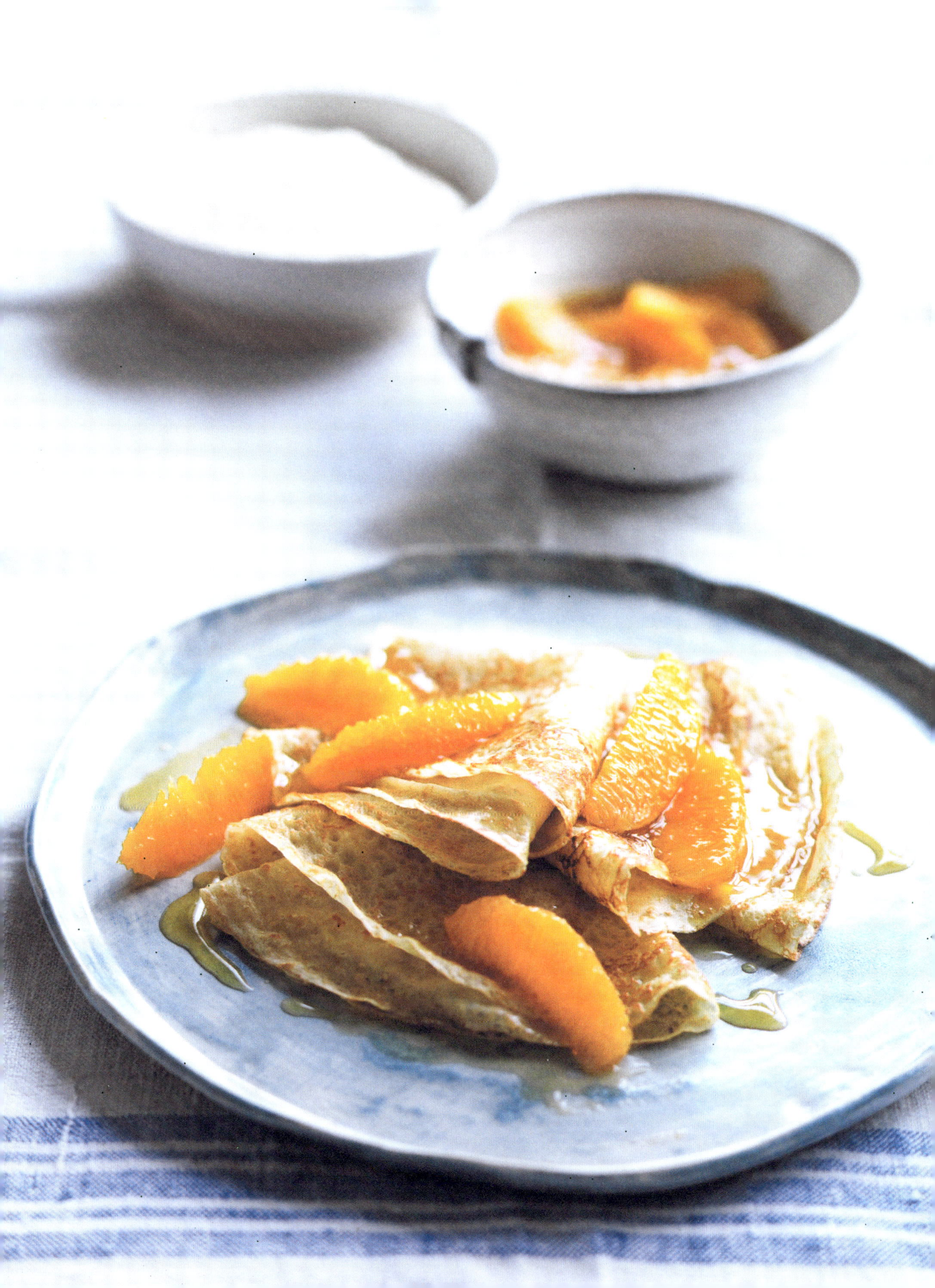

Hazelnut oat pancakes with crushed berry sauce

Makes about 12

If your child isn't a fan of oats, these pancakes are a great way of including some in his breakfast without him noticing. Teaming the oats with ground hazelnuts, eggs and berries makes this pancake recipe about one of the healthiest imaginable.

65 g (2¼ oz/⅔ cup) rolled oats or (unflavoured) quick oats
35 g (1¼ oz/⅓ cup) ground hazelnuts or ground almonds
110 g (4 oz/¾ cup) wholemeal (whole-wheat) self-raising flour
2 tablespoons hazelnut oil or olive oil
2 eggs
190 ml (6½ fl oz/¾ cup) milk

CRUSHED BERRY SAUCE
310 g (11 oz) fresh or frozen mixed berries
juice of 1 orange
2 tablespoons maple syrup (optional)

Tip *If you'd like to make a nut-free version, replace the ground nuts with a ground seed mix. Finely process a mix of seeds such as pepitas (pumpkin seeds), sunflower seeds and linseeds in a high-powered food processor (or Thermomix) and your child will also benefit from the wonderful nutritional value these seeds offer.*

Baby's serve: for a **younger baby**, wait until your baby is managing some finger foods (which may not happen until 8–9 months or older) before offering him these pancakes. When he's ready, cut into strips that he can easily hold and spread with a little butter, fruit purée or berry sauce. For an **older baby**, serve as for a younger baby, as finger food.

Toddler's serve: serve as is.

To make the crushed berry sauce, place the berries and orange juice in a small saucepan over low–medium heat and cook for about 10 minutes, or until the berries are soft. Stir through the maple syrup (if using). Depending on the texture you prefer, you can blend to a purée or use as is.

To make the hazelnut oat pancakes, place the rolled oats in a food processor (this isn't necessary if you're using quick oats). Process briefly until coarsely chopped. Transfer to a large bowl with the ground hazelnuts and flour. Make a well in the centre.

Add the oil, eggs and milk and start stirring the wet ingredients, gradually drawing in the dry ingredients until just combined. If the mixture is too thick, add a little more milk.

Heat a non-stick frying pan over medium heat. Working in batches, drop spoonfuls of the batter into the pan and shape into circles. Cook the pancakes for 2–3 minutes on each side or until golden and cooked through. Transfer to a plate and keep warm while cooking the remainder.

Serve the warm pancakes topped with the crushed berry sauce.

Breakfast

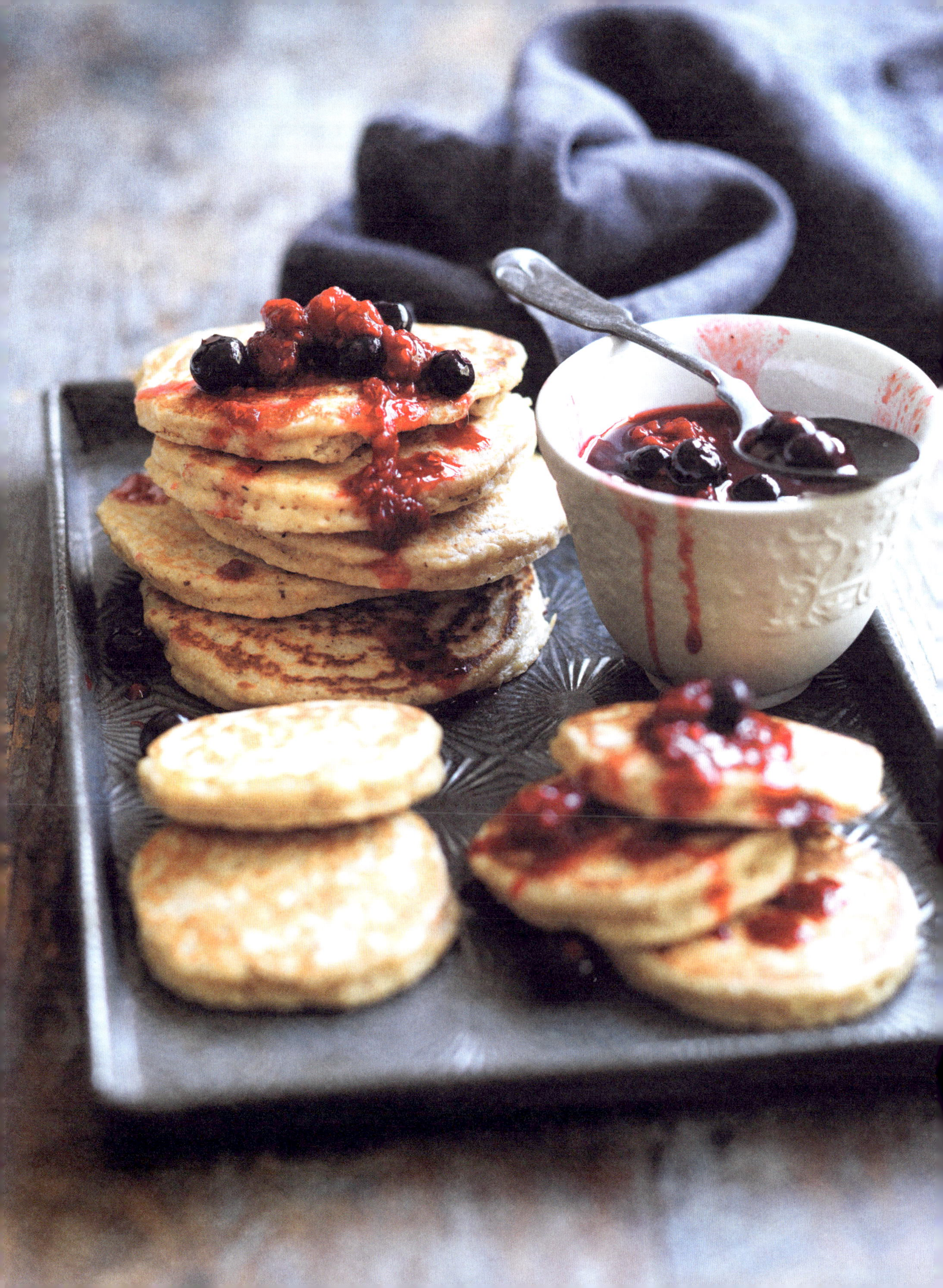

Wholemeal blueberry scones

Makes about 12

My dad is famous for his scones. He doesn't bother with cut-out round scones, which leaves too much leftover dough. He just takes a large knife and cuts them into squares for an easy, no-fuss, but still perfect outcome. He doesn't bother brushing the tops of each scone with milk either. He thinks it makes no difference, whereas I think it makes for a slightly prettier scone. You can decide for yourself which way is best!

These scones have no added sugar, which makes them perfect for kids, but if you're not serving them with jam and want a little sweetness, add a tablespoon of sugar with the flour.

450 g (1 lb/3 cups) wholemeal (whole-wheat) self-raising flour
60 g (2 oz) butter, diced
310 ml (10½ fl oz/1¼ cups) milk or buttermilk, plus extra for brushing
125 g (4½ oz/heaped ¾ cup) fresh blueberries
cream or butter, to serve

Baby's serve: for a **younger baby**, wait until your baby is managing some finger foods (which may not happen until 8–9 months or older) before offering him these scones. When he's ready, cut into pieces that he can easily hold and spread with fruit purée or a little butter. For an **older baby**, serve as for a younger baby, as finger food.

Toddler's serve: serve as is, cutting into smaller pieces.

Preheat the oven to 230°C (450°F). Line a baking tray with baking paper.

Sift the flour into a large bowl and return the sifted husks to the bowl, reserving 2 tablespoons to sprinkle over the scones. Using your fingers, rub the butter into the flour until the mixture resembles coarse crumbs. Make a well in the centre and mix in the milk. Gently knead through the blueberries. Pull the dough together into a rough ball, turn out onto a floured surface and knead lightly.

Gently pat the mixture out into a large rectangle, about 2–3 cm (¾–1¼ inches) thick. Use a large knife to cut into 5 cm (2 inch) squares. Arrange the dough squares so they are close together on the prepared tray and brush the tops with milk (or not!). Sprinkle over the reserved flour husks. Bake for 10–15 minutes, or until well risen and golden.

Serve the warm scones with cream or butter.

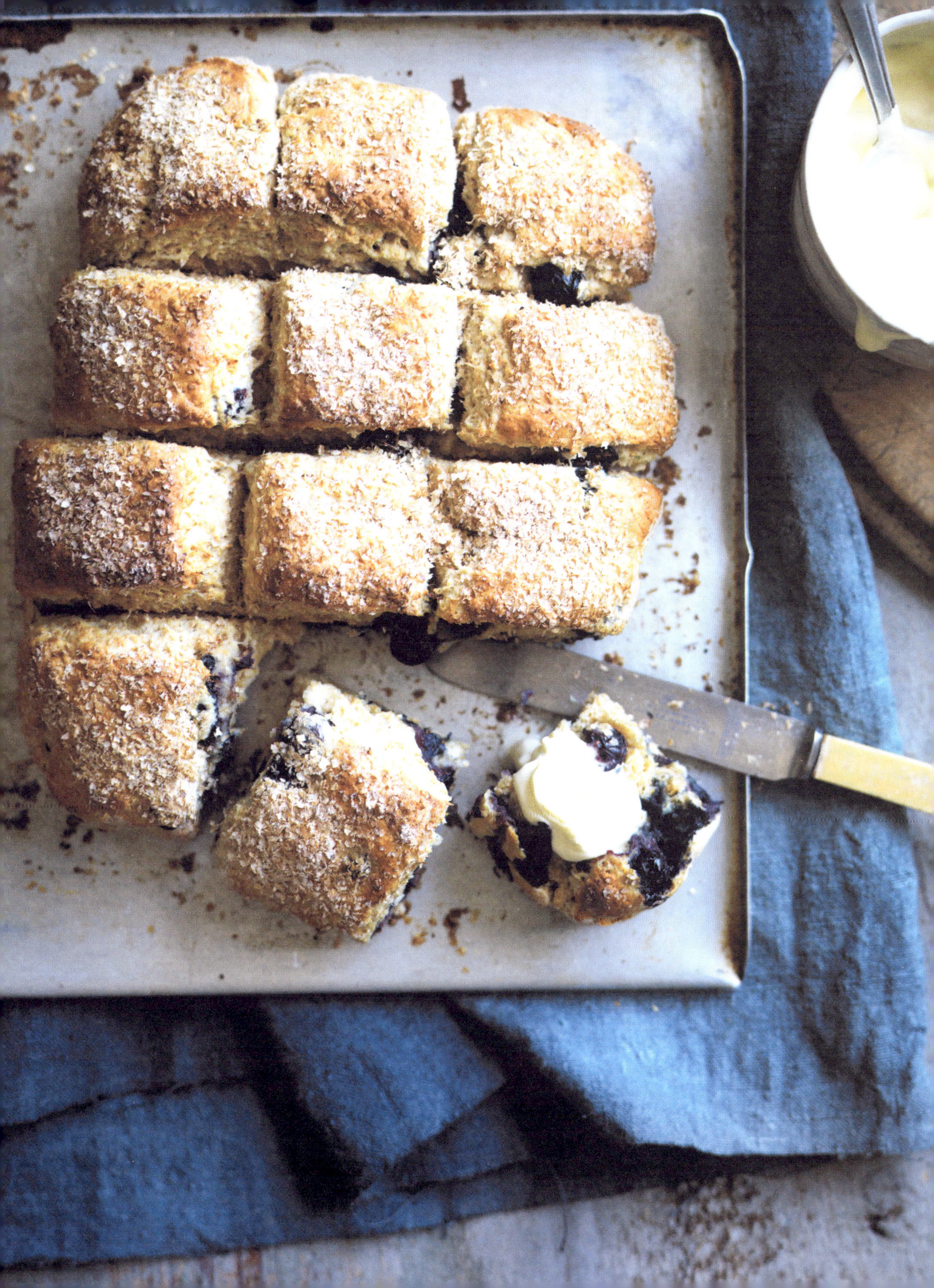

French toast with raspberry apple purée

Serves 2

French toast is a surprisingly quick breakfast to prepare and it's a great choice for children who aren't keen on eating whole eggs. Topped with fresh fruit purée instead of jam, this French toast is a healthier option for every family member.

3 eggs, lightly beaten
250 ml (8½ fl oz/1 cup) milk
½ teaspoon ground cinnamon
1 tablespoon maple syrup, plus extra to serve (optional – omit for baby's serve)
8 slices multigrain or wholemeal (whole-wheat) bread
2 teaspoons light olive oil or rice bran oil
yoghurt (optional), to serve

RASPBERRY APPLE PURÉE
3 large (or 4 small) red or pink apples, peeled, cored and chopped
155 g (5½ oz/1¼ cups) fresh or frozen raspberries

Tip Like most purées, this raspberry apple purée is ideal for freezing in individual portions. You may need to add some liquid (a little water or your baby's milk) after reheating to get the consistency just right before serving to your baby.

To make the raspberry apple purée, steam the apple for 10 minutes, or until tender. Transfer to a food processor, add the raspberries and process to a smooth purée. Refrigerate until needed.

To make the French toast, stir together the egg, milk, cinnamon and maple syrup (if using) in a shallow bowl. Soak each slice of bread in the egg mixture for 1–2 minutes, or until soaked through.

Heat the oil in a large frying pan over medium heat. Working in batches, cook the bread for 2–3 minutes on each side, or until golden and cooked through. Transfer to a plate and keep warm. Repeat with the remaining bread until all cooked.

Serve the slices of French toast topped with a spoonful of fruit purée and a little yoghurt and maple syrup, if liked.

Baby's serve: for a **younger baby**, wait until your baby is managing some finger foods (which may not happen until 8–9 months or older) before offering him the French toast. When he's ready, cut into strips that he can easily hold and spread with some raspberry apple purée. For an **older baby**, serve as for a younger baby, as finger food.

Toddler's serve: serve as is.

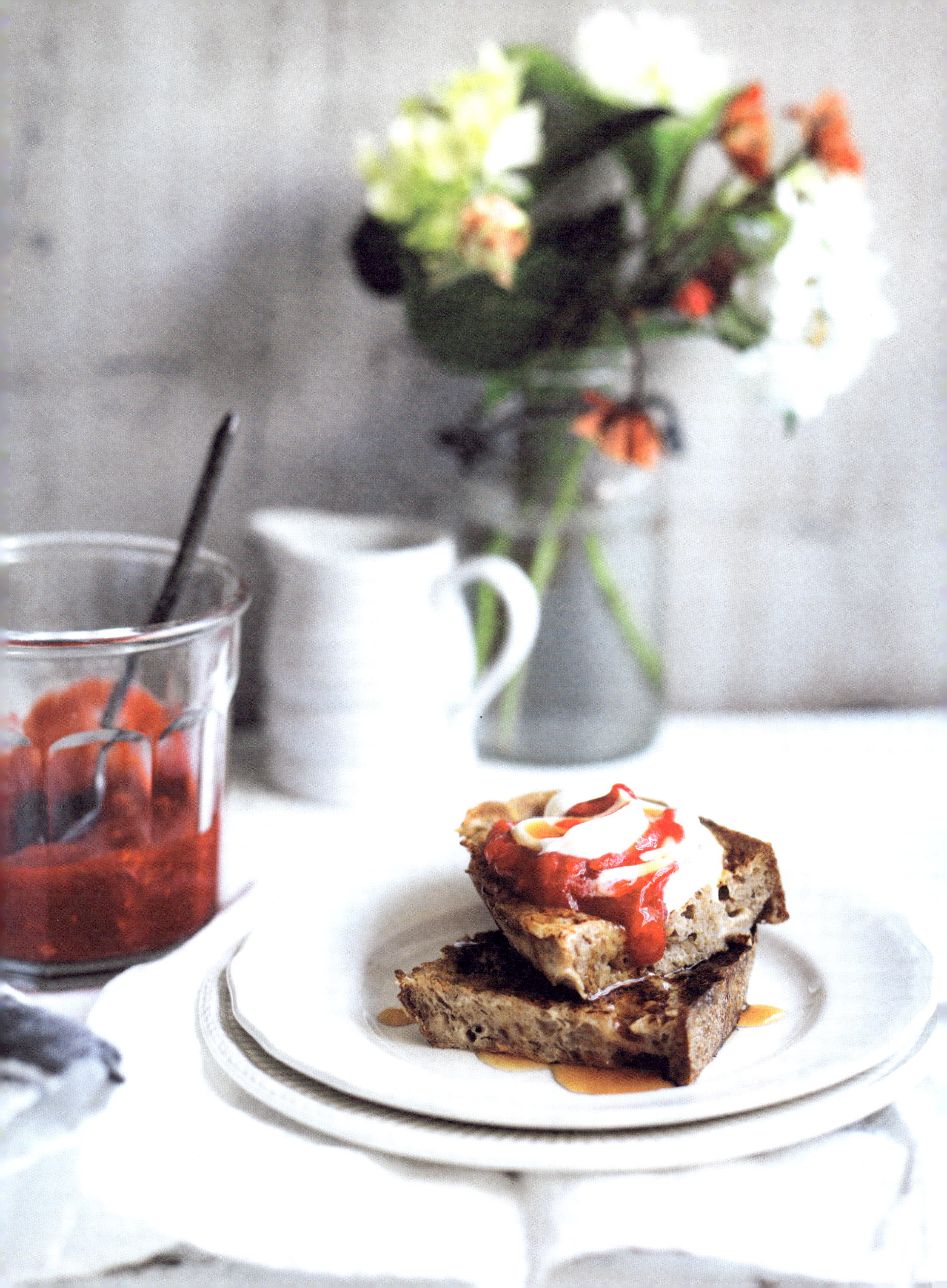

Banana oat breakfast muffins

Makes 12

It's crucial that children of every age eat a decent breakfast so they have the energy for all the growth and development that happens during the day. Without breakfast, their brains simply can't function at their optimal capacity.

On those days you have no time for a proper sit-down breakfast then having a batch of these muffins in the fridge or freezer to warm up and eat on the run is a saviour – they're definitely a better option than many commercial cereals. They also make great lunchbox snacks.

2 ripe bananas, mashed
100 ml (3½ fl oz) maple syrup
1 teaspoon ground cinnamon or cardamom (or a mixture of both)
35 g (1¼ oz/⅓ cup) rolled oats, plus extra to sprinkle
2 eggs
125 ml (4 fl oz/½ cup) milk or buttermilk
125 ml (4 fl oz/½ cup) olive oil (see note)
300 g (10½ oz/2 cups) wholemeal (whole-wheat) self-raising flour

Tip *When selecting an oil for these muffins, you might prefer to use a lighter option, as the taste of some olive oils such as extra-virgin olive oil, can be a little strong.*

Preheat the oven to 180°C (350°F). Line twelve muffin holes with silicone or paper cases.

Place all of the ingredients, except the flour, in a large bowl and mix until well combined. Add the flour and stir through until just combined.

Spoon the mixture into the prepared muffin tins and sprinkle over some extra rolled oats. Bake for about 20 minutes or until golden and cooked through. Leave in the tin for 5 minutes before transferring to a wire rack to cool.

Baby's serve: because these muffins do contain a little added sugar you might like to wait until your baby is over 12 months before offering them to him. Wait until he is managing some finger foods (which may not happen until 8–9 months or older) and break into pieces that he can easily hold. Alternatively, you could bake a couple without maple syrup or give him just a small taste. For an **older baby**, serve as for a younger baby, as finger food.

Toddler's serve: serve as is.

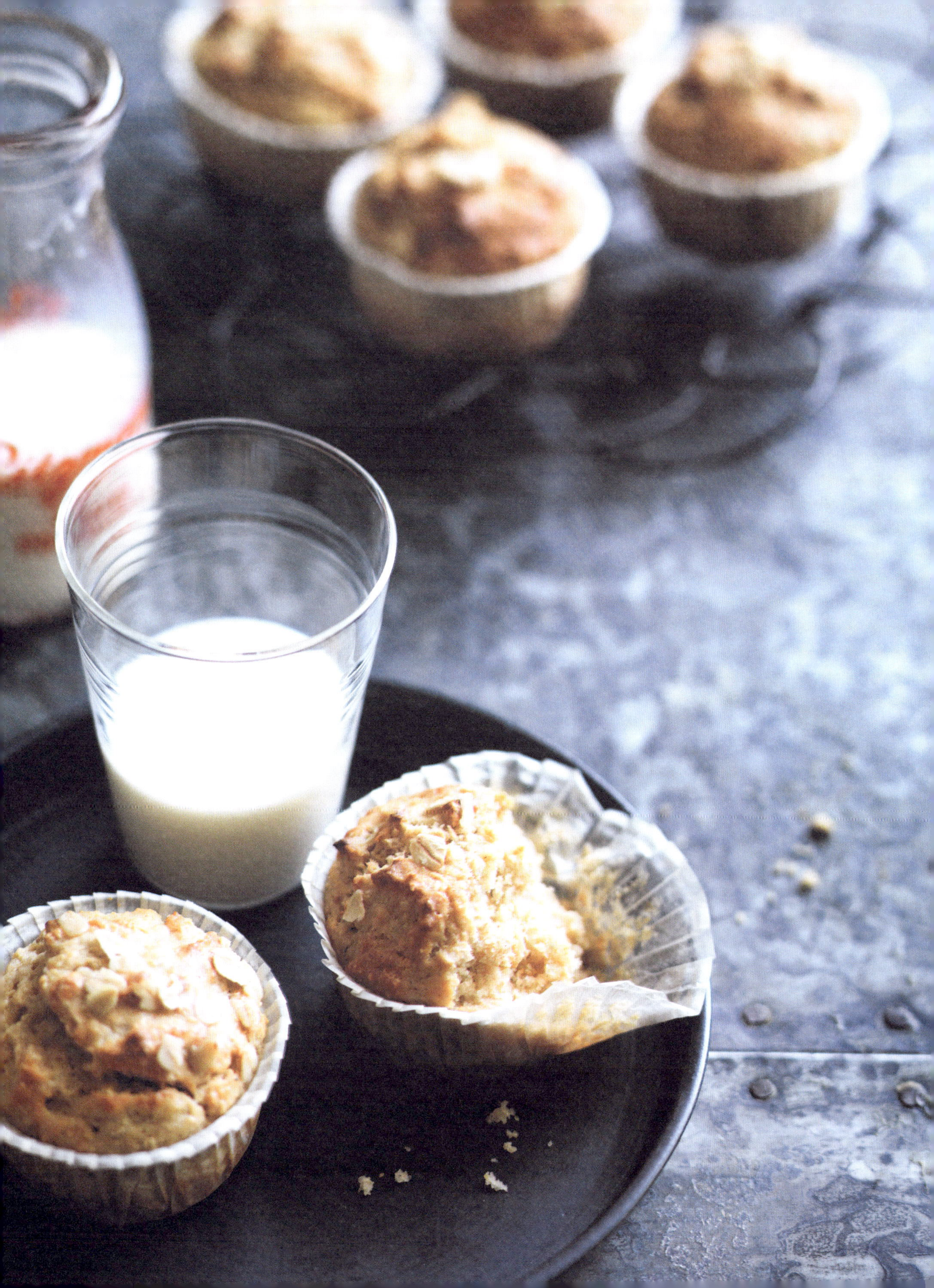

Snacks and Lunch

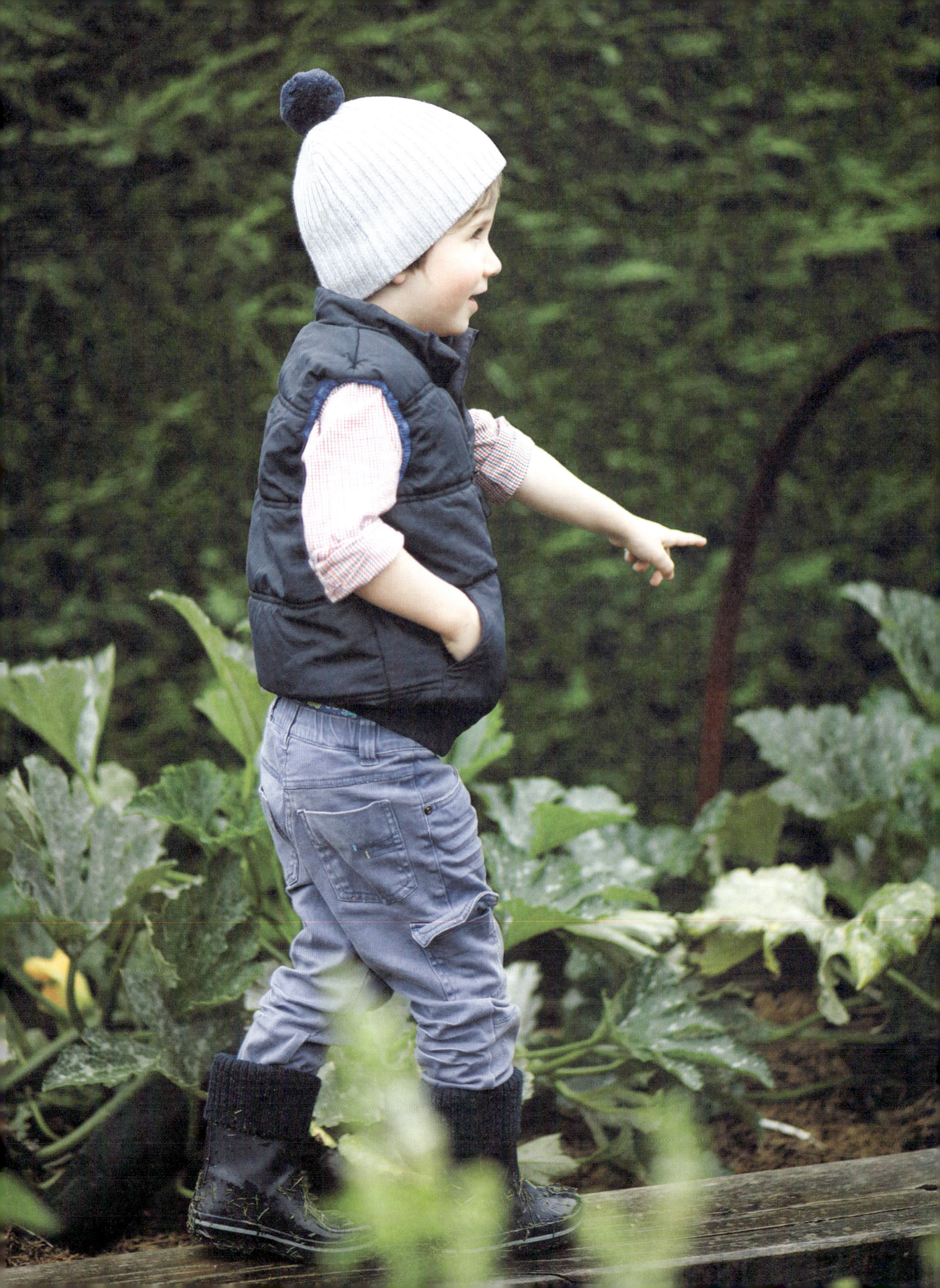

When you've got a young child, snack time and lunchtime often occur outdoors, so it's handy to have some meals up your sleeve that you can pop into a lunchbox as you run out the door. Even when you're home, it's good to have options that are easy, casual and that can be eaten with fingers. Better still, it's great if you can enjoy them as much as your child does. And that's what this chapter is all about – delicious snacks and lunch for all age groups – because like me, I'm guessing you don't have time to be preparing two meals in the middle of your busy day.

One thing to be aware of is that, because children have such little appetites, it's easy for them to fill up on snacks and then skip a main meal. This is why you need to time snacks carefully, well before your child's next meal. Ideally, snacks should also be as healthy as the rest of your child's day, and the recipes in this chapter have been designed with that in mind. That way, if she does end up eating less later on, it's not a big deal.

Straight-up edamame

Serves 4 as a snack

Despite their distinct greenness, I know children who will happily snack on these traditional Japanese soy beans in their pods, even if they're not keen on other green vegetables. I'm sure it's because of the fun of popping them out of their skins.

500 g (1 lb 2 oz) frozen edamame beans
soy sauce or tamari (choose a gluten-free brand, if needed), to serve

Steam or boil the edamame beans until tender. Refresh under cold water and set aside to cool.

Serve as is. For adults, serve with soy sauce or a sprinkle of salt.

Tip Edamame beans have twice the protein, twice the calcium and over five times the folate of green peas, so they're a great vegetable to include in your weekly shop.

Baby's serve: for a **younger baby**, prepare edamame yoghurt purée – see recipe below. For an **older baby**, keep the purée consistency lumpier or serve as is (giving your child a helping hand to shell the beans).

Toddler's serve: serve as is.

Edamame yoghurt purée

Serves 4 as a snack

This recipe is for your baby and is also lovely mixed with sweet potato (or another root vegetable) purée. Regularly serving your baby green foods will help guard against the phobia of 'all-things-green' that commonly hits at around 2 or 3 years.

250 g (9 oz) edamame beans, steamed or boiled
70 g (2½ oz) plain yoghurt
water or your baby's milk

Remove and discard the skins from the steamed edamame and place the beans in a food processor. Add the yoghurt and as much liquid as needed to reach the desired consistency.

Set aside one serving and freeze the remainder in individual portions.

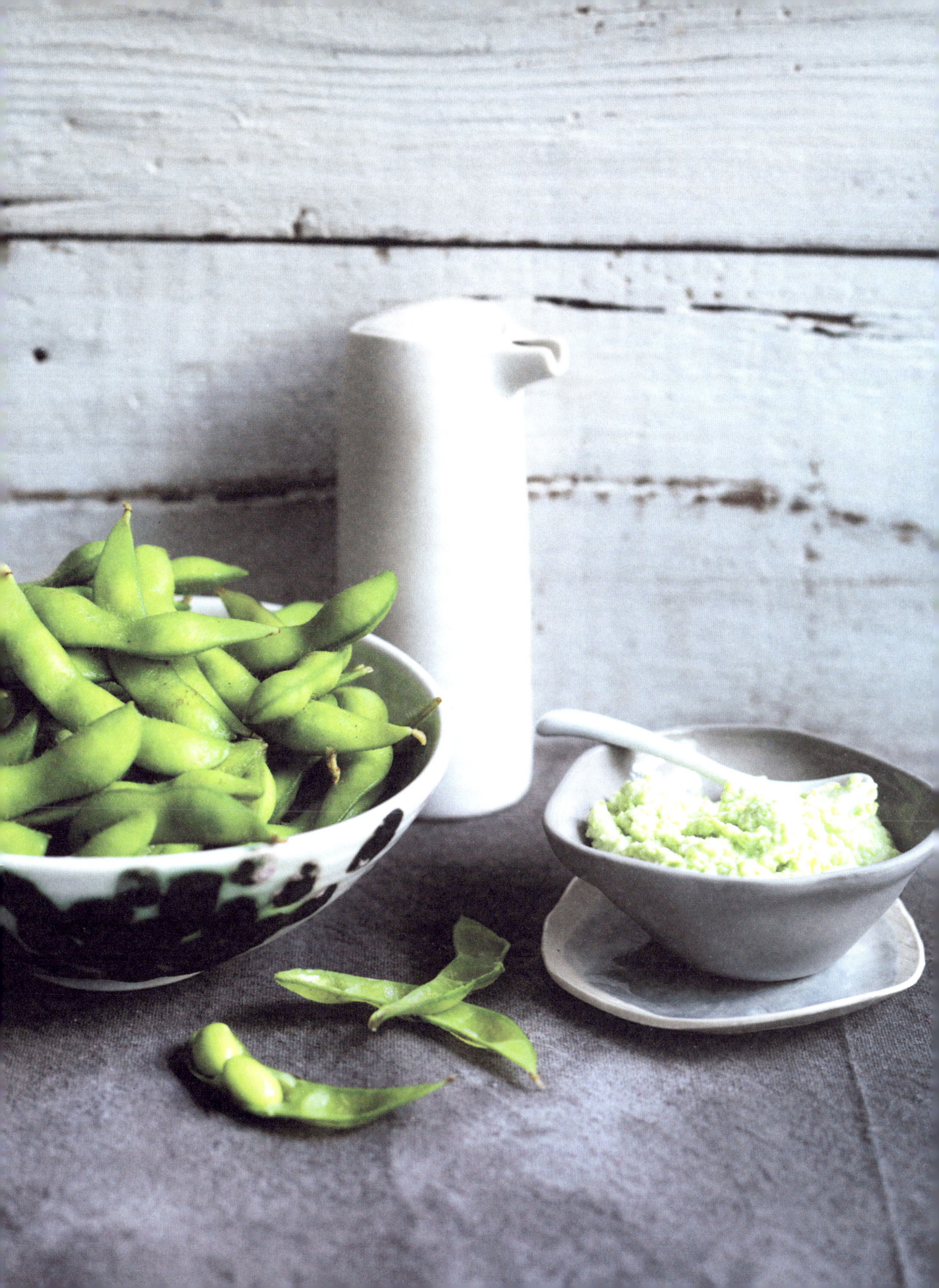

Vegetable muffins

Makes 12

These are a great, nut-free snack for school lunchboxes and a good way of including some vegetables in your child's day if she's not a fan of eating them whole. I also love them for my own morning tea – served warm with a little butter and a cup of tea on the side … bliss!

335 g (12 oz/2¼ cups) wholemeal (whole-wheat) self-raising flour
310 ml (10½ fl oz/1¼ cups) milk
80 ml (2½ fl oz/⅓ cup) olive oil
1 egg, lightly beaten
70 g (2½ oz/½ cup) grated zucchini (courgette)
80 g (2¾ oz/½ cup) grated carrot (or use sweet potato)
100 g (3½ oz) grated cheddar cheese
½ bunch chives, finely snipped
6 cherry tomatoes, halved

Preheat the oven to 190°C (375°F). Line twelve muffin holes with silicone or paper cases.

Place the flour into a large bowl, make a well in the centre, then stir through the remaining ingredients apart from the tomato, until just combined.

Spoon the batter into the muffin cases and top each one with a half tomato, cut side up. Bake for 25 minutes, or until a skewer inserted into the centre of the muffins comes out clean. Transfer to a wire rack to cool. Serve warm or at room temperature.

Baby's serve: for a **younger baby**, wait at least until your baby is managing some finger foods (which may not happen until 8–9 months or older) before offering her these muffins. Break them into pieces that she can easily hold. For an **older baby**, break into pieces that she can hold or serve as is.

Toddler's serve: serve as is, cut up if needed.

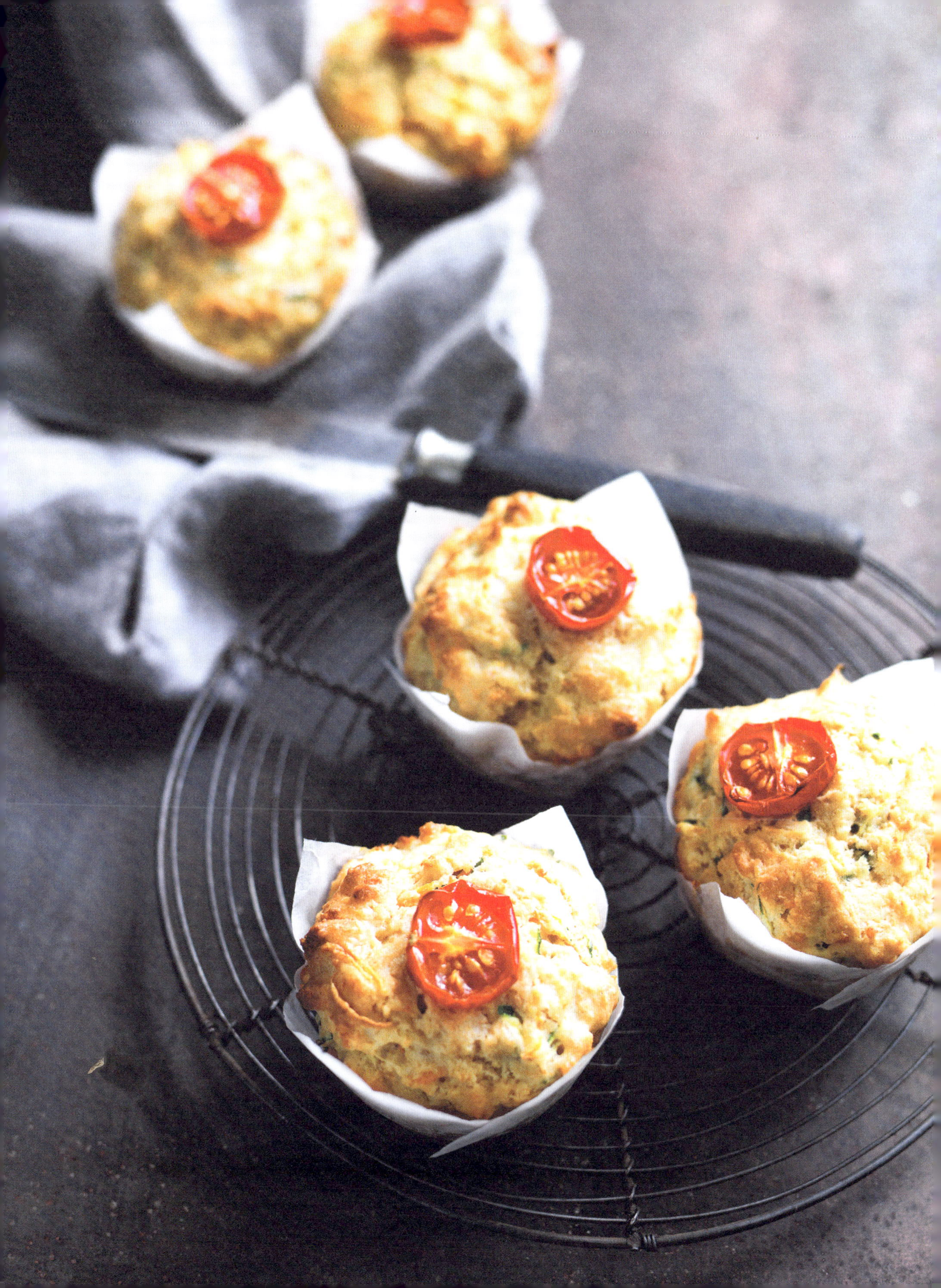

Chicken sausage rolls

Serves 36

Made with chicken, zucchini, wholemeal bread and plenty of herbs, these sausage rolls are so much healthier than any you'll buy in a shop – and a whole lot tastier too.

2 teaspoons olive oil
1 brown onion, finely diced
1 garlic clove, finely diced
2 slices wholemeal (whole-wheat) bread, roughly torn
500 g (1 lb 2 oz) chicken tenderloins, roughly chopped
3 tablespoons roughly chopped flat-leaf (Italian) parsley leaves
2 tablespoons roughly chopped chives
1 zucchini (courgette), finely grated
1 tablespoon lemon juice
3 square sheets (24 cm/9½ inch) puff pastry, partially thawed
1 egg, lightly beaten
sesame seeds, to sprinkle

HERB YOGHURT SAUCE
200 g (7 oz) plain yoghurt
2–3 tablespoons chopped fresh mixed herbs, such as mint, chives and flat-leaf (Italian) parsley
1 tablespoon lemon juice
½ garlic clove, peeled

Baby's serve: for a **younger baby**, wait at least until your baby is managing some finger foods (which may not happen until 8–9 months or older) before offering her these sausage rolls. Cut them into pieces that she can easily hold. For an **older baby**, cut into pieces that she can hold or serve as is.

Toddler's serve: serve as is, cut into halves or quarters if needed.

To make the herb yoghurt sauce, place all of the ingredients in a food processor and process until smooth. Refrigerate until needed.

Preheat the oven to 200°C (400°F). Line a large baking tray with baking paper.

Heat the oil in a small frying pan over medium heat. Add the onion and garlic and cook for 10 minutes, or until golden. Set aside to cool.

Place the bread in a food processor and process until crumbs form. Transfer to a large mixing bowl. Place the chicken, parsley and chives in the food processor and process until the mixture is minced (ground). Add to the breadcrumbs and use your hands to mix through the zucchini and lemon juice.

Cut the pastry sheets in half to create rectangles. Spoon the chicken mixture lengthways down the centre of each. Lightly brush the edges with water and fold the pastry over to form a log, pressing the edges to seal. Turn the rolls over so they are sitting seam side down. Brush the tops with egg, sprinkle with sesame seeds and cut each roll into six smaller pieces. Arrange on the tray and cook for 15 minutes, or until cooked through and the pastry is golden. Serve warm, with herb yoghurt sauce on the side.

Snacks and lunch

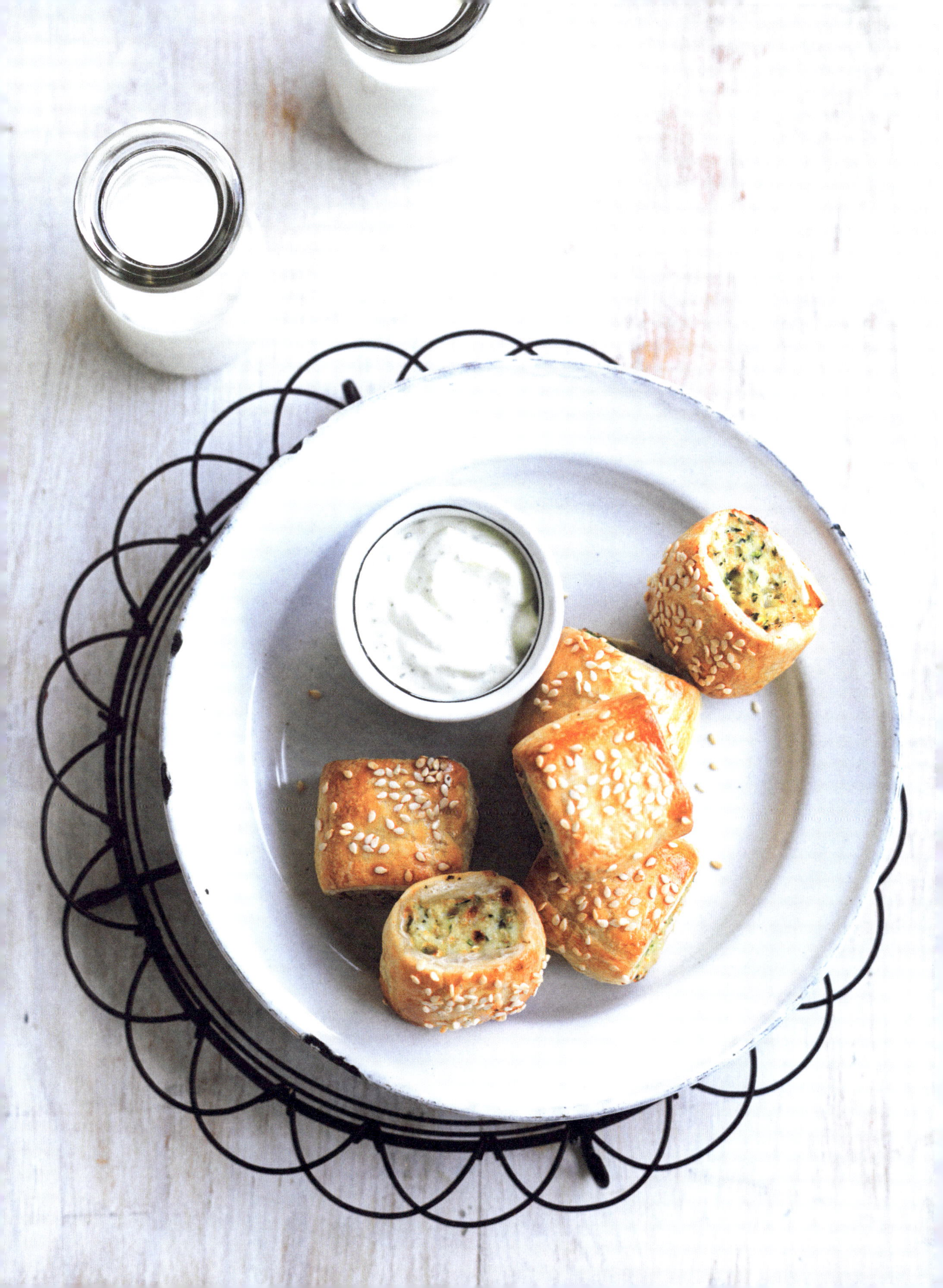

Beef meatballs with roasted eggplant dip

Makes about 40

Adding grated zucchini to meatballs is such an easy way of including an extra serve of vegetables in your child's meal. These meatballs can be served as a snack or stirred through some tomato passata (tomato purée) and served with pasta. The meatball mixture can also be used to make mini burgers (see page 112).

BEEF MEATBALLS
2 tablespoons light olive oil
1 brown onion, finely diced
3 slices wholemeal (whole-wheat) bread, chopped
60 ml (2 fl oz/¼ cup) milk
500 g (1 lb 2 oz) minced (ground) beef
135 g (5 oz/1 cup) finely grated zucchini (courgette), excess moisture squeezed out
¼ teaspoon ground paprika

ROASTED EGGPLANT DIP
2 large eggplants (aubergines), halved lengthways
1 teaspoon olive oil, plus extra to serve
1 handful flat-leaf (Italian) parsley leaves
1 garlic clove (optional)
125 g (4½ oz/½ cup) plain yoghurt
2 tablespoons tahini paste
1 tablespoon lemon juice

Baby's serve: for a **younger baby**, blend together some meatballs and eggplant dip until smooth. You may need to add some liquid (water or your baby's milk) to achieve the desired consistency. Alternatively, you can mix with a vegetable purée. For an **older baby**, keep the puréed consistency lumpier or serve as finger food.

Toddler's serve: serve as is.

Preheat the oven to 180°C (350°F). To make the roasted eggplant dip, place the eggplant halves, cut side up, in an ovenproof dish and rub over the oil. Roast for 1 hour, or until tender. Transfer the eggplant (including the skin) to a food processor with the remaining ingredients and process until smooth. Refrigerate until ready to serve – you can drizzle over a little olive oil before serving.

To make the meatballs, heat 1 tablespoon of the oil in a frying pan over medium heat. Add the onion and cook for 5 minutes, or until softened. Set aside to cool. Put the bread and milk in a large bowl and leave for 1 minute for the milk to soak in. Add the cooked onion, minced beef, zucchini and paprika and use your hands to break up the bread until well combined. Take 1 heaped tablespoonful of the mince at a time and roll into balls.

Heat the remaining oil in a frying pan over medium heat. Cook the meatballs, in batches, turning regularly until cooked through – you can partially cover the pan to help the meatballs cook through more quickly. Serve the warm meatballs with the roasted eggplant dip.

Snacks and lunch

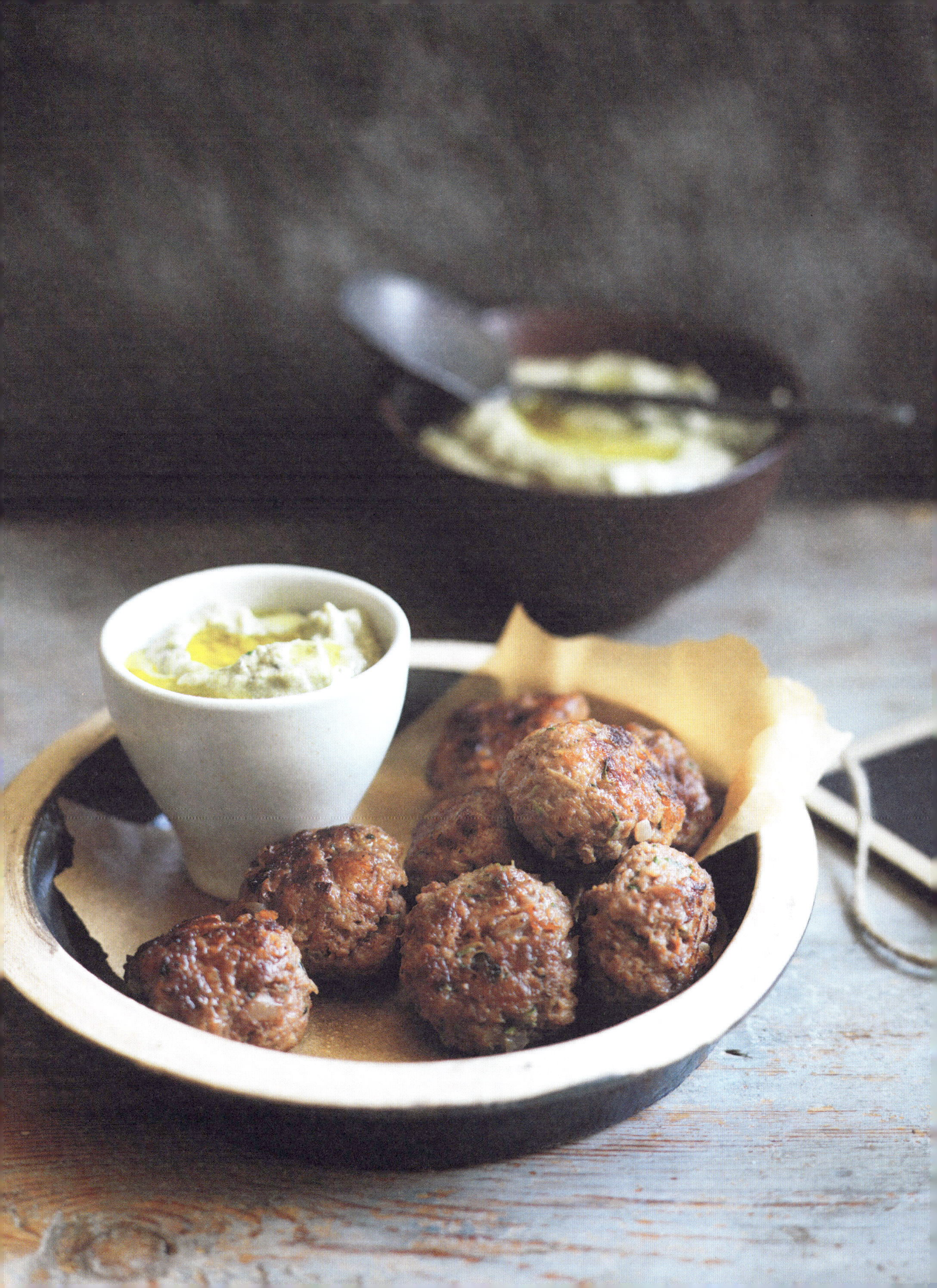

Tuna and sweet potato logs

Makes about 25

This take on conventional fish cakes makes a great portable lunch or snack. The reason I like the logs is that I've known children who won't eat them in a round shape, but will happily eat them like this – I'm sure it's because they resemble chips! If you've got a big chip fan, these are a much healthier alternative. If you have leftover cooked fish, you can use it instead of the tinned tuna. Any uncooked logs can be frozen for later use. Simply thaw and cook as needed.

500 g (1 lb 2 oz) sweet potatoes, peeled and chopped into large chunks
2 garlic cloves, peeled
185 g (6½ oz) tin tuna (in oil), drained
3 tablespoons finely grated parmesan cheese
1 tablespoon finely chopped flat-leaf (Italian) parsley
3 tablespoons wholemeal (whole-wheat) plain (all-purpose) flour
1 large egg, lightly beaten
75 g (2¾ oz) fresh wholemeal (whole-wheat) breadcrumbs
2 tablespoons light olive oil or rice bran oil
herb mayonnaise, to serve (optional – do not serve raw-egg mayonnaise to children under 2 years)

Baby's serve: for a **younger baby**, serve the (uncrumbed) sweet potato tuna mixture as a purée, blending and adding some liquid if needed for desired consistency. Alternatively, once your baby is managing some finger foods (which may not happen until 8–9 months or older) you can offer him the logs as finger food. For an **older baby**, serve as is.

Toddler's serve: serve as is.

Put the sweet potato and garlic cloves in a saucepan, pour in enough water to cover and bring to the boil. Cook for 15 minutes, or until tender. Drain, then return to the pan and cook over low heat for about 30 seconds, or until dry. Remove from the heat and mash together until smooth. Refrigerate until cool.

Mix the tuna, parmesan and parsley into the sweet potato mash, breaking up any large chunks of tuna. Using your hands, form the mixture into logs, about 7 cm (2¾ inches) long. (Set some mixture aside to purée for baby.)

Place the flour, egg and breadcrumbs in separate bowls. Dust the logs first with flour, then dip in the egg, and coat with breadcrumbs. Refrigerate for 1 hour to firm up.

Heat 1 tablespoon of the oil in a large frying pan over medium heat. Cook half of the logs for about 5 minutes, turning to cook evenly until golden all over. Repeat with the remaining oil and logs until all are cooked.

Drain on paper towels. Serve warm or cool with herb mayonnaise, if liked.

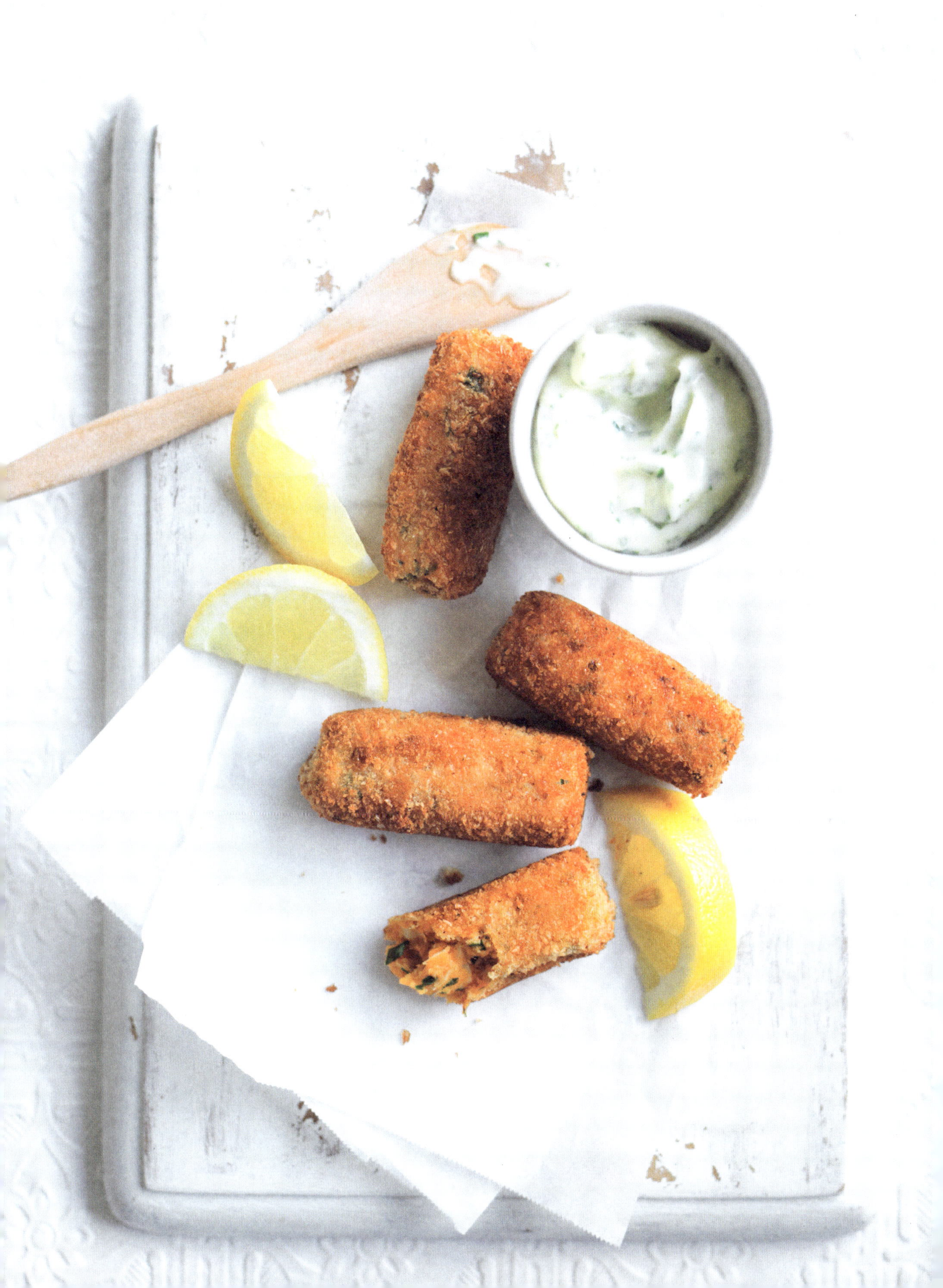

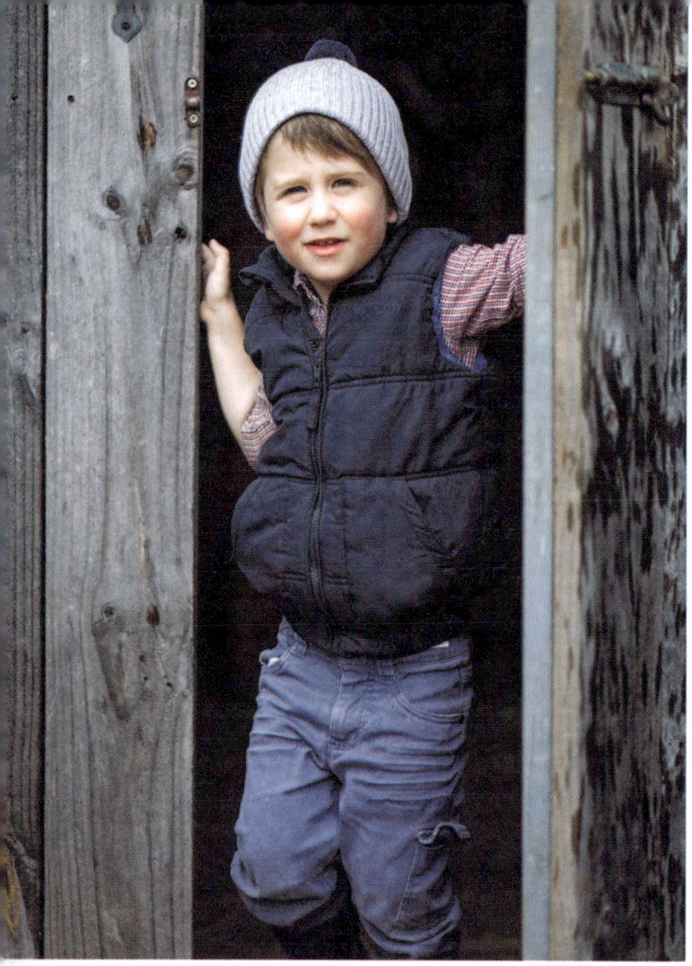
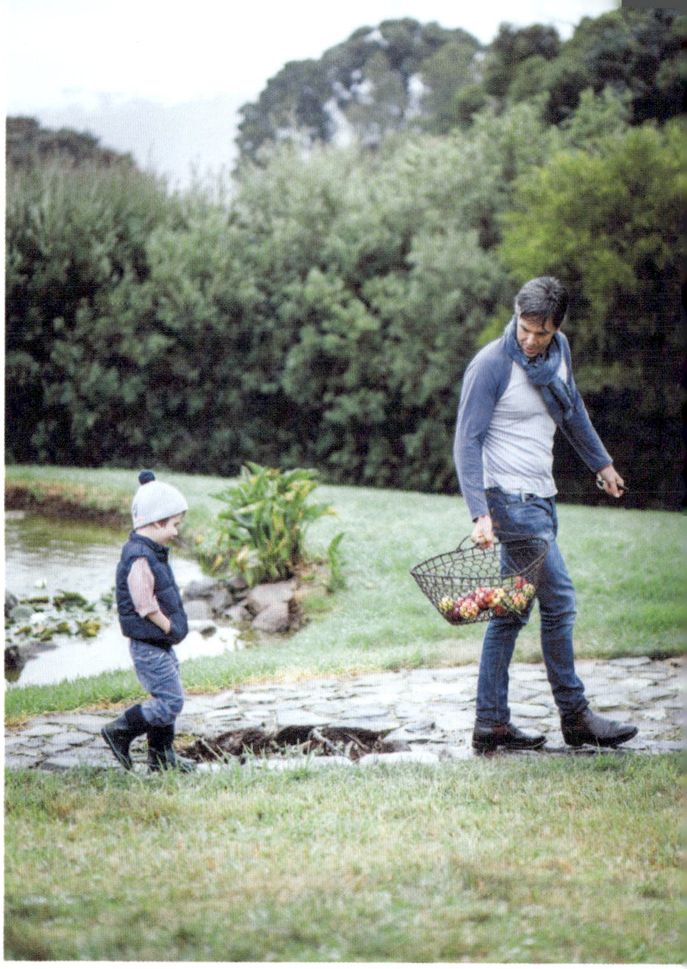
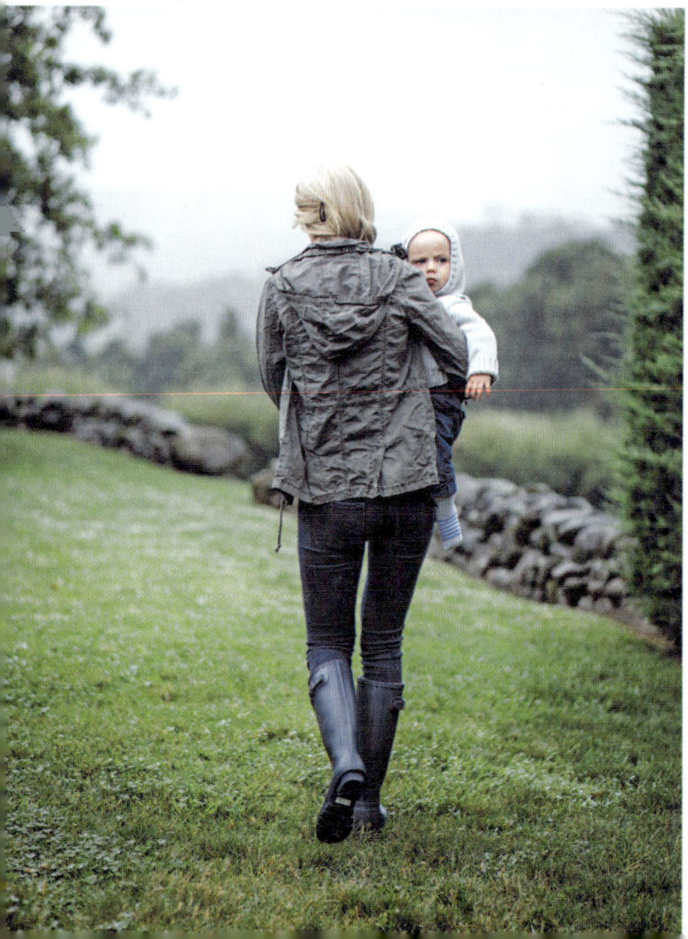
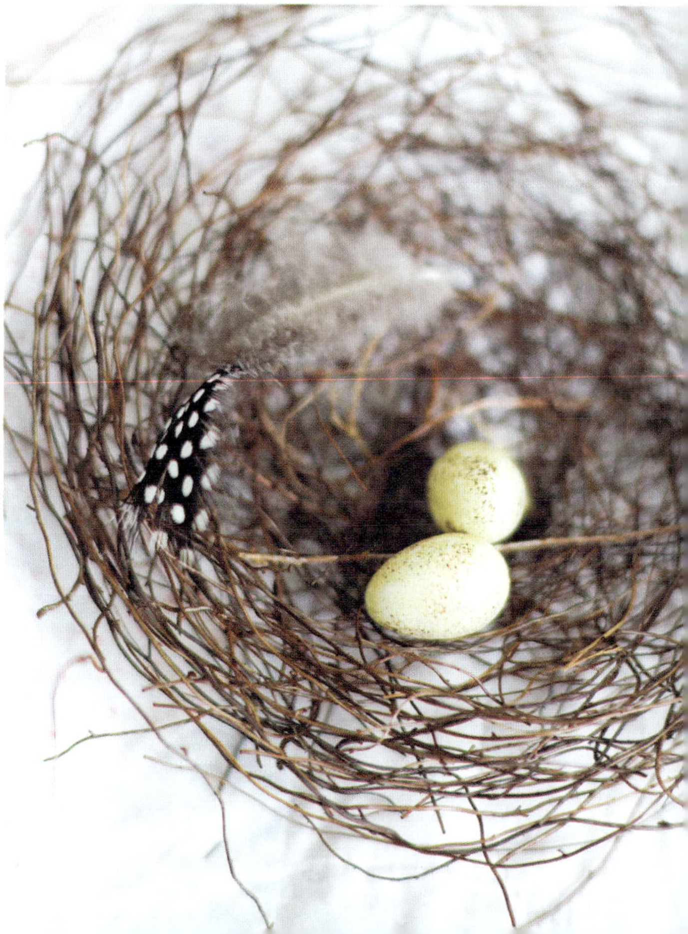

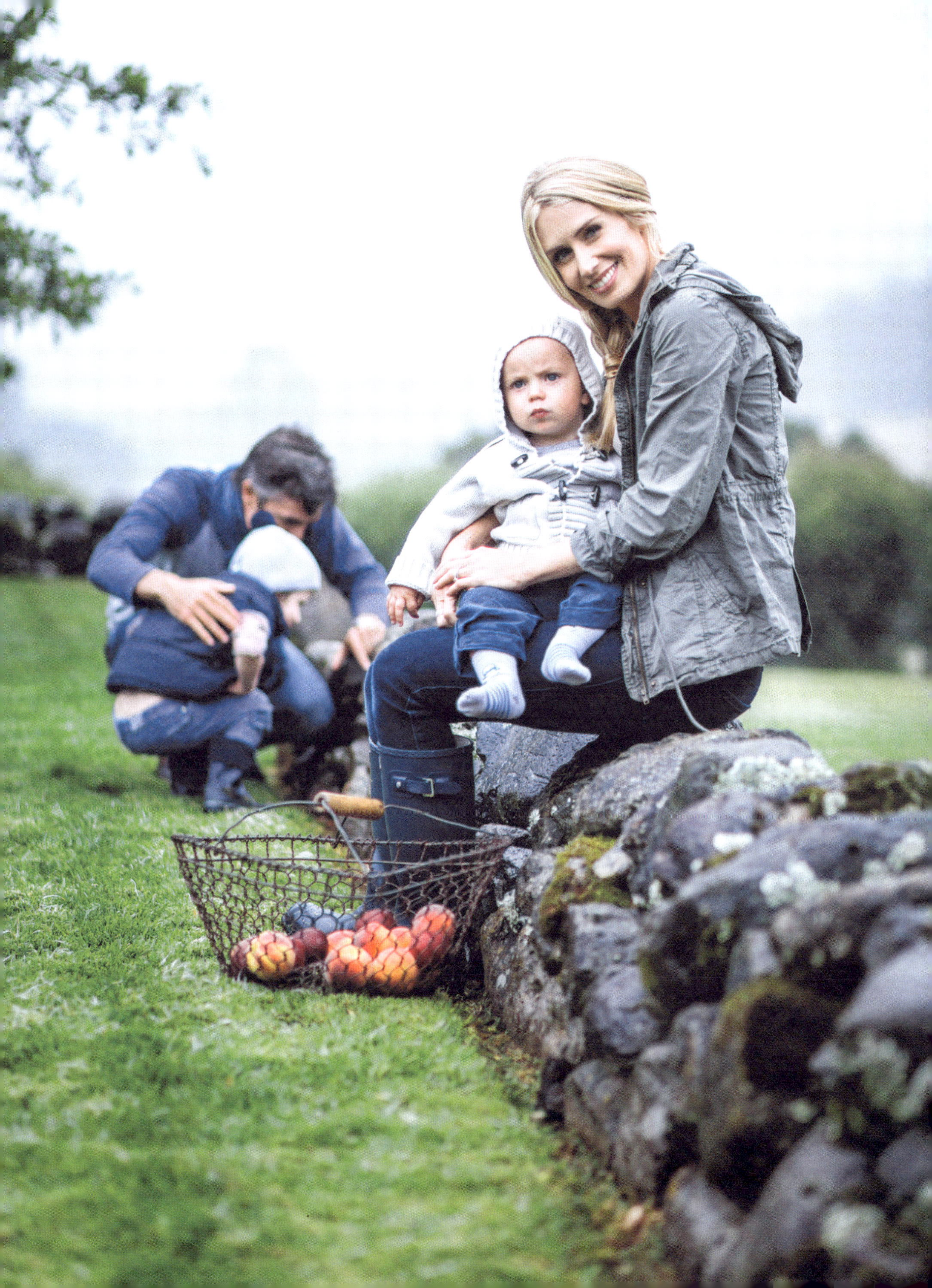

Quinoa chicken rissoles

Makes about 20

Rissoles sound so pedestrian but these are anything but. They're lovely for lunch or dinner with a salad and you can also use them in a burger. They also make a great lunchbox snack. You can use minced chicken instead of the thigh fillets if you prefer. If there's a sesame allergy in your family, omit the sesame seed coating.

135 g (5 oz/⅔ cup) white quinoa, rinsed and drained
2 tablespoons olive oil
1 brown onion, finely chopped
2 garlic cloves, crushed
330 g (11½ oz/about 3) chicken thigh fillets, trimmed and roughly chopped
1 egg
110 g (4 oz) cooked peas
1 teaspoon lemon zest (optional)
sesame seeds, to coat (optional)
mayonnaise, to serve (optional – do not serve raw-egg mayonnaise to children under 2 years)

Baby's serve: for a **younger baby**, break these rissoles up and blend or mash them with a vegetable purée, such as sweet potato. Alternatively, wait until your baby is managing some finger foods (which may not happen until 8–9 months or older) before you offer her these rissoles as finger food. For an **older baby**, serve as is or cut up into small pieces.

Toddler's serve: serve as is.

Place the quinoa in a small saucepan with 250 ml (8½ fl oz/1 cup) water. Bring to the boil and cook, covered, for 12–15 minutes, or until tender. There should be no excess moisture at this stage; if there is, drain well and set aside.

Heat 2 teaspoons of the oil in a frying pan over medium heat. Add the onion and garlic and cook for 5 minutes, or until softened. Set aside.

Place the chicken in a food processor and process until minced (ground). Transfer to a large bowl and stir through the egg, cooked peas, lemon zest (if using), quinoa, onion and garlic until well combined. Take heaped tablespoonfuls of the mixture and shape into rissoles.

Place the sesame seeds (if using) on a plate and press both sides of each rissole into the seeds to coat.

Heat the remaining oil in a frying pan over medium heat. Cook the rissoles, in batches, for about 4 minutes on each side, or until golden and cooked through. Drain on paper towel.

Serve the warm quinoa chicken rissoles with mayonnaise.

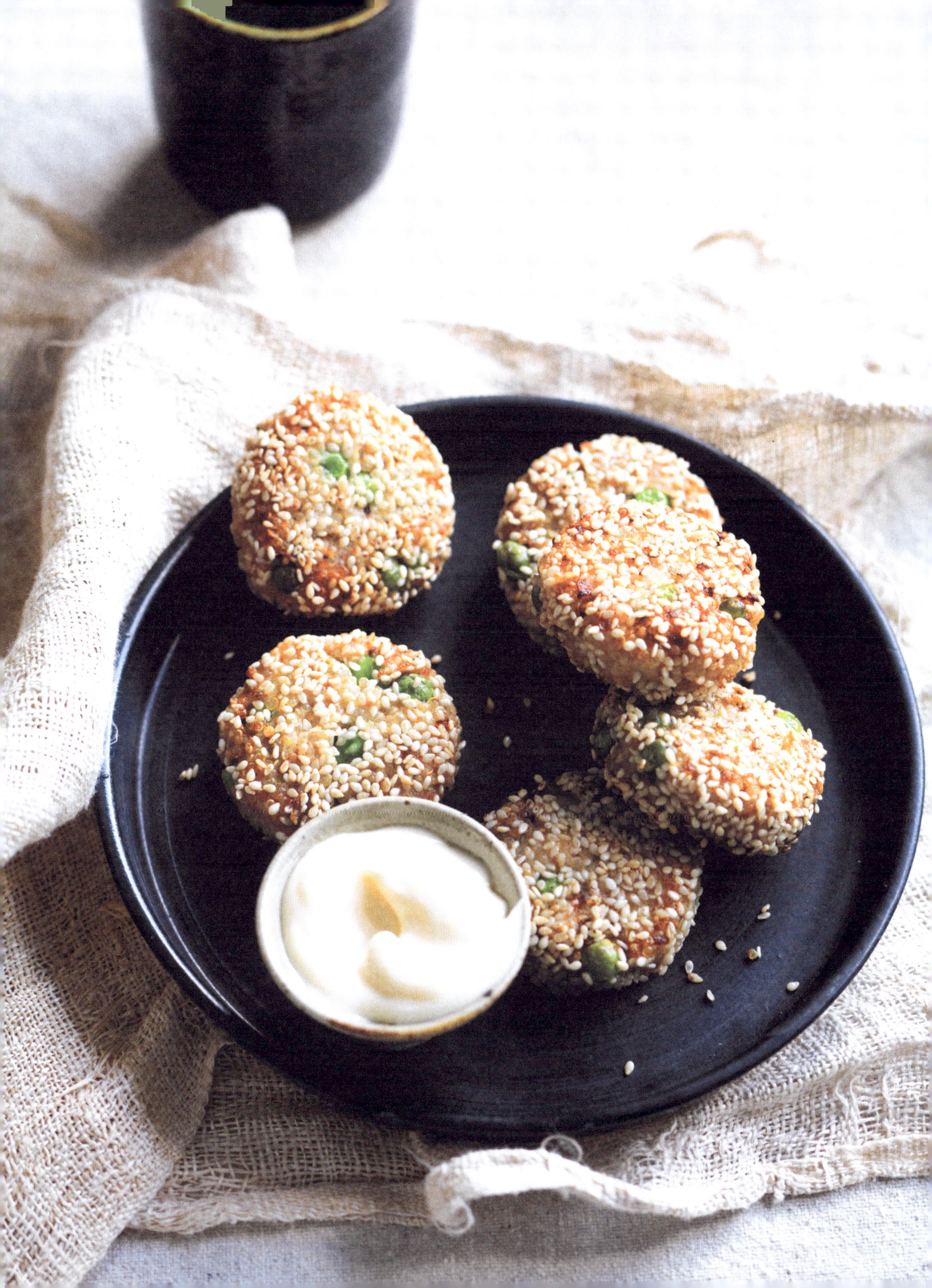

Picnic eggs

Makes 12

These eggs are very retro but they're so good that I'm officially calling for a revival! The name of this recipe says it all – they're perfect for a picnic or play date. The mustard has a very mild flavour but if you think your child may not be a fan, you can use just one teaspoon or leave it out altogether.

6 eggs
90 g (3 oz/⅓ cup) mayonnaise (optional – do not serve raw-egg mayonnaise to children under 2 years)
185 g (6½ oz) tin tuna (in oil), drained
2 teaspoons Dijon mustard
1 tablespoon finely snipped chives

Tip *If you'd like a bit more protein in your child's diet, one healthy option is to replace regular mayonnaise with tofu mayonnaise. It's really easy to make – just whizz a 300 g (10½ oz) packet of silken tofu, drained, with 1 tablespoon lemon juice and 3 tablespoons flat-leaf (Italian) parsley leaves in a food processor until very smooth.*

Place the eggs in a saucepan, cover with cold water and bring to the boil. Once the water is boiling, cook the eggs for about 5 minutes, or until hard-boiled. Run under cold water to cool. Using your fingers, carefully remove and discard the shells.

Cut each egg in half lengthways and gently remove the yolks. Set the egg whites aside. Place the egg yolks in a food processor with the mayonnaise (if using), tuna and mustard. Process until smooth.

To serve, gently spoon the tuna mixture into the yoke hole in each egg. Top with chives. Refrigerate until ready to serve.

Baby's serve: use less or no mustard in the yolk mixture. For a **younger baby**, mix the yolk mixture with a vegetable purée, such as sweet potato or pumpkin. For an **older baby**, serve eggs as is or spread the yolk mixture on some toast fingers.

Toddler's serve: serve as is.

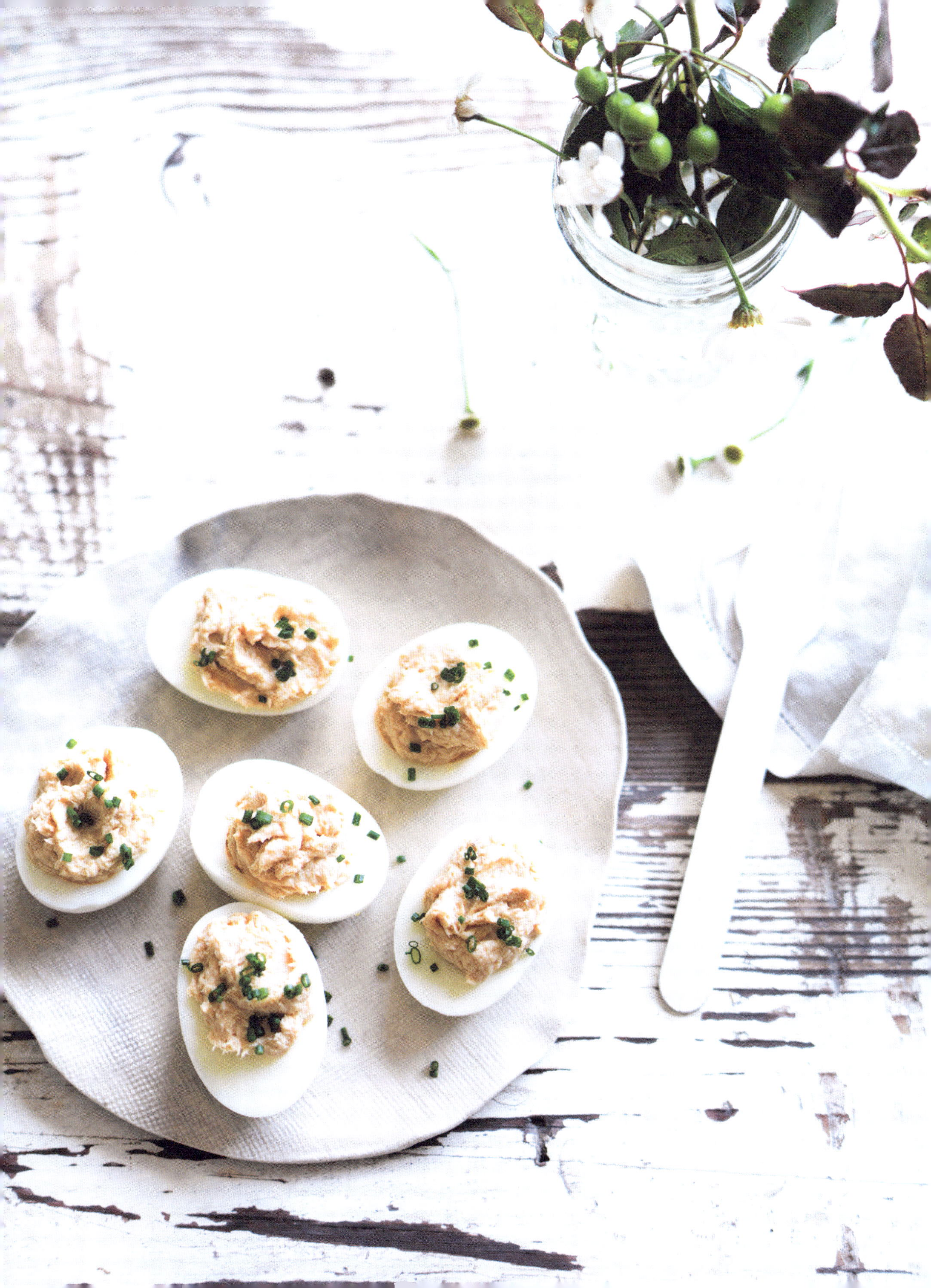

Crunchy chicken bites

Makes about 30

These little bites are perfect for a snack or lunch at home, or even at a birthday party (where I promise they'll be just as popular with the adults as the kids). Best of all, you can make them ahead and just pop them in the oven when needed. When buying cornflakes, look for a quality brand that's low in sugar and salt and high in fibre.

60 g (2 oz) parmesan cheese, roughly chopped
180 g (6½ oz) cornflakes (choose a gluten-free brand if needed)
400 g (14 oz) chicken breast fillets
400 g (14 oz) chicken thigh fillets
2 tablespoons flat-leaf (Italian) parsley leaves
2 tablespoons tomato sauce (ketchup)
2 tablespoons sesame seeds (optional – omit for sesame-free option)
75 g (2½ oz/½ cup) plain (all-purpose) flour
3 eggs, lightly beaten
olive oil spray
mayonnaise or tomato sauce (ketchup) or a blend of both, to serve (optional – do not serve raw-egg mayonnaise to children under 2 years)

Place the parmesan and cornflakes in a food processor and process until the mixture resembles fine breadcrumbs. Set aside.

Place the chicken, parsley, tomato sauce and sesame seeds (if using) into a food processor and process until minced (ground) and smooth. Take heaped tablespoonfuls of the chicken mixture and shape into nuggets.

Place the flour, egg and cornflake crumbs in three separate shallow bowls. Dust the nuggets first with flour, then dip into the egg, and roll to coat in the cornflake crumbs. Refrigerate for at least 1 hour to firm up.

Preheat the oven to 180°C (350°F). Line two baking trays with baking paper.

Arrange the chicken nuggets on the trays and lightly spray with oil. Bake in the oven for 20–25 minutes, or until golden and cooked through. Serve with your preferred dipping sauce.

Baby's serve: for a **younger baby**, wait until your baby is confidently managing finger foods (which may not happen until 8–9 months or older) before offering her these chicken bites. If it helps her, cut them into strips or halves that she can easily hold. For an **older baby**, cut into strips or halves or serve as is.

Toddler's serve: serve as is.

Snacks and lunch

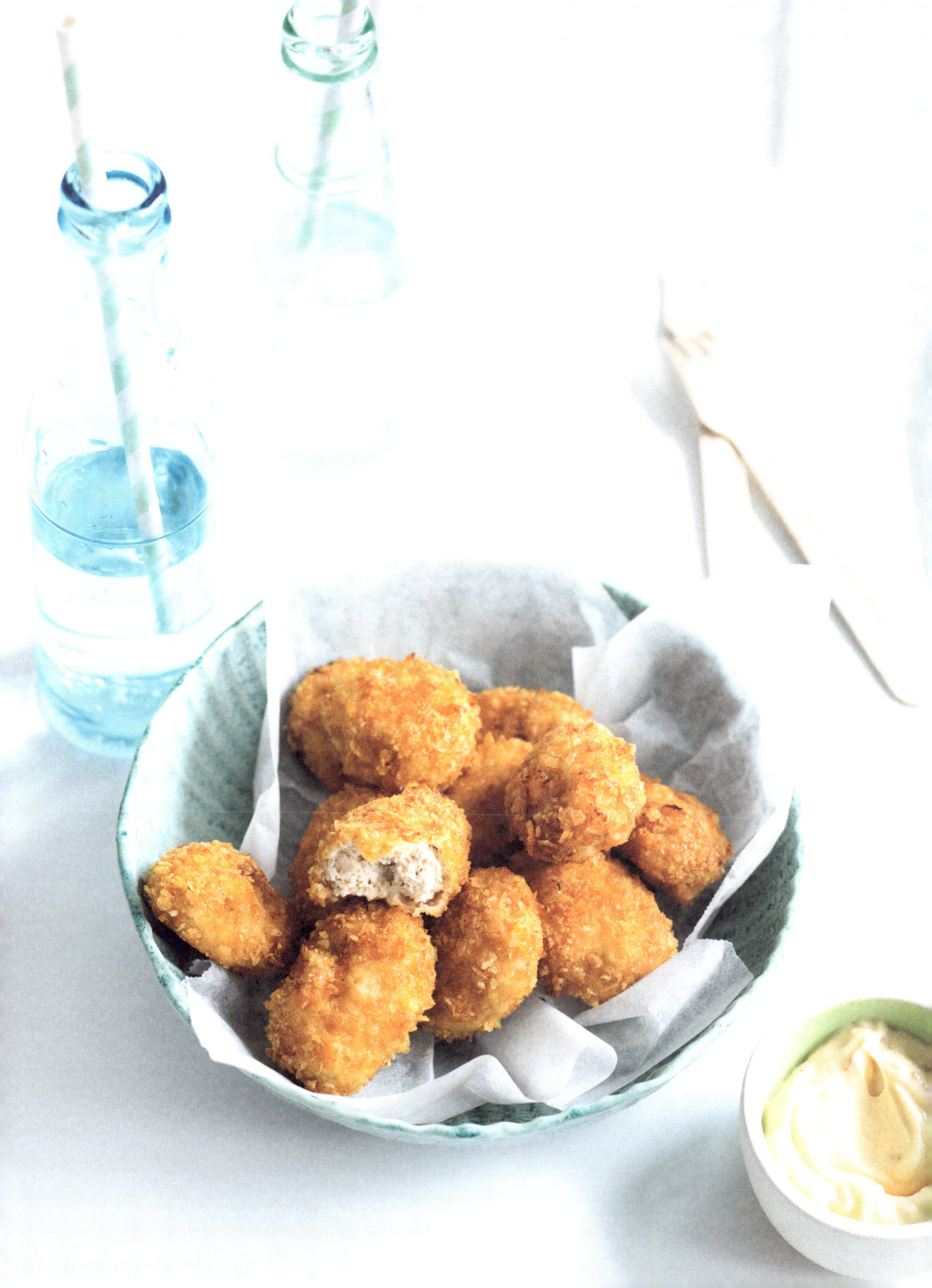

Thai fish cakes

Makes about 20

Feel free to adjust the curry paste – using just a fraction for your child, or none at all – to achieve the right taste and heat in this dish. The cucumber sauce has some sugar in it, so save it for yourself or your older child.

450 g (1 lb) firm white boneless fish fillets, chopped
½ teaspoon grated ginger
3 tablespoons chopped coriander (cilantro) leaves
2 spring onions (scallions), roughly chopped
5 green beans, trimmed and roughly chopped
1 teaspoon soy sauce or tamari (choose a gluten-free brand if needed)
1 egg
3 teaspoons red curry paste
light olive oil or rice bran oil, for shallow frying

CUCUMBER DIPPING SAUCE
60 ml (2 fl oz/¼ cup) white vinegar
75 g (2¾ oz/⅓ cup) sugar
½ Lebanese (short) cucumber, seeded and finely chopped
1 long red chilli, seeded and finely chopped
2 teaspoons fish sauce
2 tablespoons roasted peanuts, finely chopped (omit for nut-free option)

Baby's serve: for a **younger baby**, wait until your baby is managing some finger foods (which may not happen until 8–9 months or older) before offering her these fish cakes. Cut them into strips or halves that she can easily hold. For an **older baby**, cut into strips or halves or serve as is.

Toddler's serve: serve as is.

To make the cucumber dipping sauce, place the vinegar and sugar in a small saucepan with 125 ml (4 fl oz/½ cup) water. Place over low heat and cook for 4 minutes, stirring until the sugar has dissolved. Bring to a simmer and continue cooking for a further 10 minutes, or until syrupy. Remove from the heat. Add the cucumber, chilli, fish sauce and peanuts and stir to combine. Set aside to cool.

To make the Thai fish cakes, place the fish, ginger, coriander, spring onion, beans and soy sauce in a food processor and process until almost smooth. Add the egg and process until well combined. (Set aside some of the fish mixture for your baby.) Stir the red curry paste through the remaining mixture.

Heat the oil in a large frying pan over medium heat. Working in batches, drop heaped tablespoonfuls of the fish mixture into the hot pan and cook for 1–2 minutes on each side, or until cooked through and golden. Drain on paper towel and keep warm.

Serve the warm fish cakes with the cucumber dipping sauce on the side (omit the dipping sauce for your baby).

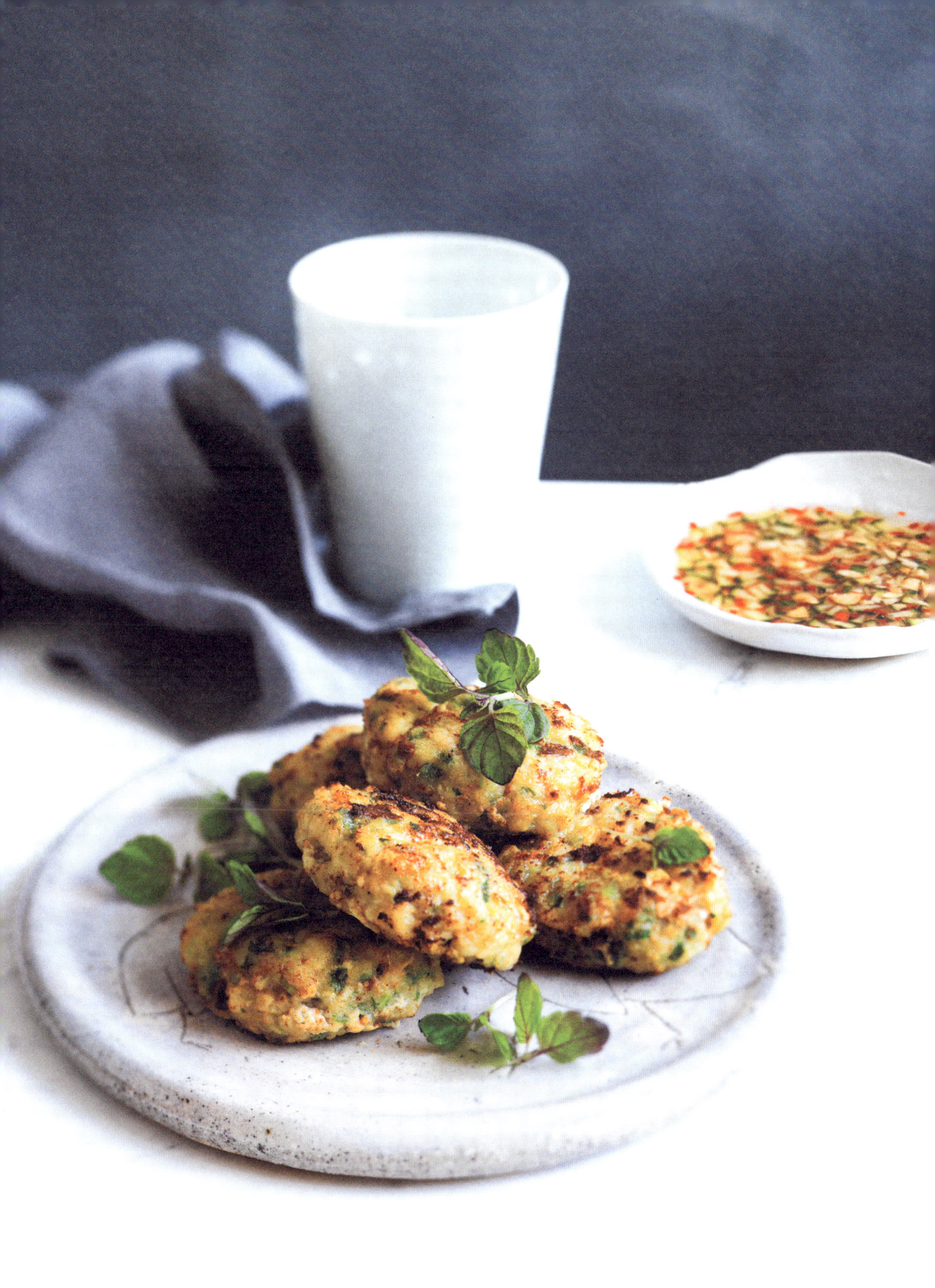

Calamari with tartare sauce

Serves 4

Calamari is a great, sustainable seafood. Lightly pan-fried it makes a healthy snack or it can be served with a salad for a more wholesome lunch. If your child isn't keen on other meats, this might be one protein source she'll happily accept.

Tartare sauce is traditionally made with a mayonnaise base, but yoghurt makes a lovely healthy alternative.

35 g (1¼ oz/¼ cup) plain (all-purpose) flour
400 g (14 oz) cleaned calamari (squid), cut into 1 cm (½ inch) strips
2 tablespoons light olive oil or rice bran oil
lemon wedges, to serve

TARTARE SAUCE
125 g (4½ oz/½ cup) Greek-style yoghurt
3 teaspoons finely chopped cornichons
2 teaspoons capers, rinsed and chopped
1 teaspoon finely chopped dill
1 teaspoon white balsamic vinegar

Tip Cooked properly, calamari should be lovely and tender. Make sure your child is confidently chewing before serving it and never leave her unattended while she's eating.

To make the tartare sauce, stir together all of the ingredients until well combined. Refrigerate until ready to serve.

To make the calamari, place the flour on a large plate. Add the calamari and toss until coated all over, shaking off any excess flour.

Heat half of the oil in a large frying pan over high heat. Add half of the calamari and cook for 2 minutes, or until golden brown and just cooked. Drain on paper towel. Repeat with the remaining oil and calamari until all cooked.

Serve the calamari with tartare sauce and lemon wedges on the side.

Baby's serve: for a **younger baby**, wait until your baby is confidently managing some finger foods (which may not happen until 8–9 months or older) before offering her this calamari. Once she's ready, simply serve as is, cut into small pieces if she prefers. For an **older baby**, serve as is.

Toddler's serve: serve as is.

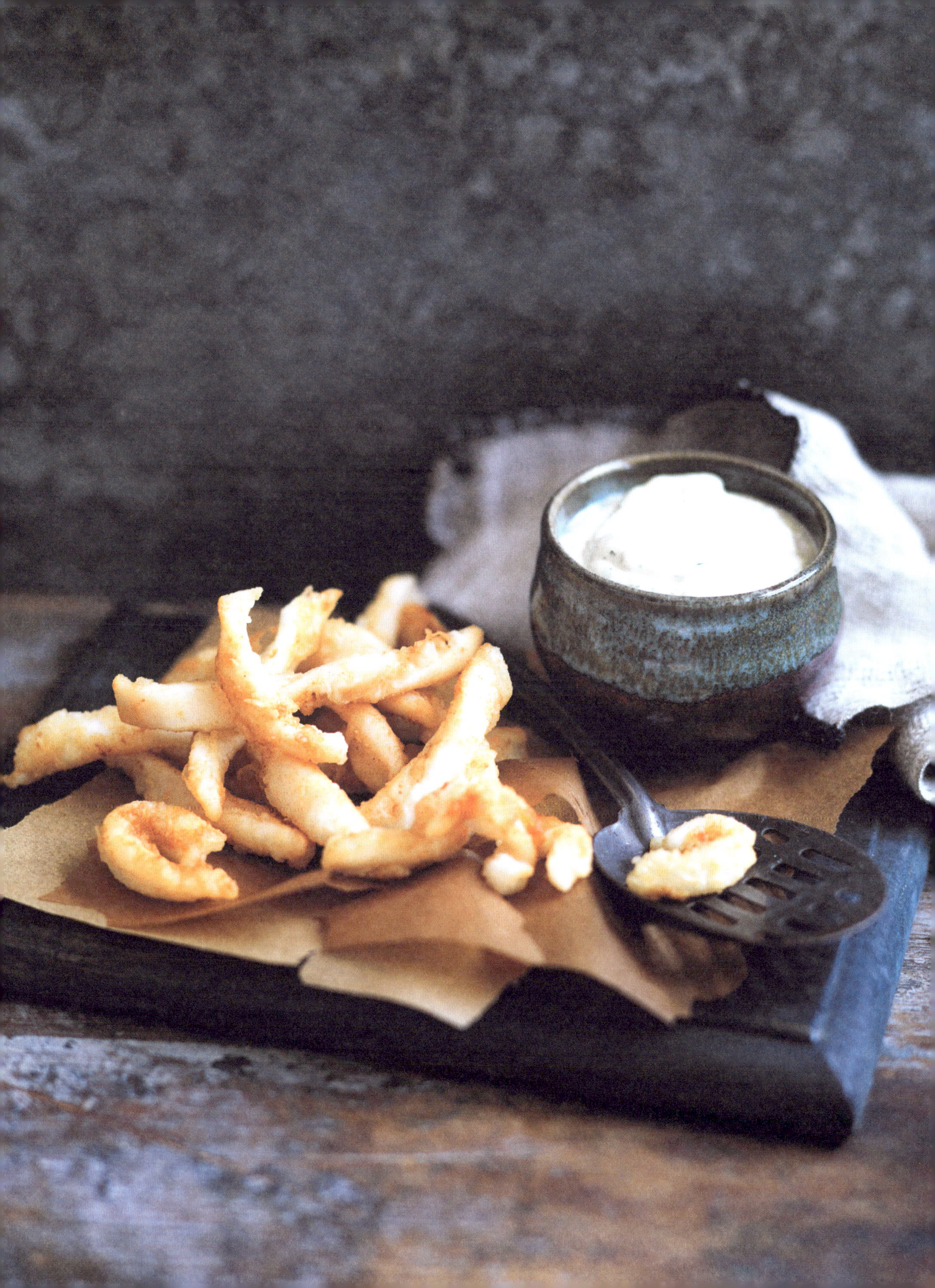

Mussel fritters

Makes 12–15

This recipe comes from New Zealand and is a favourite of my Kiwi dad, who has been cooking these fritters for our family for a few decades at least.

Among other things, mussels are a great source of omega-3 fats, selenium, iodine and iron.

1 kg (2 lb 4 oz) mussels, scrubbed, debearded and steamed, removed from shells, meat chopped (see note)
1 French shallot or ½ small red onion, finely diced
2 eggs
3 tablespoons finely chopped flat-leaf (Italian) parsley leaves
75 g (2¾ oz/½ cup) self-raising flour
1 zucchini (courgette), finely grated, lightly squeezed to remove excess moisture
light olive oil or rice bran oil, for shallow frying
1 Lebanese (short) cucumber, peeled into ribbons, to serve
lemon wedges, to serve

Note To steam the mussels, pop them in a large saucepan, covered, and cook over medium heat, stirring occasionally, until their shells open. There is no need to add water to the pot.

Place the chopped cooked mussels in a large bowl with the shallot, eggs, parsley, flour and zucchini. Mix until well combined.

Heat 1–2 tablespoons of oil in a non-stick frying pan over low–medium heat. Working in batches, drop large spoonfuls of the mussel mixture into the hot pan and lightly shape into circular fritters. Cook for 2–3 minutes on each side, or until golden and cooked through. Drain on paper towel. Repeat with the remaining mixture, using more oil if needed, until all the mixture is cooked.

Serve the warm mussel fritters with the cucumber ribbons and lemon wedges.

Baby's serve: for a **younger baby**, wait until your baby is managing some finger foods (which may not happen until 8–9 months or older) before offering her these fritters. If it helps her, cut them into strips or halves that she can easily hold. For an **older baby**, cut into strips or halves or serve as is.

Toddler's serve: serve as is.

Snacks and lunch

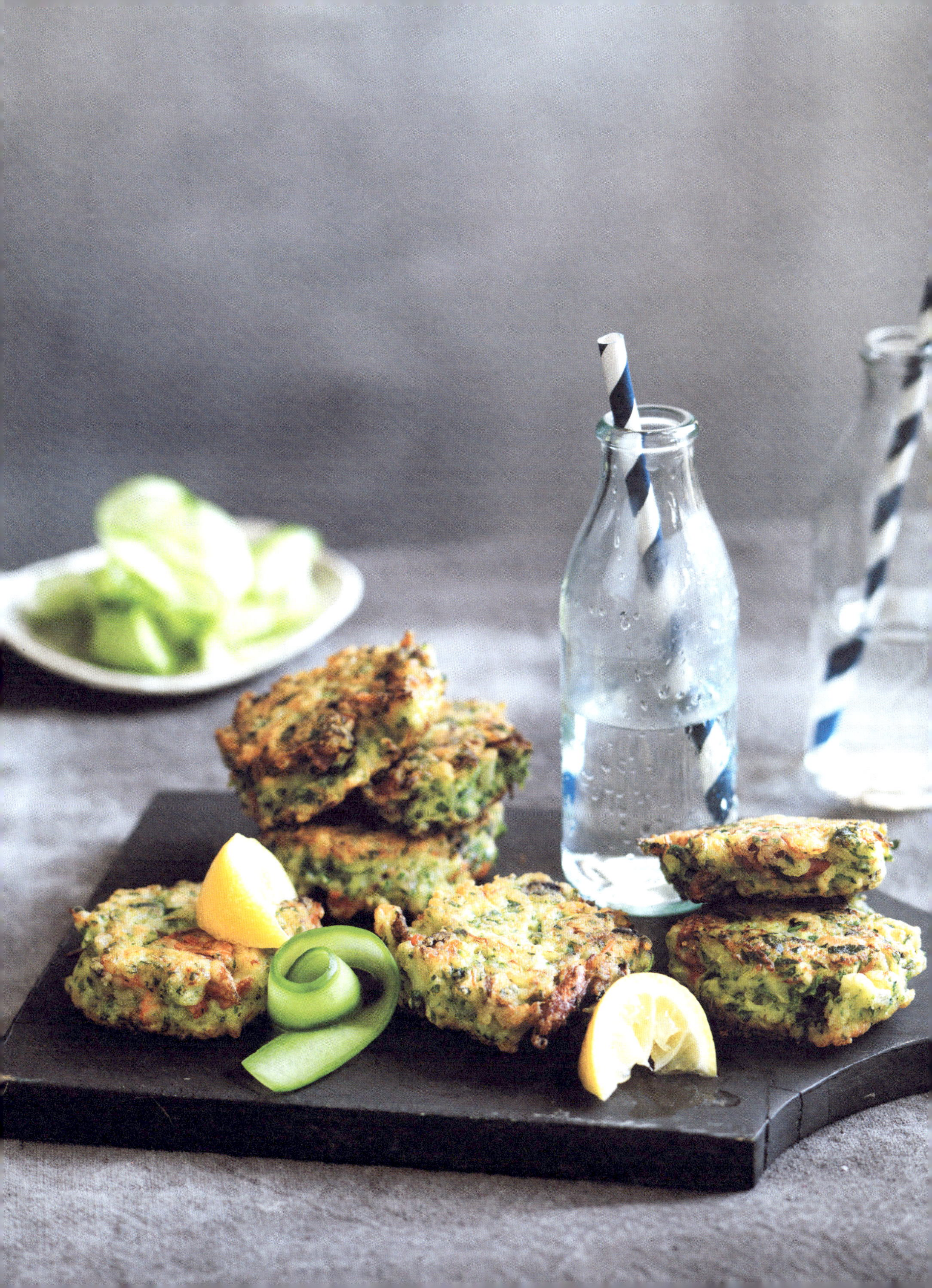

The best way to encourage a liking of green vegetables in your child is to just keep serving them – and eat them yourself. Don't always purée them or hide them in sauces. Seeing and tasting them in their whole form is a crucial part of the process.

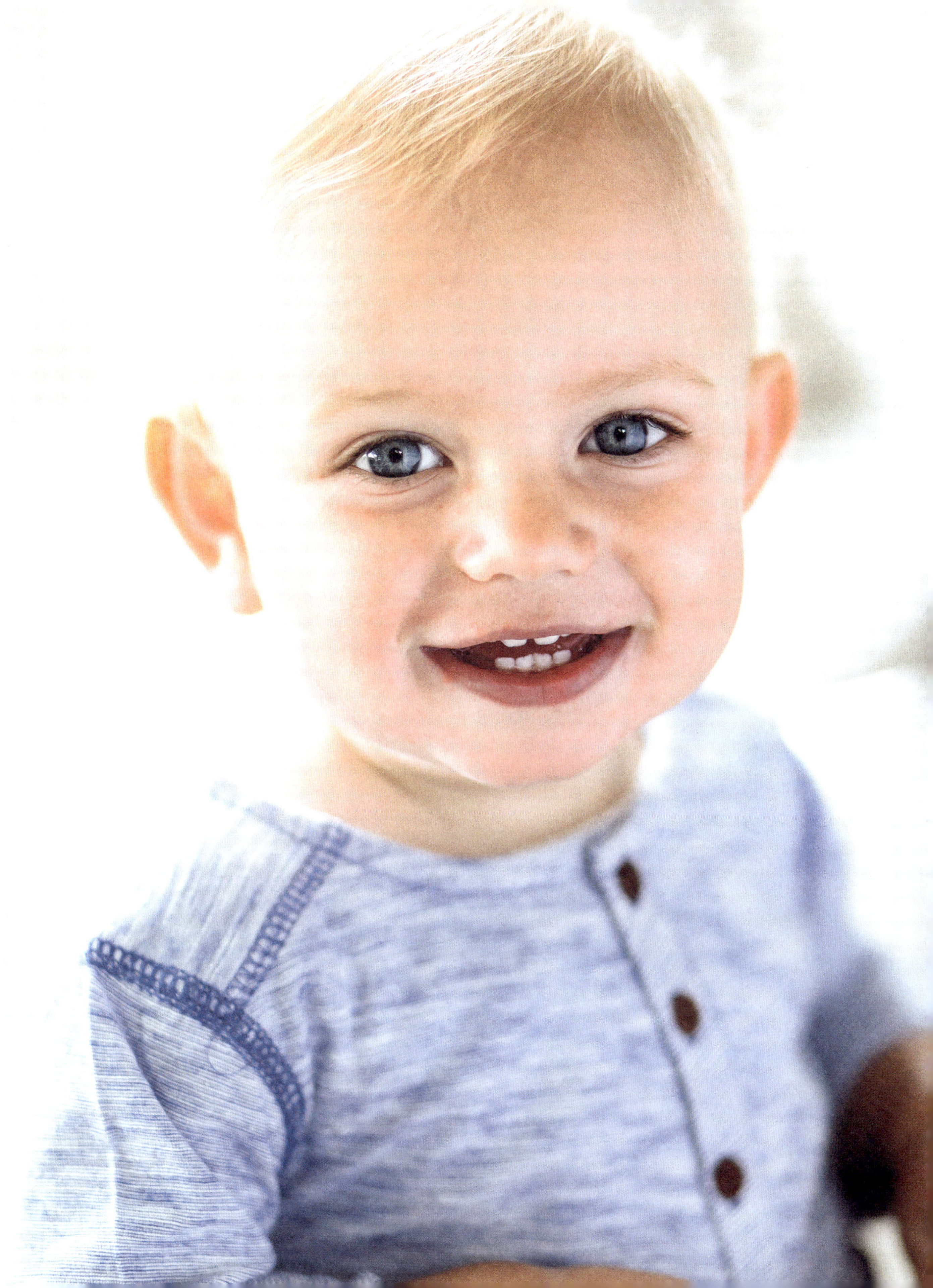

Sesame-crunch fish fingers with broad bean yoghurt sauce

Serves 4 as a snack

Step away from those frozen supermarket fish fingers! Help your child develop a liking for this nutritious, crunchy homemade version. The moreish broad bean yoghurt sauce is also a great way of adding a serve of green vegetables to your meal.

100 g (3½ oz) day-old wholemeal (whole-wheat) bread (crusts on), roughly chopped
2 tablespoons sesame seeds
2 tablespoons chopped flat-leaf (Italian) parsley
2 teaspoons finely grated lemon zest
50 g (1¾ oz/⅓ cup) wholemeal (whole-wheat) plain (all-purpose) flour
2 eggs, lightly whisked
300 g (10½ oz) flathead or other firm white fish fillets, cut into 8 cm (3¼ inch) strips
60 ml (2 fl oz/¼ cup) light olive oil or rice bran oil

BROAD BEAN YOGHURT SAUCE
200 g (7 oz) fresh or frozen broad (fava) beans
200 g (7 oz) plain yoghurt
1 tablespoon chopped fresh mint
2 teaspoons lemon juice
½ garlic clove, peeled

To make the broad bean yoghurt sauce, steam or microwave the broad beans until just tender. Refresh under cold running water. Peel and discard the skins, then place the beans in a food processor. Add the remaining ingredients and process until well combined.

To make the fish fingers, place the bread into a food processor and process until it resembles fine breadcrumbs. Transfer to a bowl and stir in the sesame seeds, parsley and lemon zest.

Place the flour, egg and breadcrumbs in three separate shallow bowls. Dust the fish strips first with flour, then dip into the egg, then roll to coat each with the crumbs.

Heat half of the oil in a frying pan over medium heat. Cook half of the fish strips for 2–3 minutes, turning until golden and cooked through. Drain on paper towel. Repeat with the remaining oil and fish until they're all cooked.

Serve the hot fish fingers with the broad bean yoghurt sauce on the side for dipping.

Baby's serve: for a **younger baby**, wait until your baby is confidently managing some finger foods (which may not happen until 8–9 months or older) before offering her these fish fingers. For an **older baby**, serve as is.

Toddler's serve: serve as is.

Snacks and lunch

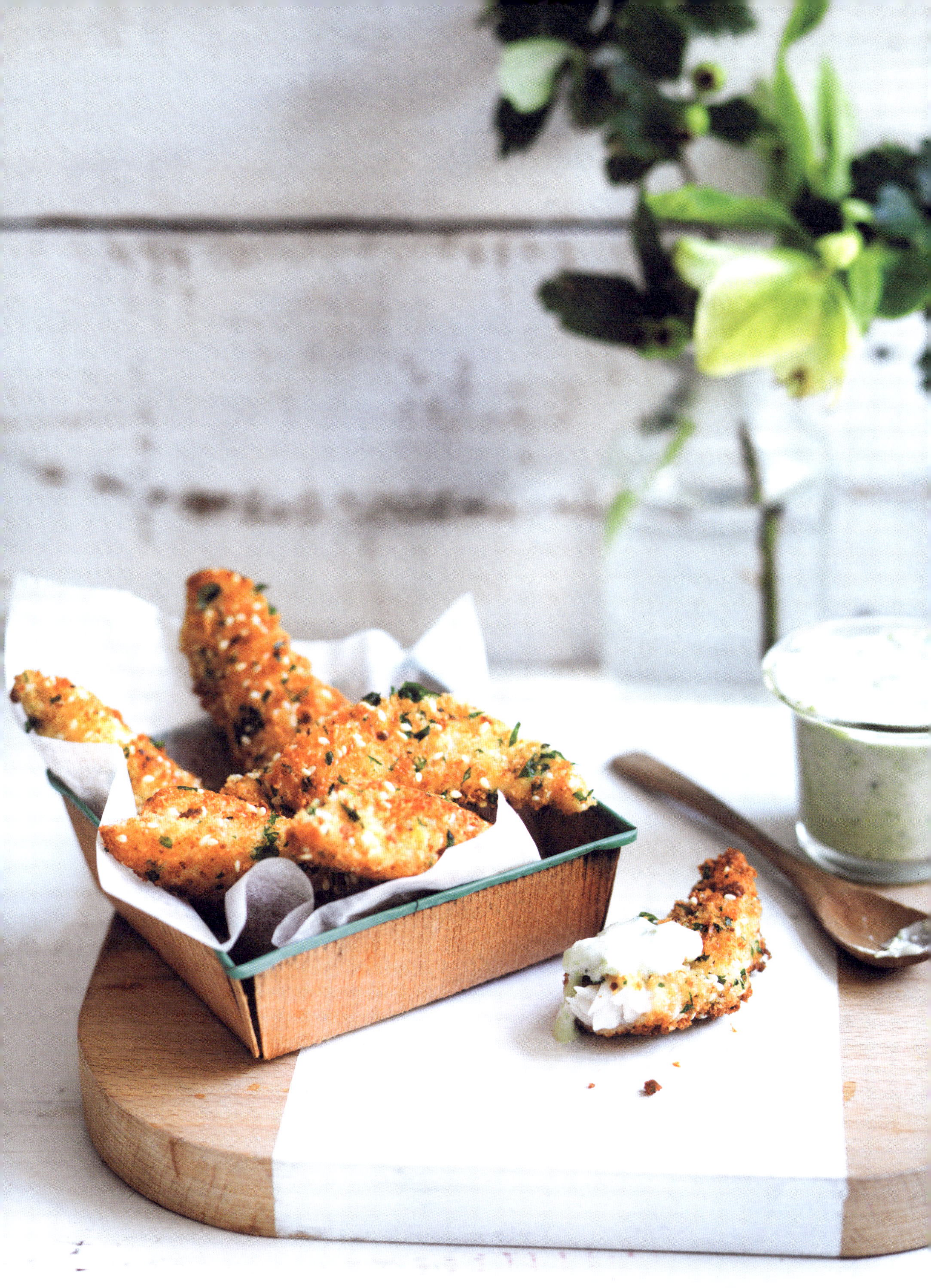

Chicken ginger wontons

Makes 30

One reason I use pretty enoki mushrooms is that I like my son to get accustomed to seeing a wide range of ingredients in our kitchen. If you have button mushrooms on hand, they're fine too.

For a flavour variation, try adding a few teaspoons of chopped fresh lemongrass.

200 g (7 oz) chicken thigh fillets, roughly chopped
200 g (7 oz) chicken breast fillets, roughly chopped
50 g (1¾ oz) enoki mushrooms (or other variety of mushroom)
1 egg
1–2 cm (½–¾ inch) piece fresh ginger, peeled
1–2 tablespoons snipped chives, plus extra to serve
1–2 tablespoons chopped coriander (cilantro) leaves (optional)
1–2 tablespoons chopped spring onions (scallions)
1 tablespoon sesame seeds, plus extra to serve
1 tablespoon soy sauce or tamari, plus extra to serve
30 wonton wrappers
sesame oil (optional), to serve

Place the chicken, mushrooms, egg, ginger, chives, coriander, spring onion, sesame seeds and soy sauce in a food processor and process until minced (ground) and smooth.

Place approximately 2 teaspoons of the filling mixture into the centre of each wonton wrapper. Wet your fingers and fold diagonally into a triangle, sealing with water. Pinch the two corners at the base together, then wrap them in front of the wonton to form dumplings.

Cut slits in a sheet of non-stick baking paper and use it to line a steaming basket. Place the wontons onto the paper, leaving space between each so they do not touch each other. Place the steamer basket over a wok of simmering water and steam for 25 minutes, or until cooked through.

Remove the basket from the heat and allow the wontons to cool for a few minutes. Serve with some soy sauce or tamari on the side. If liked, drizzle with some sesame oil and top with sesame seeds and chives, to serve.

Baby's serve: for a **younger baby**, you can steam dollops of the filling without the wrappers and then blend through your baby's favourite vegetable purée. Alternatively, you might like to wait until your baby is managing some finger foods (which may not happen until 8–9 months or older). If needed, cut into small pieces that she can easily hold. For an **older baby**, cut into small pieces or serve as is. Your baby should be having no or very little soy sauce due to the high salt content.

Toddler's serve: serve as is.

Snacks and lunch

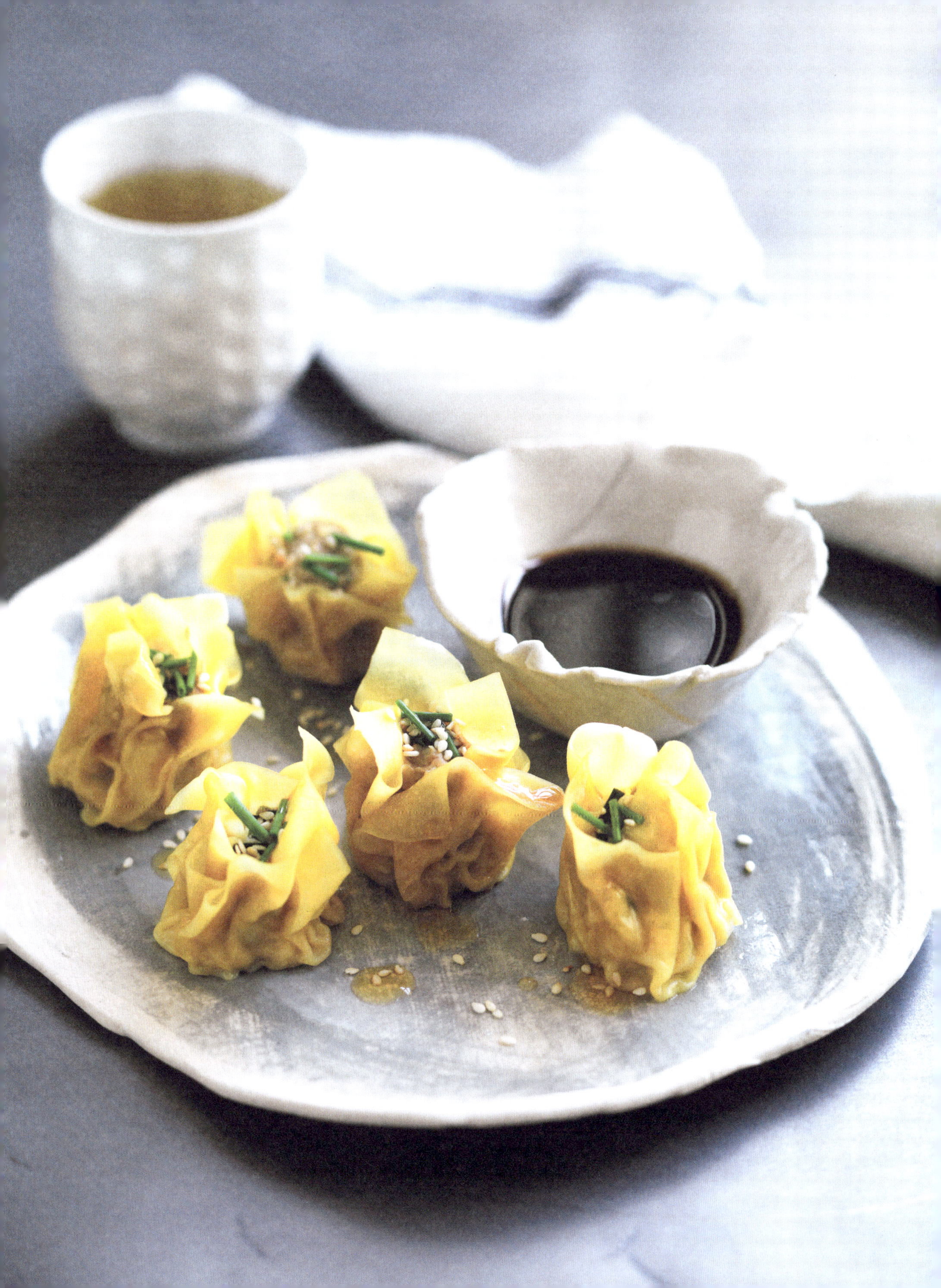

Tomato and bocconcini wholemeal pizza

Makes 6 small pizzas

Pizza is a universal favourite. Make these healthier wholemeal pizzas with your children and you'll be teaching them that even their most-beloved food can be made in their own kitchen. You can use the Five-vegetable sauce on page 142 for the pizza topping instead of the passata – it is a good way of sneaking in some more vegetables.

90 ml (3¼ fl oz) tomato passata (puréed tomatoes)
1–2 garlic cloves, finely chopped
8 button mushrooms, thinly sliced
extra-virgin olive oil, to drizzle
8 bocconcini, torn into small pieces
1 small handful basil leaves

WHOLEMEAL PIZZA BASE
300 g (10½ oz/2 cups) wholemeal (whole-wheat) plain (all-purpose) flour
1 teaspoon salt
1 teaspoon sugar
7 g (¼ oz/2 teaspoons) dried yeast
60 ml (2 fl oz/¼ cup) olive oil

Baby's serve: for a **younger baby**, wait until your baby is confidently managing finger foods (which may not happen until 8–9 months or older) before offering her some of this pizza. Cut it into strips that she can easily hold. For an **older baby**, cut into strips that she can easily hold.

Toddler's serve: serve as is, sliced as needed.

To make the pizza bases, sift the flour and salt into a large bowl and stir in the sugar and yeast. Make a well in the centre and add the oil and 200 ml (7 fl oz) lukewarm water. Mix to a dough, then turn out onto a well-floured surface and knead for 4–5 minutes, or until smooth and elastic. Put the dough in a greased bowl, cover with a tea towel (dish towel) and set aside to rise in a warm place for about 1 hour, or until doubled in size.

Preheat the oven to 220°C (430°F). Lightly flour two baking trays. Turn the dough out onto a floured surface and divide into six even-sized portions. Roll each portion into an oval shape to make 6 thin pizza bases. Carefully transfer the bases to the prepared trays.

Combine the tomato passata and garlic and spread over the pizza bases, leaving a 1 cm (½ inch) border around the edges. Scatter the mushrooms over the pizzas, drizzle with a little olive oil and bake for 7–10 minutes. Remove from the oven, top with the bocconcini, and bake for a further 5–10 minutes, or until the bases are crisp and the cheese has melted. Scatter over the basil leaves and serve immediately.

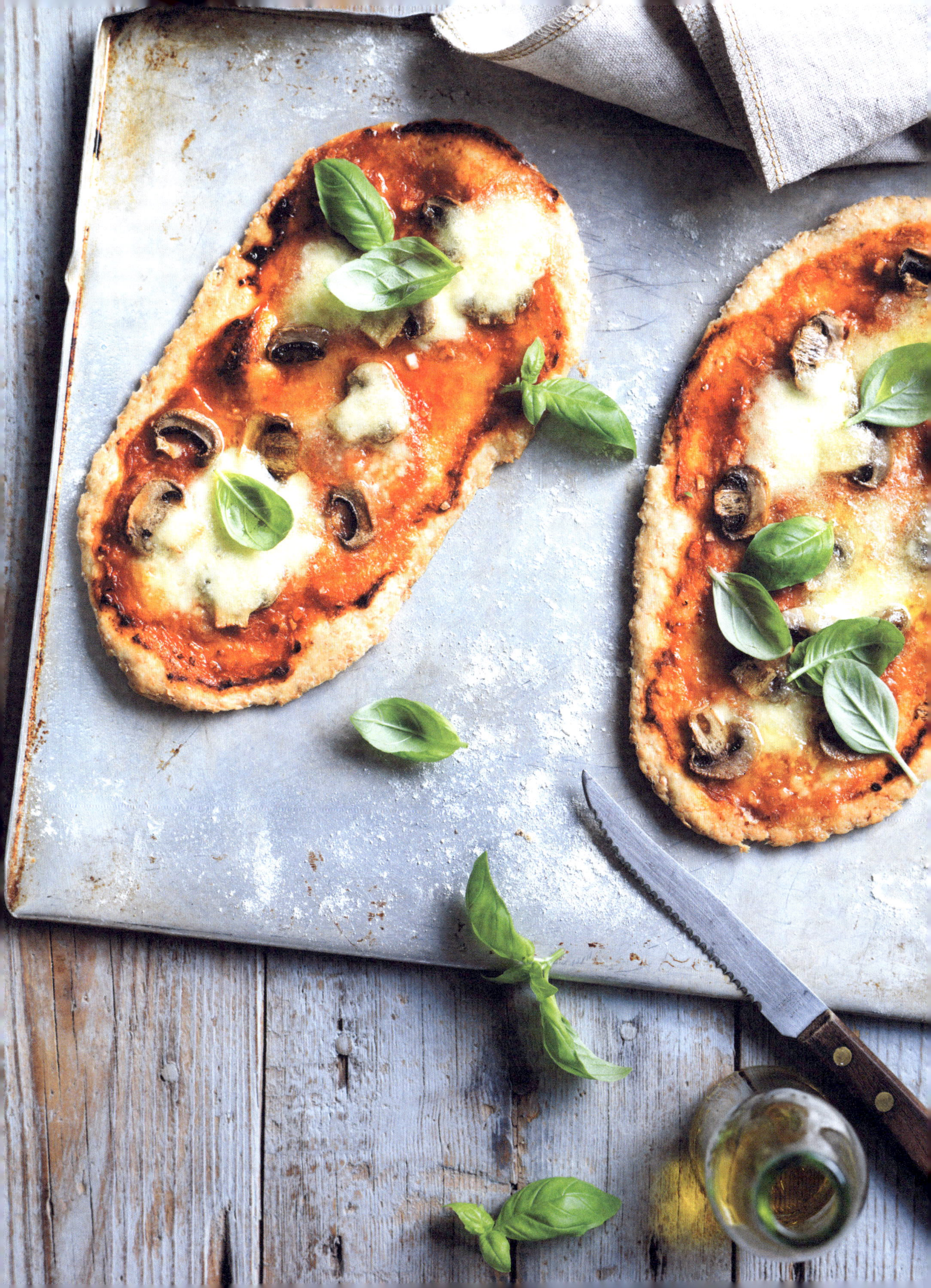

Mini burgers with guacamole

Makes 16 burgers

Burgers are a bit of a Friday night tradition in my house. Made from scratch, there is no need to feel any guilt about serving these delicious chaps. In summer, you might like to cook the beef patties on the barbecue and eat outside. You can freeze any (uncooked) leftover beef patties and then simply defrost and cook as needed.

1 quantity beef meatball mixture (see page 86)
1 tablespoon olive oil
40 g (1½ oz) cheddar cheese, thinly sliced
16 mini multigrain bread rolls, halved
small lettuce leaves, to serve

GUACAMOLE
1 ripe avocado, halved and stone removed
½ tomato, finely diced
1 tablespoon finely snipped chives
1 tablespoon lemon juice

Baby's serve: for a **younger baby**, wait until your baby is managing some finger foods (which may not happen until 8–9 months or older) before offering her some of the cooked beef patty with cheese and avocado or guacamole. Alternatively, you can mash the beef patty with avocado or guacamole. For an **older baby**, serve as for a younger baby or, if your baby is confidently managing finger food, serve as is, cut up as needed.

Toddler's serve: serve as is, cut up as needed.

To make the guacamole, scoop the avocado flesh into a large bowl and mash well. Gently stir through the remaining ingredients until combined. Refrigerate until ready to serve.

Prepare the beef mixture following the instructions for the beef meatball recipe on page 86. Instead of rolling into balls, shape the mince into 16 even-sized patties.

Preheat the oven grill (broiler) to high.

Heat the oil in a large frying pan over medium heat. Cook the beef patties for 4–5 minutes on each side, or until cooked through.

Arrange the cheddar slices over the top of each beef patty. Place under the grill (broiler) for 1 minute, or until the cheese melts.

Toast the bread rolls. Place a lettuce leaf on the base of each roll, followed by a beef patty with cheese, then top with a spoonful of guacamole. Finish assembling the burgers by placing the top half of the rolls on top and serve immediately.

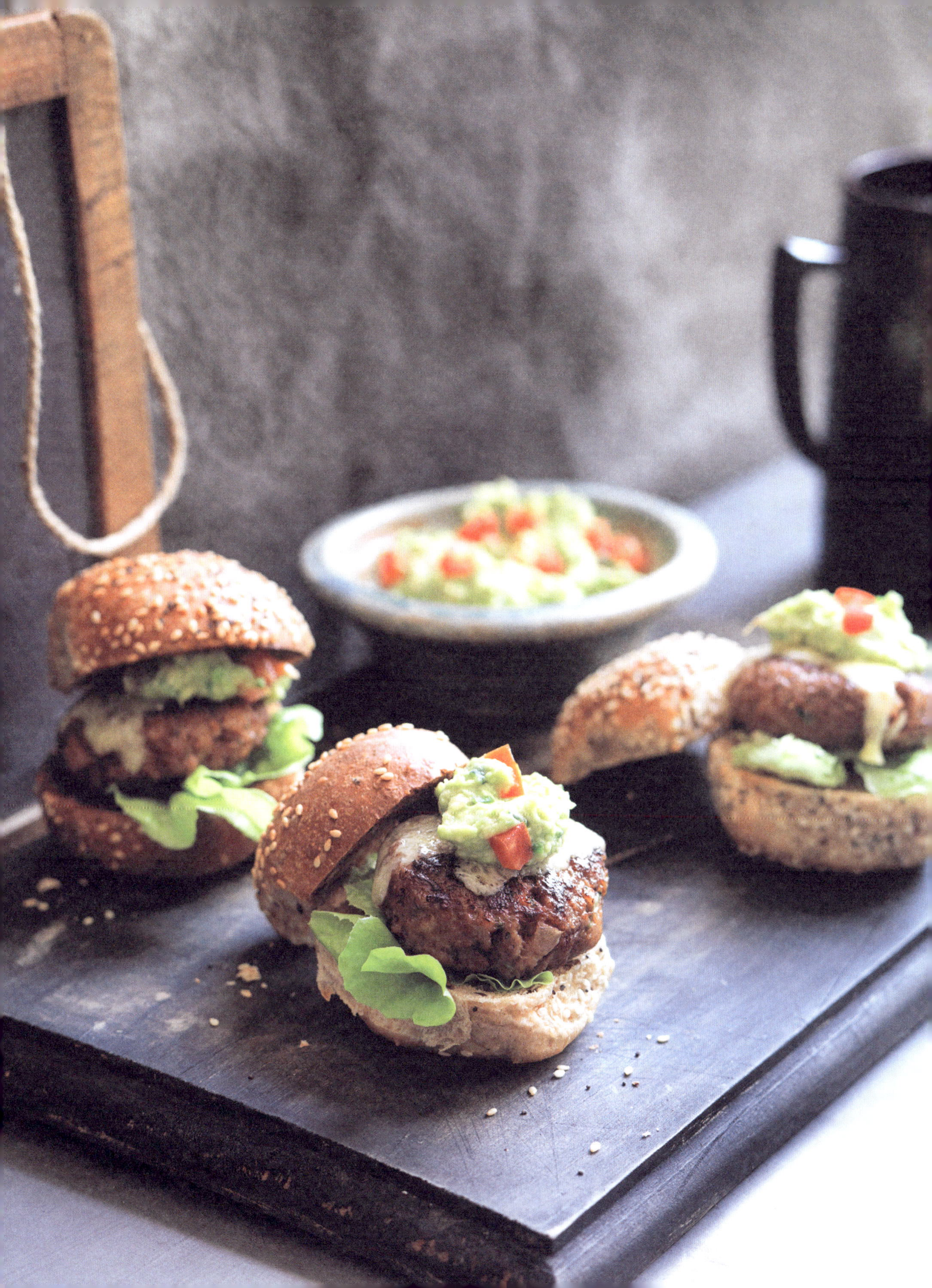

Zucchini, pea and ricotta frittata

Serves 4–6

A frittata is my go-to meal when I'm overdue for a grocery shop. If the fridge is running low, I can usually scrounge around and at least find some eggs and a couple of greens, without resorting to takeaway. It's one recipe that can be made for breakfast, lunch or dinner. It's also terrific for lunchboxes and can be eaten warm or cold as a snack any time of the day.

1 tablespoon olive oil
1 small brown onion, finely diced
1 zucchini (courgette), thinly sliced using a mandolin
140 g (5 oz) fresh or frozen peas
6 eggs
80 ml (2½ fl oz/⅓ cup) milk
100 g (3½ oz) fresh ricotta (see note, page 38)
fresh herbs, to serve (optional)

Preheat the oven grill (broiler) to high.

Heat the oil in a large non-stick ovenproof frying pan over medium heat. Add the onion and cook for 5 minutes, or until softened. Add the zucchini and peas and cook for a further 2–3 minutes, or until the zucchini has softened.

Whisk together the eggs and milk in a bowl, then pour over the zucchini and pea mixture in the pan, stirring gently to mix the eggs through the greens. Crumble the ricotta evenly over the top, reduce the heat to low and cook for a further 6 minutes, or until the egg is nearly set.

Transfer the frying pan to the grill (broiler) and cook for 5 minutes, or until the top is set and golden.

Cut the frittata into slices and serve with fresh herbs sprinkled on top, if liked.

Baby's serve: for a **younger baby**, wait at least until your baby is managing some finger foods (which may not happen until 8–9 months or older), before offering her this frittata. Cut into fingers that she can easily hold. For an **older baby**, serve as for a younger baby.

Toddler's serve: serve as is, cut into fingers.

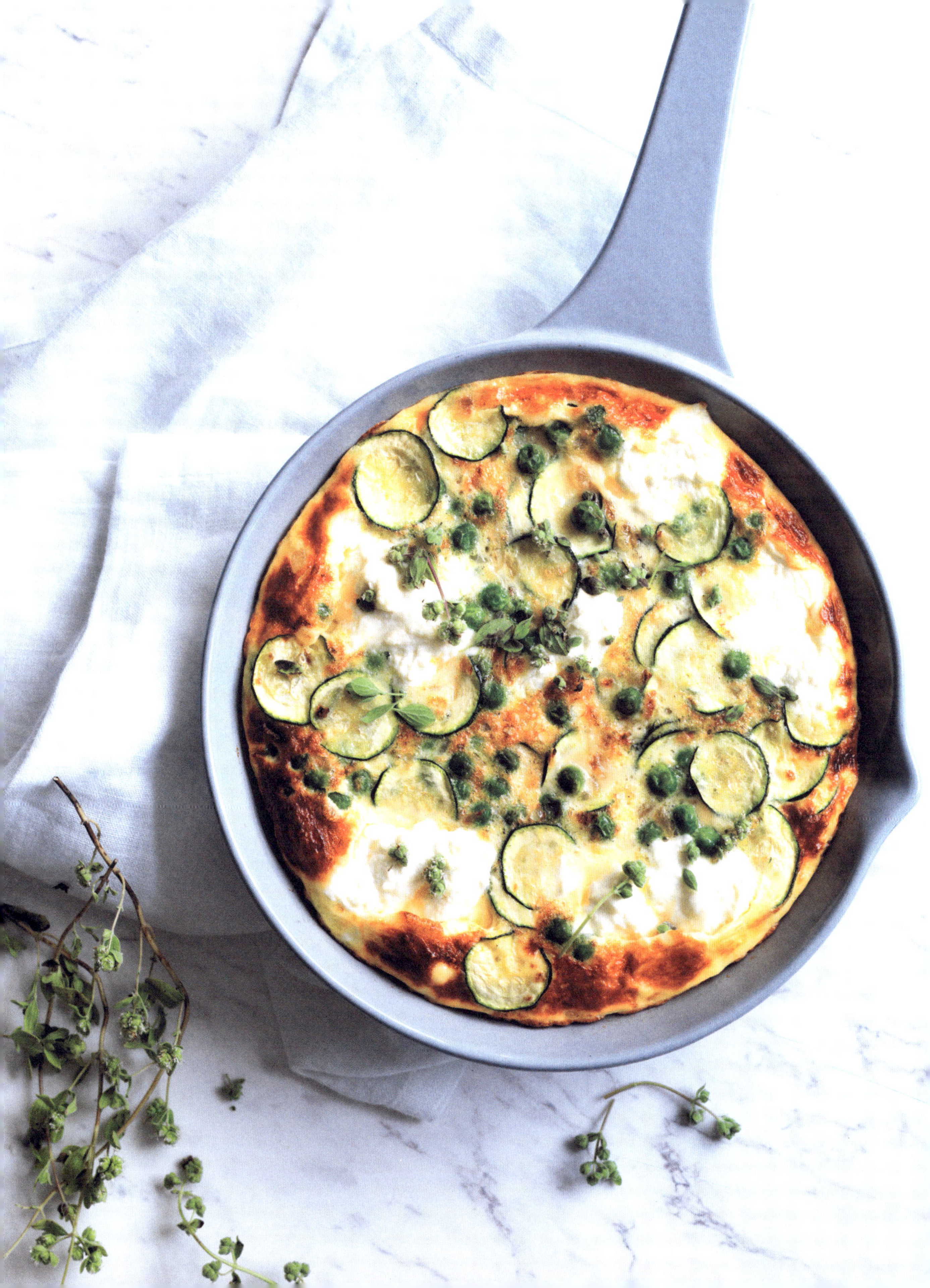

Lamb souvlaki with tzatziki

Serves 4

Pop these on the barbecue for a much healthier alternative to sausages for your family. Unlike sausages (which sometimes contain only half meat and often include fillers and preservatives), you know what you're getting with these delicious souvlaki.

½ teaspoon ground coriander
½ teaspoon ground cumin
½ teaspoon sweet paprika
1 tablespoon olive oil
800 g (1 lb 12 oz) lean lamb, cubed
4 tomatoes, diced
2 teaspoons red wine vinegar
2 tablespoons extra-virgin olive oil
fresh mint leaves, to serve
4 pitta breads, to serve (choose a gluten-free brand if needed)

TZATZIKI
1 Lebanese (short) cucumber, grated
½ garlic clove, finely chopped
2 tablespoons mint leaves, finely chopped
200 g (7 oz) Greek-style yoghurt

To make the tzatziki, combine all of the ingredients in a bowl. Refrigerate until ready to serve.

To make the lamb souvlaki, place the spices and oil in a large bowl. Add the lamb, tossing to coat, and leave in the refrigerator to marinate for at least 30 minutes or overnight.

Preheat a chargrill pan or barbecue grill to medium–high. Thread the lamb onto 8 wooden skewers. Cook the lamb skewers for 10–12 minutes, turning regularly until browned and cooked to your liking. Transfer to a plate, cover loosely with foil and allow to rest for 5–10 minutes.

In a bowl, stir together the tomatoes, vinegar and olive oil until combined. Transfer to a serving bowl and scatter over a few fresh mint leaves.

Serve the lamb souvlaki with the pitta breads, tzatziki and tomatoes.

Baby's serve: for a **younger baby**, blend together some cooked lamb and yoghurt until smooth. You may need to add some liquid (water or your baby's milk) to achieve the desired consistency. Alternatively, if your baby is managing finger foods, cut into small pieces. For an **older baby**, keep the puréed consistency lumpier or serve as finger food.

Toddler's serve: serve as is, cut into smaller pieces if needed.

Snacks and lunch

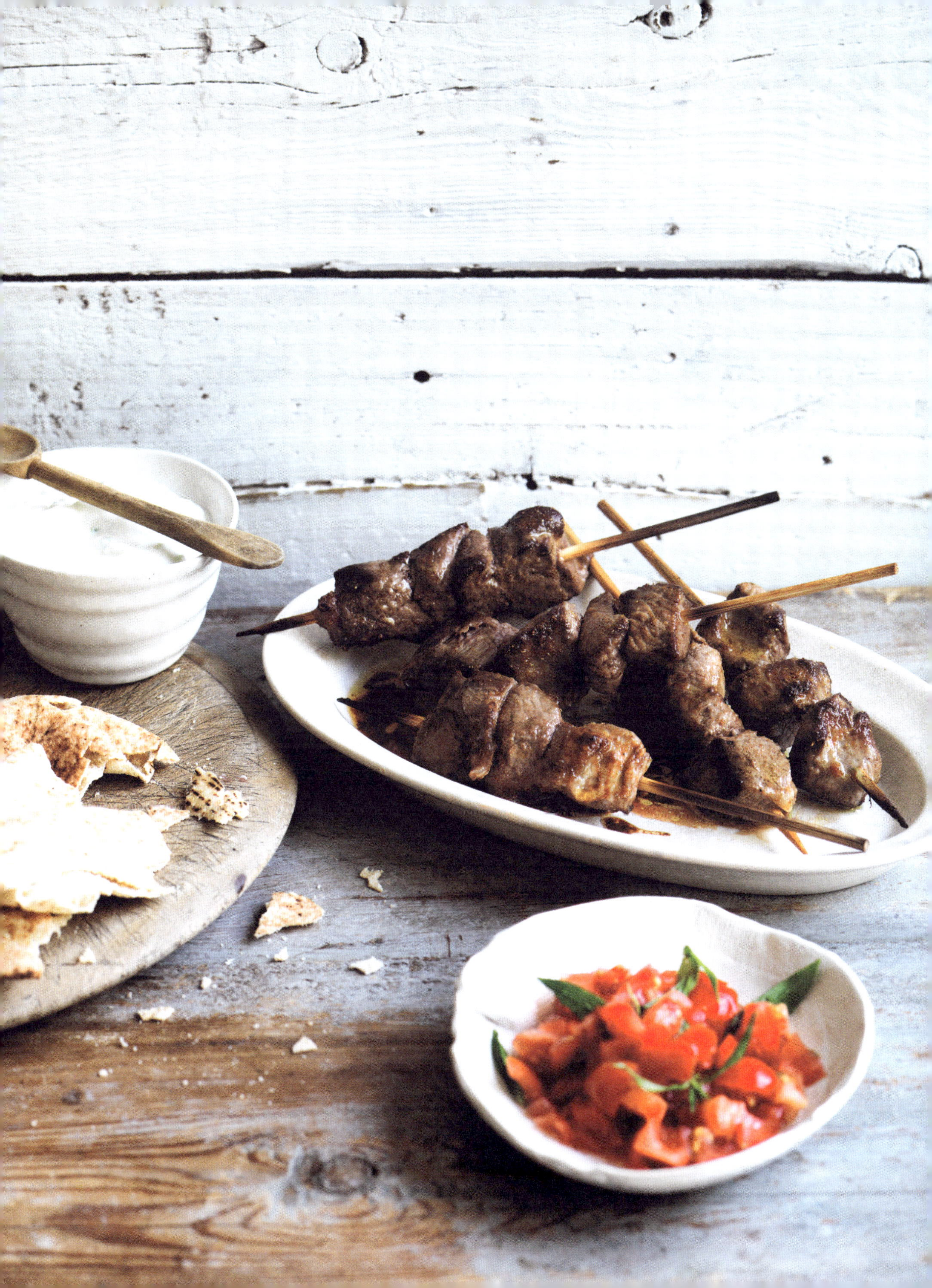

Baby beetroot salad with orange, avocado and walnuts

Serves 4

If fresh beetroot is not an item that ever appears on your grocery list, try giving it a go. I buy a few bunches a week, steam and peel them, and have them ready-to-eat in the fridge to add to salads and sandwiches.

While this may not seem like a kid-friendly dish at first glance, if you take away the leaves, the remaining ingredients – beetroot, avocado, orange, cream cheese, nuts – are all things that many children will happily eat. If yours isn't one of them, give her a chance. If she's accustomed to seeing these foods, she's more likely to eventually try them. Puréed, they also make a perfect baby food.

2 bunches baby beetroots (beets), trimmed, leaves reserved
1 orange, cut into segments, juice reserved
1 avocado, peeled, stone removed and sliced
80 g (2¾ oz) cream cheese, broken into pieces
40 g (1½ oz/⅓ cup) chopped walnuts
2 tablespoons extra-virgin olive oil

Steam the baby beetroots for 30 minutes, or until tender. Set aside to cool slightly. Select some of the pretty beetroot leaves, rinse well and set aside.

Using your fingers, slip the skins off the beetroot. Cut into wedges and arrange on serving plates. Top with the orange segments, avocado slices, cream cheese, walnuts and beetroot leaves. Drizzle over the reserved orange juice and olive oil just before serving.

Baby's serve: for a **younger baby**, blend the beetroot, avocado, cheese and walnuts until smooth, adding as much liquid as required to achieve the desired consistency. (Avocado doesn't freeze well so omit the avocado if you intend to freeze the purée.) For an **older baby**, keep the puréed consistency lumpier or serve as finger food, cut into small pieces.

Toddler's serve: serve as is, omitting the beetroot leaves if your child isn't keen on them.

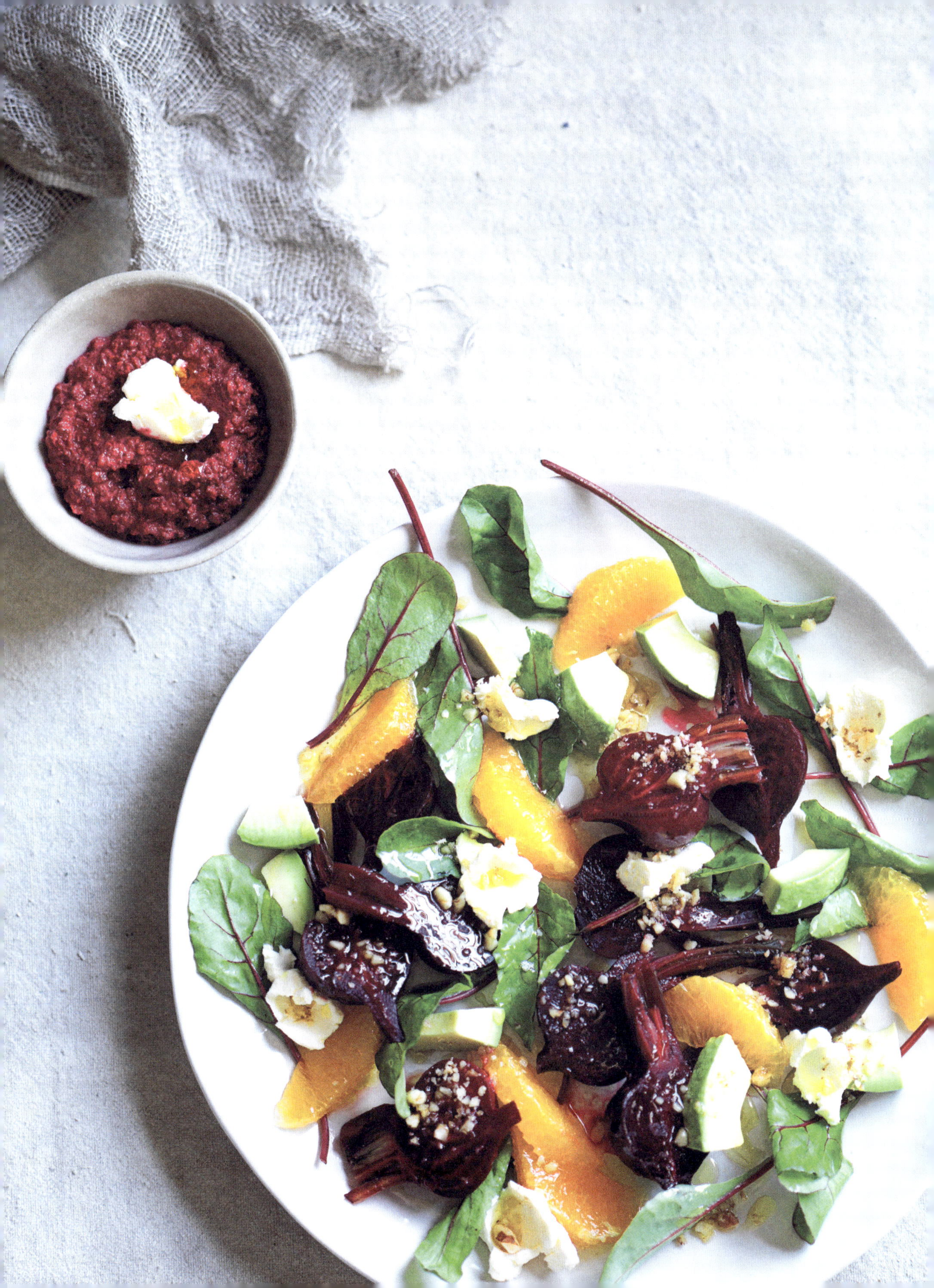

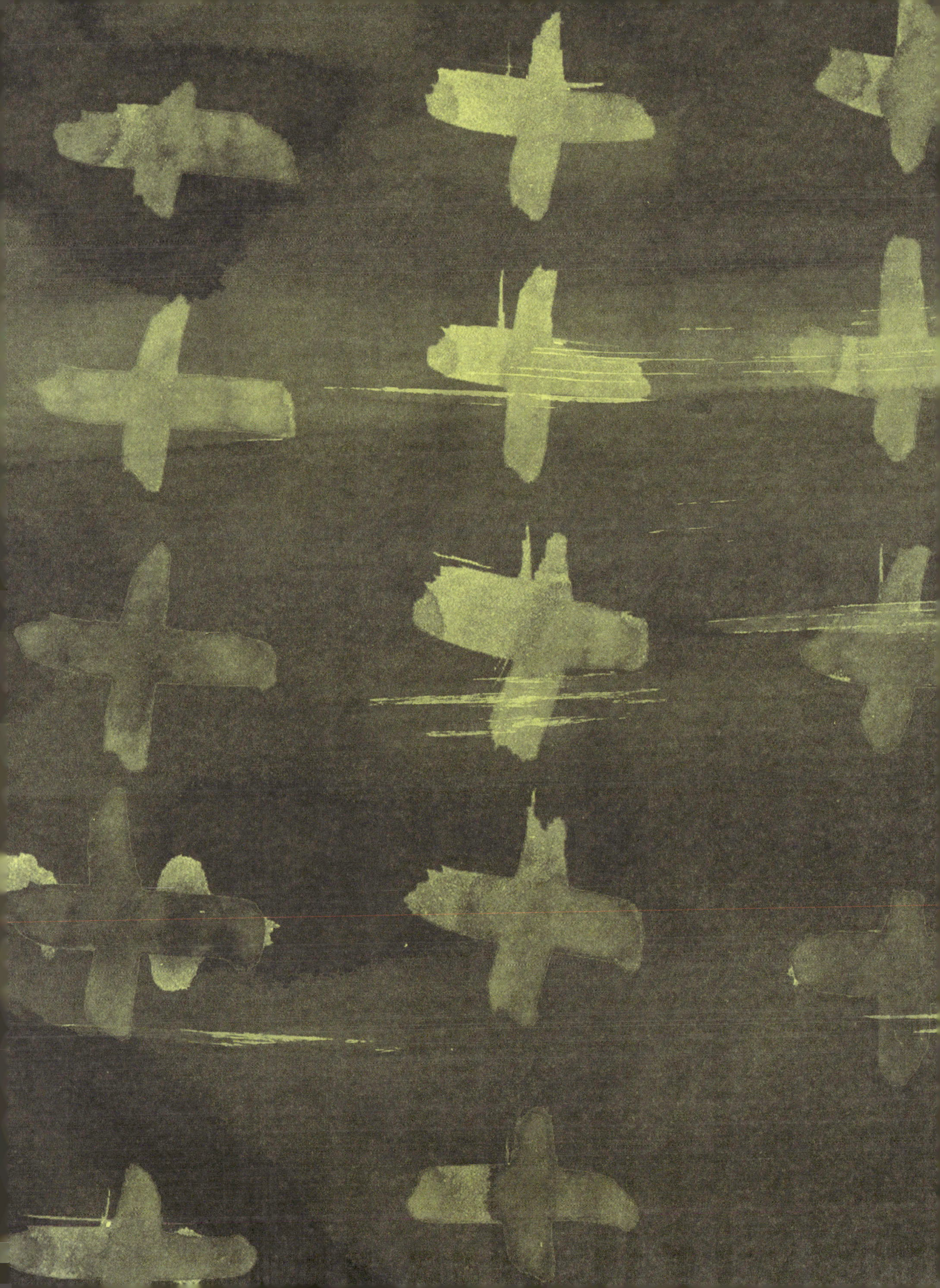

Dinner

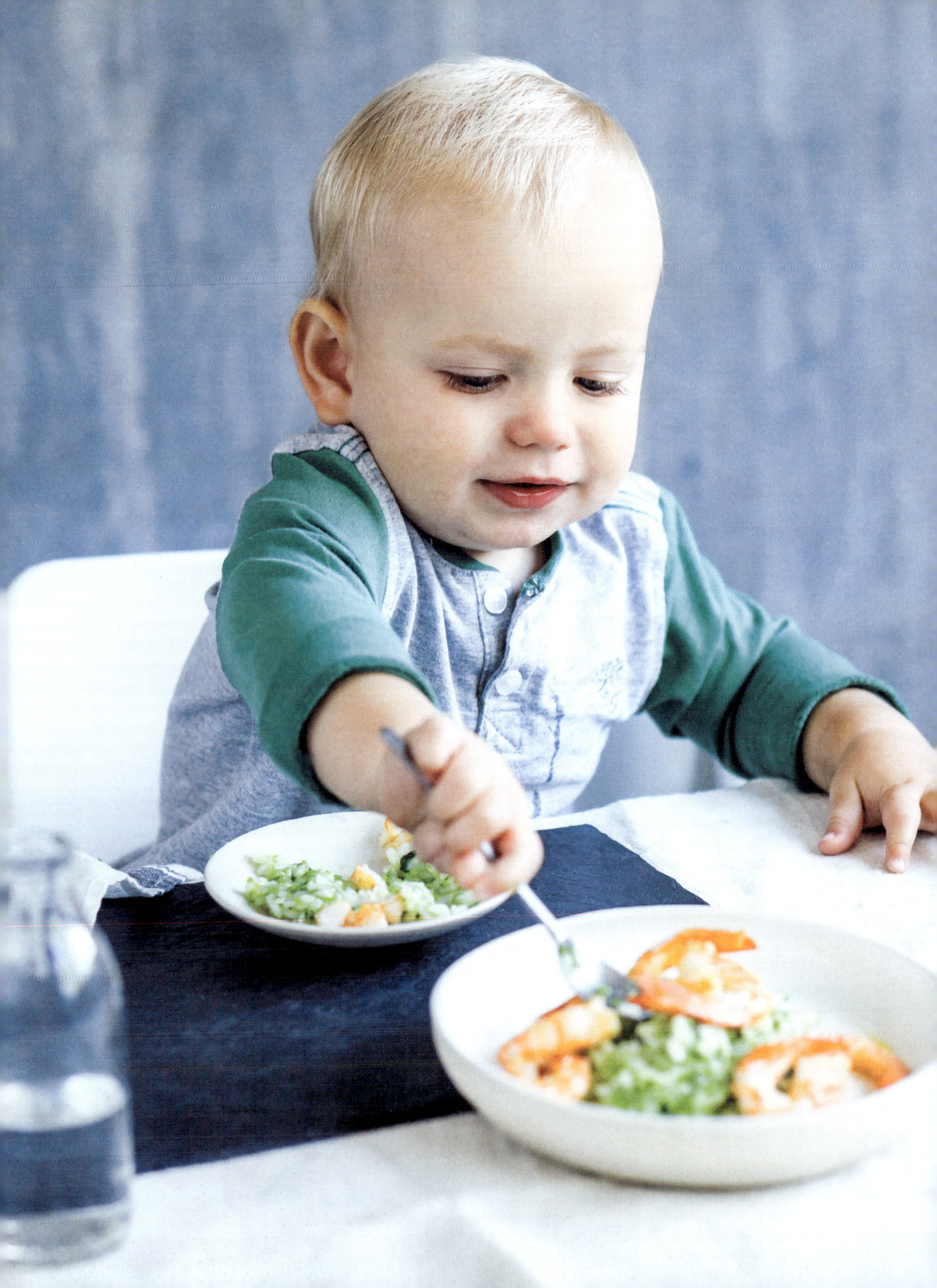

In many families, dinner is often the first point of the day where everyone has a chance to come together and have a chat. While it can be bedlam getting a meal on the table and gathering your troops to sit down to eat it, the long-term outcomes suggest that it's well worth the effort. It's something my working mum and dad managed to do through my childhood and I'm sure it's one of the reasons we're still so close now.

One way to make the evening witching hour easier, is to prepare ahead and make enough for another meal. Many of the recipes in this chapter – soups, pies, casseroles – are perfect for just that. Another saviour is sharing with your children the same meal that you're having, as all these recipes are designed to do. Ultimately, if they can develop a liking for your cooking and the food you like eating, it will save you years of having to cook two dinners every night.
Bon appétit!

Zucchini, pea and mint soup

Serves 4–6

This delicious green soup is a great way to include some freshness in the middle of winter. Not all children like the mint, so feel free to adjust the amount.

- 2 tablespoons olive oil
- 1 onion, finely chopped
- 2 garlic cloves, finely chopped
- 2 bacon rashers (slices), rind removed, finely chopped (optional – see note, page 126)
- 3 large (or 4 small) zucchini (courgettes), roughly chopped
- 500 g (1 lb 2 oz) fresh or frozen peas
- 1 litre (34 fl oz/4 cups) reduced-salt chicken or vegetable stock (see note)
- 1 tablespoon chopped mint leaves (optional), plus extra to garnish (or you can use chives)
- cream or plain yoghurt (optional), to serve

Note When making soups for your children, always use a reduced-salt, preferably home-made, stock. Babies' developing kidneys, in particular, can't handle much salt and it can cause them to become dehydrated.

Heat the oil in a large saucepan over medium heat. Add the onion, garlic and bacon (if using) and cook for about 5 minutes, or until the onion has softened. Add the zucchini and peas and cook, stirring, for a further 2 minutes. Add the stock and bring to the boil, then reduce the heat to low and simmer, covered, for 15 minutes, or until the zucchini is tender.

Remove the pan from the heat and allow the soup to cool a little before transferring to a food processor (or you can use a stick blender). Add the mint (if using) and blend or process until smooth. Return the soup to the pan and stir over medium heat for 3 minutes, or until warmed through.

Divide the soup among serving bowls, add a little cream or yoghurt (if using) and some extra mint or chives, to serve.

Baby's serve: for a **younger baby**, stir through a little rice cereal or some cooked quinoa or couscous to soften the flavour and thicken the soup. You may also like to stir through a little yoghurt. An **older baby** may like to eat as per a younger baby or with toast fingers for dipping.

Toddler's serve: serve as is, with toast fingers for dipping and a short-handled spoon. As with baby's serve, you may like to stir through some cooked quinoa or couscous to thicken.

Dinner

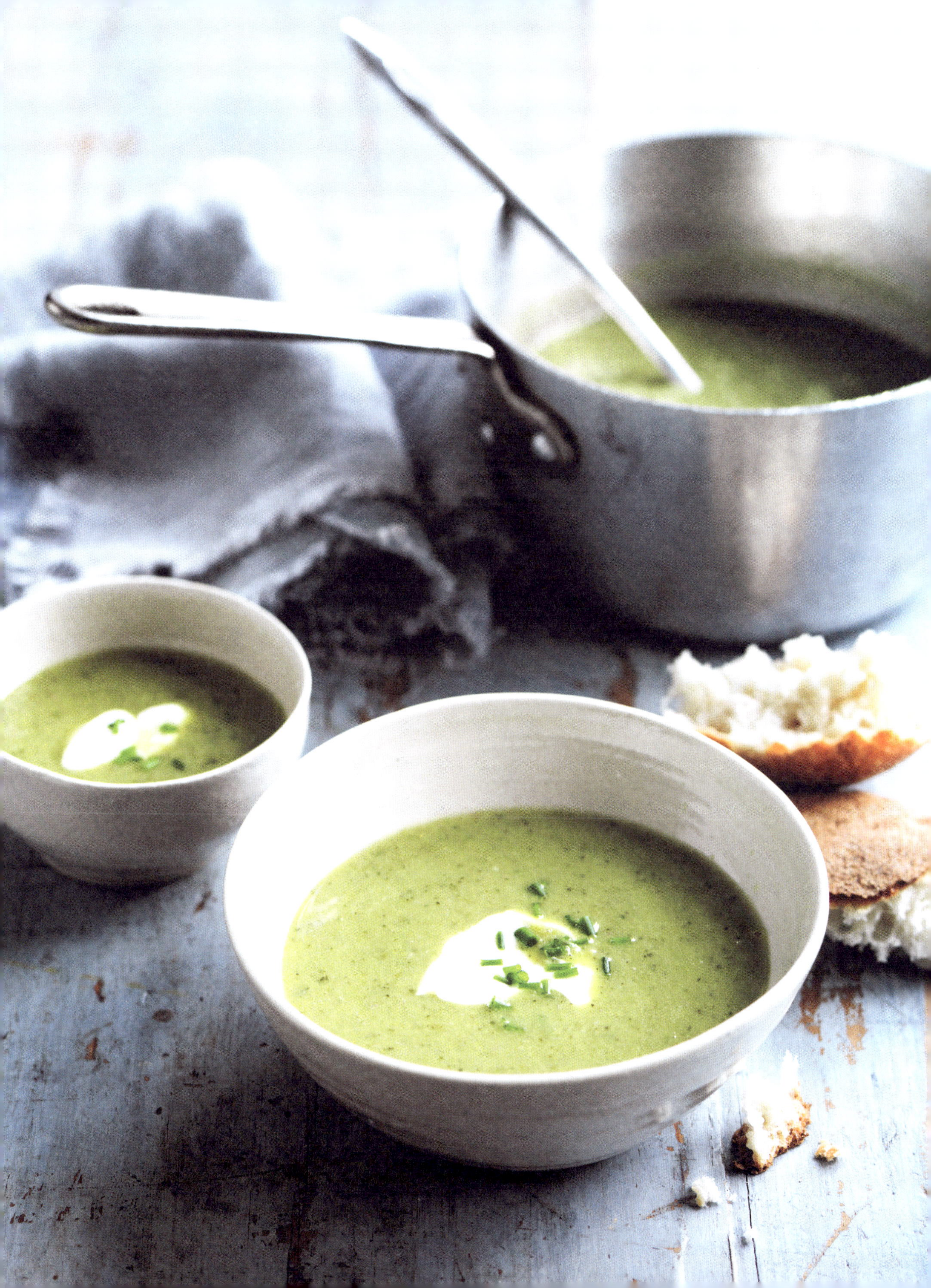

Seafood chowder

Serves 4–6

I adore a good chowder – it takes me straight to Boston where I was lucky enough to spend some time studying. If you're making this dish for six people, use 2 kilograms (4 lb 8 oz) mussels. Your kids, like mine, might love to dip in chunks of bread to mop up the yummy soup at the end.

1 tablespoon olive oil
2 bacon rashers (slices), rind removed and diced (optional – see note)
2 onions, finely chopped
2 celery stalks, thinly sliced
1 garlic clove, crushed
2 tablespoons plain (all-purpose) flour
500 ml (17 fl oz/2 cups) milk
2 large desiree potatoes, peeled and cut into 1.5 cm (½ inch) dice
500 ml (17 fl oz/2 cups) reduced-salt fish or chicken stock (see note, page 124)
2 corn cobs, kernels cut from cobs
500 g (1 lb 2 oz) firm white boneless fish fillets, cut into bite-sized chunks
1 kg (2 lb 3 oz) mussels, scrubbed and debearded
½ bunch chives, finely snipped, to garnish

Note *Processed meats, such as bacon, have been linked with a higher cancer risk, so I prefer to use them sparingly. I also use organic whenever available.*

Heat the oil in a large saucepan over medium heat. Add the bacon (if using) and cook until starting to crisp. Add the onion, celery and garlic and cook for 5 minutes, or until softened. Add the flour and stir for 1 minute.

Stir in the milk, add the potato and stock, cover, and cook for 5–10 minutes, or until the potato is almost tender. Stir in the corn and fish, cover and cook for a further 5 minutes, or until the fish is cooked through.

Meanwhile, place the mussels in a separate large saucepan over medium heat. Cover and cook for 5 minutes, stirring occasionally, until the mussels open. Drain and discard any mussels that have not opened.

Remove half of the mussels from their shells and keep the remaining mussels on the half-shell. Add them to the chowder. Divide among serving bowls and garnish with chives, to serve.

Baby's serve: for a **younger baby**, blend the soup to a smooth consistency, using as much liquid (water or your baby's milk) as needed to achieve the desired consistency. For an **older baby**, keep the blended texture lumpier or simply chop up the mussels (remove the shells) and potato and serve as is.

Toddler's serve: chop up the mussels and serve as is, with a short-handled spoon.

Dinner

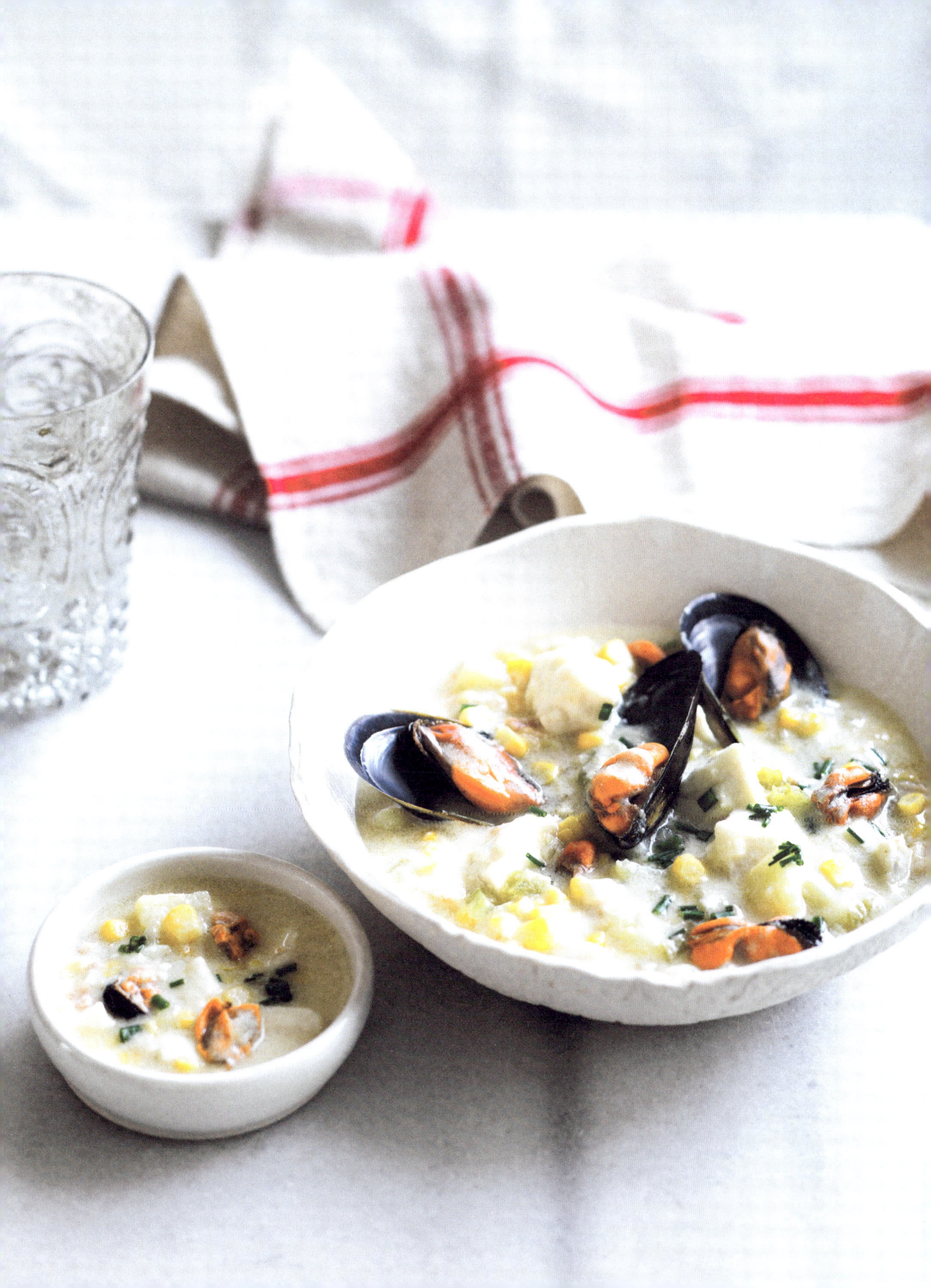

Best pumpkin soup

Serves 4–6

This is my favourite pumpkin soup recipe – and I've made my fair share! When you're a busy parent it's a saviour to make a big batch and keep a couple of portions handy in the freezer. With some grilled cheese on toast and a big green salad, it's a perfect dinner on a busy weeknight.

1 tablespoon olive oil
1 brown onion, chopped
2 garlic cloves, chopped
3 bacon rashers (slices), rind removed and diced (optional – see note, page 126)
½ teaspoon ground cumin
½ teaspoon freshly grated nutmeg
½ teaspoon ground coriander
1.2 kg (2 lb 10 oz) pumpkin (winter squash), peeled and roughly chopped
1 litre (34 fl oz/4 cups) reduced-salt chicken stock (see note, page 124)
2 tablespoons cream, plus extra to serve
2 tablespoons snipped chives or chopped coriander (cilantro) leaves (optional), to garnish

Heat the oil in a large saucepan over medium heat. Add the onion, garlic and bacon and cook for 5 minutes, or until the onion has softened. Add the spices and cook gently for a further 1 minute.

Add the pumpkin and stock and bring to the boil. Reduce the heat to low, cover, and simmer for 15 minutes. Remove the lid and continue simmering for a further 10 minutes, or until the pumpkin is very tender.

Remove the pan from the heat and allow the soup to cool a little before transferring to a food processor (or you can use a stick blender) and process until smooth. Return the soup to the pan and stir through the cream. Stir the soup over medium heat for 3 minutes, or until warmed through.

Divide the soup among serving bowls and garnish with extra cream (or use plain yoghurt) and herbs, if liked.

Baby's serve: for a **younger baby**, stir through a little rice cereal or some cooked quinoa to thicken the soup. You may also like to stir through a little yoghurt. An **older baby** might like to eat as per a younger baby or with toast fingers for dipping.

Toddler's serve: serve as is, with toast fingers for dipping and a short-handled spoon. As with baby's serve, you may like to stir through some cooked quinoa to thicken.

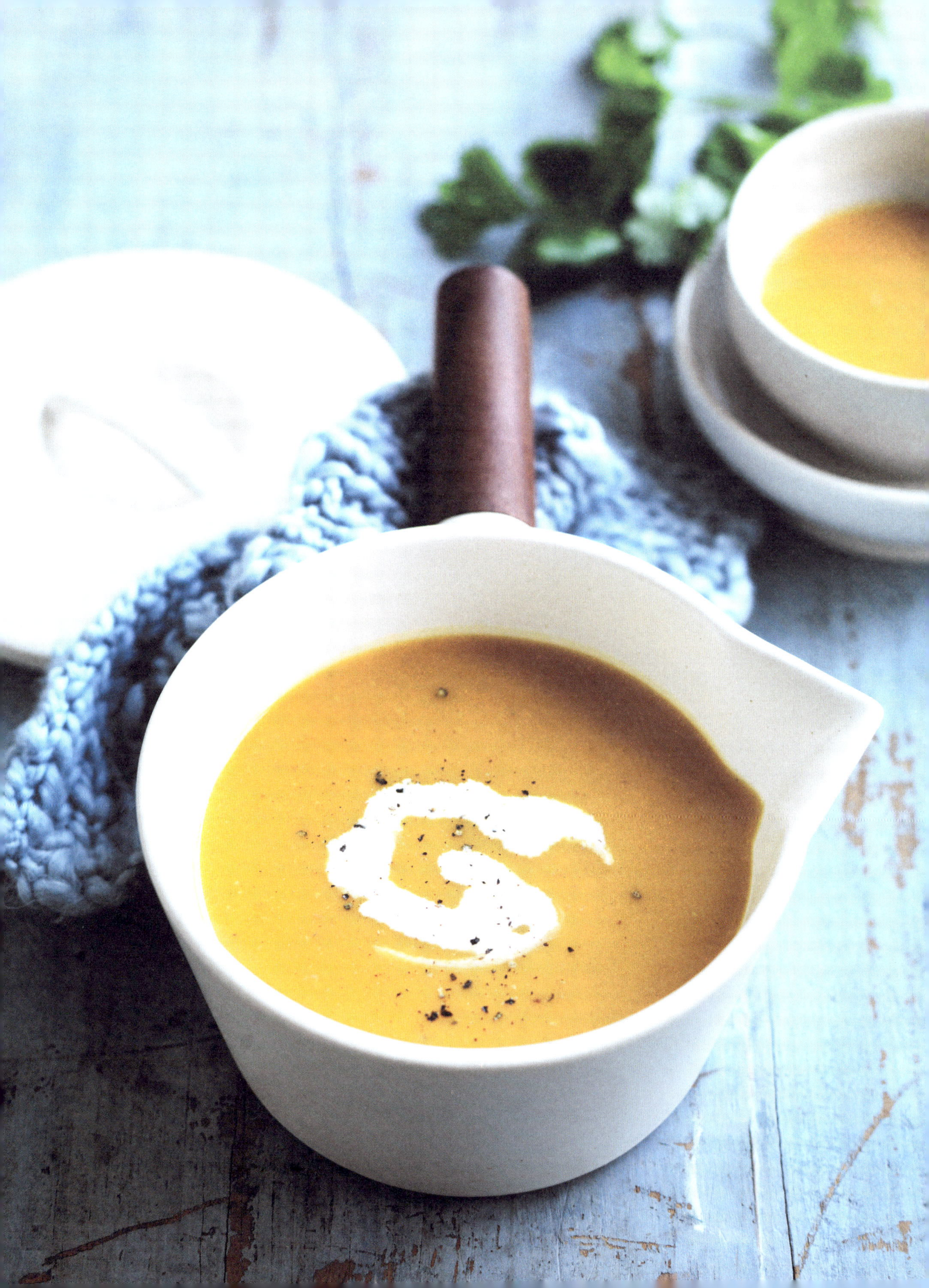

Lamb and barley soup

Serves 8

Similar to a Scotch broth (which often has dried pulses added to it), this soup gets the thumbs-up from my Scottish grandma. If barley is not a grain you cook with much, give it a go – it has a lovely texture and is also a good source of fibre and protein.

2 tablespoons olive oil
6 trimmed lamb shanks
2 large onions, chopped
4 garlic cloves, diced
2 celery stalks, diced
2 litres (68 fl oz/8 cups) reduced-salt beef or chicken stock (see note, page 124)
250 g (9 oz) pearl barley
1 tablespoon chopped rosemary
3 carrots, diced
2 small parsnips, peeled and diced
1 tablespoon chopped Italian (flat-leaf) parsley, to garnish

Heat the oil in a large saucepan over medium–high heat. Add the lamb shanks and cook for about 5 minutes, turning to brown all over. Remove the shanks from the pan and set aside. Add the onion, garlic and celery to the pan and cook for 5 minutes, or until the onion has softened.

Return the shanks to the pan and add the stock, barley, rosemary and 500 ml (17 fl oz/2 cups) water. Bring to the boil, then reduce the heat to low, cover, and simmer for 2 hours. Add the carrot and parsnip for the final 20 minutes of cooking – they should be tender when done.

Remove the shanks from the soup and set aside to cool slightly. Remove the meat from the bone and flake into pieces, discarding the bones. Return the meat to the soup and stir through.

Divide the soup among serving bowls and serve garnished with a little parsley.

Baby's serve: for a **younger baby**, blend the soup until smooth, using as much of the broth as needed to achieve the desired consistency. For an **older baby**, keep the blended texture lumpier or simply chop up the lamb and vegetables (if needed) and serve as is.

Toddler's serve: serve as is, with toast fingers for dipping and a short-handled spoon.

Dinner

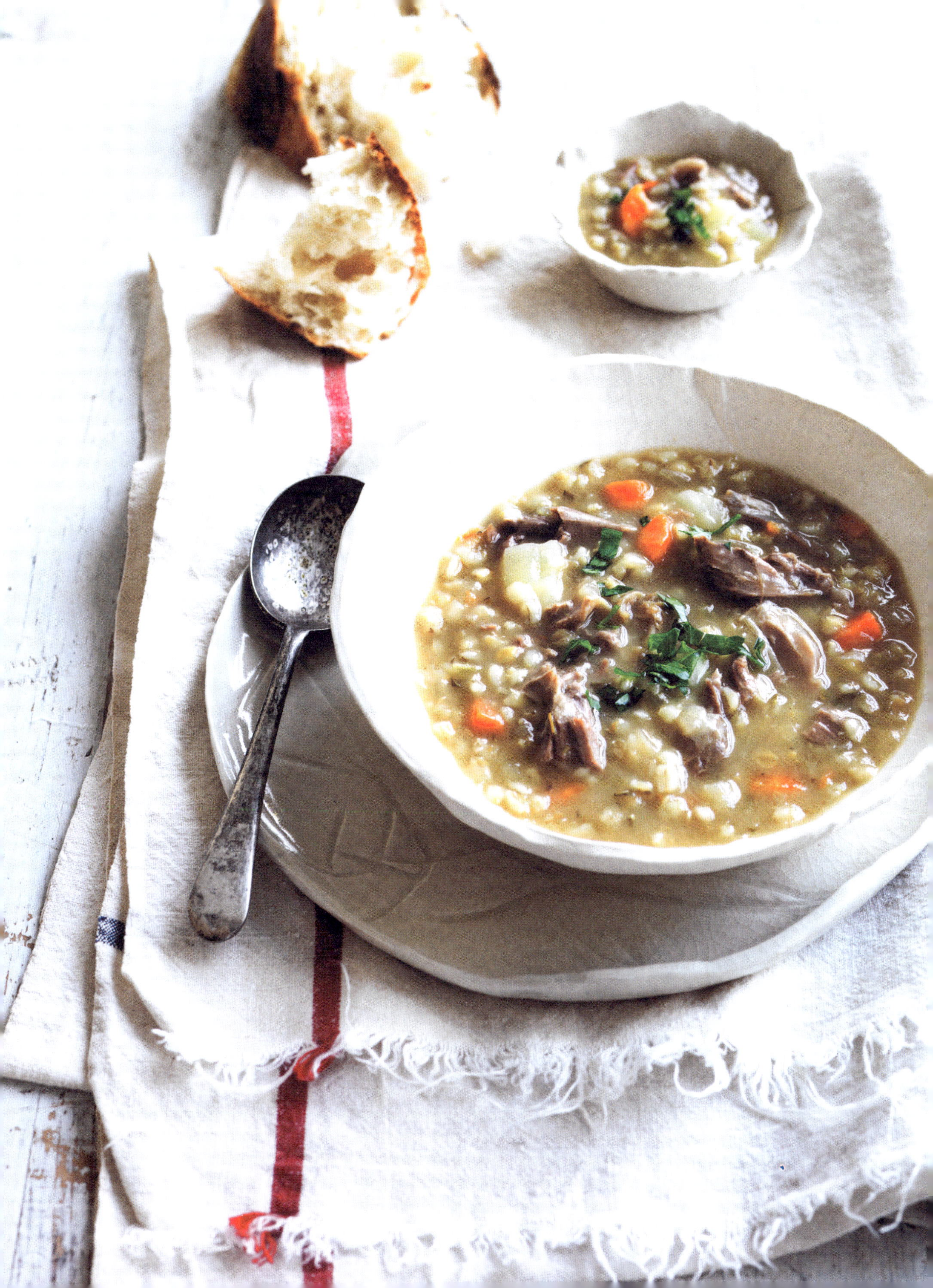

Chicken and soba noodle soup

Serves 3–4

I make this dinner in about 15 minutes flat, so it's great for those days (and there's plenty of them!) when I'm too exhausted to make a more substantial meal. For a variation, substitute the snow peas with bok choy (pak choy).

- 250 g (9 oz) buckwheat soba noodles (choose a gluten-free brand if needed)
- 1.5 litres (52 fl oz/6 cups) reduced-salt chicken stock (see note, page 124)
- 2 tablespoons reduced-salt soy sauce or tamari (choose gluten-free if needed)
- 1 whole star anise
- 2 garlic cloves, thinly sliced
- ¼ teaspoon finely grated ginger
- 1 tablespoon brown sugar (optional – omit for baby's serve)
- 360 g (12½ oz) chicken breast fillets, thickly sliced
- 200 g (7 oz/2 cups) shredded snow peas (mangetout) or green beans
- 2 spring onions (scallions), trimmed and sliced

Note *If you prefer your snow peas raw and crunchy, simply pop them on top of the soup just before serving.*

Cook the noodles according to the packet instructions. Drain and set aside.

Place the stock, soy sauce, star anise, garlic, ginger and sugar (if using) in a saucepan and bring to the boil. Reduce the heat to low, add the chicken and snow peas, and simmer for 5–7 minutes, or until the chicken is cooked through.

To serve, divide the noodles among serving bowls. Pour over the hot soup and garnish with spring onion.

Baby's serve: for a **younger baby**, blend the soup until smooth, using as much of the liquid as needed to achieve the desired consistency. For an **older baby**, keep the blended texture lumpier or simply serve some of the chicken, noodles and snow peas as finger food, without the broth. You may like to cut the snow peas into larger pieces, or not at all, so they're easier to hold.

Toddler's serve: serve as for an older baby or as is, with a short-handled spoon.

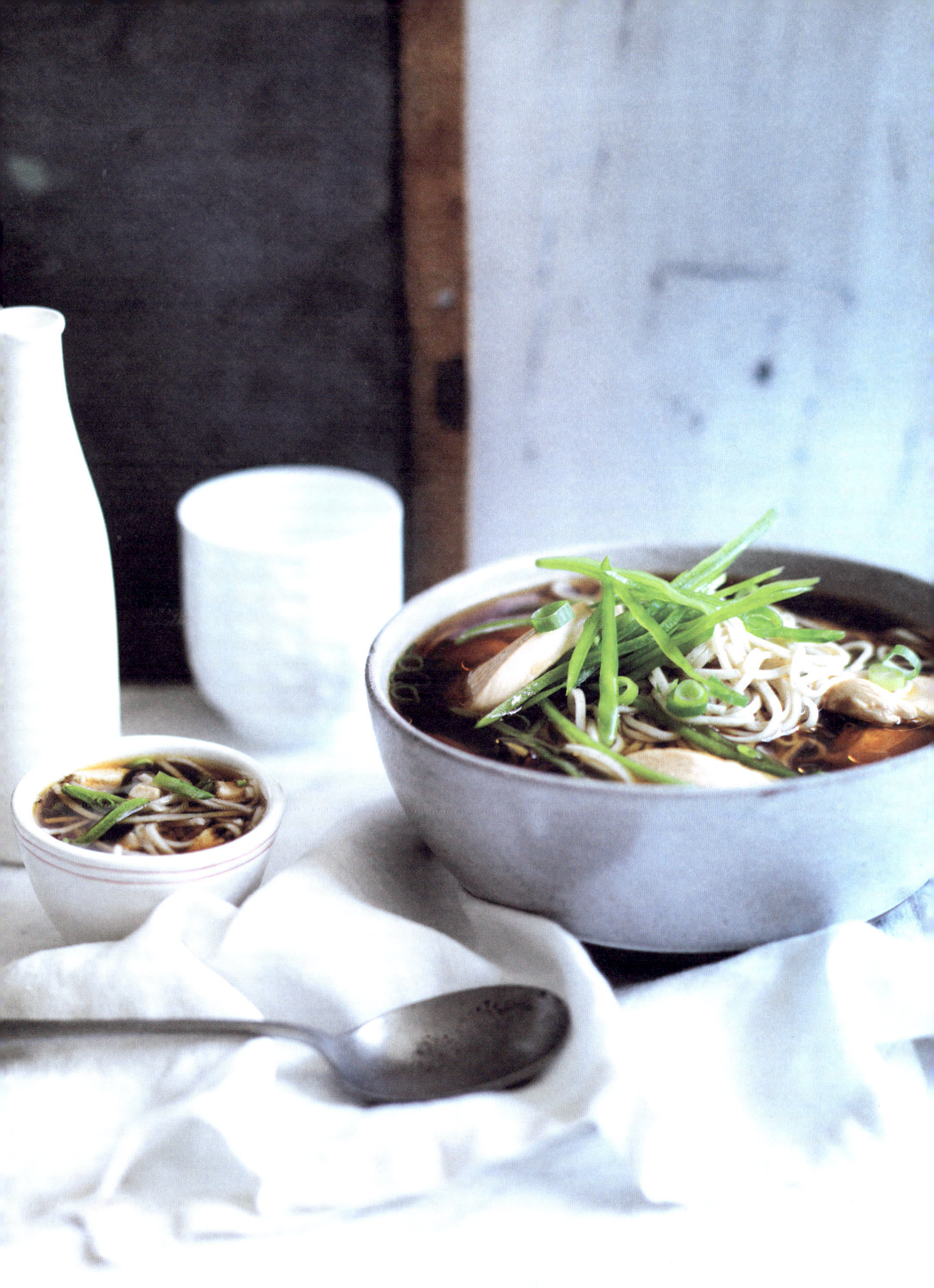

Red quinoa and chicken salad

Serves 4

I call this my superfoods salad because of the wonderfully nutritious quinoa, broccoli and blueberries. We often have it for a weekend dinner but it's also great served for lunch.

200 g (7 oz/1 cup) red quinoa
60 g (2 oz/1 cup) steamed broccoli florets
125 g (4½ oz/heaped ¾ cup) fresh blueberries
120 g (4½ oz) marinated reduced-salt feta (see note, page 38)
400 g (14 oz) cooked chicken, shredded
1 small handful mint leaves, torn

HAZELNUT DRESSING
1 teaspoon Dijon mustard
1 teaspoon white wine vinegar
1 teaspoon honey (optional – honey is not suitable for babies under 12 months)
2 tablespoons hazelnut oil or olive oil

Place the quinoa in a saucepan with 500 ml (17 fl oz/2 cups) water. Cover and cook over low–medium heat for about 15 minutes, or until the quinoa is tender. Drain any excess liquid and set aside to cool slightly.

To make the hazelnut dressing, whisk together the mustard, vinegar and honey (if using). Slowly add the hazelnut oil, continuing to whisk until the ingredients are well combined.

Transfer the quinoa to a large bowl and toss through the broccoli, blueberries and half of the dressing. Divide the salad among serving plates and arrange the feta, chicken and mint leaves on top. Drizzle the remaining dressing over the top.

Baby's serve: for a **younger baby**, blend together some quinoa, chicken, broccoli and blueberries until smooth, adding as much liquid (water or your baby's milk) as needed to achieve the desired consistency. For an **older baby**, keep the puréed consistency lumpier or serve as finger food.

Toddler's serve: serve as is with a short-handled spoon.

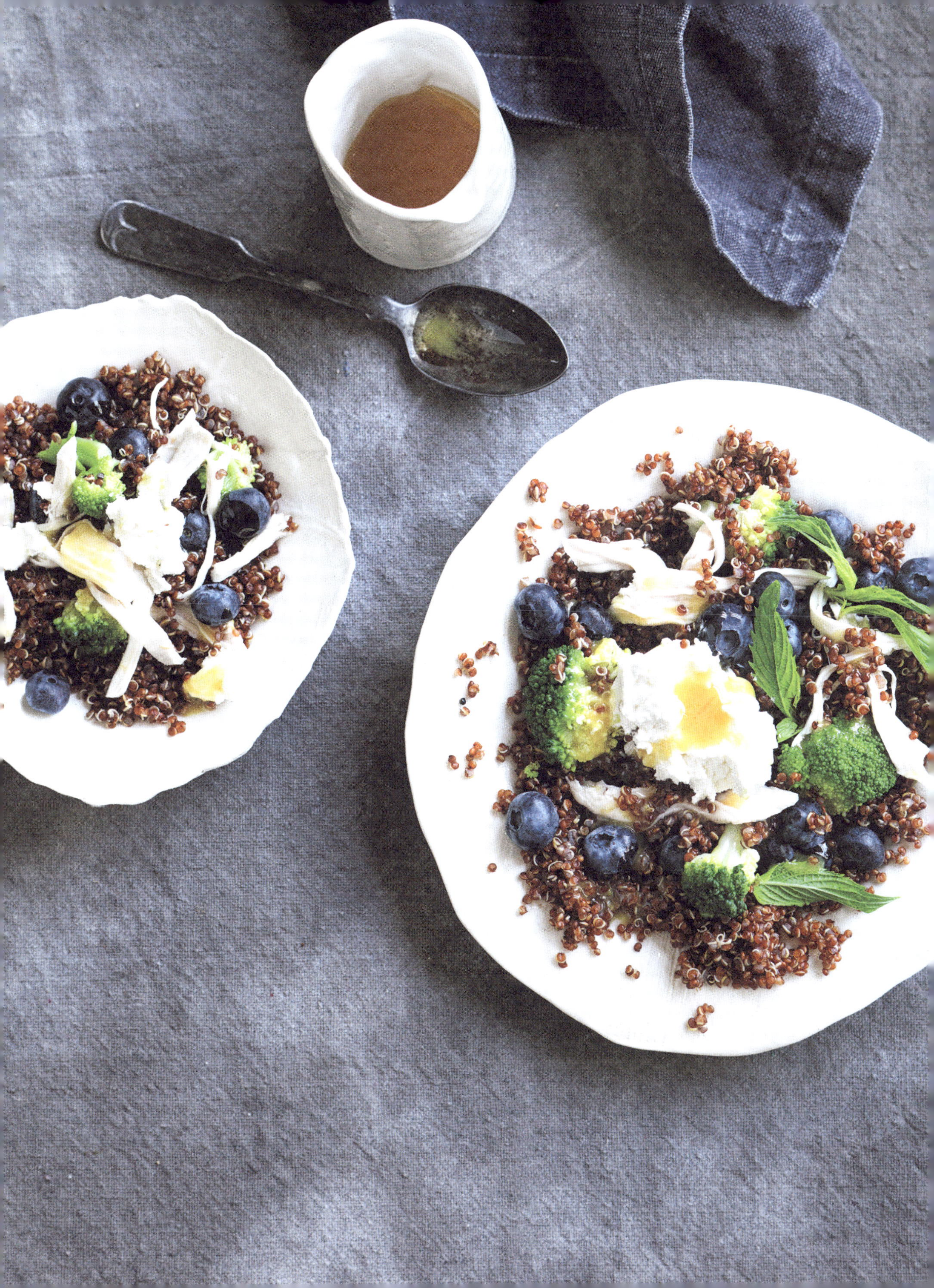

Wild rice, prawn and mango salad

Serves 4

You can use either wild rice for this salad or a rice blend, such as a mix of black, brown and red rice. These rices have quite a diverse nutritional profile (wild rice is actually a species of grass, not a true rice), so they're great to include in your child's diet.

285 g (10 oz/1½ cups) wild rice or coloured rice blend
1 tablespoon olive oil or rice bran oil
20 raw prawns (shrimp), peeled and deveined, tails intact
2 spring onions (scallions), shredded
2 large handfuls coriander (cilantro) leaves
1 Lebanese (short) cucumber, halved lengthways and thinly sliced
1 mango, peeled, stone removed and flesh sliced
1 long red chilli, seeded and finely chopped (optional)
1 tablespoon sesame seeds, toasted

SESAME DRESSING
1 tablespoon rice wine vinegar
3 teaspoons maple syrup
1 teaspoon soy sauce or tamari (choose a gluten-free brand if needed)
½ teaspoon sesame oil
2 tablespoons olive oil

Tip *If you can't source fresh mango, peach and papaya are both lovely alternatives in this salad.*

To make the sesame dressing, mix together all of the ingredients in a small bowl until well combined. Set aside.

Cook the rice according to the packet instructions. Transfer to a serving platter and set aside.

Heat the oil in a large frying pan over high heat. Add the prawns and cook for 3 minutes, turning occasionally, until cooked through.

To serve, top the rice with the spring onion, coriander, cucumber, mango and chilli (if using). Add the prawns, then drizzle over the sesame dressing and sprinkle with the toasted sesame seeds.

Baby's serve: for a **younger baby**, blend some cooked prawns, rice, mango and coriander until smooth, adding as much liquid (water or your baby's milk) as needed to achieve the desired consistency. For an **older baby**, chop the prawns (remove the tails) and serve with rice, mango and cucumber.

Toddler's serve: prepare as for an older baby. Serve the spring onion, coriander and dressing according to your child's preferences.

Dinner

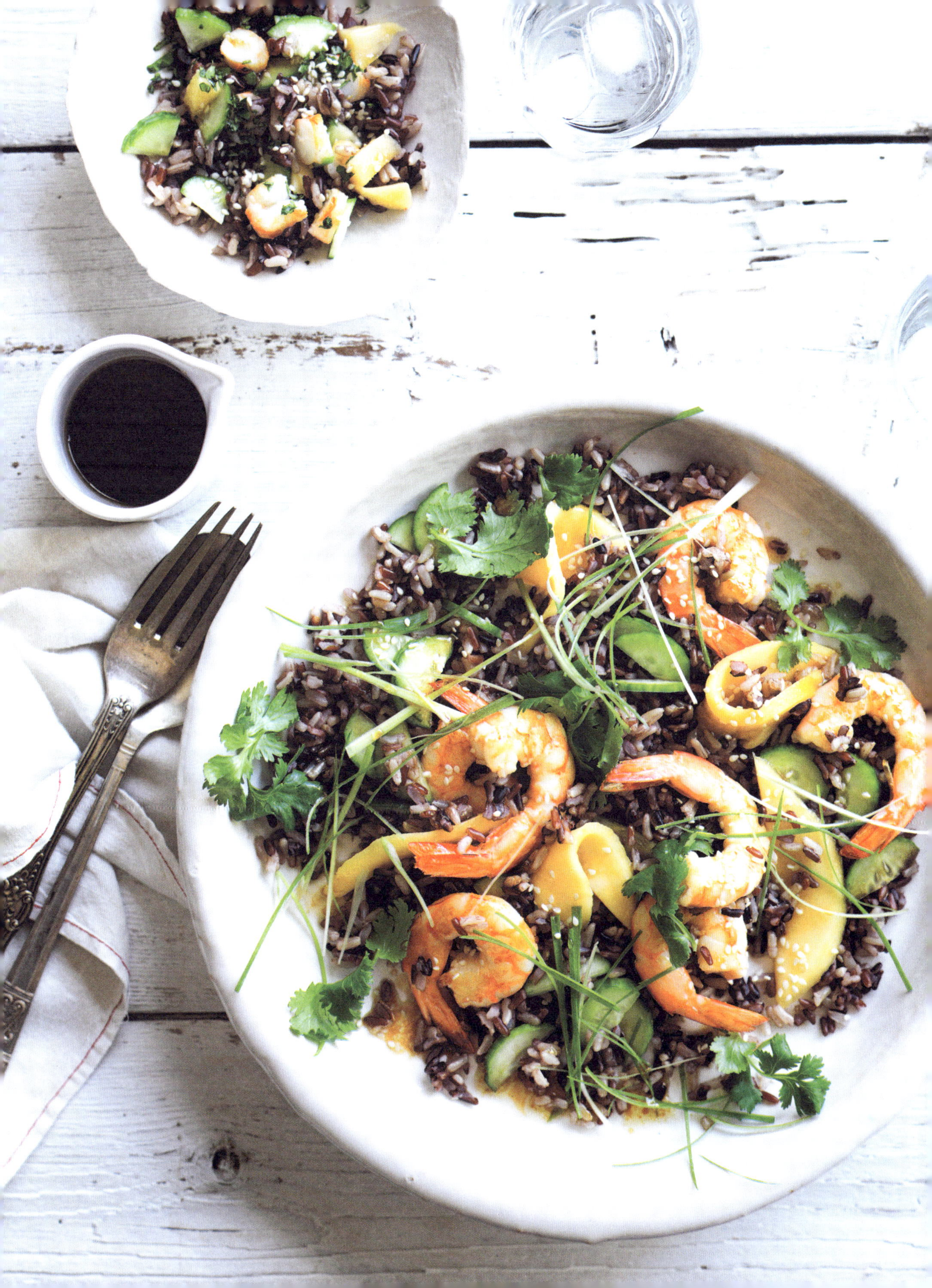

Fried brown rice with chicken and snow peas

Serves 4

If fried rice is a firm favourite in your household, try switching to brown rice occasionally. It has a little more fibre and it also helps your child become accustomed to seeing and tasting different foods. Another favourite is fried quinoa – yum!

200 g (7 oz/1 cup) brown rice
3 teaspoons olive oil
400 g (14 oz) chicken thigh fillets, diced
200 g (7 oz) red cabbage, core removed and leaves finely shredded
2 teaspoons grated fresh ginger
2 garlic cloves, crushed
4 spring onions (scallions), green part only, thinly sliced
100 g (3½ oz) snow peas (mangetout), halved lengthways
2 tablespoons sesame seeds
1½ tablespoons reduced-salt soy sauce or tamari (choose a gluten-free brand if needed)
coriander (cilantro) leaves, to serve

Tip *If there are no egg allergies in your family, this dish is also delicious topped with a fried egg or with an omelette, cut into strips.*

Cook the rice according to the packet instructions. Set aside to cool.

Heat 1 teaspoon of the oil in a wok over high heat. Add half of the chicken and stir-fry for 4 minutes, or until browned and cooked through. Transfer to a plate. Repeat with another 1 teaspoon of the oil and the remaining chicken. Set aside.

Heat the remaining oil in the wok over medium–high heat. Add the cabbage with 1 tablespoon water and stir-fry for 2 minutes, or until softened. Add the ginger, garlic, spring onion, snow peas and a further 1 tablespoon water. Stir-fry for a further 2 minutes, or until the snow peas have softened. Return the chicken to the wok with the rice, sesame seeds and soy sauce. Stir-fry for 1–2 minutes further, or until heated through and well combined.

To serve, divide the fried rice among serving bowls and garnish with coriander leaves.

Baby's serve: for a **younger baby**, blend some of the fried rice until smooth, adding as much liquid (water or your baby's milk) as needed to achieve the desired consistency. For an **older baby**, keep the texture lumpier or serve as is, with the chicken, cabbage and snow peas cut into smaller pieces.

Toddler's serve: serve as is, with the chicken, cabbage and snow peas cut into smaller pieces.

Dinner

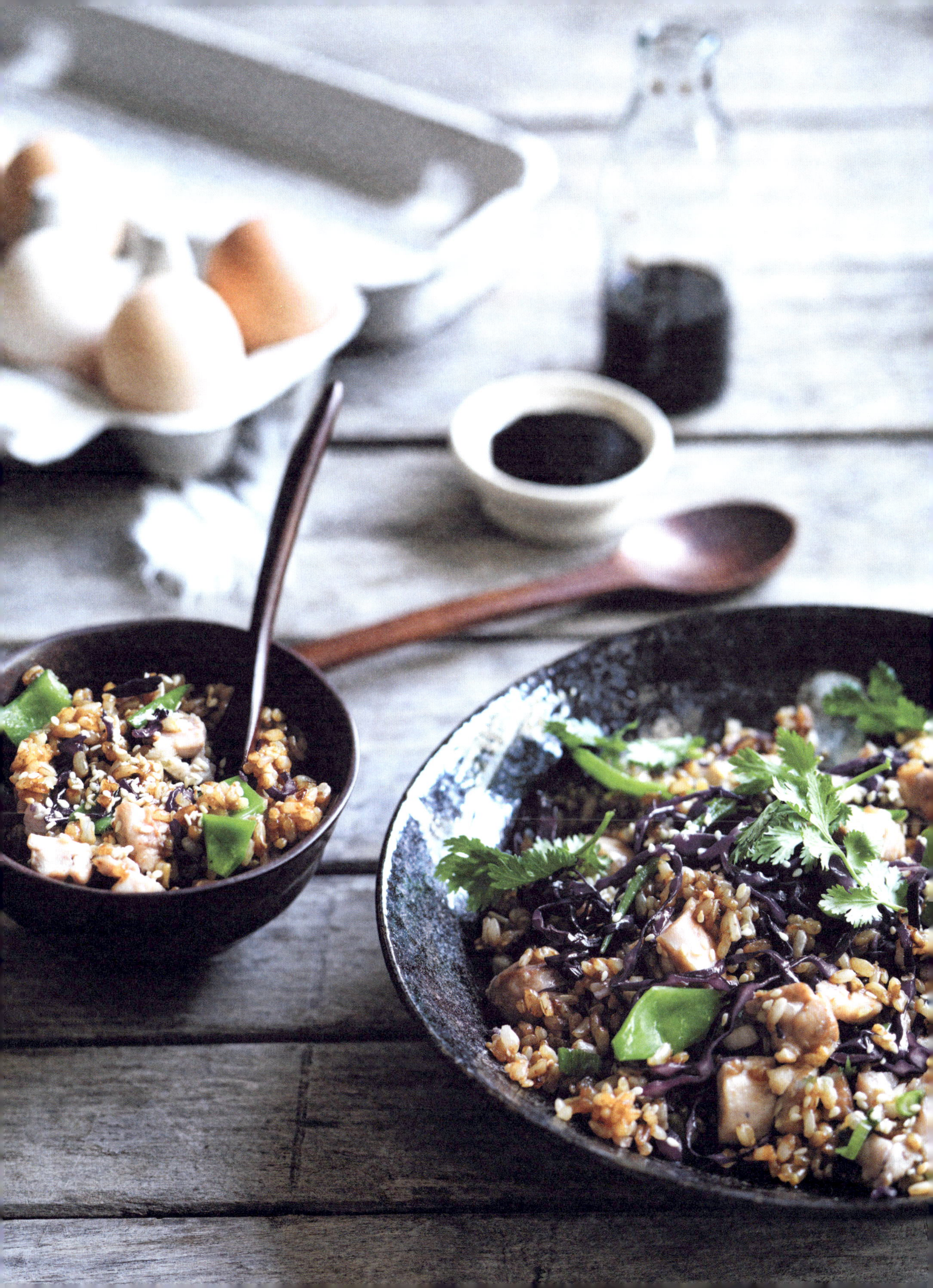

Pea and prawn risotto

Serves 4

As a general rule, I'm not a big fan of risotto, but the peas and mint in this one have thoroughly won me over. The risotto will thicken on standing, so have some extra stock handy if you don't intend to eat it right away.

- 215 g (7½ oz) fresh or frozen peas, thawed
- 2 spring onions (scallions), roughly chopped
- 1 small handful flat-leaf (Italian) parsley leaves
- 1–2 tablespoons fresh mint leaves
- 2 garlic cloves, roughly chopped
- 1 litre (34 fl oz/4 cups) reduced-salt chicken stock (see note, page 124)
- 2 tablespoons olive oil
- 1 small onion, diced
- 330 g (11½ oz/1½ cups) arborio rice
- 35 g (1¼ oz/⅓ cup) grated parmesan cheese
- 500 g (1 lb 2 oz) raw prawns (shrimp), peeled and deveined, tails intact
- micro herbs (optional), to garnish

Baby's serve: for a **younger baby**, blend the risotto and prawns (remove the tails) until smooth, adding a little extra liquid (water or your baby's milk) to achieve the desired consistency. An **older baby** will probably be able to manage as is, although you may need to cut up the prawns.

Toddler's serve: remove the tails from the prawns, chop them a little if needed, and serve as is.

Place the peas, spring onion, parsley, mint and garlic in a food processor and process to a coarse paste. Set aside.

Pour the stock and 375 ml (12½ fl oz/1½ cups) water into a saucepan and bring to the boil. Reduce the heat to low, cover, and simmer.

Heat half of the oil in a large saucepan over low heat. Add the onion and cook for 5 minutes, or until softened. Add the rice and cook, stirring, for 1 minute. Add 250 ml (8½ fl oz/1 cup) of the hot stock and stir until all of the liquid has been absorbed. Continue adding the hot stock, 1 cup at a time, stirring until the stock has been absorbed before adding more – the total cooking time should be about 25 minutes. Stir through the pea mixture and parmesan and remove from the heat. Keep warm.

Meanwhile, heat 2 teaspoons of the remaining oil in a large frying pan over high heat. Add half of the prawns and cook for 3 minutes, or until cooked through. Repeat with the remaining oil and prawns until all are cooked.

Divide the risotto among serving plates and top with the cooked prawns. Garnish with a few micro herbs, if liked.

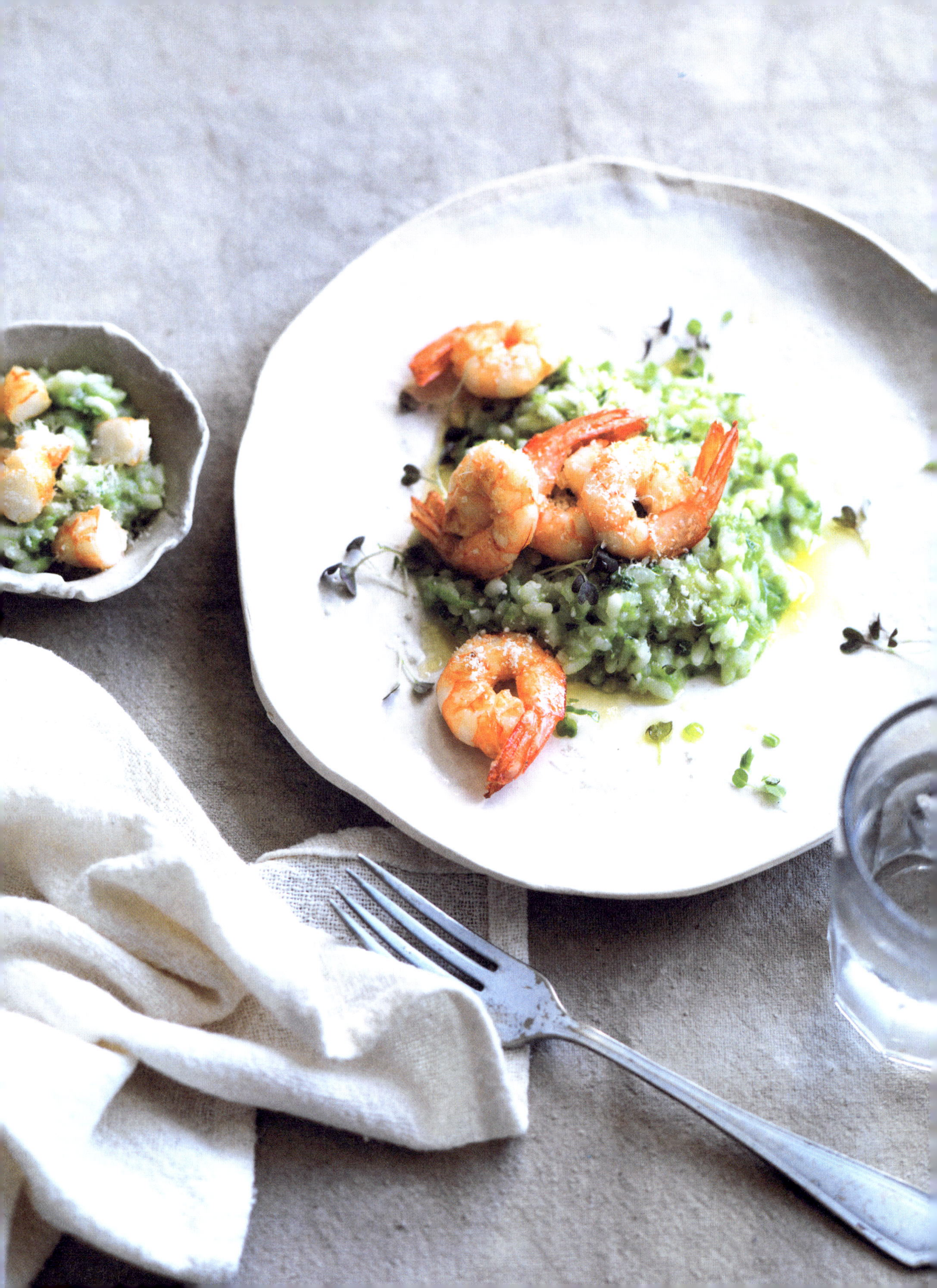

Five-vegetable pasta

Serves 4–6

I'm generally not keen on sneaking hidden vegetables into children's meals, only because I think it can exacerbate fussy eating if vegetables aren't seen in their whole form. Having said that, this pasta sauce is definitely a handy way of boosting vegetable variety. If you serve some steamed beans on the side, you will have ticked both boxes.

1 tablespoon olive oil
1 onion, diced
1 garlic clove, halved
1 large carrot, diced
155 g (5½ oz/1 cup) diced pumpkin (winter squash)
1 tablespoon tomato paste (concentrated purée)
100 g (3½ oz) diced cauliflower
1 zucchini (courgette), diced
6 button mushrooms, sliced
600 g (1 lb 5 oz) ripe tomatoes, diced
1 teaspoon brown sugar (optional – omit for baby's serve)
1 small handful basil or oregano leaves
cooked pasta, to serve (choose a gluten-free brand if needed)
grated parmesan cheese, to serve (omit for dairy-free)

Heat the oil in a large saucepan over medium heat. Cook the onion, garlic, carrot and pumpkin for 6–8 minutes, stirring occasionally, until the onion has softened.

Stir in the tomato paste, then add the cauliflower, zucchini, mushroom, tomato, sugar (if using) and 80 ml (2½ fl oz/⅓ cup) water. Bring to the boil, then reduce the heat to low and simmer for 25–30 minutes, stirring occasionally, until the vegetables are tender.

Remove the pan from the heat and allow to cool slightly before transferring to a food processor (or use a stick blender). Add the basil, then blend or process to your desired consistency.

Divide the cooked pasta among serving bowls and top with the five-vegetable sauce. Sprinkle over the parmesan, if liked.

Baby's serve: for a **younger baby**, blend the pasta and sauce to a smooth consistency, or stir smaller pasta shapes (such as stars) through the sauce. For an **older baby**, chop up the pasta, or use smaller shapes, and stir through the sauce.

Toddler's serve: serve as for an older baby or simply as is.

Dinner

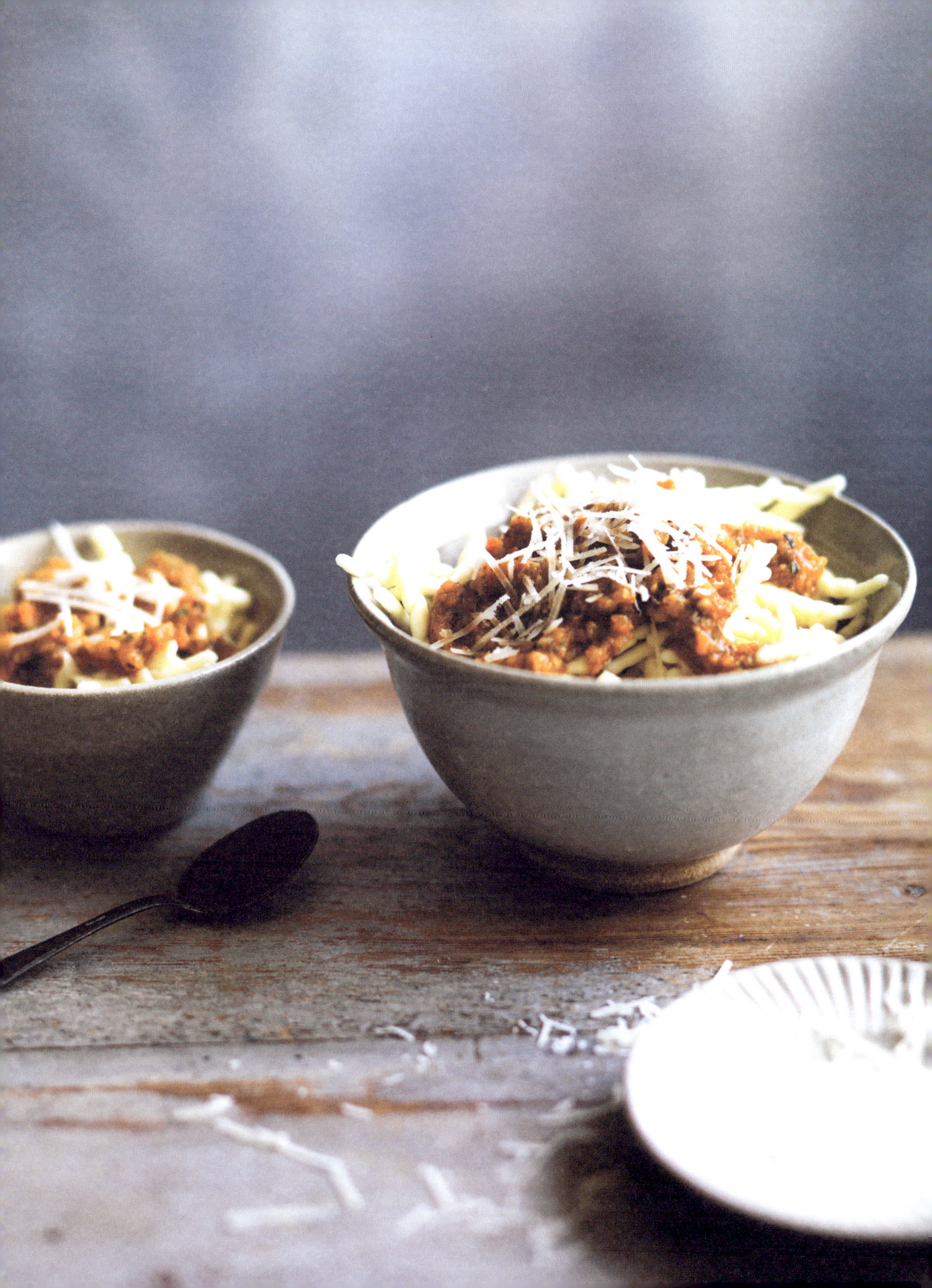

Ricotta gnocchi with cherry tomato sauce

Serves 3–4

This recipe comes from my gorgeous mum, who is the best cook I know (my grandma agrees). She makes everything look so easy, but in the case of this delicious gnocchi, it actually is. Try to find the sweetest, most perfectly ripe tomatoes you can for the sauce.

250 g (9 oz/1 cup) fresh ricotta (see note, page 38)
60 g (2 oz) freshly grated parmesan cheese, plus extra to serve
1 egg
150 g (5½ oz/1 cup) plain (all-purpose) flour, sifted

CHERRY TOMATO SAUCE
2 tablespoons olive oil
1 small onion, diced
1 garlic clove, sliced
400 g (14 oz) cherry tomatoes, halved
2 tablespoons torn basil leaves

Baby's serve: for a **younger baby**, wait until your baby is managing some finger foods (which may not happen until 8–9 months or older) before you offer him this gnocchi as finger food, chopped into smaller pieces if needed. For an **older baby**, chop up the gnocchi and stir through the sauce or serve as finger food.

Toddler's serve: serve as for an older baby.

Lightly flour a baking tray. Place the ricotta, parmesan and egg in a mixing bowl, then gradually add 110 g (4 oz/¾ cup) of the flour, lightly mixing after each addition. Use only as much of the remaining flour as you need to create a firm enough dough to roll – you may not need to use it all (if the dough is too firm it can become tough). Divide into four even-sized portions and roll out on a clean floured surface to make four logs, each with a 2 cm (¾ inch) diameter. Cut each log at 2 cm (¾ inch) intervals to make the gnocchi pieces. With the back of a fork, press down lightly on top of each gnocchi. Transfer to the baking tray and, if not using immediately, store in the refrigerator for up to 24 hours.

To make the cherry tomato sauce, heat the oil in a saucepan over medium heat. Cook the onion and garlic for 5 minutes, or until softened. Add the tomatoes, cover, and simmer over low heat for 15 minutes.

Bring a large saucepan of water to the boil. Working in batches, cook the gnocchi for 3 minutes, or until cooked through.

Serve the gnocchi with the tomato sauce and basil. Top with a little extra parmesan, if liked.

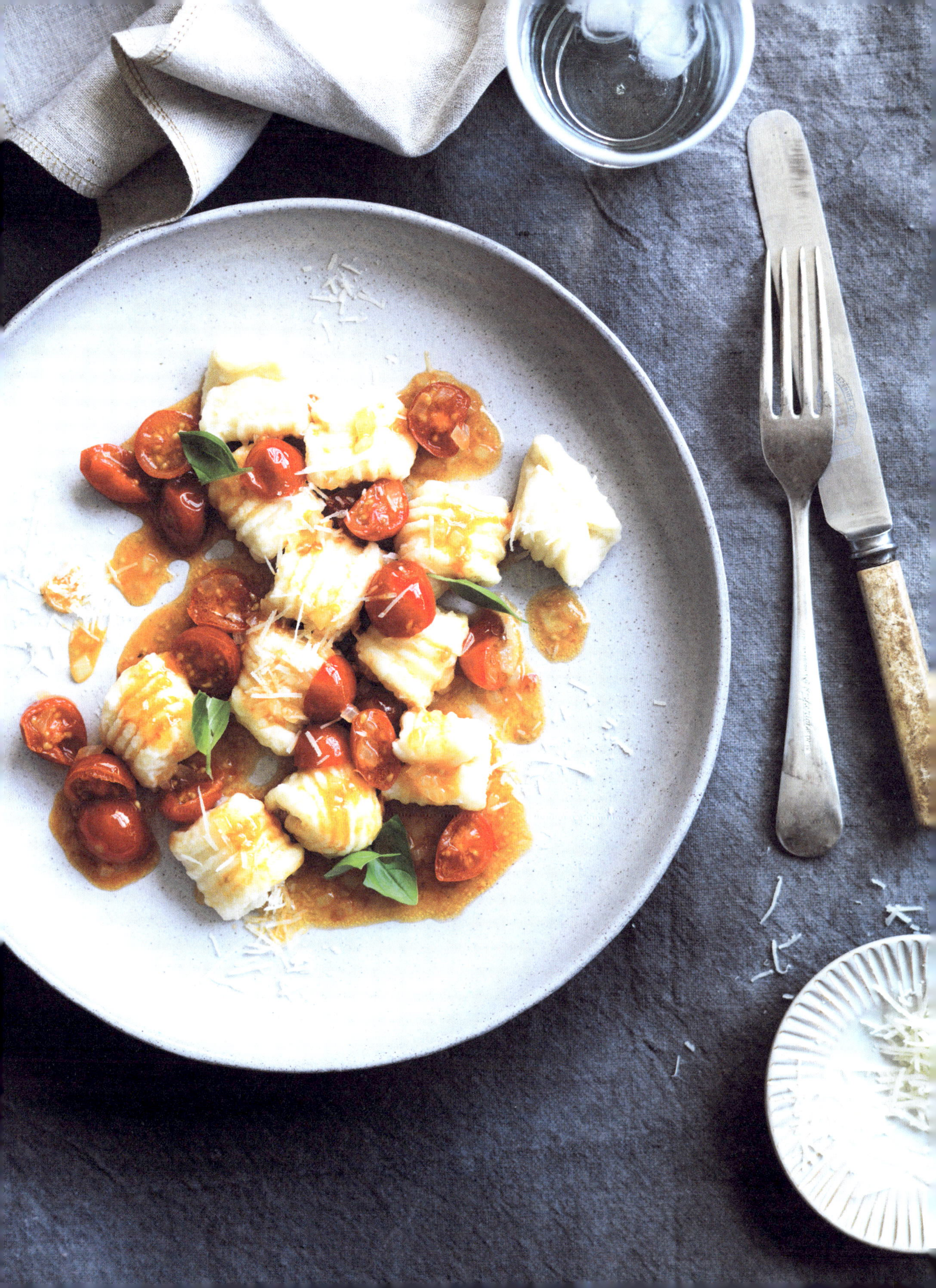

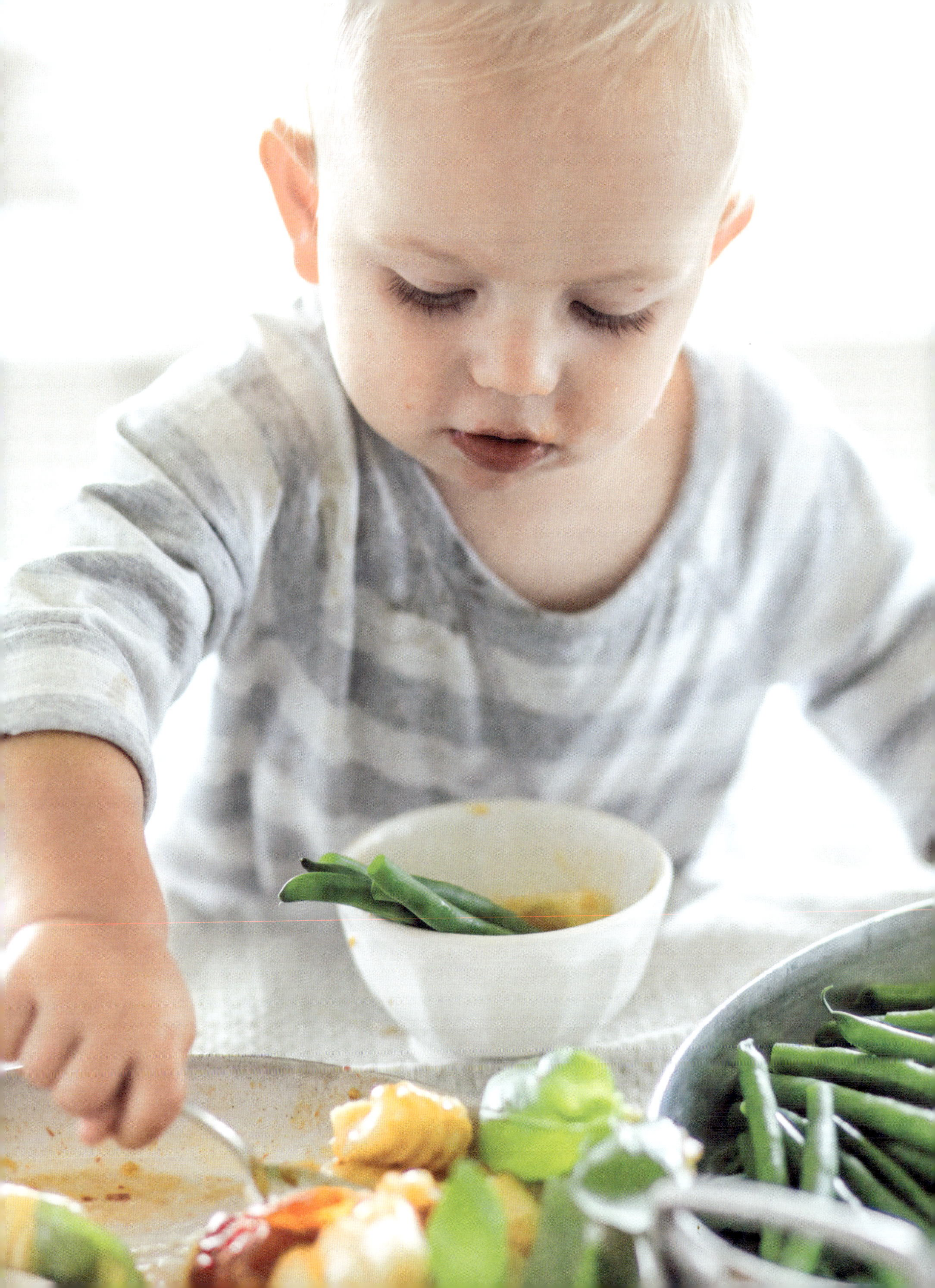

Most children have an inherent ability to regulate their own appetites, which we often interfere with. Give your child the freedom to serve himself healthy foods and to choose how much he eats and he'll grow up with a better sense of his appetite and its limits.

Mushroom and spinach lasagne

Serves 4–6

---

15 g (½ oz/⅔ cup) dried porcini mushrooms
200 g (7 oz) spinach leaves, stalks removed
500 g (1 lb 2 oz) field mushrooms, quartered
2 tablespoons olive oil
200 g (7 oz) Swiss brown mushrooms, sliced
1 onion, finely diced
2 garlic cloves, diced or crushed
1 tablespoon oregano leaves
375 ml (12½ fl oz/1½ cups) tomato passata (puréed tomatoes)
460 g (1 lb) ricotta cheese
2 eggs
60 g (2 oz) grated parmesan cheese
250 g (9 oz) fresh lasagne sheets

Preheat the oven to 180°C (350°F). Lightly grease a 2 litre (68 fl oz/8 cup) capacity baking dish.

Soak the porcini mushrooms in 125 ml (4 fl oz/½ cup) boiling water for 10 minutes. Strain and reserve the soaking liquid. Chop the mushrooms and set aside.

Place the spinach in a microwave-proof bowl and microwave for 2 minutes, or until the leaves have just wilted. Drain and set aside.

Place the field mushrooms into a food processor and blend to a coarse paste. Set aside.

Heat half of the oil in a large deep frying pan. Add the Swiss brown mushrooms and sauté for 5 minutes, or until golden. Remove and set aside.

Add the remaining oil, onion and garlic to the pan and cook over medium heat for 5 minutes, or until the onion has softened. Add the field mushroom paste and the chopped porcini mushrooms and cook for 5 minutes, stirring until tender. Add the oregano, tomato passata and the reserved porcini soaking liquid and continue to simmer for 5 minutes. Finally, stir through the reserved Swiss brown mushrooms. Remove from the heat and set aside.

To assemble the lasagne, place the ricotta, eggs and half of the parmesan in a food processor and process until well combined and smooth.

Place one-third of the mushroom mixture in the bottom of the baking dish to make an even layer. Layer one-third of the spinach leaves on top, followed by one-third of the lasagne sheets, then one-quarter of the ricotta mixture. Repeat a further two times brushing the final lasagne sheets with some water and using all of the remaining ricotta mixture. Top with the remaining parmesan.

Bake the lasagne for 45 minutes, or until golden on top and cooked through. Cut into portions and serve immediately.

Baby's serve: for a **younger baby**, set aside a little of the mushroom mixture and blend it with a vegetable purée, such as sweet potato. Alternatively, if your baby is managing some finger foods (which may not happen until 8–9 months or older), he may be able to manage a piece of the lasagne chopped up. For an **older baby**, cut into smaller pieces.

Toddler's serve: serve as for an older baby.

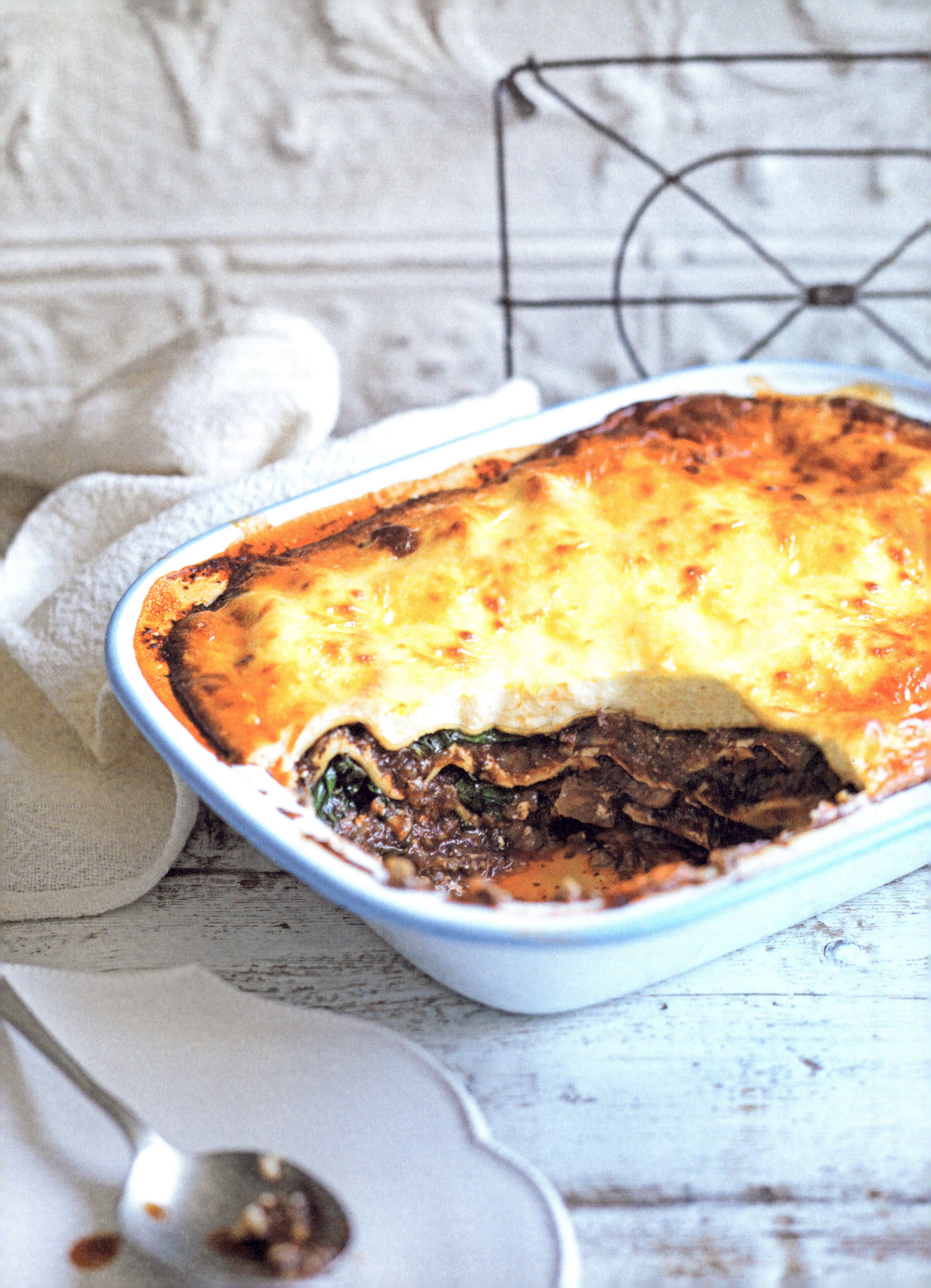

Cauliflower macaroni cheese

Serves 4

This dish is a combination of two of my favourites – macaroni cheese and cauliflower cheese. Topped with toasty breadcrumbs … aah, you can make it for me any time! You might like to grate some extra parmesan to pop on your serving for an added flavour hit.

400 g (14 oz) cauliflower florets
200 g (7 oz/1⅓ cups) wholemeal (whole-wheat) macaroni
20 g (¾ oz) butter
2 tablespoons plain (all-purpose) flour
375 ml (12½ fl oz/1½ cups) milk
40 g (1½ oz/⅓ cup) grated cheddar cheese
25 g (1 oz/¼ cup) grated parmesan cheese
50 g (1¾ oz) fresh wholemeal (whole-wheat) breadcrumbs
1 tablespoon olive oil
green salad, to serve

Tip *If you don't have wholemeal (whole-wheat) macaroni or wholemeal breadcrumbs on hand, don't worry. Regular versions of both will also work perfectly.*

Preheat the oven to 180°C (350°F).

Cook the cauliflower and macaroni in a large saucepan of boiling water for 8–10 minutes, or until both are just tender. Drain and transfer to a large ovenproof baking dish.

Melt the butter in a saucepan over low heat. Stir in the flour and cook for 1 minute. Gradually add the milk, stirring over low–medium heat until the sauce thickens. Stir in the cheeses and cook for 1 minute. Pour the sauce over the pasta and cauliflower.

Toss the breadcrumbs in a bowl with the olive oil and scatter over the cauliflower macaroni. Bake in the oven for 15–20 minutes, or until golden on top. Serve with green salad.

Baby's serve: for a **younger baby**, blend some cauliflower, macaroni and sauce to a smooth consistency, adding as much liquid (water or your baby's milk) as needed to achieve the desired consistency. For an **older baby**, chop into small pieces or serve as finger food.

Toddler's serve: serve as for an older baby.

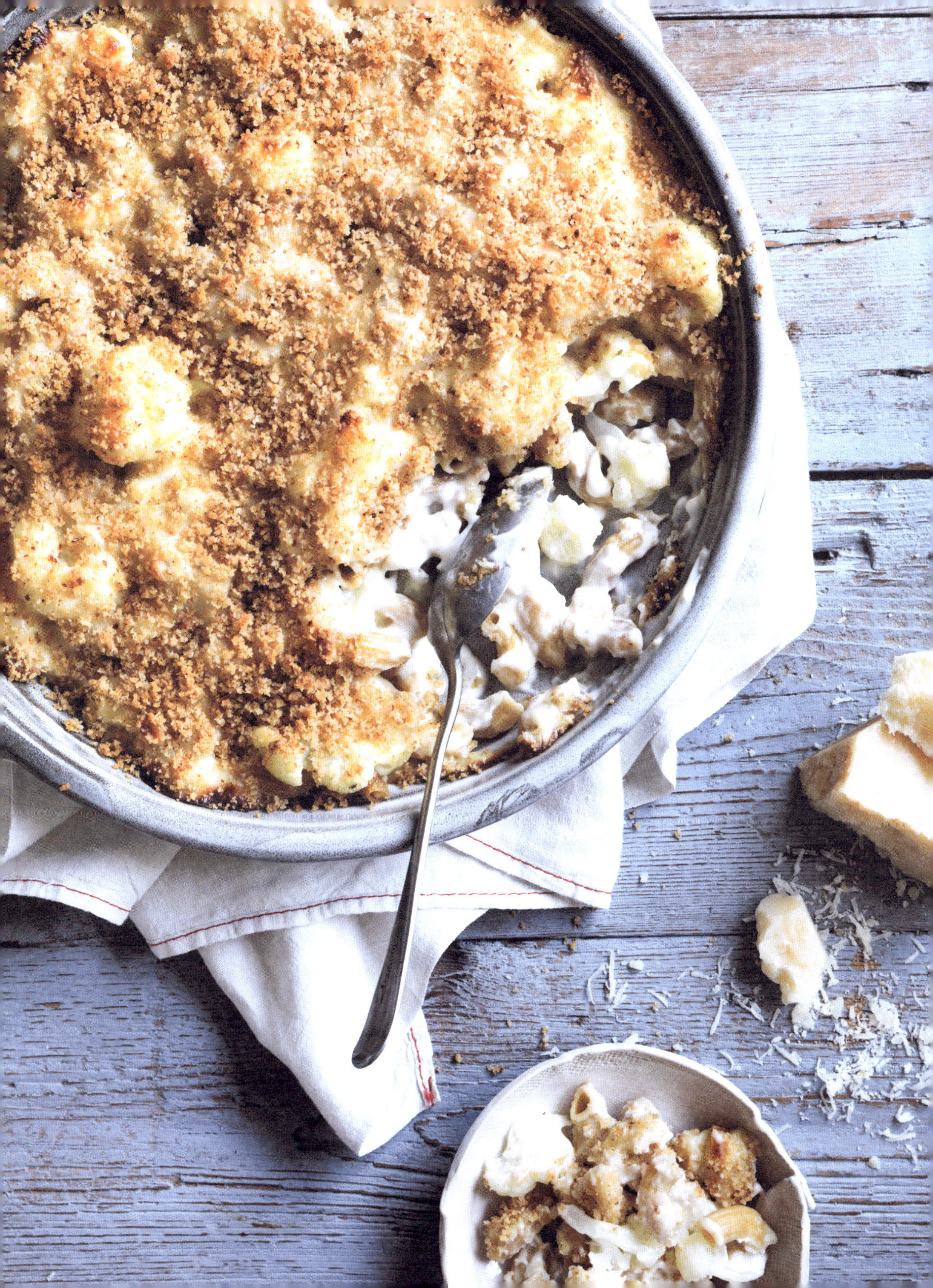

Slow-cooked beef ragu with penne

Serves 4–6

Made with steak instead of minced (ground) beef, this is the more delicious cousin of the basic bolognese. If you've got any leftover sauce, it's perfect for freezing and using for another meal.

1 tablespoon olive oil
1 kg (2 lb 3 oz) chuck steak, cut into 3 cm (1¼ inch) cubes
2 brown onions, finely diced
2 celery stalks, diced
1 large carrot, diced
1 garlic clove, diced
2 × 400 g (14 oz) tins chopped tomatoes or 1 kg (2 lb 3 oz) fresh tomatoes, chopped
3–4 thyme sprigs
cooked penne, to serve (choose a gluten-free brand if needed)
freshly grated parmesan cheese, to serve (optional – omit for dairy-free)
finely chopped flat-leaf (Italian) parsley, to serve

Tip *If you'd like to include some more vegetable variety in this pasta sauce, add 155 g (5½ oz/ 1 cup) fresh or frozen peas during the final few minutes of cooking.*

Heat half of the oil in a large saucepan over high heat. Add half of the steak and cook for 5 minutes, stirring occasionally, until browned all over. Transfer to a plate. Repeat with the remaining oil and beef and set aside.

Add the onion, celery, carrot and garlic to the pan and cook for 5 minutes, or until the onion has softened. Return the beef to the pan, stir in the tomatoes, 250 ml (8½ fl oz/1 cup) water and the thyme sprigs, and bring to the boil. Reduce the heat to low, cover, and simmer for 1½ hours.

Remove the lid from the pan and continue to simmer for a further 1 hour, or until the meat is tender and the sauce has thickened. Discard the thyme sprigs. Add the cooked pasta to the ragu and toss for 1 minute.

Serve the beef ragu and penne with parmesan (if using) and parsley, to garnish.

Baby's serve: for a **younger baby**, blend the pasta sauce and stir through some smaller pasta shapes, such as pasta stars, or some quinoa or couscous. For an **older baby**, chop up the penne and stir through the sauce or serve as finger food.

Toddler's serve: serve as for an older baby.

Dinner

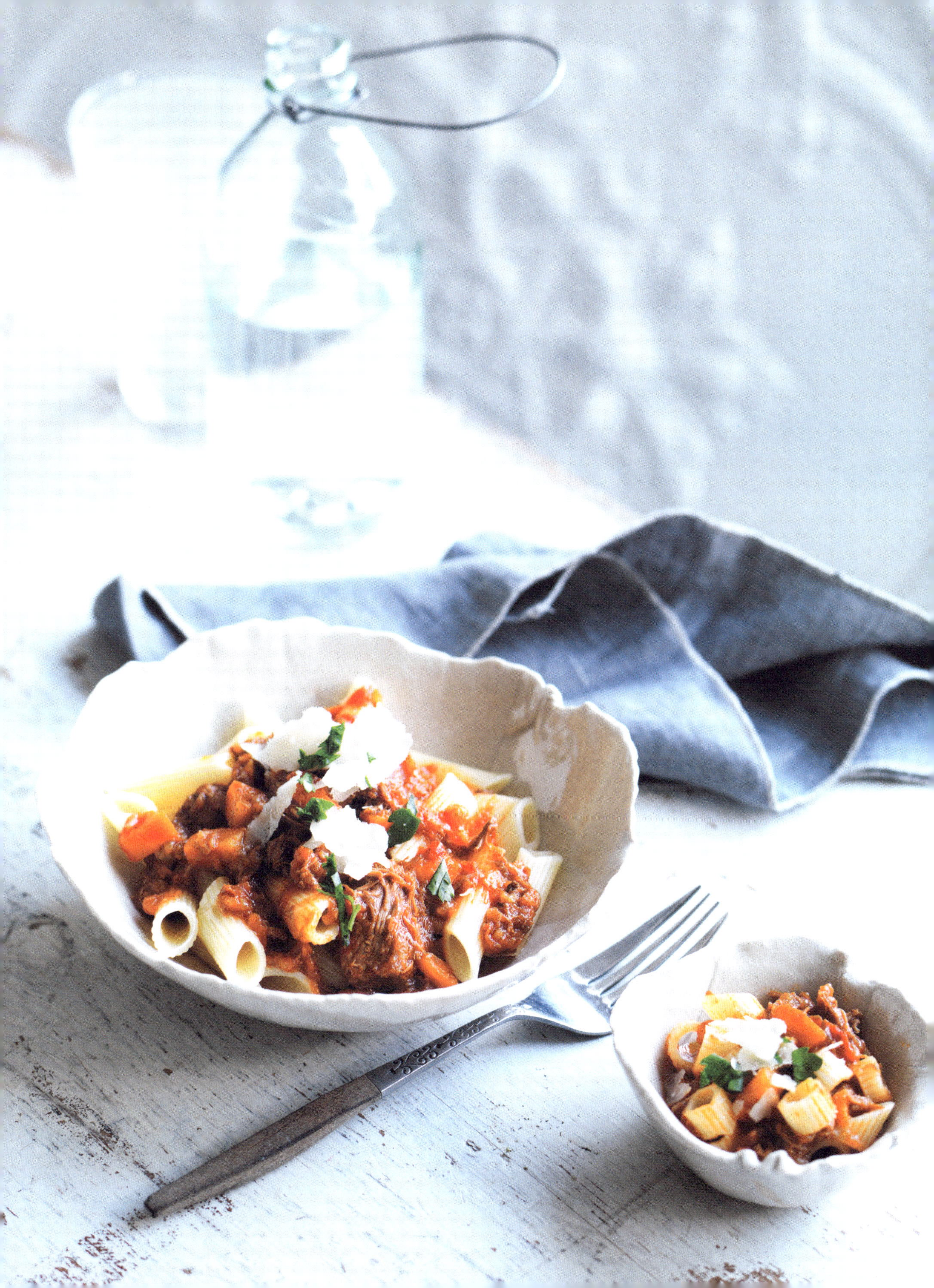

Pumpkin cauliflower dal

Serves 4

Most of us could probably do with eating a little less meat and this dal feels like a more-than-satisfactory replacement. The spices are really mild, so don't worry if your child isn't accustomed to eating them.

1 tablespoon olive oil
1 onion, finely diced
1 teaspoon finely grated ginger
1 carrot, finely diced
¼ teaspoon ground cumin
¼ teaspoon ground coriander
¼ teaspoon ground turmeric
200 g (7 oz) split red lentils, rinsed and drained
270 ml (9 fl oz) tin light coconut milk
310 g (11 oz/2 cups) diced pumpkin (winter squash)
150 g (5½ oz) diced cauliflower
150 g (5½ oz/1 cup) fresh or frozen peas
2 tablespoons lemon juice
1 tablespoon finely chopped coriander (cilantro) leaves
steamed basmati rice, to serve
plain yoghurt, to serve (optional – omit for dairy-free)
cooked pappadums, to serve (optional)

Tip *The pappadums can have sharp points when broken so just watch your child with them. You might like to wait until he's 2 years or older before offering them to him.*

Heat the oil in a large saucepan over low heat. Add the onion, ginger and carrot and cook for about 5 minutes, or until the onion has softened. Stir in the spices and lentils and cook for a further 2 minutes.

Add the coconut milk and 435 ml (15 fl oz/ 1¾ cups) water. Cover and simmer for 5 minutes. Stir through the pumpkin and cauliflower, cover, and simmer for a further 20 minutes, or until the vegetables are tender, adding the peas during the final 5 minutes of cooking.

Remove the pan from the heat and stir through the lemon juice and coriander. Serve with basmati rice, yoghurt (if using) and pappadums (if using), on the side.

Baby's serve: for a **younger baby**, blend together some dal and rice until smooth, or blend the dal and then stir through some rice for a more textured consistency. For an **older baby**, chop up the dal to a consistency that can easily be eaten with a spoon and stir through some of the rice.

Toddler's serve: serve as for an older baby or as is.

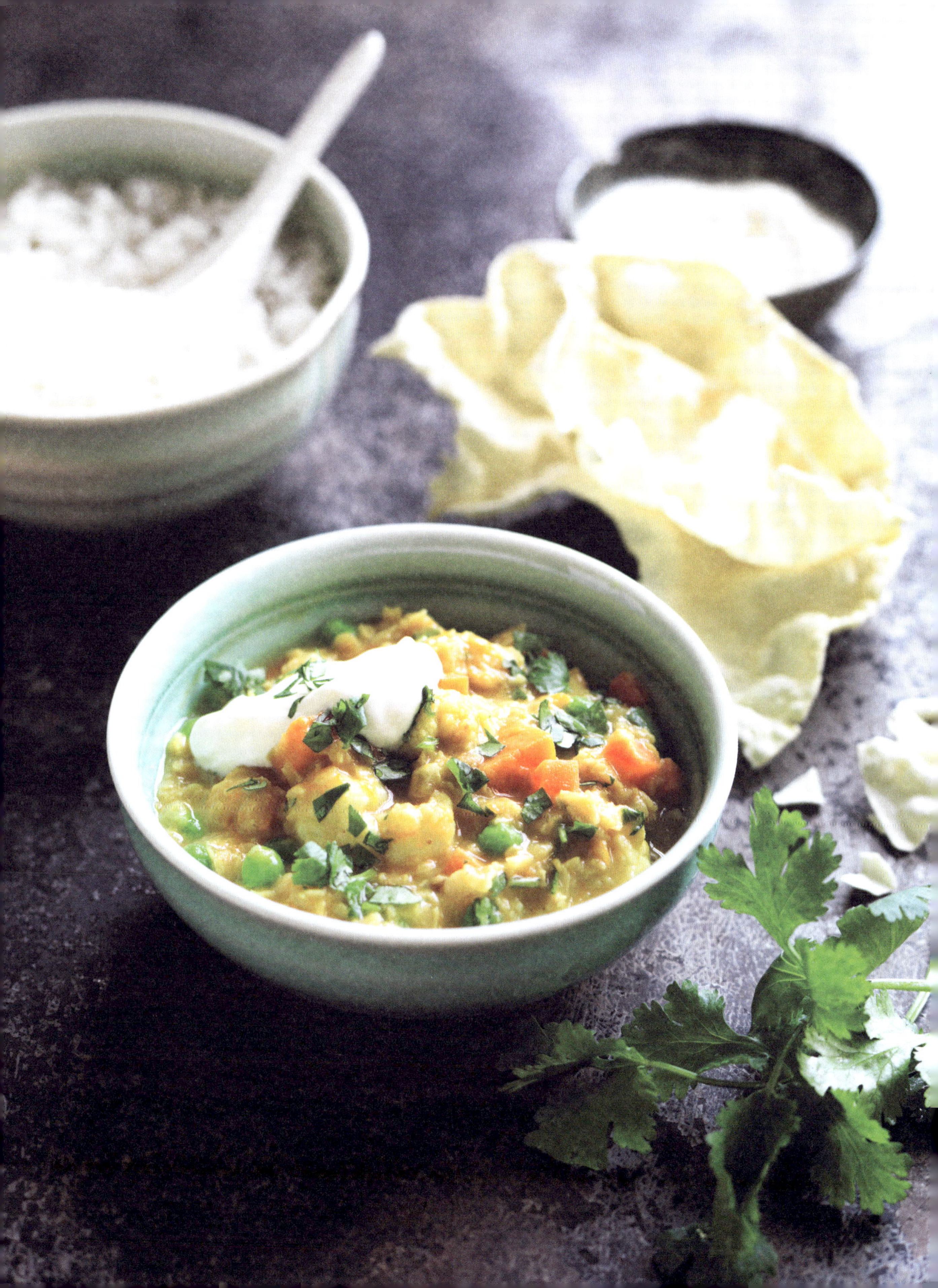

Flathead fillets with pepita pesto

Serves 4

If your child loves fish and chips, it should be easy enough to win him over to this healthier version. The pepita pesto may be a bigger ask, but offer it to him even so. He may surprise you and have a taste.

1 large sweet potato, peeled and cut into wedges
600 g (1 lb 5 oz) cauliflower, cut into florets
2 tablespoons light olive oil or rice bran oil
100 g (3½ oz/⅔ cup) plain (all-purpose) flour
2 eggs, lightly whisked
700 g (1 lb 9 oz) boneless flathead fillets

PEPITA PESTO
1 bunch coriander (cilantro) or flat-leaf (Italian) parsley, leaves picked
40 g (1½ oz/¼ cup) pepitas (pumpkin seeds)
1 tablespoon sesame seeds
1 garlic clove, peeled
60 ml (2 fl oz/¼ cup) extra-virgin olive oil
1–2 tablespoons lemon juice

Baby's serve: for a **younger baby**, blend together some fish, sweet potato and cauliflower until smooth, adding as much liquid (water or your baby's milk) as needed to achieve the desired consistency. Alternatively, if your baby is managing some finger foods (which may not happen until 8–9 months or older), cut into small pieces. For an **older baby**, keep the puréed consistency more textured or serve as finger food.

Toddler's serve: serve as is.

To make the pepita pesto, place the herbs, seeds and garlic in a food processor and process until the mixture is coarsely blended. Add the oil and process until well combined and finely blended. Add the lemon juice and 1–2 tablespoons water and blend until smooth, adding a little more oil or water if needed to achieve the desired consistency – the mixture should not be too thick. Refrigerate until needed.

Preheat the oven to 200°C (400°F). Arrange the sweet potato and cauliflower on a baking tray and roast in the oven for 30–40 minutes, or until tender – the sweet potato may take a little longer to cook than the cauliflower. Remove from the oven and keep warm.

Heat 1 tablespoon of the oil in a frying pan over medium heat. Place the flour and egg in separate shallow bowls. Dust the fish first with flour, then dip into the egg to coat on each side. Working in batches, cook the fish for about 5 minutes, turning halfway, until golden and cooked through. Drain on paper towel.

Serve the flathead fillets with the roasted vegetables and pepita pesto on the side.

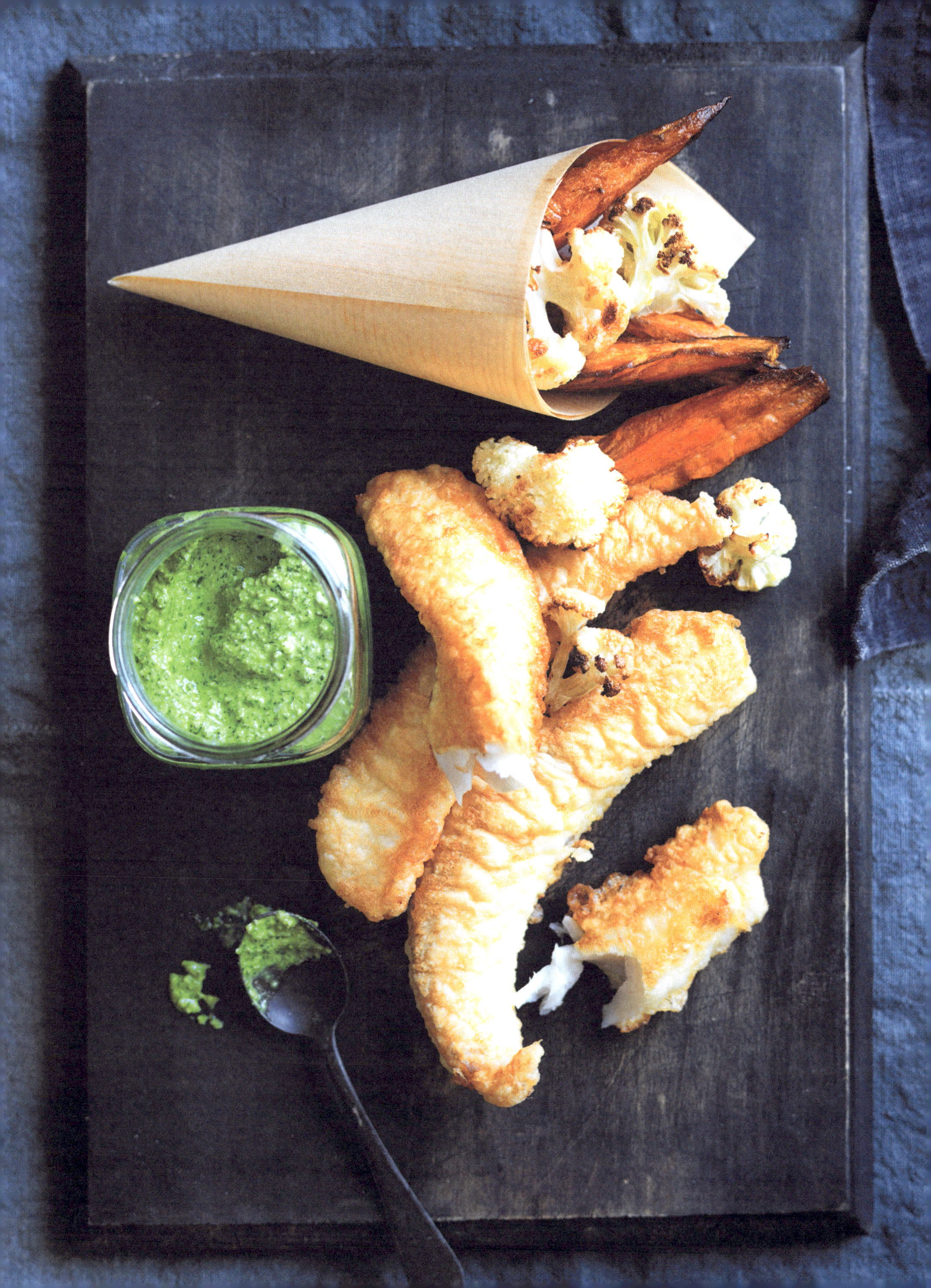

Seafood and pearl couscous stew

Serves 4–6

This makes a wonderfully tasty winter alternative to a beef casserole. If you have fresh cherry tomatoes on hand you can use them instead of tinned – just add a little extra water.

1 tablespoon olive oil
1 small leek, white part only, trimmed and diced
2 carrots, diced
2 garlic cloves, crushed
400 g (14 oz) tin cherry tomatoes (or use chopped tomatoes)
2 tablespoons lemon juice
150 g (5½ oz) pearl (Israeli) couscous
400 g (14 oz) firm white boneless fish fillets, cut into chunks
12 raw prawns (shrimp), peeled and deveined, tails intact
1 handful coriander (cilantro) leaves, finely chopped
steamed green beans, to serve

Heat the oil in a heavy-based saucepan over medium heat. Cook the leek, carrot and garlic for 5 minutes, or until the leek has softened. Add the tomatoes, lemon juice and 500 ml (17 fl oz/2 cups) water and bring to the boil.

Add the couscous to the pan, reduce the heat to low, cover, and simmer for 15 minutes, stirring occasionally until the couscous and carrot are just tender.

Add the fish and prawns, cover, and continue to simmer gently for a further 5–6 minutes, or until cooked through. Stir through the coriander.

Divide the seafood and pearl couscous stew among serving bowls and serve with steamed green beans on the side.

Baby's serve: for a **younger baby**, blend the stew (remove the tails from the prawns) until smooth, adding as much liquid (water or your baby's milk) as needed to achieve the desired consistency. An **older baby** may be able to manage as is, although you might like to cut up the prawns and fish.

Toddler's serve: remove the tails from the prawns, chop the prawns and fish into smaller pieces (if needed) and serve as is.

Dinner

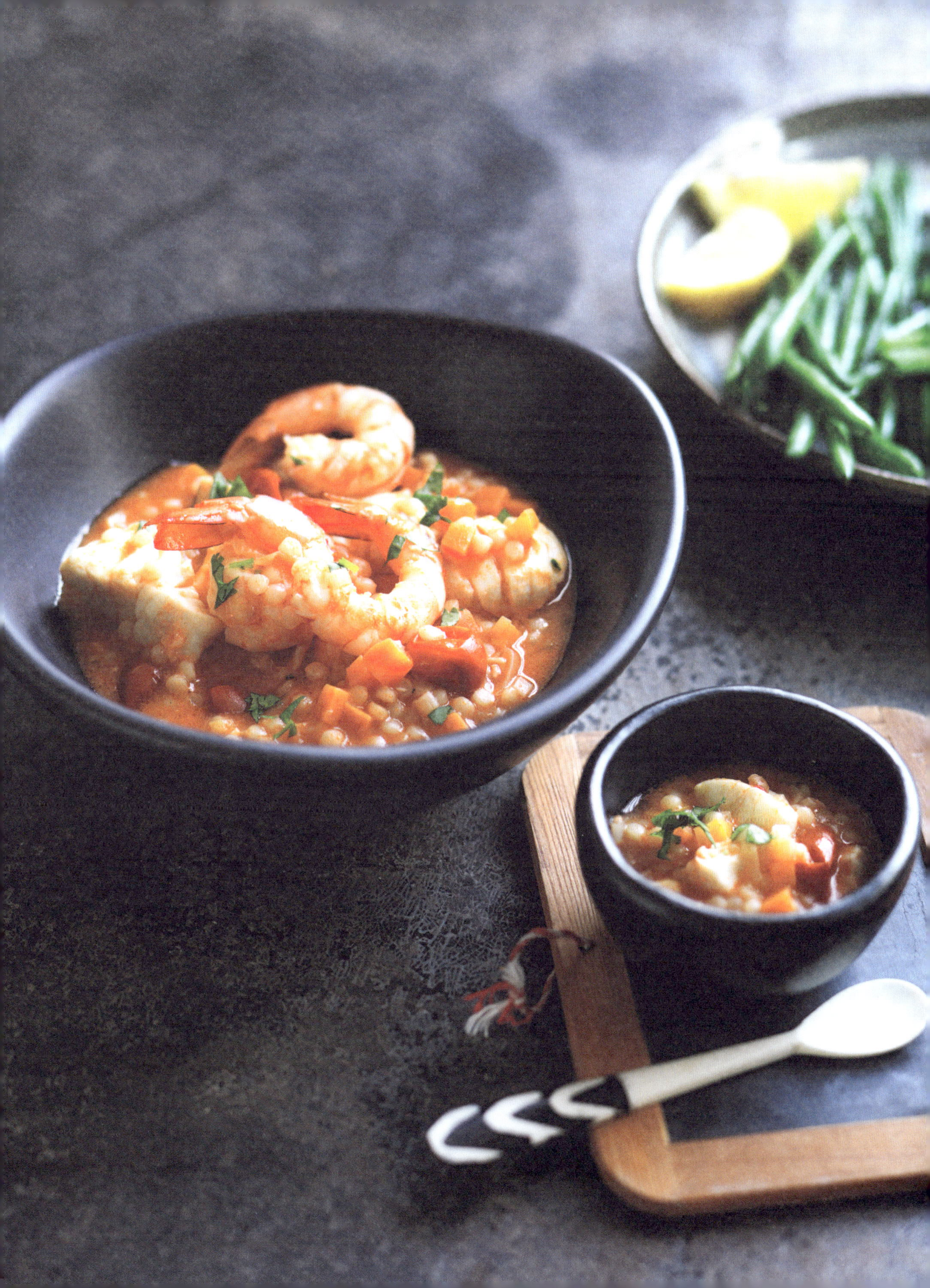

Salmon with roasted fennel purée and crispy smashed potatoes

Serves 4

This fennel purée is best made with large fennel, as the baby ones tend to be less fleshy and a bit fibrous. If you'd like to soften the flavour or texture, add some steamed cauliflower, sweet potato or another root vegetable.

12 baby red delight potatoes, unpeeled, boiled and patted dry with paper towel
600 g (1 lb 5 oz) fennel, trimmed and chopped
3 garlic cloves, unpeeled
60 ml (2 fl oz/¼ cup) olive oil
20 g (¾ oz) butter
60 ml (2 fl oz/¼ cup) milk, warmed
4 × 150 g (5½ oz) boneless salmon or ocean trout fillets
1 bunch asparagus, woody ends trimmed, steamed
lemon cheeks, to serve

Baby's serve: for a **younger baby**, blend some of the fish (remove the skin), fennel purée, asparagus and potato until smooth, adding as much liquid (water or your baby's milk) as needed to achieve the desired consistency. For an **older baby**, mash or cut up the fish, potatoes and asparagus into small pieces and serve as finger food with the fennel purée.

Toddler's serve: serve as is, cut up into small pieces.

Brush a large baking tray with a little oil. Arrange the potatoes on the tray and, using a potato masher, press down gently on each one to flatten. Refrigerate for 1–2 hours to cool and dry out the potatoes.

Preheat the oven to 180°C (350°F). Arrange the fennel and garlic in a separate baking dish. Toss through 1 tablespoon of the oil. Add 80 ml (2½ fl oz/⅓ cup) water, cover with foil, and roast for 40–45 minutes, or until tender. Remove from the oven.

Meanwhile, drizzle the remaining oil over the potatoes. Roast for 20 minutes, or until crispy and golden, turning once during cooking.

While the potatoes are cooking, remove and discard the garlic skins. Transfer the garlic and fennel to a food processor, add the butter and warm milk and process until smooth.

Heat a large non-stick frying pan over medium–high heat. Cook the fish for about 3–4 minutes on each side, or until cooked to your liking.

Serve the salmon fillets with the fennel purée, roasted potatoes, steamed asparagus and lemon cheeks.

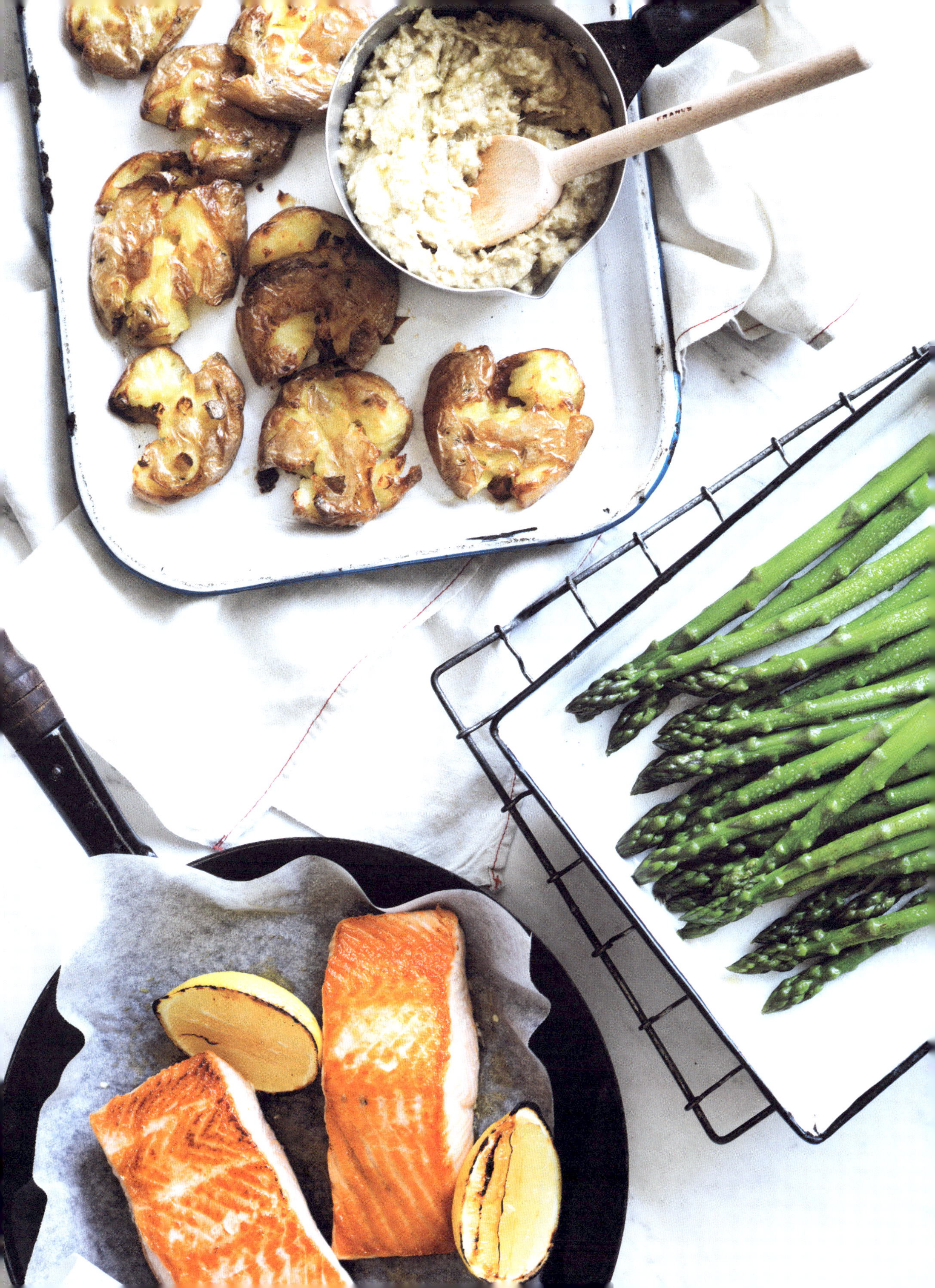

Thai green chicken curry with eggplant

Serves 4

I've seen babies in South-East Asia with a better tolerance for chilli than me, because of their exposure to it in the womb and through their mum's breastmilk. If your child is accustomed to chilli, by all means feel free to let him share in the hotter portion of this meal. Otherwise, the recipe allows you to have a Thai green curry while your child has a delicious coconut chicken dinner.

2 tablespoons olive oil
1 medium eggplant (aubergine), cut into 3 cm (1¼ inch) cubes
1 onion, diced
800 g (1 lb 12 oz) chicken thigh fillets, cut into strips
400 ml (13½ fl oz) tin light coconut milk
250 g (9 oz) green beans, cut in half crossways
2–3 tablespoons Thai green curry paste
steamed basmati or wild rice, to serve
Thai basil and fresh lime, to serve (optional)

Baby's serve: for a **younger baby**, blend the non-curried portion of the meal and some rice, adding as much liquid (water or your baby's milk) as needed to achieve the desired consistency. For a more textured version, stir through the rice after blending. For an **older baby**, chop the chicken and vegetables (or serve as finger food), and serve with the rice.

Toddler's serve: prepare as for an older baby or simply serve as is.

Heat 1½ tablespoons of the oil in a large deep frying pan or saucepan over medium–high heat. Add the eggplant and cook for 3–5 minutes, turning until golden all over. Transfer to a plate and set aside. Add the onion to the pan and cook for 5 minutes, or until softened. Add the chicken and stir-fry for a further 3 minutes.

Return the eggplant to the pan and add 350 ml (12 fl oz) of the coconut milk. Cover and cook for 10 minutes over low heat. Add the beans and cook for a further 5–10 minutes, uncovered, or until the chicken is cooked and the beans are tender. At this stage you can set aside baby's serve.

Meanwhile, for the adult servings, heat the remaining oil in a small frying pan over low–medium heat. Add the green curry paste and cook, stirring for 1–2 minutes (you may need to adjust the quantity of curry paste according to the strength of the brand). Add the remaining coconut milk. Pour over the chicken and vegetables and stir through. Transfer to a serving platter and serve with steamed rice, and Thai basil and lime (if using).

Dinner

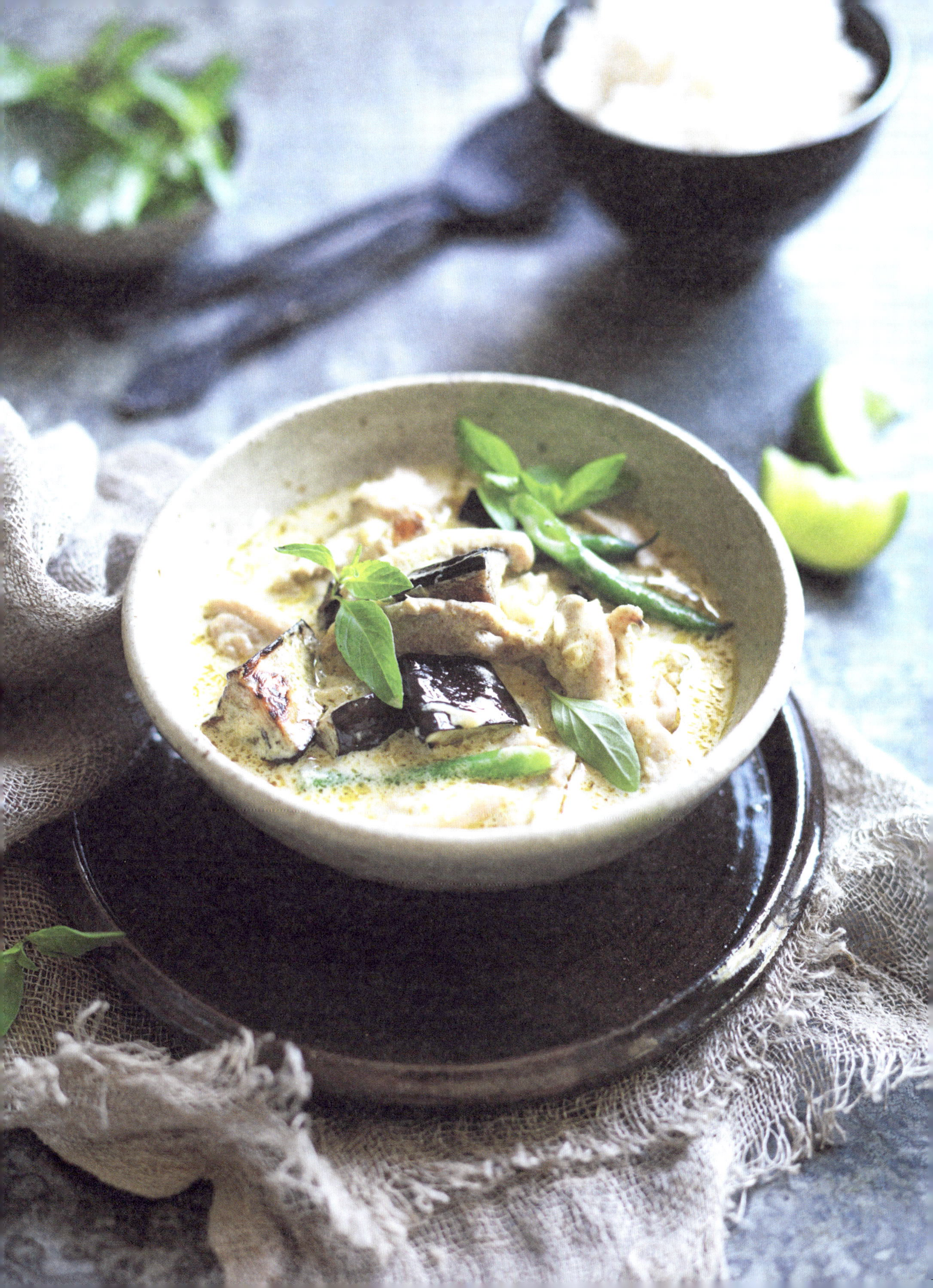

Chicken schnitzel with mushy peas and purple carrots

Serves 4

Schnitzel with mushy peas is one of my ultimate comfort meals. It's especially welcome on a chilly night. The peas are a healthier twist on potato mash.

700 g (1 lb 9 oz) chicken breast fillets
50 g (1¾ oz/⅓ cup) plain (all-purpose) flour
2 eggs
1 tablespoon milk
150 g (5½ oz) fresh breadcrumbs
1 small handful mixed fresh herbs, such as flat leaf (Italian) parsley, basil, thyme and oregano, finely chopped
35 g (1¼ oz/⅓ cup) finely grated parmesan cheese
1 teaspoon finely grated lemon zest
light olive oil or rice bran oil, for shallow-frying
1 bunch baby purple carrots, trimmed and steamed
lemon cheeks (optional), to serve

MUSHY PEAS
2 teaspoons olive oil
1 brown onion, diced
500 g (1 lb 2 oz) fresh or frozen peas
80 ml (2½ fl oz/⅓ cup) reduced-salt chicken stock (see note, page 124) or water
20 g (¾ oz) butter
1 tablespoon sour cream (optional)

Baby's serve: for a **younger baby**, the mushy peas make a lovely purée. You may also wish to blend in some of the carrots. Wait until your baby is able to eat finger foods (which may not happen until 8–9 months or older) before offering him the schnitzel, cut into strips. For an **older baby**, cut the chicken and carrot into strips and serve with the mushy peas.

Toddler's serve: prepare as for an older baby.

Cut each chicken breast in half horizontally through the centre to create two thinner fillets. Place between two sheets of plastic wrap (cling film) and gently pound with a meat mallet until about 5 mm (¼ inch) thick.

Place the flour in a shallow bowl. In another bowl, lightly beat together the eggs and milk. Combine the breadcrumbs, herbs, parmesan and lemon zest in a separate bowl. Coat the chicken first in the flour, then in the egg mixture, and then coat with the breadcrumb mixture. Refrigerate until required.

To make the mushy peas, heat the oil in a saucepan over medium heat. Add the onion and cook for 5 minutes, or until softened. Add all of the remaining ingredients, except the sour cream, and cook for 20 minutes, stirring occasionally. Remove from the heat and add the sour cream (if using). Transfer to a food processor (or use a stick blender) and process to a rough purée. Set aside and keep warm.

Meanwhile, heat the oil in a large frying pan over medium–high heat. Cook the chicken until golden brown on both sides and cooked through. Drain on paper towel. Serve the schnitzel with the mushy peas and steamed baby carrots on the side. Squeeze over a little fresh lemon juice (if using).

Dinner

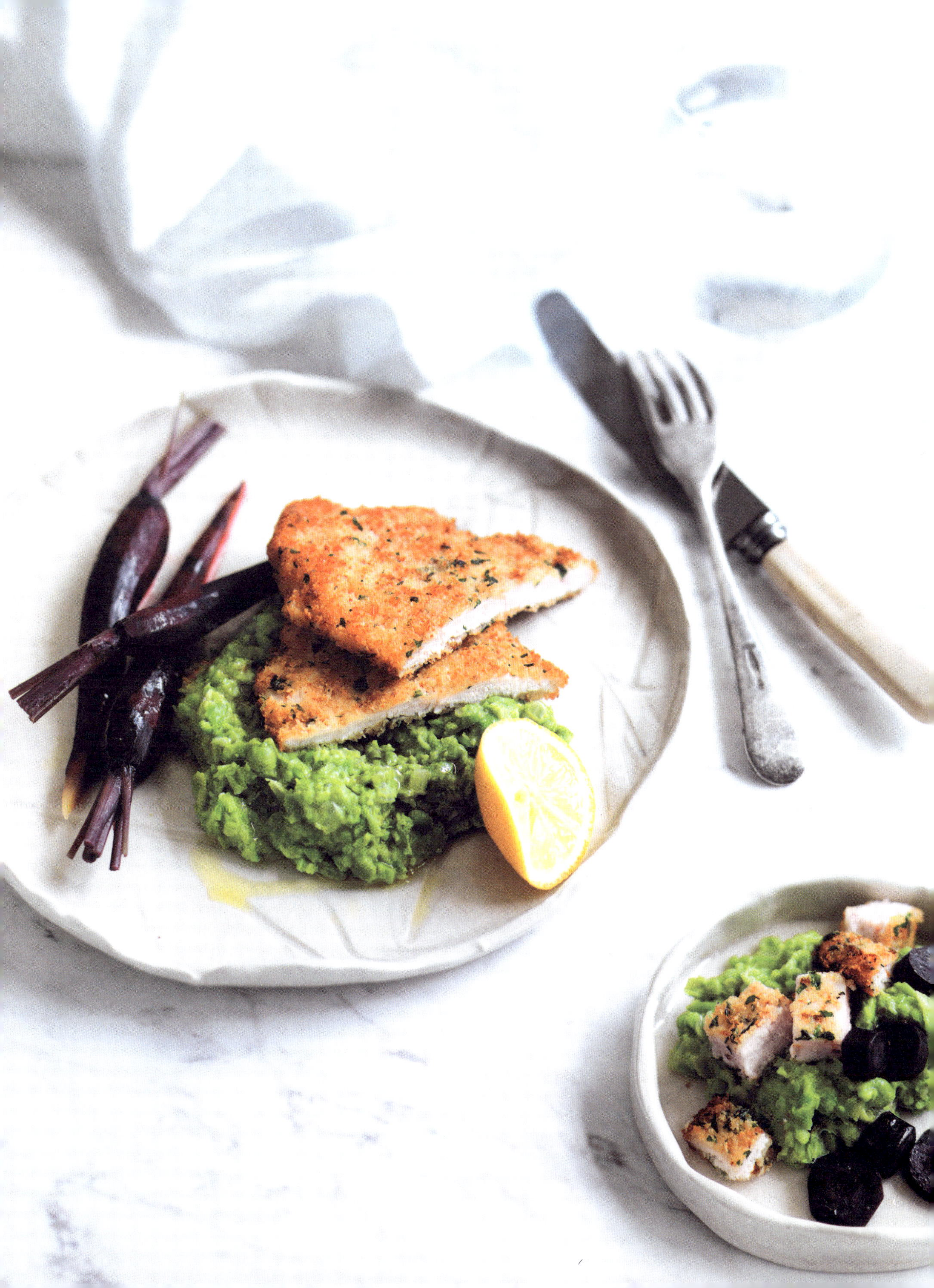

Growing your own herbs is a great way to teach children about where food comes from. Better still, we know from the research that children who have grown their own food are more likely to eat and enjoy it.

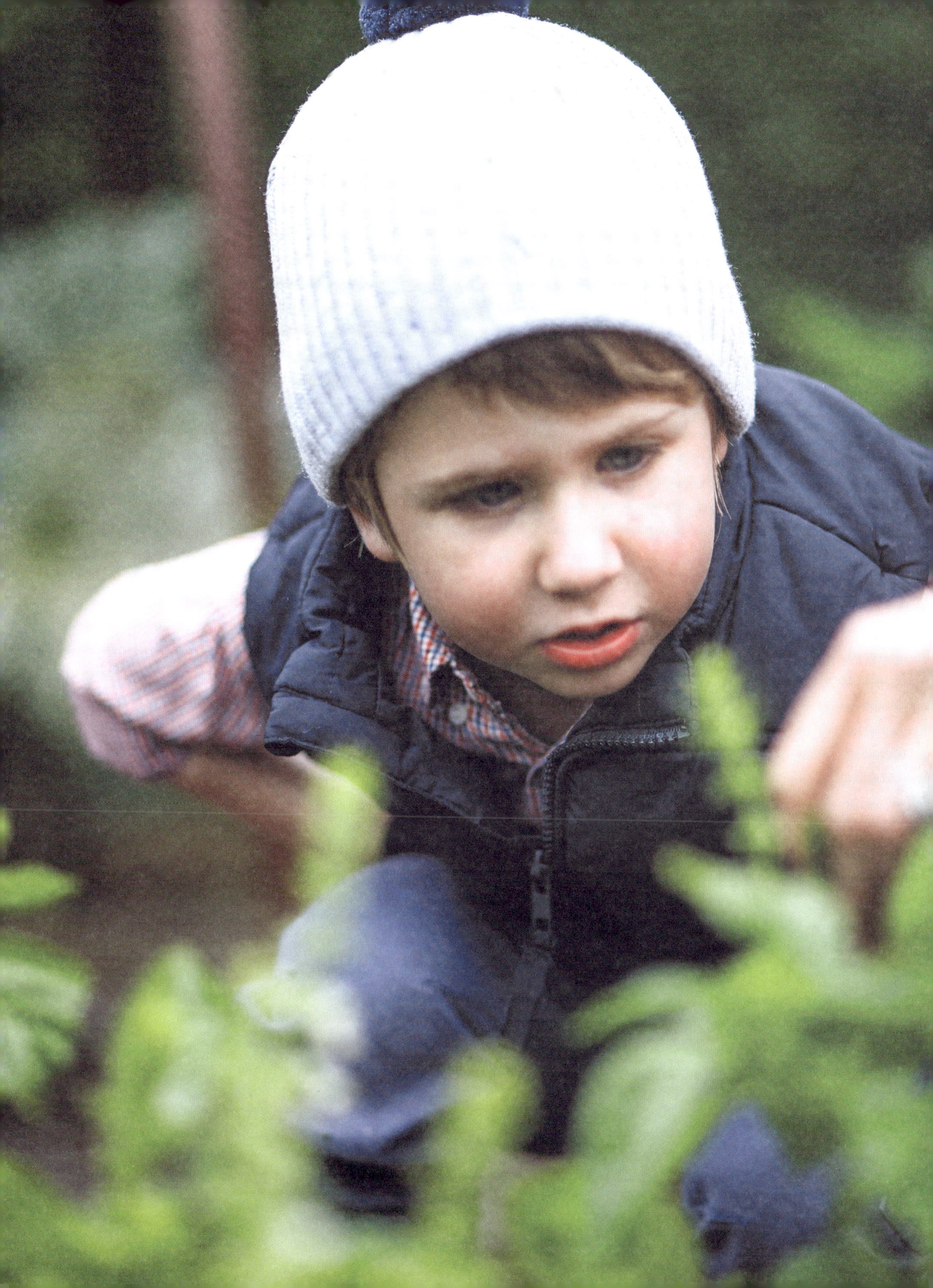

Chicken, mushroom and leek pot pies

Makes 4 pies

This is a dish that tends to be loved by people of every age, from the baby of the family right through to Great Grandma. I prefer to use chicken thigh fillets over breast fillets, because they don't dry out and contain twice as much iron and zinc as the white meat – something many of us need more of.

1 tablespoon olive oil
700 g (1 lb 9 oz) chicken thigh fillets, trimmed and diced
200 g (7 oz) button mushrooms, quartered
1 leek, white part only, trimmed and sliced
2 garlic cloves, crushed
2 tablespoons plain (all-purpose) flour
375 ml (12½ fl oz/1½ cups) reduced-salt chicken stock (see note, page 124)
150 g (5½ oz/1 cup) fresh or frozen peas
2 teaspoons chopped tarragon or flat-leaf (Italian) parsley
1–2 tablespoons lemon juice
1 sheet frozen puff pastry, partially thawed
milk, for brushing

Preheat the oven to 180°C (350°F).

Heat half of the oil in a large, deep frying pan over medium–high heat. Add the chicken and cook, stirring occasionally, for 5 minutes or until browned. Set aside. Add the remaining oil and the mushroom, leek and garlic and cook for 5 minutes, or until the leek has softened. Return the chicken to the pan. Stir through the flour and cook for 1 minute.

Stir in the stock and bring to the boil. Reduce the heat to low–medium, cover, and simmer for 5 minutes, stirring occasionally until the chicken is cooked through and the sauce has thickened. Stir through the peas, tarragon or parsley and lemon juice, then spoon the chicken mixture into four 375 ml (12½ fl oz/1½ cup) capacity ramekins or individual baking dishes.

Cut the pastry sheet into quarters and top each dish with a pastry square, pinching around the edges to seal, and trimming any excess pastry. Brush the tops with a little milk and bake for about 20 minutes, or until the pastry is crisp and golden. Serve immediately.

Baby's serve: for a **younger baby**, reserve some of the chicken pie filling and blend until smooth, adding as much liquid (water or your baby's milk) as needed to achieve the desired consistency. For an **older baby**, keep the puréed consistency more textured or simply chop up the chicken pieces and serve as is.

Toddler's serve: serve as is, ensuring the pie is cool enough to eat, and chopping up the chicken a little if needed.

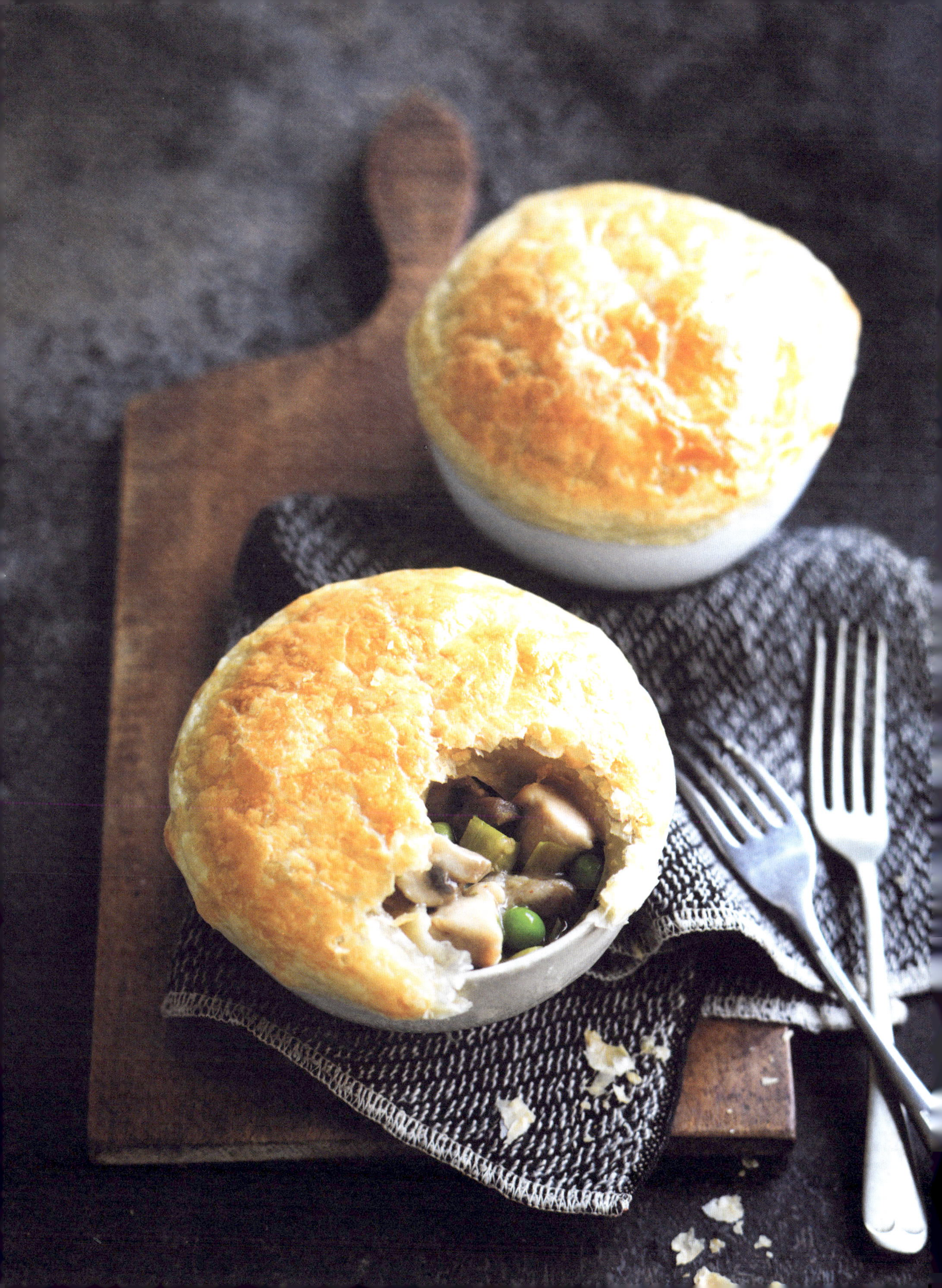

Chicken with cherry tomatoes and butter beans

Serves 4

Those of you who have my book *Cooking For Your Baby and Toddler* will know that I like to make a similar dish using fish, which I learnt on a trip to the Ligurian coast in Italy. This adaptation is just as good, if not better.

If you don't have a mandolin, it's worth investing in one (it won't break the bank). Once you have these perfectly, thinly sliced potatoes you'll be hooked! Unless you're a particularly nifty cook, it's tricky to get quite the same result by hand.

4 chicken leg quarters (marylands)
6 desiree potatoes, skin on, thinly sliced using a mandolin
4 small zucchini (courgettes), thinly sliced using a mandolin
1 brown onion, thinly sliced using a mandolin
60 ml (2 fl oz/¼ cup) olive oil
4 garlic cloves, unpeeled
2 rosemary sprigs
12–18 truss cherry tomatoes
400 g (14 oz) tin butter or cannellini (lima) beans, rinsed and drained

Preheat the oven to 180°C (350°F). Heat a large non-stick frying pan (or flameproof baking dish which you can continue to use for cooking the vegetables) over high heat. Add the chicken and cook for 4–5 minutes on each side, or until golden brown. Set aside.

Arrange the potato, zucchini and onion slices evenly in the base of a large baking dish. Toss through 2 tablespoons of the olive oil and place the browned chicken, garlic and rosemary sprigs on top. Bake for 20 minutes, or until the chicken and potato are almost cooked.

Remove the dish from the oven and scatter over the tomatoes and beans. Drizzle over the remaining olive oil. Return the dish to the oven and bake for a further 5–10 minutes, or until the chicken and vegetables are cooked through.

Baby's serve: for a **younger baby**, blend together some of the chicken (remove any bones), beans, vegetables and tomato until smooth, adding as much liquid (water or your baby's milk) as needed to achieve the desired consistency. For an **older baby**, keep the puréed consistency more textured or simply chop up the chicken and serve as finger food.

Toddler's serve: serve as is, chopping into smaller pieces as needed.

Dinner

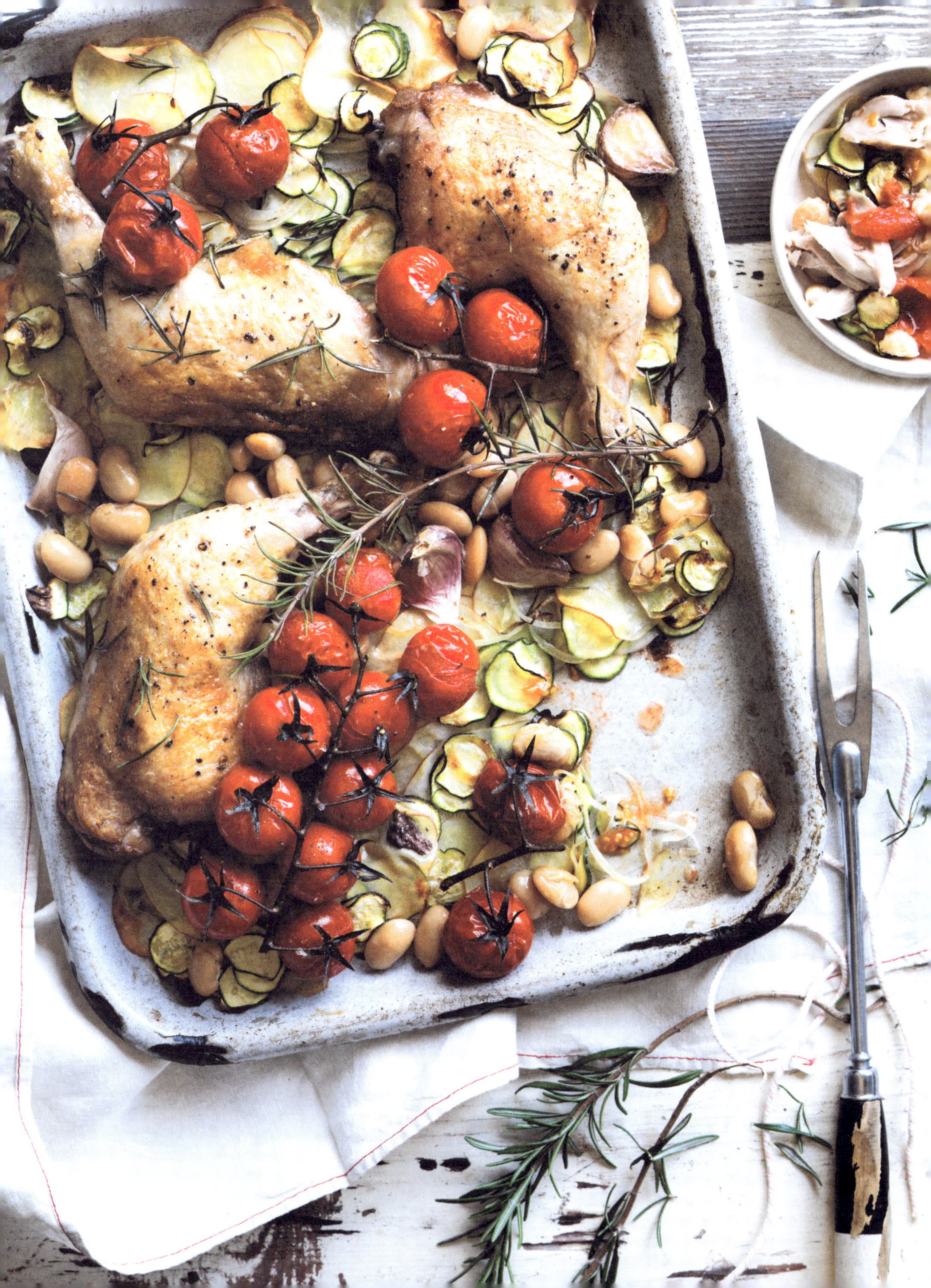

Shepherd's pie with parsnip and pumpkin topping

Serves 4–6

The parsnip and pumpkin topping on this pie offers more vegetable variety than conventional potato topping, plus it helps your children become accustomed to seeing a variety of colours on their plate. You can serve this pie in a large dish or in smaller individual dishes. I often divide the mixture between two smaller dishes so we have one for dinner and one to freeze for another night.

1 tablespoon olive oil, plus extra for drizzling
1 onion, finely diced
1 carrot, finely diced
2 garlic cloves, crushed
500 g (1 lb 2 oz) minced (ground) lamb
2 tablespoons tomato paste (concentrated purée)
400 g (14 oz) tin chopped tomatoes or 500 g (1 lb 2 oz) fresh tomatoes, chopped
2 zucchini (courgettes), finely diced
2 tablespoons chopped flat-leaf (Italian) parsley
400 g (14 oz) pumpkin (winter squash), peeled, seeded and diced
400 g (14 oz) parsnip, peeled and diced
30 g (1 oz) butter
50 g (1¾ oz) grated cheddar cheese

Baby's serve: for a **younger baby**, blend together the shepherd's pie filling and topping, adding as much liquid (water or your baby's milk) as needed to achieve the desired consistency. For an **older baby**, chop up to a consistency that can be easily eaten with a spoon.

Toddler's serve: prepare as for an older baby or simply serve as is.

Preheat the oven to 180°C (350°F).

Heat the oil in a large saucepan over medium heat. Add the onion, carrot and garlic and cook for 5 minutes, stirring until softened. Add the lamb and cook for 5 minutes, stirring with a wooden spoon to break up any lumps, until the lamb has browned all over.

Stir in the tomato paste, tomatoes and 190 ml (6½ fl oz/¾ cup) water. Simmer for 10 minutes, or until the sauce has thickened. Stir in the zucchini and parsley.

Meanwhile, steam or boil the pumpkin and parsnip for 10–15 minutes, or until tender. Drain and return to the pan. Mash (or blend using a stick blender) until smooth, then stir through the butter.

Spoon the beef mixture into a 2 litre (68 fl oz/ 8 cup) ovenproof dish (or use two dishes or six smaller ramekins). Top with the pumpkin and parsnip mixture. Sprinkle over the cheese and drizzle over a little oil. Bake the pie in the oven for 25 minutes, or until the top is lightly browned.

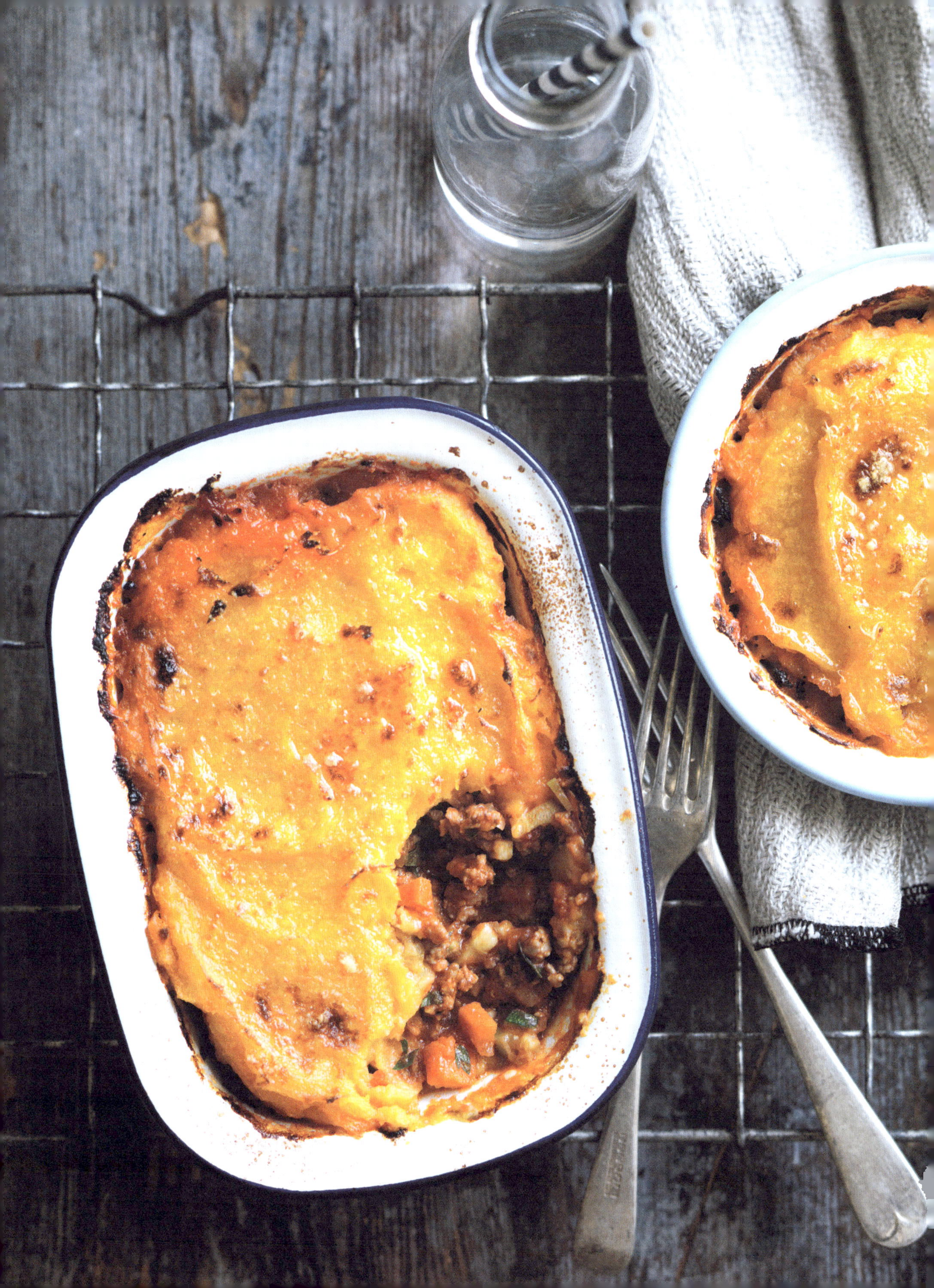

Herb-crusted lamb racks with roast pumpkin and cauliflower purée

Serves 4–6

If a crusted rack of lamb is not part of your usual repertoire, don't be scared. Preparing the crust is really pretty simple and adds so much flavour. Try it once and you'll have perfected it for the next time your in-laws come over for dinner.

11–15 garlic cloves, unpeeled
80 g (2¾ oz/½ cup) macadamia nuts
80 g (2¾ oz/½ cup) almonds
3 tablespoons flat-leaf (Italian) parsley leaves
3 tablespoons coriander (cilantro) leaves
1 teaspoon finely grated lemon zest (optional)
2½ tablespoons olive oil, plus extra for drizzling
2 lamb racks (8 cutlets on each rack), French-trimmed (ask your butcher to do this for you)
400 g (14 oz) pumpkin (winter squash), peeled, seeded and cut into 1 cm (½ inch) slices
800 g (1 lb 12 oz) cauliflower, cut into florets, steamed
2 tablespoons milk

Tip *If you'd like a lemon parsley sauce to drizzle over the mash (as pictured), simply whizz some parsley leaves in a blender with some lemon juice and olive oil.*

Preheat the oven to 200°C (400°F). Peel 1 garlic clove and place in the bowl of a food processor along with the macadamia nuts, almonds, herbs, lemon zest (if using) and 1½ tablespoons of the oil. Process to a coarse paste.

Place the lamb racks on a wire rack in a baking dish and firmly press the nut mixture over the lamb to coat. Arrange the pumpkin and remaining garlic around the lamb. Cook in the oven for 20–25 minutes (for medium-rare), or until cooked to your liking. Remove from the oven, cover the lamb loosely with foil, and set aside to rest for 10 minutes before serving.

Meanwhile, transfer the steamed cauliflower to a food processor (or use a stick blender). Squeeze the roasted garlic flesh from 2 of the cloves and add to the cauliflower, with the pumpkin, milk and remaining oil. Process until smooth. Serve the cutlets with the vegetable purée, remaining garlic cloves and an extra drizzle of olive oil.

Baby's serve: for a **younger baby**, the pumpkin cauliflower purée can be served as is, or you can add some lamb to it and re-blend to a smooth consistency. For an **older baby**, keep the blended consistency more textured, or cut the lamb into strips and allow your child to have a chew on the cutlet.

Toddler's serve: chop up the lamb as needed or simply serve as is.

Dinner

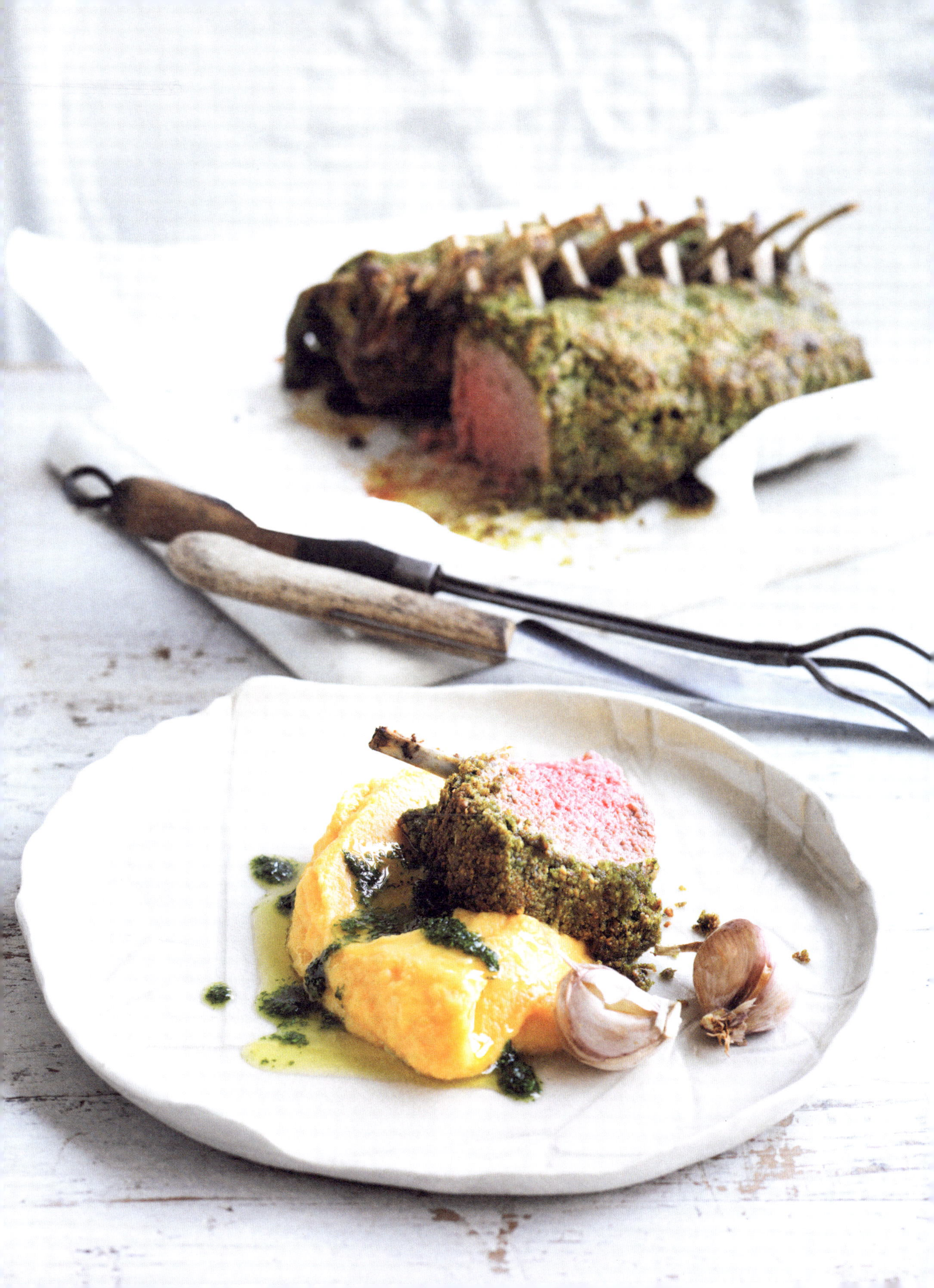

Oven-braised lamb shanks with creamy polenta

Serves 4

These slow-cooked lamb shanks are just the thing for a weekend lunch or dinner. Because they cook for over two hours, you can make them ahead of time and sit and relax in the lead-up to dinner. You can serve with mash instead of the polenta.

4–8 (depending on their size) lamb shanks
35 g (1¼ oz/¼ cup) plain (all-purpose) flour
2 tablespoons olive oil
1 celery stalk, sliced
1 brown onion, chopped
2 garlic cloves, chopped
1 tablespoon balsamic vinegar
310 ml (10½ fl oz/1¼ cups) reduced-salt chicken, beef or vegetable stock (see note, page 124)
400 g (14 oz) tin chopped tomatoes
juice of 1 lemon
4 anchovy fillets, finely chopped (optional)
4 thyme sprigs
1 bunch baby carrots, stems trimmed
flat-leaf (Italian) parsley leaves, to serve

CREAMY POLENTA
750 ml (25½ fl oz/3 cups) milk
100 g (3½ oz) polenta
60 g (2 oz/½ cup) grated cheddar cheese

Baby's serve: for a **younger baby**, blend together some lamb (no bone), carrots, polenta and cooking juices until smooth. For an **older baby**, keep the purée more textured and give him a short-handled spoon, or let him pick up pieces of lamb and carrot in his hands.

Toddler's serve: serve as for an older baby, above.

Preheat the oven to 180°C (350°F). Dust the lamb shanks with flour, shaking off any excess.

Heat the oil in a large flameproof casserole dish over high heat. Add the shanks, in batches if necessary, and cook until brown all over. Set aside. Reduce the heat to low–medium and cook the celery, onion and garlic for 5 minutes, or until softened.

Increase the heat, add the balsamic vinegar and boil briskly for a few seconds. Add the stock, tomatoes and lemon juice and bring back to the boil. Add the anchovy (if using), then return the shanks to the dish with the thyme sprigs. Cover, and cook in the oven for 1½ hours. Add the carrots and cook for a further 30 minutes, or until the meat is falling-off-the-bone tender. Remove the lid and return to the oven for a further 15 minutes.

Meanwhile, to make the polenta, pour the milk into a large saucepan with 500 ml (17 fl oz/2 cups) water and bring to the boil. Gradually add the polenta to the pan, stirring continuously. Reduce the heat to very low and simmer, stirring regularly, for about 10 minutes, or until the polenta thickens. Stir in the cheese until melted and combined.

Divide the polenta among four serving dishes. Top with the lamb shanks and carrots, and spoon over a little of the cooking juices from the casserole dish. Scatter over the parsley leaves and serve.

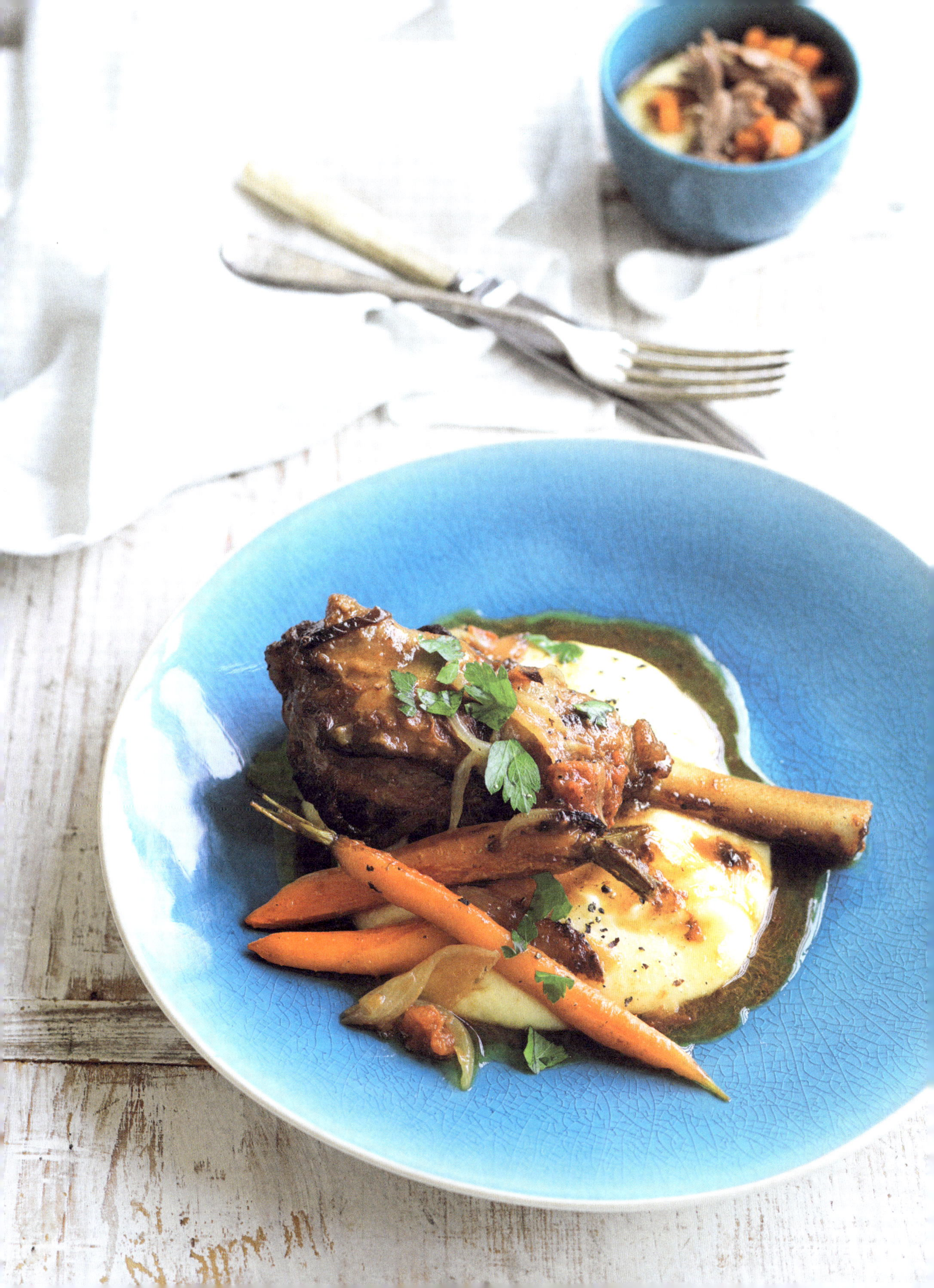

Beef and vegetable pie

Serves 4

When I was about seven years old, my family took a winter road trip to stay with friends in Bathurst. I have the most vivid memory of arriving at their farmhouse in the evening, exhausted and cold, to be greeted with a beef pie – exactly like this one – being pulled from the oven. It was the most perfect act of hospitality and, even though I was so young, I've never forgotten how good it tasted.

1½ tablespoons olive oil
1 kg (2 lb 3 oz) chuck steak, cut into 3 cm (1¼ inch) cubes
1 brown onion, finely diced
2 large carrots, diced
1 garlic clove, diced
400 g (14 oz) tin chopped tomatoes
3 thyme sprigs (optional)
400 g (14 oz) tin lentils, rinsed and drained – or use 150 g (5½ oz/1 cup) fresh or frozen peas
1 sheet frozen puff pastry, just thawed
milk, for brushing

Baby's serve: for a **younger baby**, reserve some of the beef pie filling and blend until smooth, adding as much liquid (water or your baby's milk) as needed to achieve the desired consistency. For an **older baby**, keep the puréed consistency more textured or simply chop up the beef pieces and serve as is.

Toddler's serve: serve as is, ensuring the pie is cool enough to eat, and chopping the beef into smaller pieces if needed.

Heat 2 teaspoons of the oil in a large saucepan over high heat. Add half of the beef and cook for 5 minutes, stirring occasionally, until browned. Transfer to a plate and set aside. Repeat with another 2 teaspoons of the oil and the remaining beef.

Add the remaining oil to the pan with the onion, carrot and garlic and cook for 6 minutes, or until softened. Return the beef to the pan, stir in the tomatoes, then add the thyme sprigs (if using) and 125 ml (4 fl oz/½ cup) water and bring to the boil. Reduce the heat to low, cover, and simmer for 2 hours, or until the beef is tender. Discard the thyme sprigs and stir through the lentils or peas. At this stage you can set aside your baby's serve.

Transfer the remaining mixture to a 1.5 litre (51 fl oz/6 cup) capacity baking dish and allow to cool for 10 minutes.

Meanwhile, preheat the oven to 180°C (350°F). Press the pastry over the beef, tucking in the edges. Brush the top with a little milk and bake for 15 minutes, or until golden.

Dinner

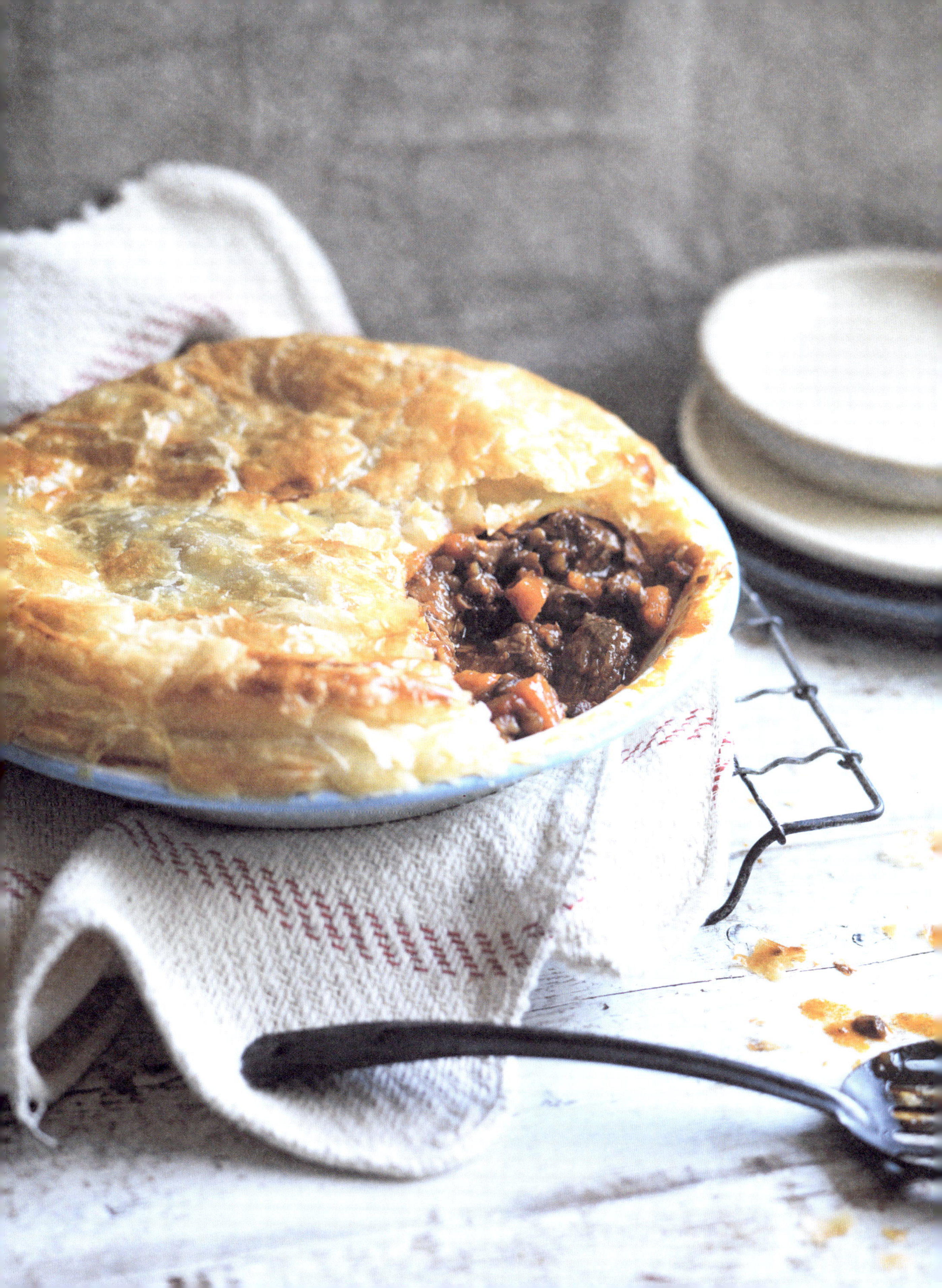

Osso bucco with white bean purée

Serves 6

If your child still has daytime sleeps, this is a great dish to make while he's down. It means dinner will be well and truly ready when that evening witching hour comes around!

6 large osso bucco
50 g (1¾ oz/⅓ cup) plain (all-purpose) flour
60 ml (2 fl oz/¼ cup) olive oil
2 carrots, diced
1 celery stalk, diced
1 onion, diced
2 garlic cloves, crushed
500 ml (17 fl oz/2 cups) reduced-salt beef stock
400 g (14 oz) tin chopped tomatoes or 500 g (1 lb 2 oz) fresh tomatoes, chopped
1 tablespoon balsamic vinegar
steamed green beans, to serve
micro herbs (optional), to serve

WHITE BEAN PURÉE

2 × 400 g (14 oz) tins cannellini (lima) beans, rinsed and drained
70 g (2½ oz/⅔ cup) ground almonds
2 tablespoons lemon juice
1 garlic clove
125 ml (4 fl oz/½ cup) olive oil

Baby's serve: for a **younger baby**, blend together some of the osso bucco (no bone), white bean purée and green beans, adding as much liquid (water or your baby's milk) as needed to achieve the desired consistency. For an **older baby**, keep the purée more textured, and let him pick up the beef and carrot in his hands.

Toddler's serve: serve as for an older baby.

To make the white bean purée, place the beans, ground almonds, lemon juice and garlic in a food processor and process to combine. Add the oil and process until smooth. Transfer to a bowl and set aside until needed.

Wipe the osso bucco dry with paper towel and dust with the flour to coat. Heat the oil in a large saucepan or flameproof casserole over medium–high heat. Working in batches, add the osso bucco and cook for 3 minutes on each side, or until brown all over. Remove the osso bucco to a plate and set aside.

Reduce the heat to low, add the carrot, celery and onion and cook for 5 minutes, or until softened. Stir in the garlic and cook for a further 3 minutes. Add the stock, tomatoes and 375 ml (12½ fl oz/1½ cups) water. Using a spatula, lightly scrape the base of the dish to loosen any cooked-on flour. Return the osso bucco to the dish, stir through the balsamic vinegar and bring to the boil. Reduce the heat to low, cover, and simmer for 2 hours. Remove the lid and cook for a further 20 minutes, or until the meat is tender and the sauce has thickened.

Serve the osso bucco on serving plates with the white bean purée, steamed green beans and micro herbs (if using).

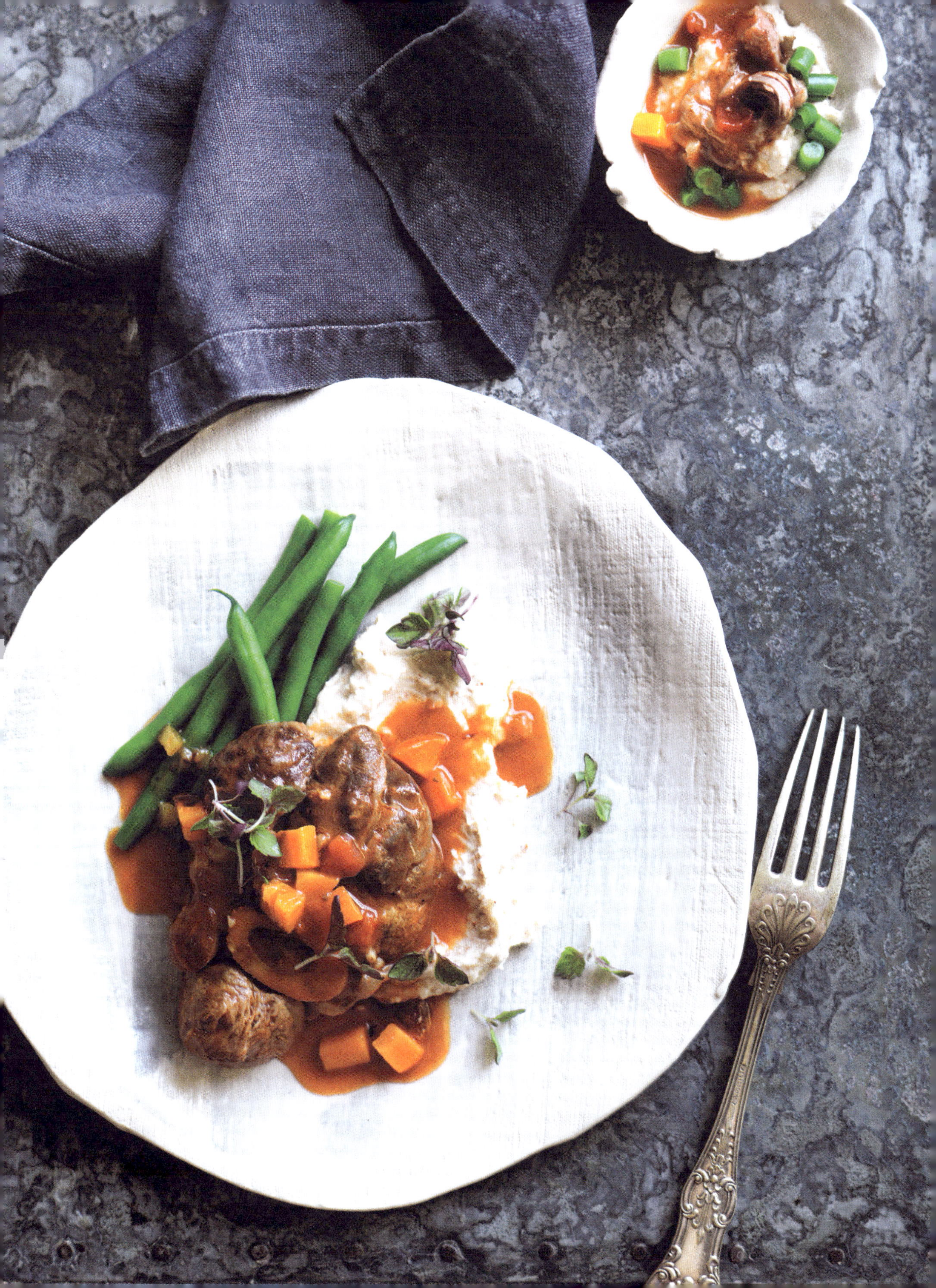

Desserts and Baking

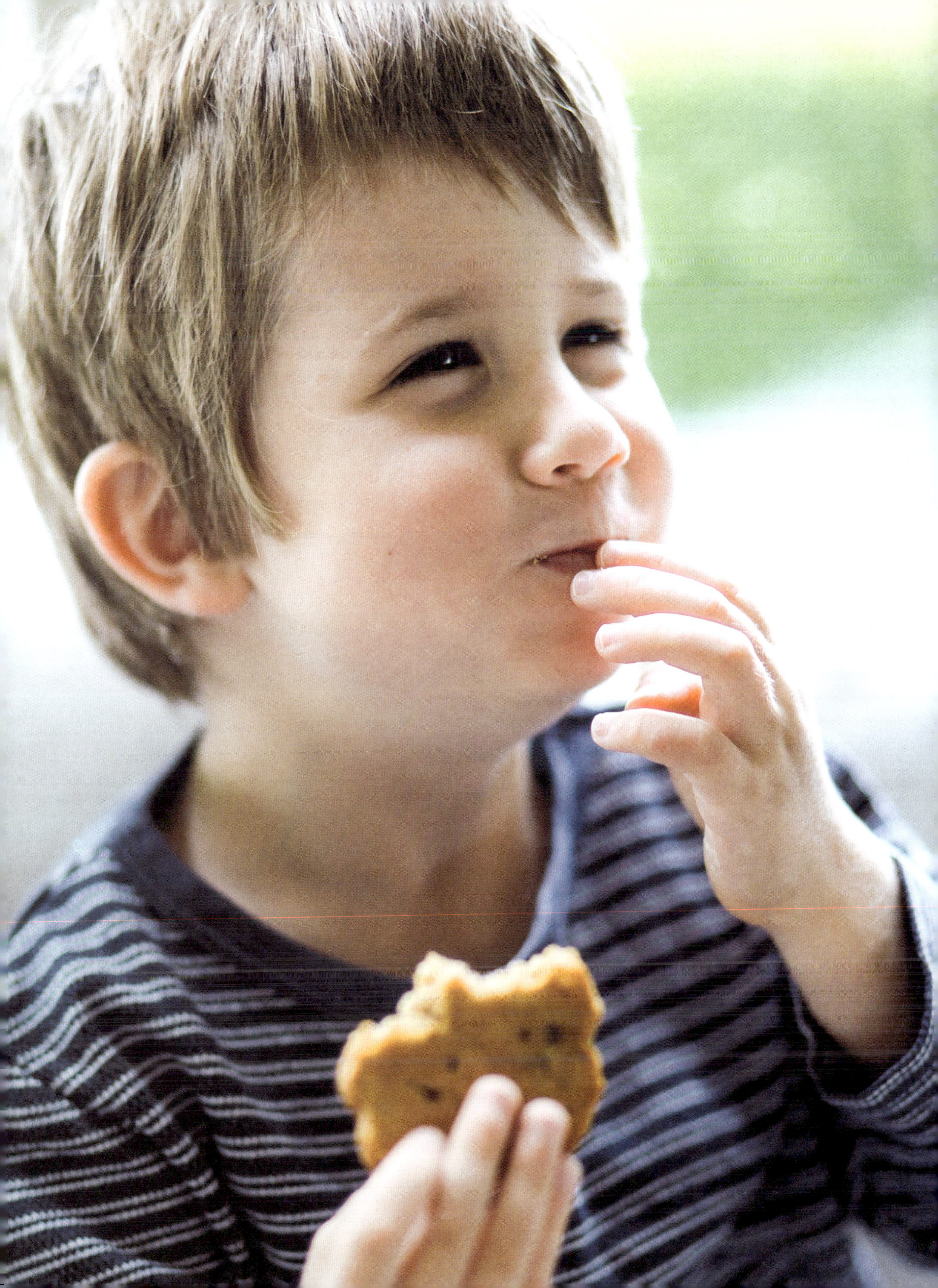

I'm a firm believer in balance and moderation. So although my focus is healthy eating, I don't believe that means skipping dessert. I have so many fond childhood memories of baking scones with my dad and cakes with my grandma, I couldn't bear it if my own children missed out on the joy of pulling a freshly baked sweet treat from the oven.

The trick is to make your desserts and baking as nutritious as possible, which is what the recipes in this chapter are all about. By cutting back on sugar and adding fruit (and even vegetables) where possible, there's no reason your baking should cause you any guilt.

If you're looking to bring your children into the kitchen to teach them some cooking basics, the recipes in this chapter might be the best place to start. There's something about making cupcakes or biscuits that seems to captivate every age.

Roasted rhubarb and strawberry

Serves 4

If you have any space in your garden, rhubarb is a super-easy plant to grow, and can be used in so many ways in the kitchen, from pies and compotes, to jams and this lovely dessert. Rhubarb can be quite tart, so feel free to adjust the honey or maple syrup quantities – you can add a little more at the end of cooking, if needed.

1 bunch (about 300 g/10½ oz) rhubarb, leaves removed
1–2 tablespoons honey or maple syrup (honey is not suitable for babies under 12 months)
250 g (9 oz/1⅔ cups) strawberries
Whole-egg custard (page 188), to serve (or use plain yoghurt for an egg-free option; omit for dairy-free option)

Preheat the oven to 180°C (350°F). Line a baking dish with baking paper.

Cut the rhubarb stalks into 10 cm (4 inch) lengths. Place in the prepared baking dish. Drizzle over the honey or maple syrup. Roast in the oven for 15 minutes, or until just tender. Add the strawberries to the dish and cook for a further 3–5 minutes, or until tender.

Serve the warm roasted rhubarb and strawberries with custard or yoghurt.

Baby's serve: because this dish has a little added sugar, you should ideally wait until your baby is over 12 months before offering it to her. If you do give your baby a small taste (using the maple syrup, not the honey), you can purée until smooth or you can offer it as finger food.

Toddler's serve: serve as is, cut up as needed.

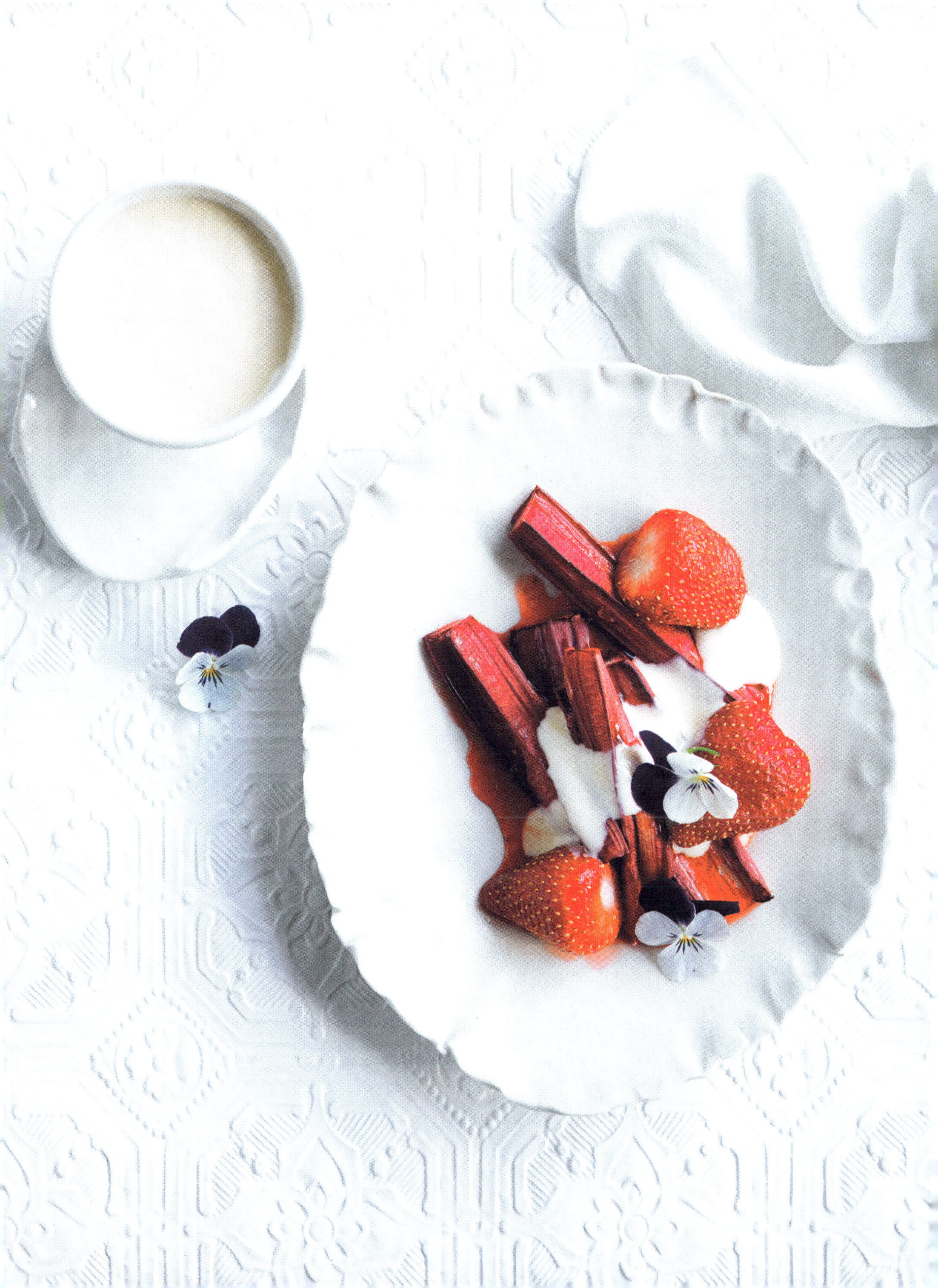

Poached pears with whole-egg custard

Serves 4–6

These poached pears are also lovely served with yoghurt – in many ways it allows you to enjoy the delicious cinnamon syrup more. But for most children, the simplicity of the chopped pear with custard is a firm favourite.

POACHED PEARS
250 ml (8½ fl oz/1 cup) fresh orange juice
2 tablespoons maple syrup
1 cinnamon stick
6 small Packham pears, peeled

WHOLE-EGG CUSTARD
3 eggs
1½ tablespoons maple syrup
1 tablespoon cornflour (cornstarch)
 (use a gluten-free brand if needed)
500 ml (17 fl oz/2 cups) milk
½ teaspoon natural vanilla extract

To make the poached pears, place the orange juice, maple syrup and cinnamon stick in a saucepan. Add the pears and 190 ml (6½ fl oz/¾ cup) water and bring to the boil. Reduce the heat to low, cover, and simmer for 45 minutes, turning occasionally, until the pears are tender. Use a slotted spoon to transfer the pears to a heatproof bowl.

Increase the heat to high and bring the pear cooking liquid to the boil. Cook, stirring occasionally, for 20 minutes or until the liquid becomes syrupy. Pour over the pears and set aside for 10 minutes to cool slightly.

Meanwhile, make the custard. Place the eggs, maple syrup and cornflour in a mixing bowl. Use a hand-held whisk to combine. Heat the milk and vanilla in a small saucepan until it is just starting to simmer. Slowly pour into the bowl with the egg mixture, whisking continuously until combined. Return to the saucepan and cook, stirring, over low heat for about 5 minutes, or until the mixture thickens and coats the back of a spoon. Remove from the heat. Strain to remove any lumps.

Serve the poached pears and syrup with the warm custard or yoghurt, if liked.

Baby's serve: because this dish does have some added sugar, you should ideally wait until your baby is over 12 months before offering it to her. If you do wish to give her a little taste, you can blend together some of the pear and custard until smooth, or cut up the pear into small pieces.

Toddler's serve: cut up the pear into small pieces and serve with the custard.

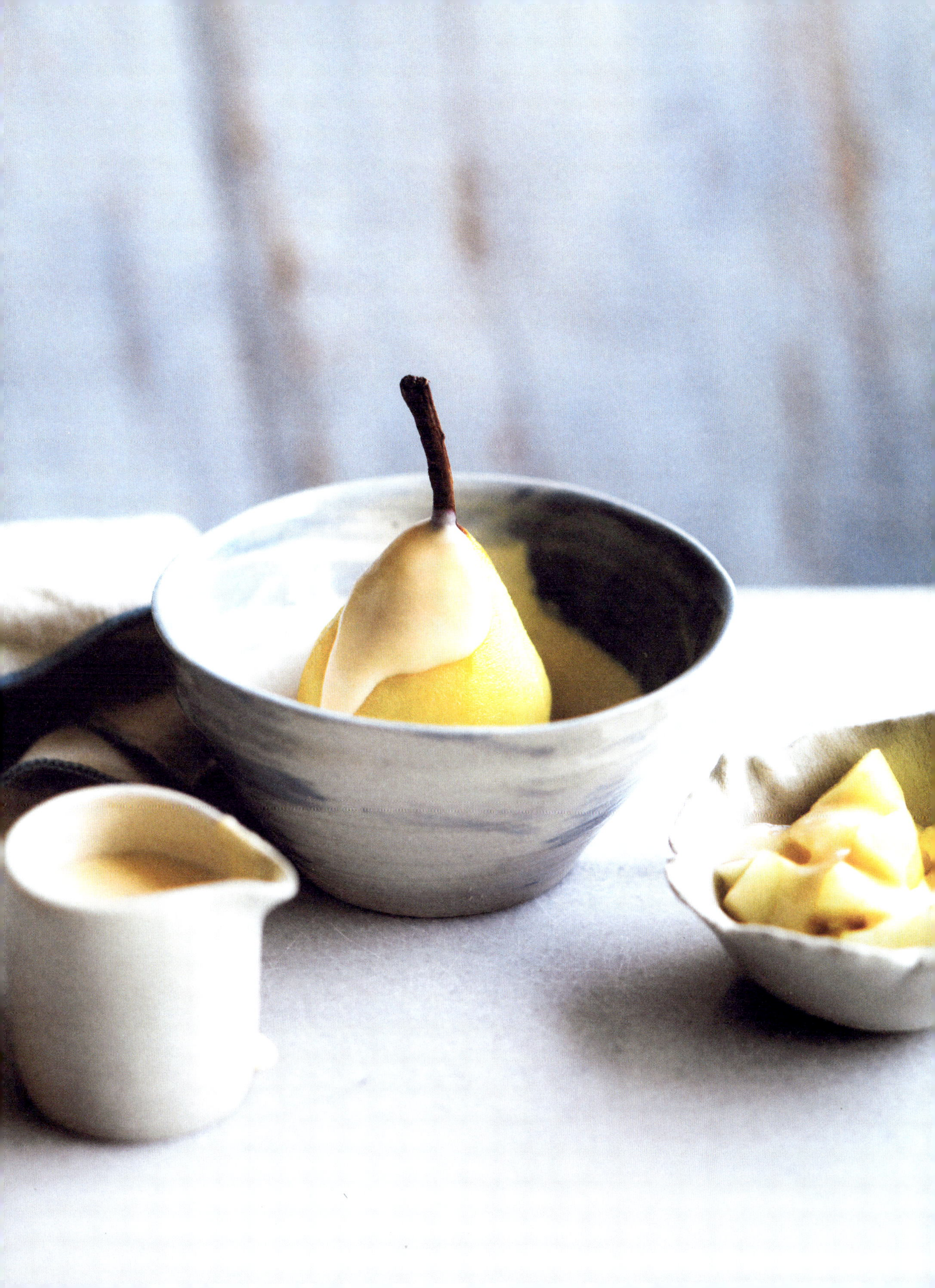

Peach almond crumble

Serves 4–6

One of my guilty pleasures is to make a crumble for dessert and then eat the leftovers for breakfast the next morning. While people often think of a crumble as an autumn or winter dessert, I also like to use stone fruits in the warmer months.

4–5 large ripe peaches, stones removed and flesh diced
2½ tablespoons brown or rapadura sugar (see note)
100 g (3½ oz/1 cup) rolled oats
50 g (1¾ oz/⅓ cup) wholemeal (whole-wheat) plain (all-purpose) flour
50 g (1¾ oz) flaked almonds
2 tablespoons desiccated (shredded) coconut
½ teaspoon ground cinnamon
80 g (2¾ oz) butter, diced
plain yoghurt (optional), to serve

Note *Rapadura sugar comes from the dried whole natural juice of the sugar cane. Because it's not separated from its molasses content, it retains its natural nutrients. Brown sugar, on the other hand, typically has the molasses stripped out and then some of it is added back in. It also tends to be cheaper and more readily available. Nutritionally, the difference between them is not immense, but if you want a less processed sugar, rapadura is a good option. When purchasing, take note of its country of origin. It can be difficult to source local rapadura sugar, so you might prefer to choose brown to avoid using an imported product.*

Preheat the oven to 180°C (350°F).

Place the peach in a 1 litre (34 fl oz/4 cup) capacity ovenproof dish. Toss through 1 tablespoon of the sugar. Set aside.

In a mixing bowl, combine the rolled oats, flour, almonds, coconut, cinnamon and remaining sugar. Using your fingertips, rub in the butter until well combined. Sprinkle the crumble over the peaches and bake in the oven for 20–25 minutes, or until the crumble is golden and the peaches are tender. Serve warm on its own or with yoghurt (if using).

Baby's serve: this crumble does have a little added sugar so you should ideally wait until your baby is over 12 months before offering it to her. However, a small taste as an occasional treat, with some yoghurt stirred through, is a nice way to include her in family mealtimes. You can blend or mash it to the right consistency.

Toddler's serve: simply serve as is with some custard or yoghurt.

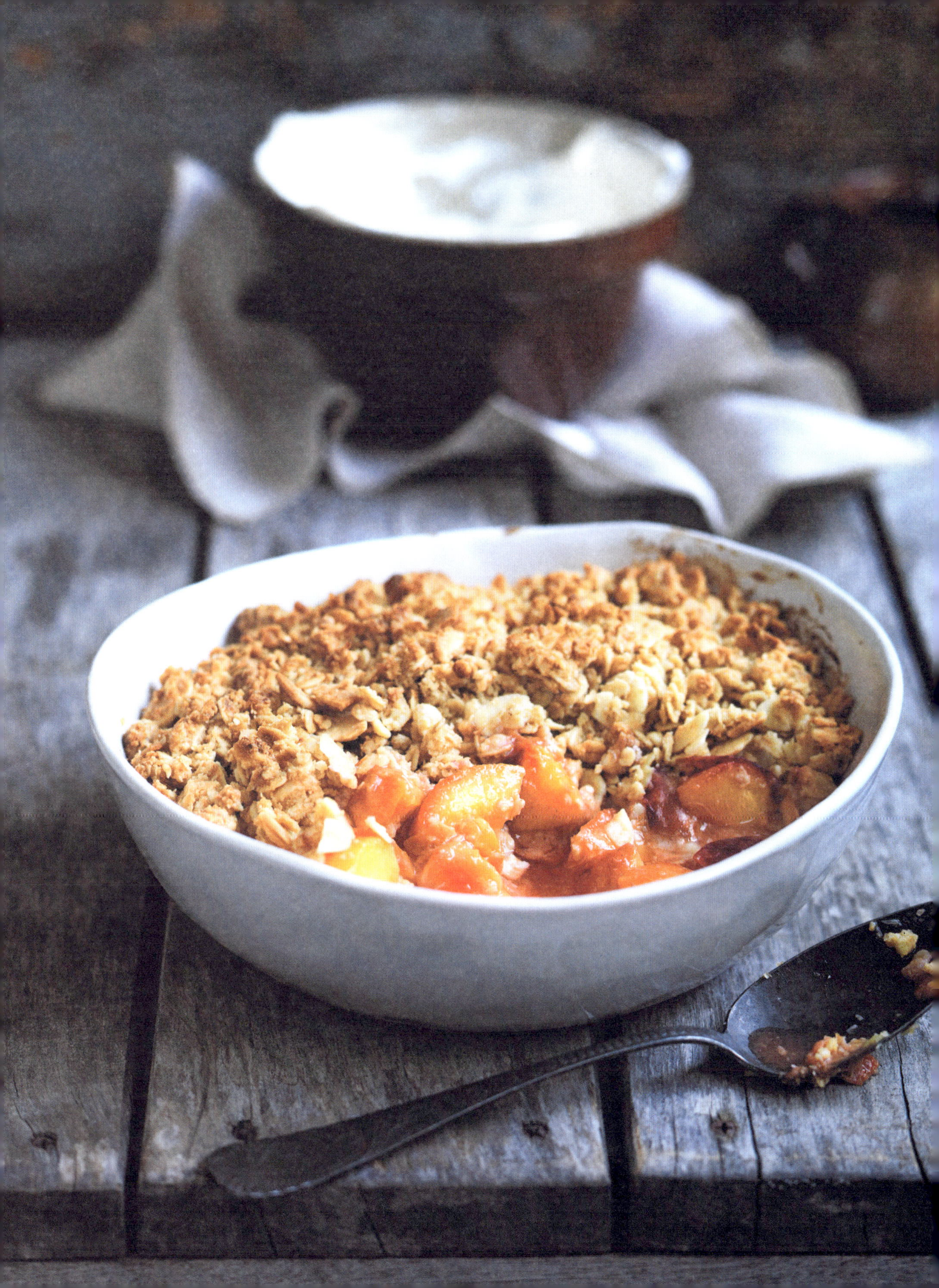

By cooking with your children, you're opening their eyes to the extraordinary potential of the kitchen and equipping them with one of life's most precious skills — being able to prepare themselves a meal.

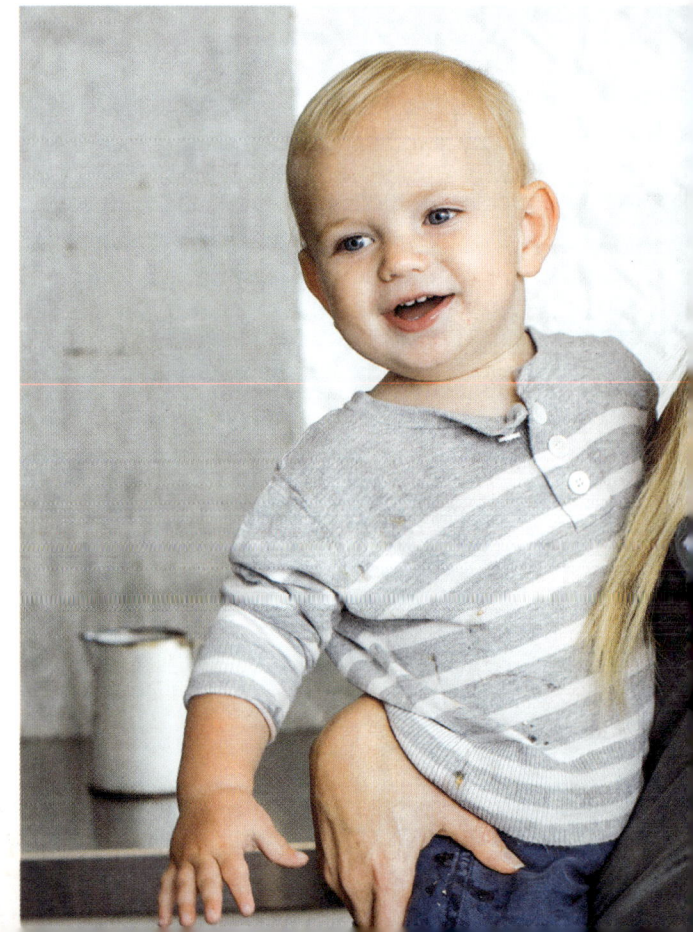

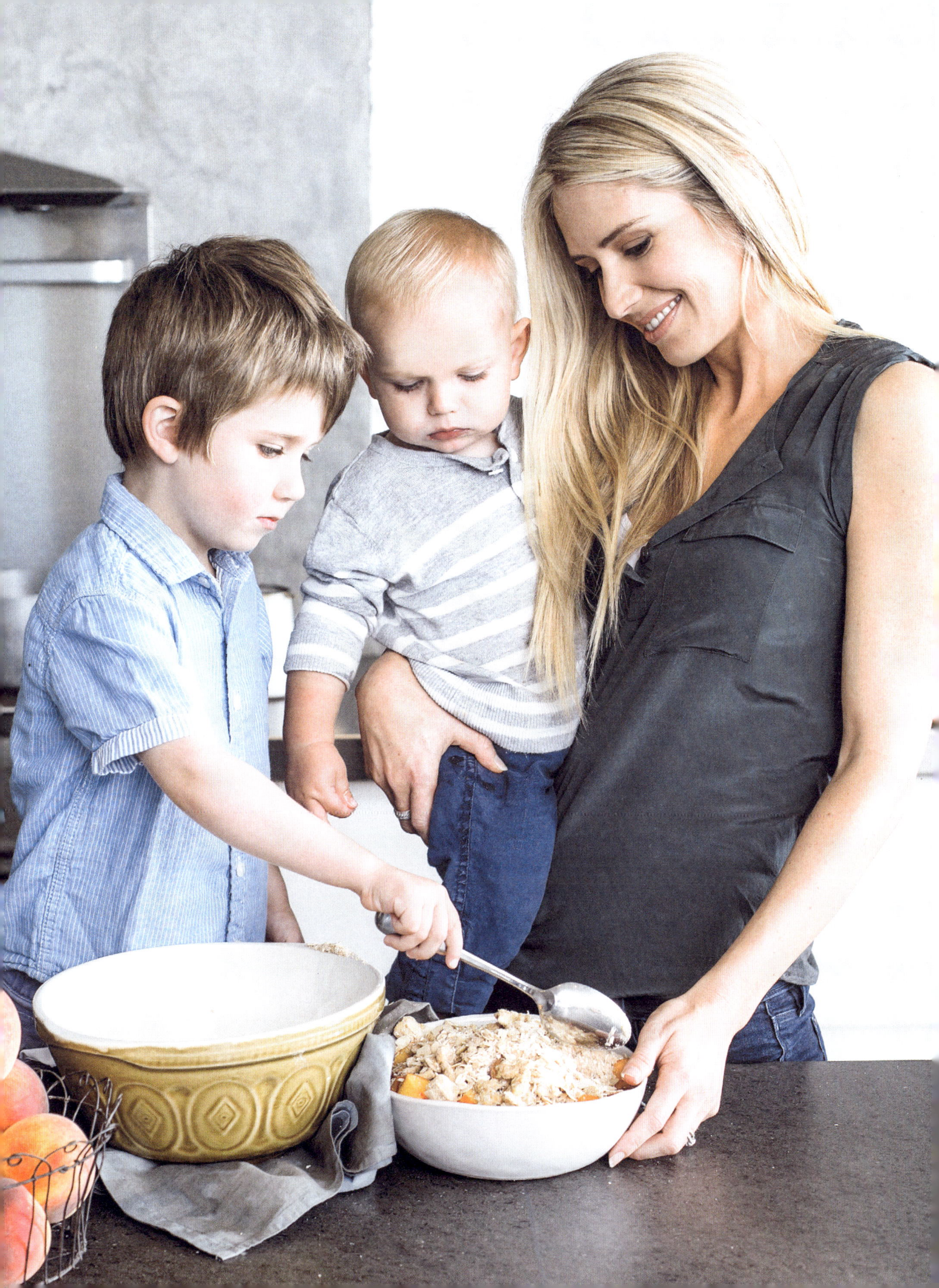

Cardamom rosemary baked custards

Serves 6

If I was living on a desert island and had to choose five dishes to survive on for the rest of my life, this would be one of them. Served warm or cold, the flavours are ridiculously good. Sometimes I even sneak one for breakfast.

Take care not to overcook them – either with the oven too hot or leaving them in too long – or they may start to 'weep' and won't retain their lovely, silky texture. They also go well with the Spiced fruit compote on page 50.

625 ml (21 fl oz/2½ cups) milk
3 cardamom pods, lightly crushed
2 rosemary sprigs
2 eggs
2 egg yolks
60 ml (2 fl oz/¼ cup) maple syrup (optional – omit for baby's serve)
ground cardamom or cinnamon, to serve

Baby's serve: because these custards do have some added sugar, you should ideally wait until your baby is over 12 months before offering some to her. Alternatively, you can make her a maple-free option or just give her a small taste.

Toddler's serve: serve as is.

Place the milk, cardamom pods and rosemary sprigs in a saucepan and bring to scalding point (just below the boil). Remove from the heat and set aside for 20 minutes.

Preheat the oven to 160°C (320°F).

Place the eggs, yolks and maple syrup (if using) in a bowl and whisk until well combined. Pour the mixture through a sieve to strain, then slowly add the milk mixture and whisk gently to combine.

Strain the mixture into a jug and divide between six 170 ml (5½ fl oz/⅔ cup) ramekins or small bowls. Place the ramekins in a deep baking dish and pour in enough hot water to come halfway up the sides of the ramekins. Bake for 35 minutes – you can test if the custard is set by inserting a knife into the centre; it should come out clean. The custard will still have a slight wobble and a softness when set.

Serve the custards warm or cool dusted with ground cardamom or cinnamon.

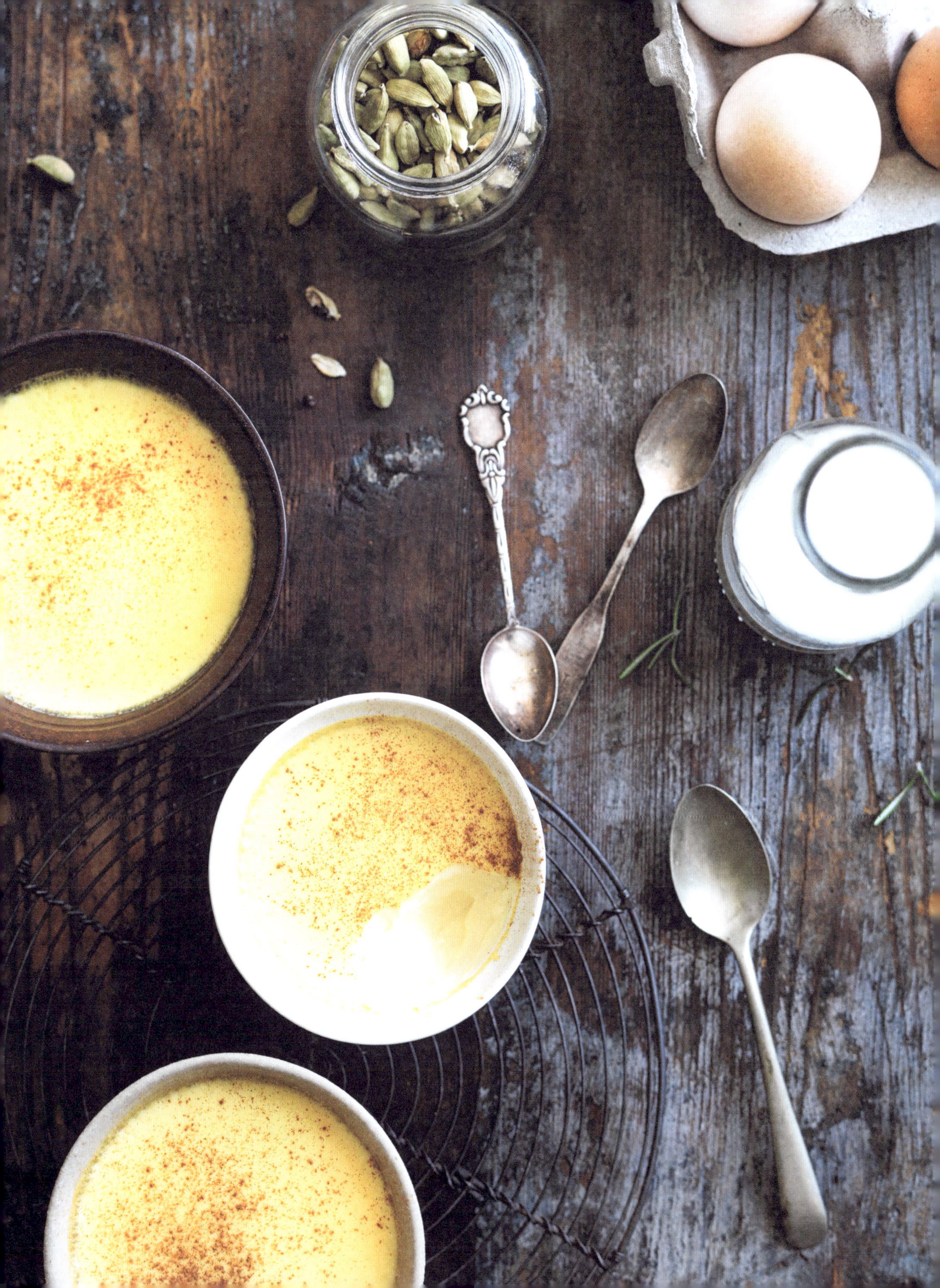

Yoghurt panna cotta with mango

Makes 8

Traditional panna cotta is loaded with sugar and cream. These are a much healthier option made with milk and yoghurt, and sweetened with a little maple syrup. Don't be fooled by their fanciness – they are honestly one of the simplest desserts to make. If you want to make a sugar-free version, simply omit the maple syrup.

340 ml (11½ fl oz/1⅓ cups) milk
2 tablespoons maple syrup (optional – omit for baby's serve)
3 teaspoons powdered gelatine
600 g (1 lb 5 oz) Greek-style or plain yoghurt
1 teaspoon natural vanilla extract
fresh mango, peeled, stone removed and flesh sliced, to serve

MANGO PURÉE
1–2 mangoes, peeled and stones removed
1 tablespoon maple syrup (optional – omit for baby's serve)

To make the mango purée, place the mango and maple syrup in a food processor and process until smooth. Refrigerate until needed.

Place the milk and maple syrup in a saucepan over low heat. Heat gently for about 6 minutes, stirring occasionally until hot but not quite simmering – do not allow to boil. Remove from the heat and sprinkle in the gelatine. Whisk until the gelatine dissolves, then set aside for 10 minutes to cool.

Place the yoghurt and vanilla in a large bowl and stir to combine. Slowly strain the milk mixture into the yoghurt mixture and stir well. Pour the mixture into eight 125 ml (4 fl oz/½ cup) moulds and refrigerate for at least 3 hours, or until set.

To serve, run a small knife or spatula around the side of each mould and turn out the panna cotta onto serving plates. Serve with fresh mango and a drizzle of mango purée.

Baby's serve: leave out the maple syrup for your baby's serve. Simply serve as is with the mango purée, mashing the panna cotta a little if needed.

Toddler's serve: serve as is.

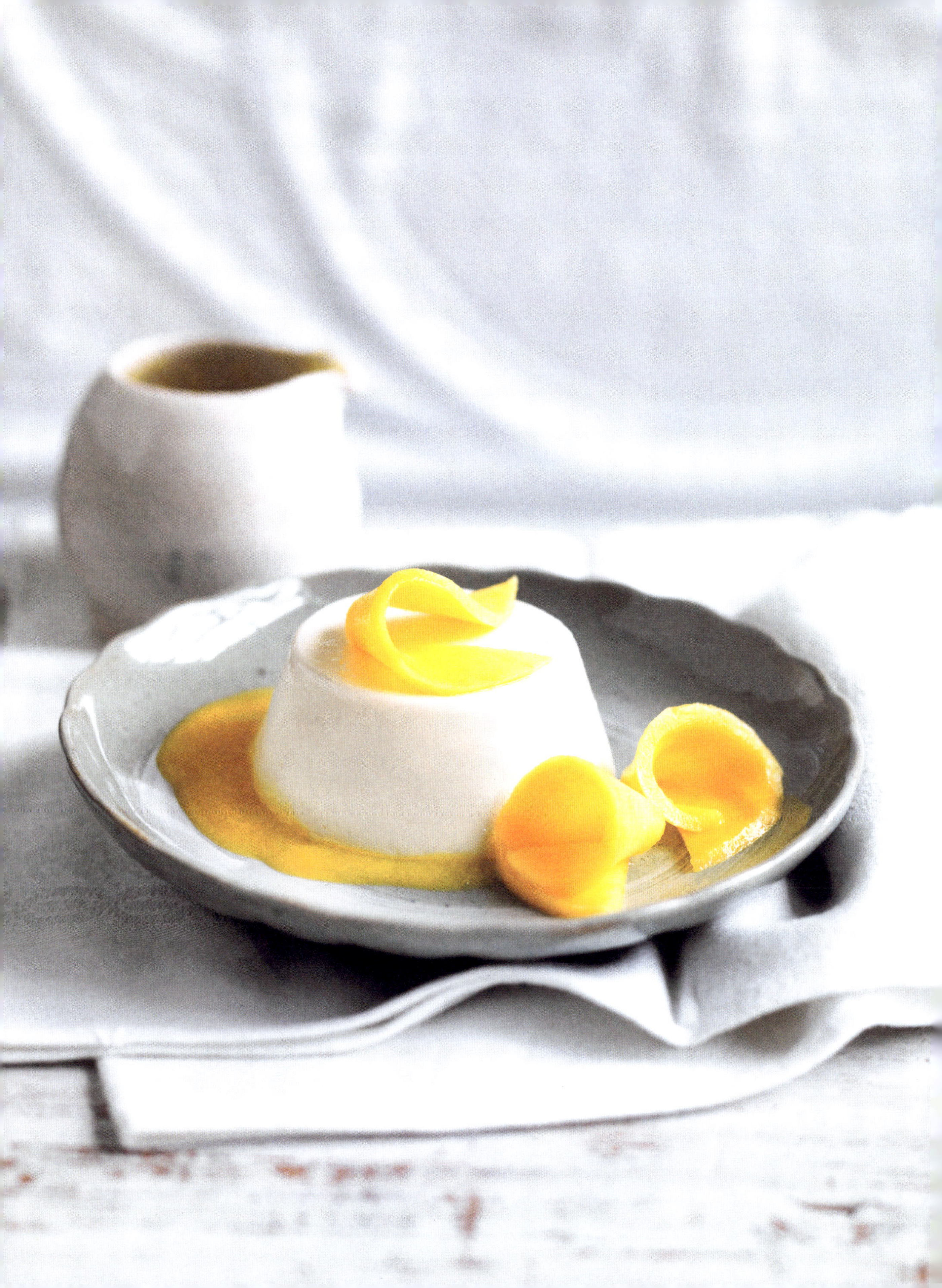

Black coconut rice

Serves 4–5

This is a cheat's version of a black coconut rice pudding, which is typically made with palm sugar (jaggery). This version is infinitely easier to make and I think the taste is just as lovely. It makes the perfect ending to a Thai meal – you might like to have it after the Thai green chicken curry with eggplant on page 162.

200 g (7 oz/1 cup) black rice
1 tablespoon maple syrup, plus extra to drizzle (optional – omit for baby's serve)
200 g (7 oz) coconut yoghurt (choose a dairy-free brand if needed)
sliced banana, to serve
black sesame seeds or toasted coconut, to serve

Cook the rice according to the packet instructions (use the absorption method). Set aside a small serving of rice for baby. Add the maple syrup (if using) to the remaining rice, stirring until well combined.

Divide the rice mixture among serving glasses or bowls. Top with the coconut yoghurt, banana slices and black sesame seeds or toasted coconut. Drizzle over a little extra maple syrup, if liked.

Note Black rice is sometimes called 'forbidden rice' – it is believed to have once been set aside solely for the Chinese emperor, because of its health benefits. Black rice is packed with anthocyanins, the same antioxidants that give blueberries their colour. While research is still unfolding, it is believed anthocyanins may have potent disease-fighting properties.

Baby's serve: mix your baby's rice with coconut yoghurt and black sesame seeds. For a **younger baby**, blend until smooth or simply serve as is. For an **older baby**, serve as is.

Toddler's serve: serve as is.

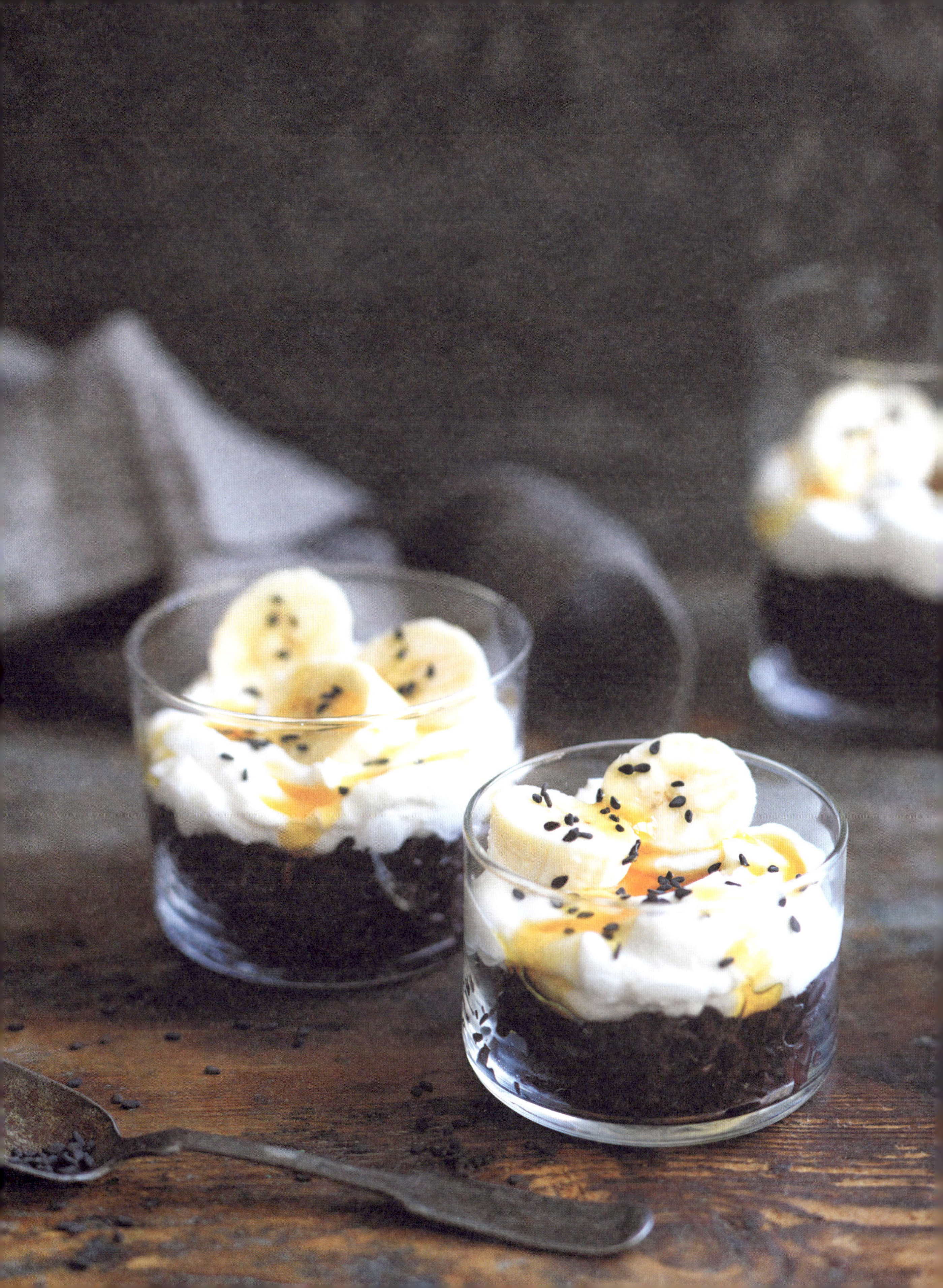

Banana date puddings

Serves 6

These individual puddings are a healthier take on the traditional and much-loved sticky date pudding. Served with a splash of cream or custard, they've got just the right amount of sweetness and gooeyness to please everyone at the table.

I adore hazelnut oil and use it wherever I can, but it can be a bit pricey and tricky to source, so feel free to use olive oil instead.

50 g (1¾ oz) whole hazelnuts
160 g (5½ oz/1 cup) fresh pitted dates, chopped
1 teaspoon bicarbonate of soda (baking soda)
2 large bananas, chopped
125 g (4½ oz/⅔ cup lightly packed) brown or rapadura sugar (see note, page 190)
80 ml (2½ fl oz/⅓ cup) hazelnut or olive oil
185 g (6½ oz/1¼ cups) self-raising flour
cream or Whole-egg custard (page 188) (optional), to serve

Baby's serve: because these puddings do have some added sugar, you should ideally wait until your baby is over 12 months before offering some to her.

Toddler's serve: serve as is, cutting up as needed.

Preheat the oven to 180°C (350°F). Grease six 375 ml (12½ fl oz/1½ cup) ramekins or small ovenproof bowls and place a small square of baking paper in the base of each.

Place the hazelnuts on a baking tray and cook for 8 minutes, or until lightly toasted. Finely chop and set aside.

Place the dates, bicarbonate of soda and 310 ml (10½ fl oz/1¼ cups) boiling water in a bowl. Leave to stand for 5 minutes. Transfer to a food processor and add the banana, sugar and oil. Process until almost smooth. Add the flour and pulse for 2–3 seconds until just combined. Divide the mixture between the prepared ramekins or bowls. Top each with some of the chopped hazelnuts.

Bake for 40–50 minutes, or until a skewer inserted in the centre of the puddings comes out clean. (Place a sheet of foil over the puddings if they start to get too brown during cooking.)

Serve the warm puddings in their bowls with cream or custard, if liked.

Desserts and baking

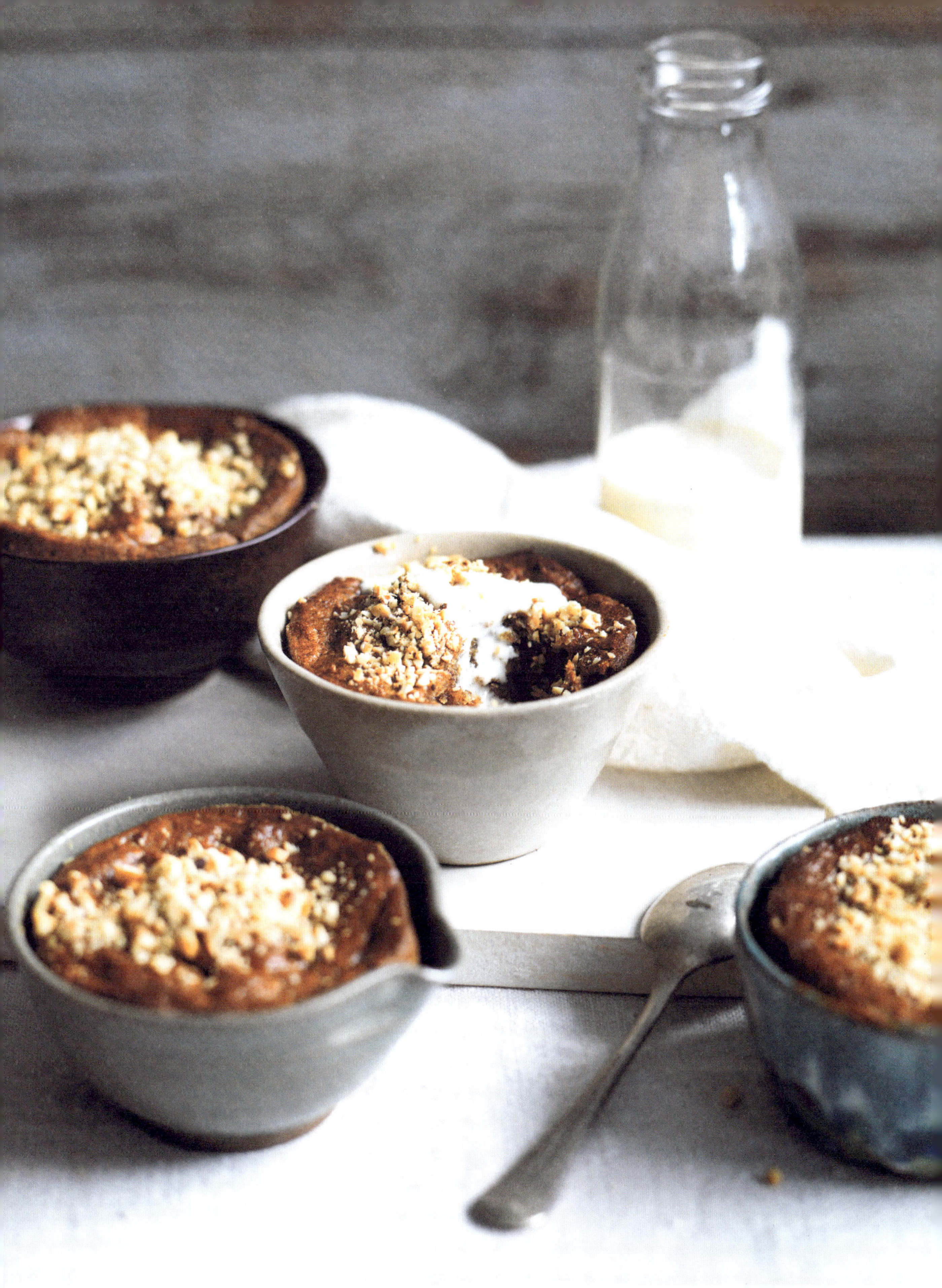

Stone fruit almond tarts

Serves 8

Despite looking rather impressive, these lovely individual tarts couldn't be simpler to prepare. I even let my four-year-old son help me if I'm feeling patient. You can use whichever stone fruits you have on hand.

The apricot glaze is not essential, but it does give a lovely shiny finish (see note).

2 sheets frozen puff pastry, just thawed
2 tablespoons ground almonds
1–2 nectarines, stones removed and flesh sliced
2 plums, stones removed and flesh sliced
2 apricots, stones removed and flesh sliced
100 g (3½ oz) fresh raspberries
redcurrants, to serve (optional)
maple syrup, to serve

Tip *If you'd like your pastry edges to have a shiny glaze, melt 1 tablespoon apricot jam in the microwave until it is a syrupy consistency and brush the edges as soon as the tarts come out of the oven.*

Preheat the oven to 190°C (375°F). Line a baking tray with baking paper. Cut out eight pastry circles – each with a 12 cm (4¾ inch) diameter. Place on the prepared tray.

Sprinkle 1 teaspoon of ground almonds over each pastry base, leaving a 5 mm (¼ inch) border around the edges. Arrange the sliced stone fruit in overlapping circles over the ground almonds. Top with the raspberries. (Prepare some fruit for your baby at the same time – put some additional diced stone fruit and raspberries in a small baking dish.) Bake the tarts (and baby's fruit) for 12–15 minutes, or until the pastry is golden and the fruit is tender.

To serve, place the warm tarts on serving plates. Top some of the tarts with redcurrants (if using) and drizzle over some maple syrup.

Baby's serve: prepare the baked fruit as per baby's serve in the recipe. For a **younger baby**, purée the baked fruit until smooth, adding as much liquid (water or your baby's milk) as needed to achieve the desired consistency. If it is a little tart, you can mix it with a sweeter purée such as apple or some Whole-egg custard (page 188). For an **older baby**, keep the purée more textured or simply serve as is, cut up as needed.

Toddler's serve: prepare as per baby's serve in the recipe or serve as is, cut up as needed.

Desserts and baking

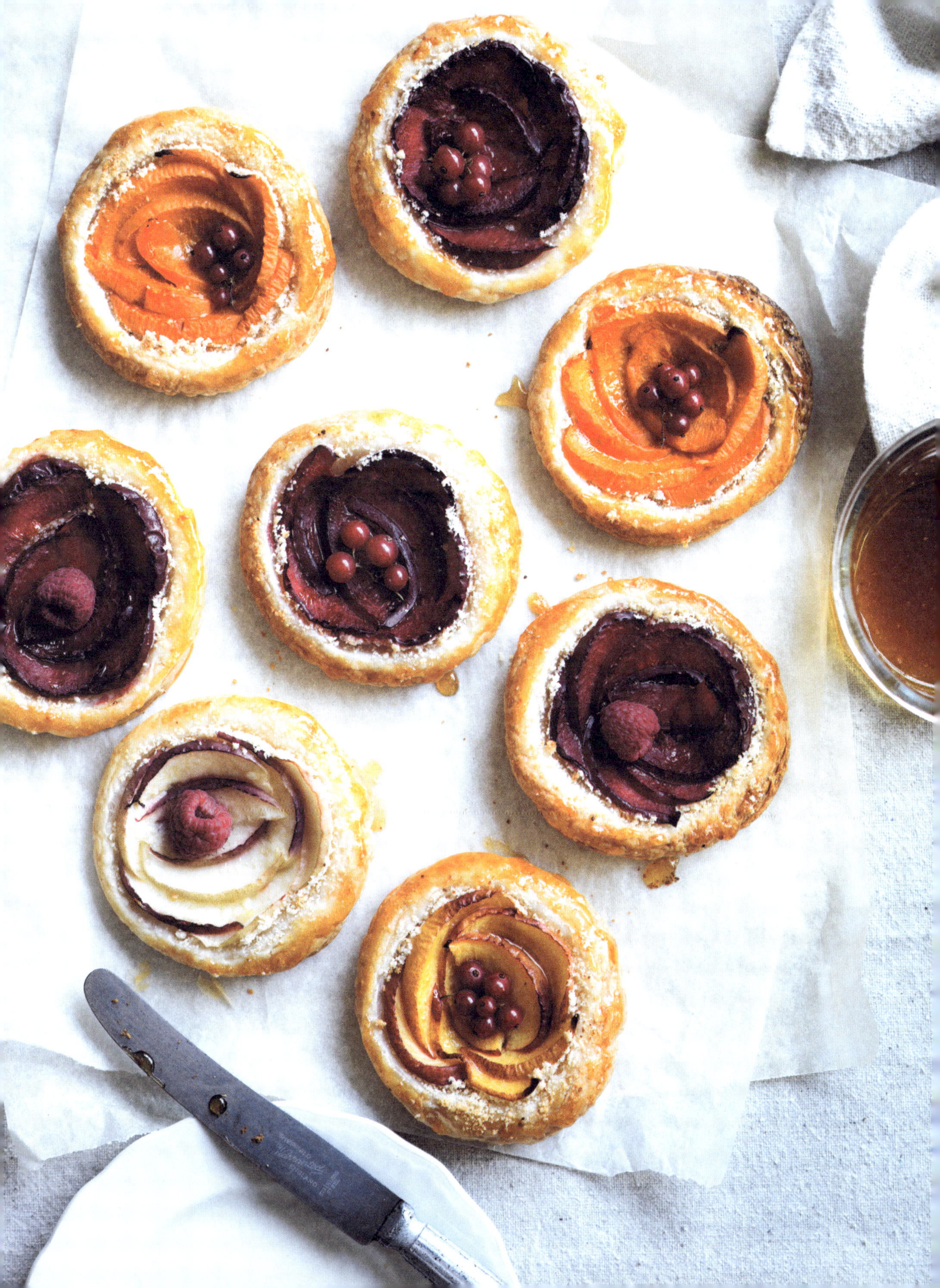

Strawberry jellies

Makes 3 large jellies or 8 small jellies

I buy a lovely good-quality apple and strawberry juice from my local supermarket to make these jellies. However, if you're not able to source it, any other clear juice will work, such as apple and blackcurrant. Similarly, you can use other types of fresh fruit if you prefer (except for pineapple, kiwi fruit and papaya, because they contain enzymes which prevent jelly from setting).

750 ml (25½ fl oz/3 cups) apple and strawberry juice
1 tablespoon powdered gelatine
12 strawberries, hulled and sliced, plus extra to serve
whipped cream, to serve (optional – omit for dairy-free option)

Tip *If you're not fussed about layering the strawberries through the jelly, you can simply place the strawberries in the moulds and then fill the moulds with the jelly mixture.*

Place 125 ml (4 fl oz/½ cup) of the juice in a bowl and microwave for about 45 seconds, or until hot. Sprinkle the gelatine into the hot juice and stir until dissolved. Add the remaining juice and stir well.

One-quarter fill three large or eight small jelly moulds and refrigerate until just set – this may take up to a few hours. Keep the remaining juice mixture at room temperature so it doesn't start setting.

Add some of the sliced strawberries to the moulds over the already-set jelly and pour over a little more juice mixture. Return the moulds to the refrigerator until just set. Continue layering until the strawberries and jelly mixture is used up. Refrigerate until completely set.

To serve, carefully turn each jelly from its mould and serve with whipped cream and extra fresh strawberries, if liked.

Baby's serve: there is no point blending these jellies because the texture will be lost, so wait until your child can manage larger pieces of fruit before offering them to her. You can cut up the strawberries into smaller pieces if you wish.

Toddler's serve: serve as is, cut into smaller pieces if needed.

Desserts and baking

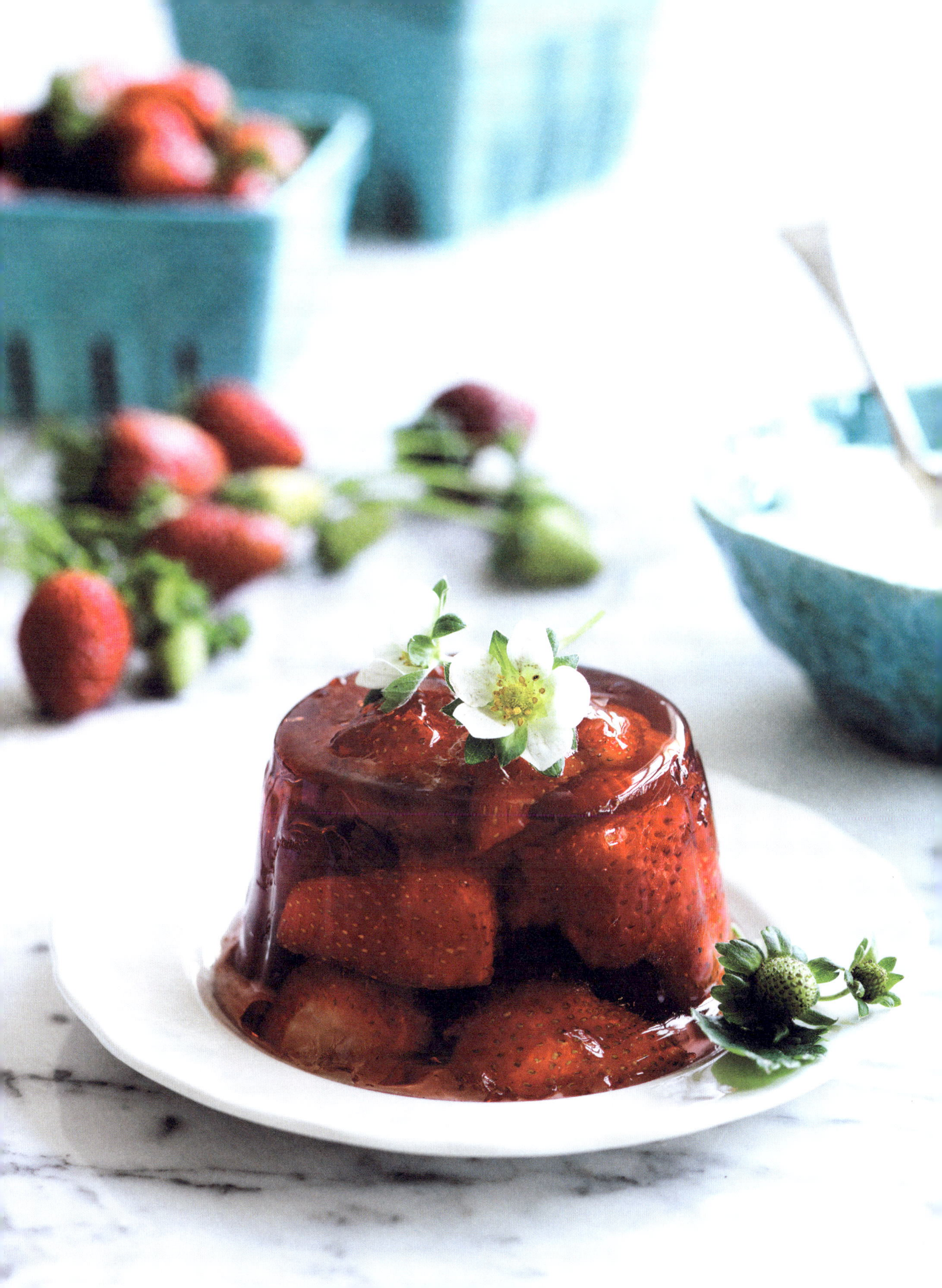

Pink grapefruit raspberry ices

Makes 6–12

These are great to make with your children in the summer months to help fill the seemingly endless school holidays.

If your child isn't keen on pink grapefruit, you can switch to fresh orange juice or whichever other juice she prefers. Sometimes I also add a splash of rosewater to the pink grapefruit juice for a deliciously different iceblock – it's a lovely way to introduce your child to a new flavour.

625 ml (21 fl oz/2½ cups) freshly squeezed pink grapefruit juice
3 tablespoons maple syrup
24 raspberries, washed

Stir together the grapefruit juice and maple syrup with 125 ml (4 fl oz/½ cup) water.

Place half of the raspberries in the bottom of six 125 ml (4 fl oz/½ cup) iceblock moulds or use twelve 60 ml (2 fl oz/¼ cup) moulds.

Pour half the grapefruit mixture into the moulds over the berries and freeze for 1–2 hours, or until partially frozen. Repeat with remaining raspberries and grapefruit mixture. Freeze overnight or until frozen solid. (If you are using iceblock sticks, you will need to freeze the second round of mixture for 1–2 hours until partially frozen, insert the sticks, then return to the freezer overnight.)

Baby's serve: if you like, you can make a maple-free version of these for your baby, but they might be a little sour for her. Switching the grapefruit juice for freshly squeezed orange juice will make a naturally sweeter iceblock. Many babies will find these too cold and you might prefer to wait until your baby is over 12 months before offering them to her.

Toddler's serve: serve as is.

Desserts and baking

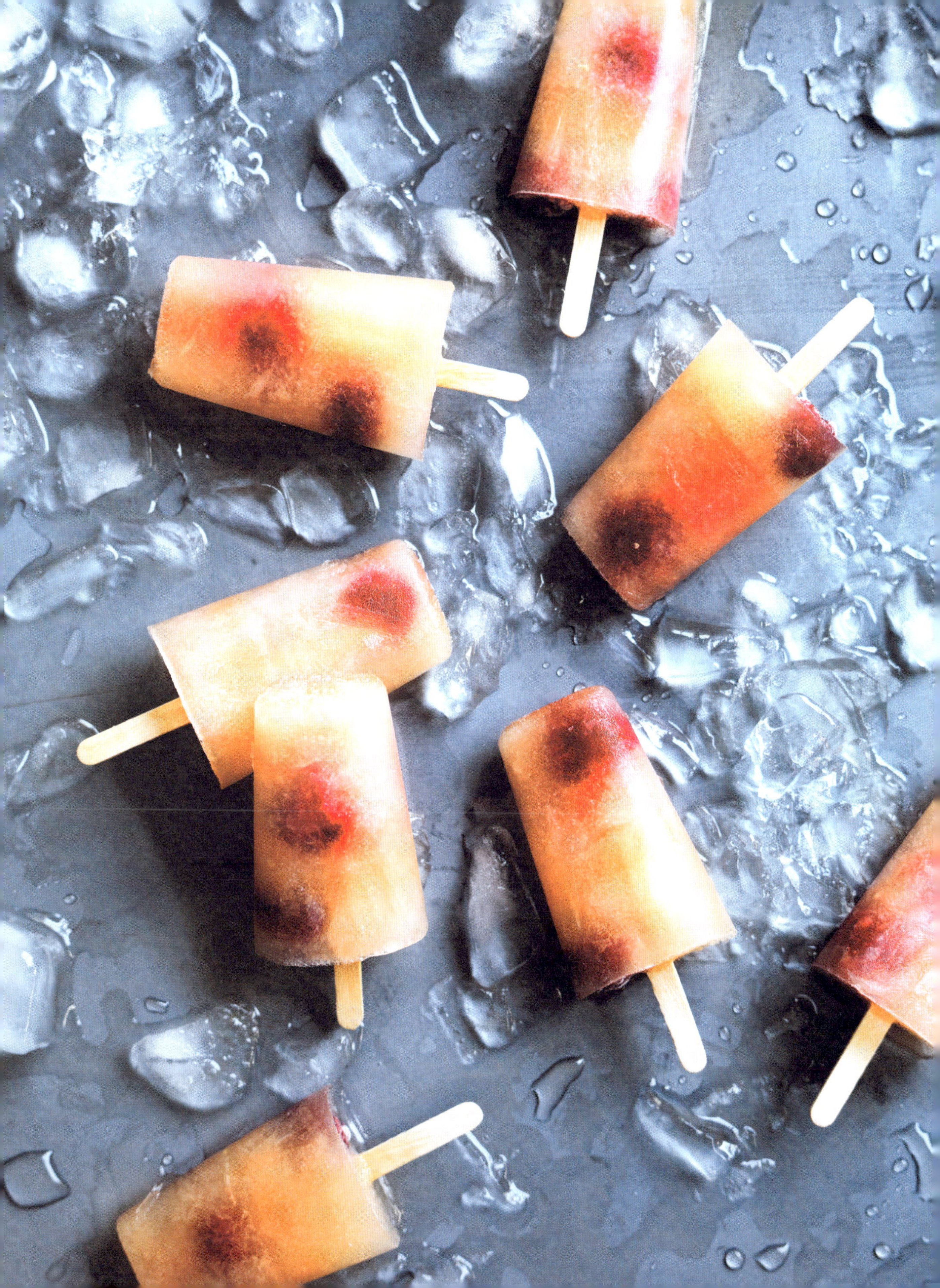

Carrot quinoa muffins

Makes 15

With a serving of carrot and quinoa, these are definitely one of the healthier sweet treats you can give your child. Don't worry – their nutrition credentials don't stop them from being really delicious. My husband often requests a batch because he likes them as a work snack.

You can also turn them into cupcakes with the lemon cream cheese icing from page 226.

65 g (2¼ oz/⅓ cup) white quinoa
4 eggs
150 g (5½ oz/⅔ cup) brown or rapadura sugar (see note, page 190)
190 ml (6½ fl oz/¾ cup) olive oil (see note)
310 g (11 oz/2 cups) grated carrot
55 g (2 oz/⅓ cup) chopped pitted dates (optional)
225 g (8 oz/1½ cups) self-raising flour
1 teaspoon ground cinnamon
1 teaspoon mixed (pumpkin pie) spice

Tip *When selecting an oil for these muffins, you might prefer to use a lighter option, as the taste of some olive oils such as extra-virgin olive oil, can be a little strong.*

Preheat the oven to 180°C (350°F). Line 15 muffin holes with paper or silicone cases.

Place the quinoa in a small saucepan with 125 ml (4 fl oz/½ cup) water. Bring to the boil, then reduce the heat to low, cover, and cook for 12–15 minutes, or until tender. There should be no excess moisture, but if there is, drain well and set aside.

In a mixing bowl, whisk together the eggs, sugar and oil. Stir in the carrot, dates (if using) and reserved quinoa. Add the flour and spices, and gently stir to combine.

Divide the mixture among the muffin holes and bake for about 20 minutes, or until a skewer inserted into the centre of the muffins comes out clean. Leave in the tin for 5 minutes, before transferring to a wire rack to cool.

The muffins can be stored in an airtight container and also freeze well.

Baby's serve: because these muffins do have some added sugar, you should ideally wait until your baby is over 12 months before offering some to her.

Toddler's serve: serve as is, cutting up as needed.

Desserts and baking

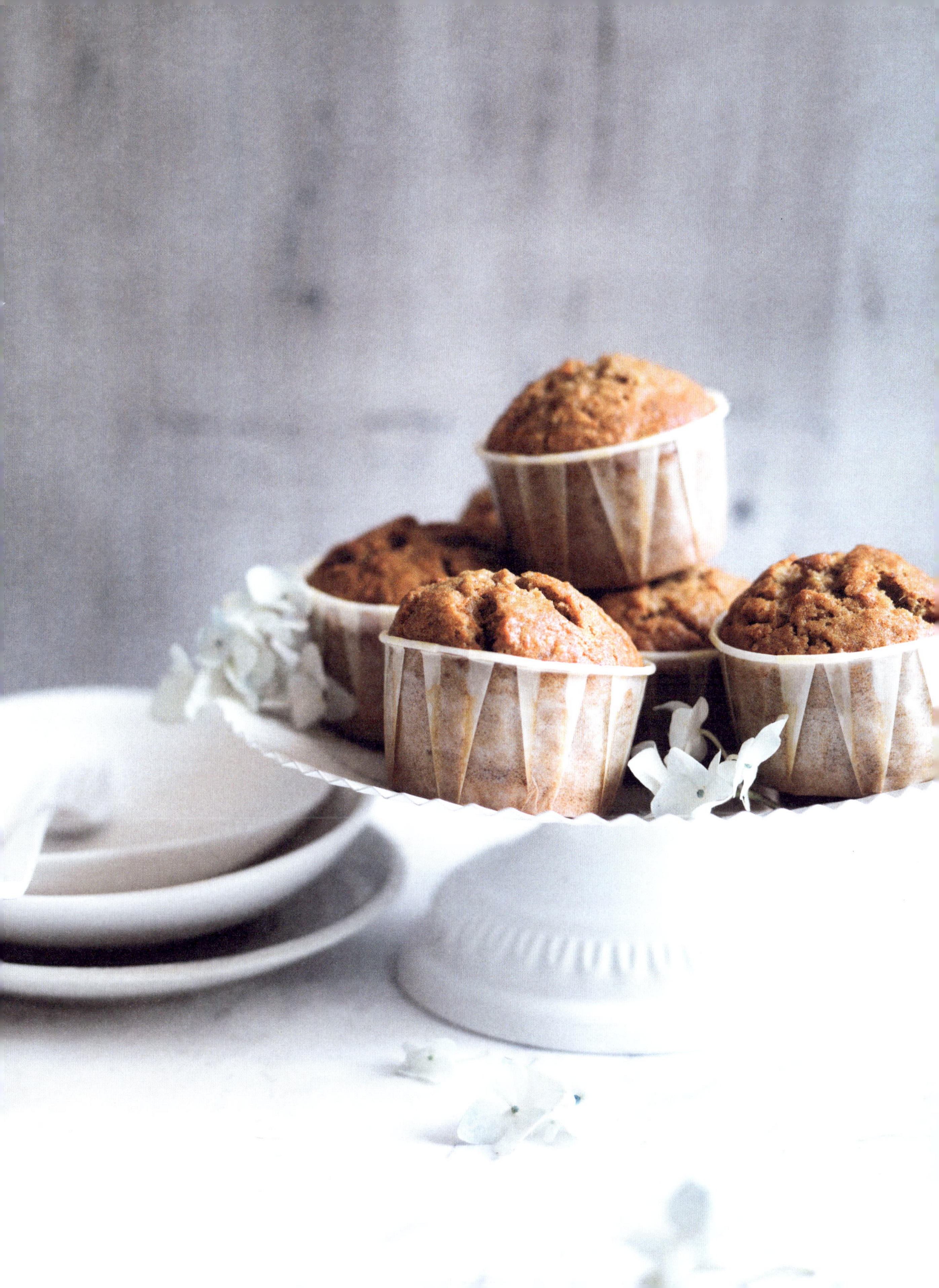

Banana, hazelnut and honey bread

Makes 1 loaf

Easy to make and totally delicious, you'll feel like a domestic goddess (or god) for having made your very own instead of picking it up from your local café. You can cut the loaf into thick slices, wrap them in plastic wrap (cling film) and freeze. Simply defrost and heat in the toaster or microwave when you're ready to eat.

- 225 g (8 oz/1½ cups) self-raising flour
- 50 g (1¾ oz/½ cup) ground hazelnuts
- 3 tablespoons brown or rapadura sugar (see note, page 190)
- ½ teaspoon ground cinnamon
- 240 g (8½ oz/1 cup) mashed banana (about 2 bananas)
- 60 ml (2 fl oz/¼ cup) milk
- 125 ml (4 fl oz/½ cup) hazelnut oil, olive oil or coconut oil
- 2 eggs, lightly beaten
- 2 tablespoons honey (honey is not suitable for babies under 12 months)
- 120 g (4½ oz/¾ cup) chopped pitted dates
- 2 tablespoons chopped hazelnuts (optional)

Tip *When selecting coconut oil, choose a virgin coconut oil. Coconut oil will turn from a liquid to a solid at 24°C (76°F), so if your oil has solidifed, gently melt it before using it.*

Preheat the oven to 170°C (340°F). Grease a 25 cm (10 inch) loaf (bar) tin. Line the base and the two longest sides with baking paper, leaving the ends overhanging to make it easier to remove the loaf from the tin.

Sift the flour into a mixing bowl and add the ground hazelnuts, sugar and cinnamon. Make a well in the centre and add the remaining ingredients, stirring until the mixture is just combined.

Pour the mixture into the prepared tin and bake for about 1 hour, or until a skewer inserted into the centre of the loaf comes out clean. Remove from the oven and leave in the tin for 5 minutes, before transferring to a wire rack to cool.

Cut the bread into slices and serve warm or cool.

Baby's serve: because this bread contains a little added sugar, wait until your baby is over 12 months before offering it to her. If you do wish to give her a small taste, use maple syrup in place of the honey.

Toddler's serve: serve as is, cut up as needed.

Desserts and baking

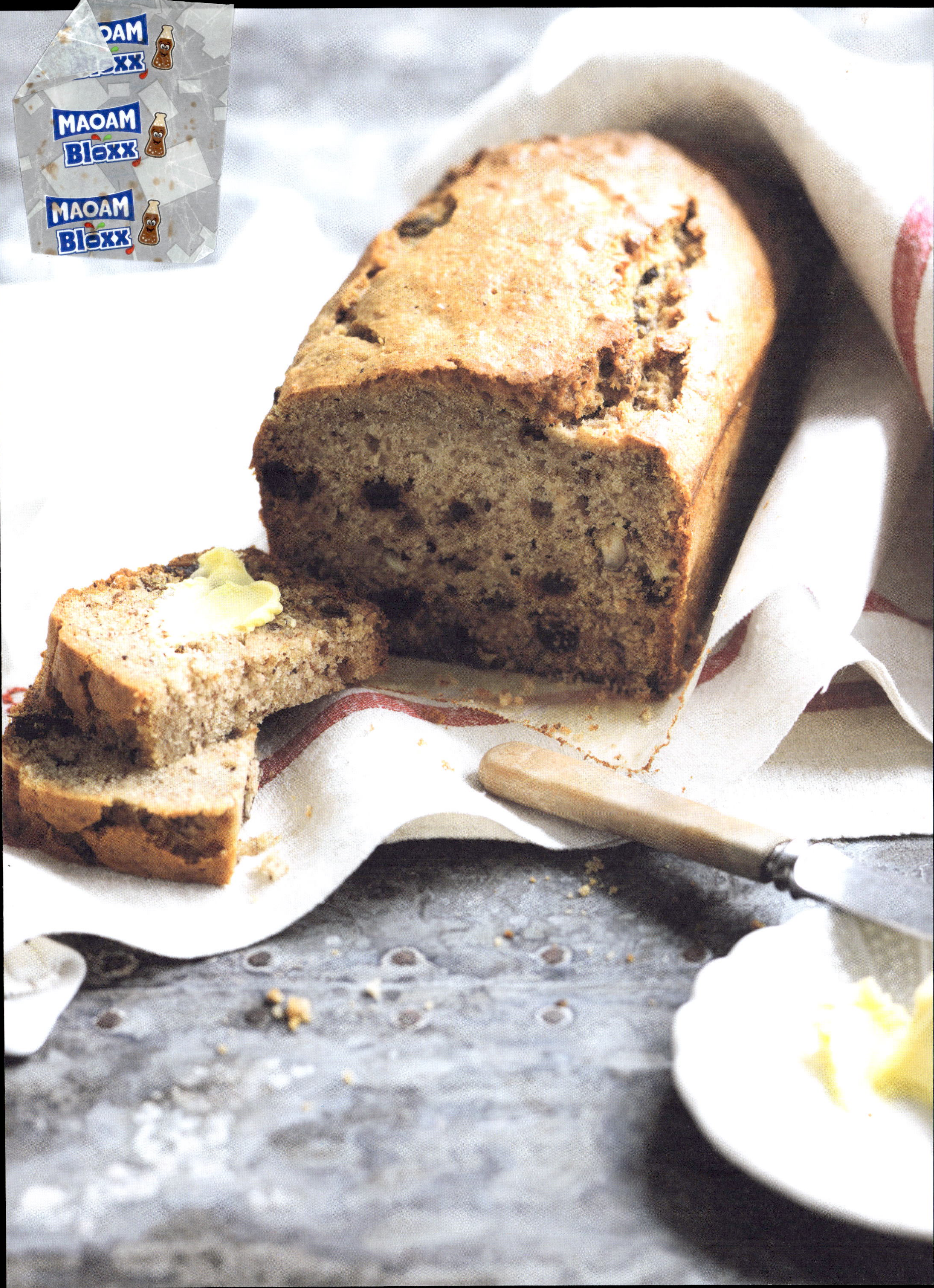

Pumpkin and walnut cupcakes

Makes 12

These are particularly moist and delicious cupcakes – the pumpkin flavour is barely noticeable. If you prefer, you can use lemon instead of orange for the icing. Alternatively, you can skip the icing altogether and eat them more like a muffin. If you'd like to freeze these, don't put the icing on until after they've thawed.

2 eggs
60 ml (2 fl oz/¼ cup) milk
100 g (3½ oz/½ cup) brown or rapadura sugar (see note, page 190)
125 ml (4 fl oz/½ cup) walnut oil, olive oil or coconut oil (see tip, page 210)
125 g (4½ oz/1 cup) grated pumpkin
55 g (2 oz/½ cup) ground almonds
40 g (1½ oz/⅓ cup) chopped walnuts (optional)
150 g (5½ oz/1 cup) wholemeal (whole-wheat) self-raising flour
½ teaspoon ground cinnamon or cardamom, or a mixture of both

ORANGE CREAM CHEESE ICING (FROSTING)
150 g (5½ oz) cream cheese, softened
40 g (1½ oz/⅓ cup) icing (confectioners') sugar, sifted
3 teaspoons fresh orange juice
finely grated zest of 1 orange (optional)

Baby's serve: because these cupcakes contain some added sugar, I recommend waiting until your baby is over 12 months before offering them to her. If you do wish to give her a small taste, skip the icing and offer them to her as a muffin, broken into pieces.

Toddler's serve: as with baby's serve, you may wish to skip the icing to avoid the extra sugar. Simply serve as is, cut up as needed.

Preheat the oven to 180°C (350°F). Line a twelve-hole muffin tin with paper or silicone cases.

In a mixing bowl, whisk together the eggs, milk, sugar and oil. Stir in the grated pumpkin, ground almonds and walnuts (if using). Add the flour and cinnamon, and stir until just combined.

Divide the mixture among the paper cases and bake for about 20 minutes, or until a skewer inserted into the centre of the cupcakes comes out clean. Leave in the tin for 5 minutes, before transferring to a wire rack to cool completely.

To make the orange cream cheese icing, beat the cream cheese, icing sugar and orange juice together in a mixing bowl until well combined and smooth. Add a little more orange juice if you like a stronger flavour.

Spread the icing over the top of the cooled cupcakes, topping each with a little orange zest, if liked. The cupcakes can be stored in an airtight container.

Tip: For a nut-free version you can replace the almonds with a ground seed mix (see tip on page 68).

Desserts and baking

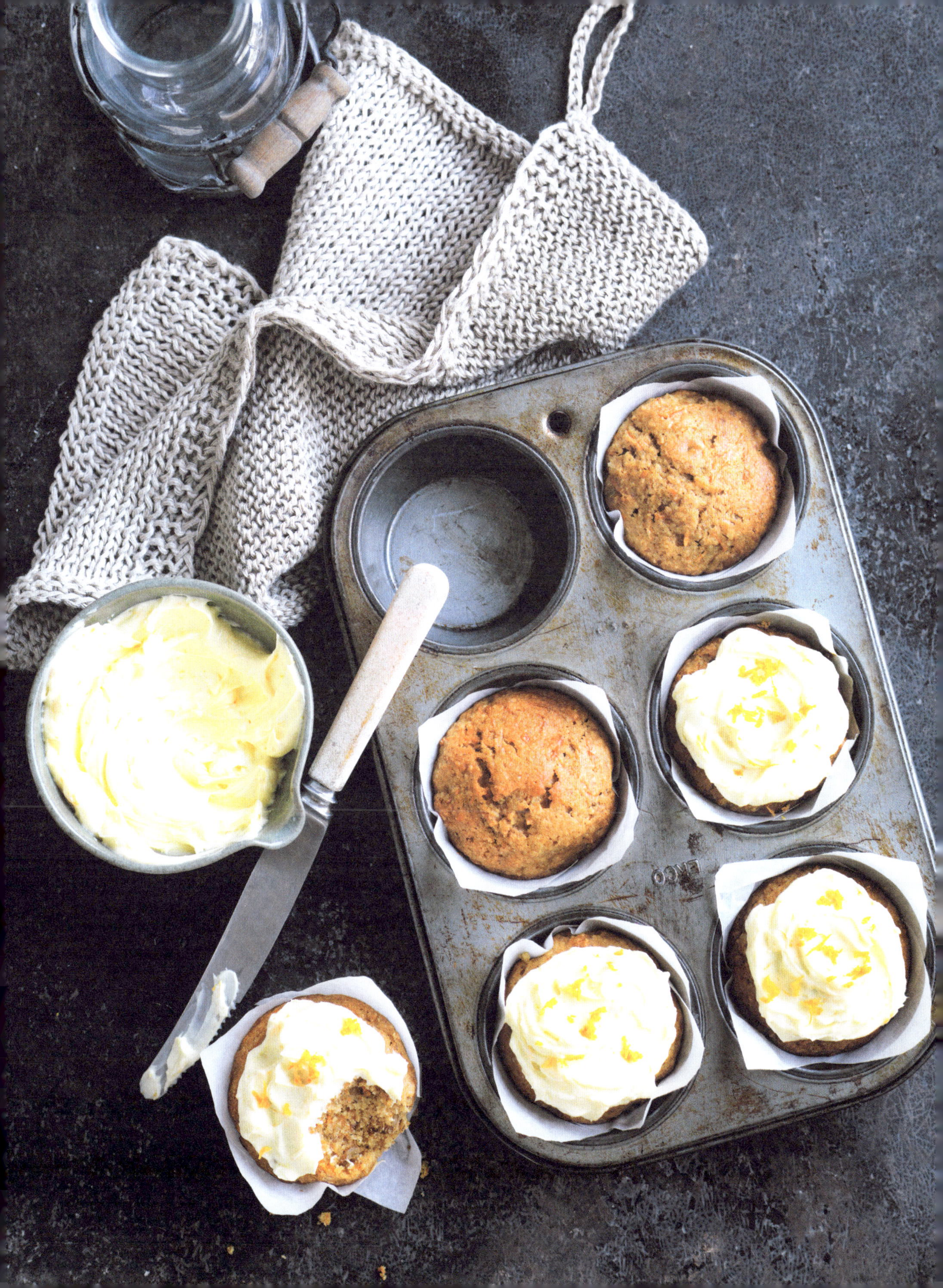

Chocolate beetroot cupcakes

Makes 15

These cupcakes are not too sweet – just perfect in my book, although the icing adds some extra sweetness. If you're having them without icing, feel free to add a dash of extra maple syrup, although I don't think they need it.

If you don't have wholemeal flour on hand, regular self-raising flour is also fine.

2 eggs
170 ml (5½ fl oz/⅔ cup) maple syrup
125 ml (4 fl oz/½ cup) olive oil or coconut oil (see tip, page 210)
225 g (8 oz) grated beetroot (beet)
2 tablespoons milk
225 g (8 oz/1½ cups) wholemeal (whole-wheat) self-raising flour
½ teaspoon baking powder
30 g (1 oz/¼ cup) cocoa powder

CHOCOLATE CREAM CHEESE ICING (FROSTING)
60 g (2 oz) butter, softened
125 g (4½ oz/½ cup) cream cheese, softened
90 g (3 oz/¾ cup) icing (confectioners') sugar, sifted
40 g (1½ oz/⅓ cup) cocoa powder or raw cacao powder
1 tablespoon milk

Baby's serve: because these cupcakes contain some added sugar, I recommend waiting until your baby is over 12 months before offering them to her. If you do wish to give her a small taste, skip the icing (frosting) and offer them to her as a muffin, broken into pieces she can easily hold.

Toddler's serve: as with baby's serve, you may wish to skip the icing to avoid the extra sugar. Simply serve as is, cut up as needed.

Preheat the oven to 170°C (340°F). Line a muffin tin with 15 paper or silicone cases.

In a large bowl, whisk together the eggs, maple syrup and oil. Stir in the beetroot and milk. Sift in the flour, baking powder and cocoa and stir until combined.

Divide the batter among the paper cases and bake in the oven for 20 minutes, or until a skewer inserted into the centre of the cupcakes comes out clean. Leave in the tin for 5 minutes, before transferring to a wire rack to cool completely.

To make the chocolate cream cheese icing, use an electric mixer to beat the butter and cream cheese until well combined and smooth. Add the icing sugar, cocoa and milk and beat until light and fluffy. Spread over the top of the cooled cupcakes and serve. The cupcakes can be stored in an airtight container.

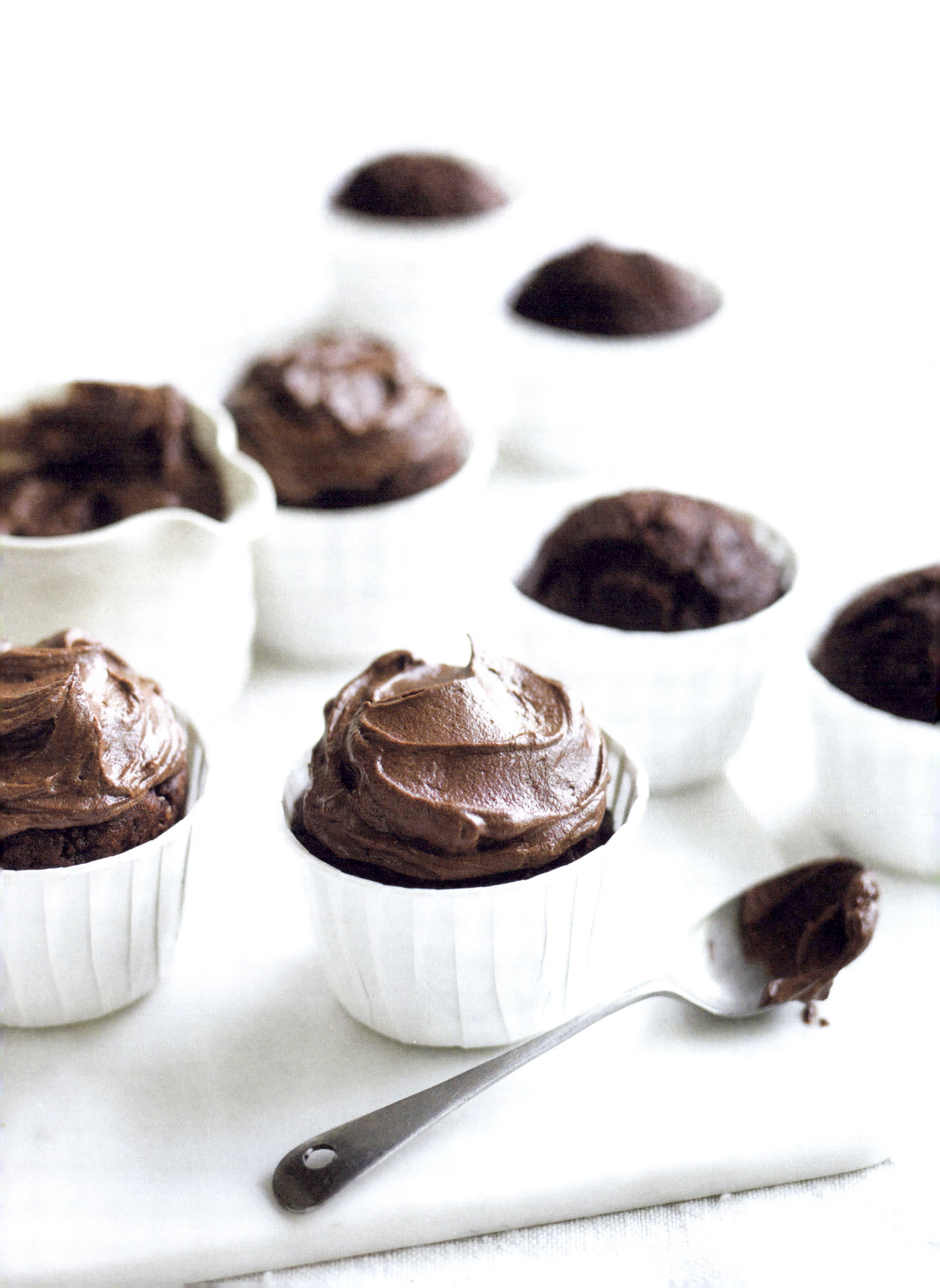

Jam thumbprint biscuits

Makes about 45

I used to make these with my mum when I was a little girl and I remember relishing the task of pressing thumbprints into the dough and filling the holes with jam. It somehow felt so naughty to be sticking my finger straight into the middle of a perfectly rolled ball of dough. Chilling the dough is not absolutely crucial, but it does stop the biscuits from spreading too much.

250 g (9 oz) butter, softened
150 g (5½ oz/¾ cup lightly packed) brown or rapadura sugar (see note, page 190)
1 teaspoon natural vanilla extract
1 egg
260 g (9 oz/1¾ cups) wholemeal (whole-wheat) plain (all-purpose) flour
55 g (2 oz/½ cup) ground hazelnuts
raspberry and apricot jam

Tip *The wholemeal flour makes these biscuits a healthier option, but if you don't have any on hand, you can use regular plain flour.*

Baby's serve: because these biscuits contain some added sugar, you should ideally wait until your baby is over 12 months before offering them to her.

Toddler's serve: because of the sugar content, serve only as an occasional treat. Simply serve as is, broken up if needed.

Preheat the oven to 180°C (350°F). Line two baking trays with baking paper.

Using an electric mixer, cream the butter and sugar until pale and fluffy. Add the vanilla and egg and beat until combined.

With the mixer on low speed, add the flour and ground hazelnuts, mixing until the dough just comes together to form a ball. Refrigerate for at least 1 hour.

Take 2 teaspoons of the dough at a time and roll into balls. Arrange on the prepared baking trays and flatten slightly by pressing your thumb or index finger (or the end of a wooden spoon) into the centre of each dough ball to make an indent.

Fill each indent with about ¼ teaspoon jam. Bake in the oven for 10–15 minutes, or until golden.

Remove from the oven and allow to cool for 5 minutes, before transferring to a wire rack to cool completely. Top up each indent with more jam, if needed, while they're still hot.

Desserts and baking

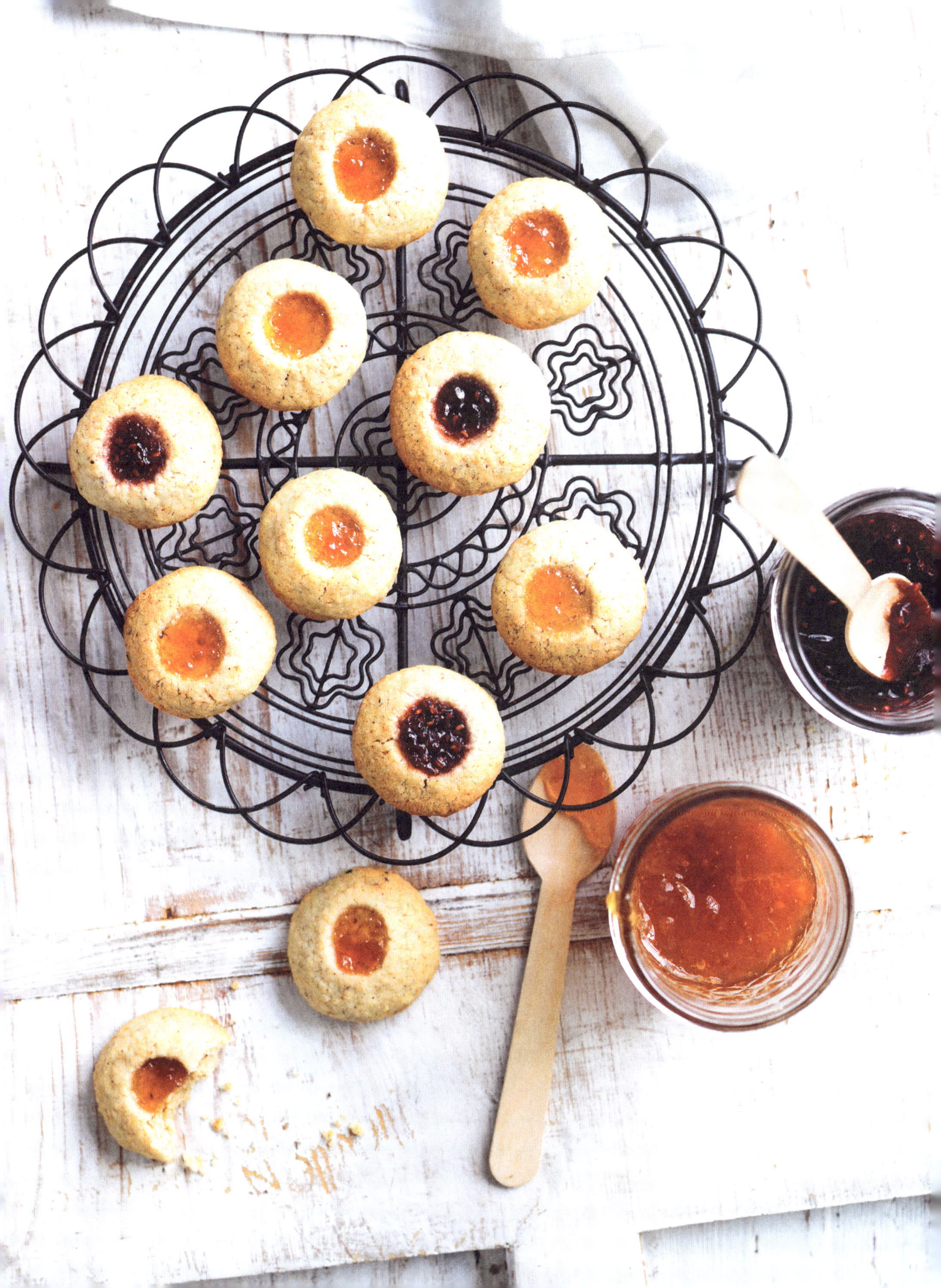

Chocolate coconut balls

Makes about 36

These look and taste like a delicious chocolatey treat, but actually they're filled with goodness from the fruit, almonds and coconut and there's very little chocolate in them. Plus, because of the natural sweetness of the dried fruit, they have no added sugar.

The best bit is they're incredibly easy to make – your child could happily get involved. If you need to make a nut-free version, replace the ground almonds with extra coconut or some nutritious wheatgerm, or you could use a ground seed mix (see tip on page 68).

100 g (3½ oz) pitted dates
170 g (6 oz) raisins or sultanas (golden raisins)
55 g (2 oz/½ cup) ground almonds
2 tablespoons raw cacao powder or cocoa powder (see note)
2½ tablespoons fresh orange juice
45 g (1½ oz/½ cup) desiccated coconut, plus extra for coating

Place the dates and raisins in a food processor and process until finely chopped. Add the ground almonds, cacao powder, orange juice and coconut and blend until the mixture forms a smooth paste.

Spread the extra coconut onto a clean surface. Using your hands, separate the mixture into small balls and roll in the coconut to coat. Store the chocolate coconut balls in an airtight container in the refrigerator for up to 1 week.

Tip *Raw cacao is similar to regular cocoa – both come from the cocoa bean – except that it's less processed and hasn't been heated to high temperatures, so it retains more nutrients including vitamin C, iron, fibre, polyphenols and other antioxidants. Just like cocoa, raw cacao does contain some caffeine and another stimulant called theobromine, so it should still be consumed in moderation.*

Baby's serve: because the cacao does contain small amounts of caffeine, you should ideally wait until your baby is over 12 months before offering these to her.

Toddler's serve: serve as is, broken up if needed. Again, because of the small amounts of caffeine in the cacao and the high levels of natural sugars in the dried fruit, offer these in moderation.

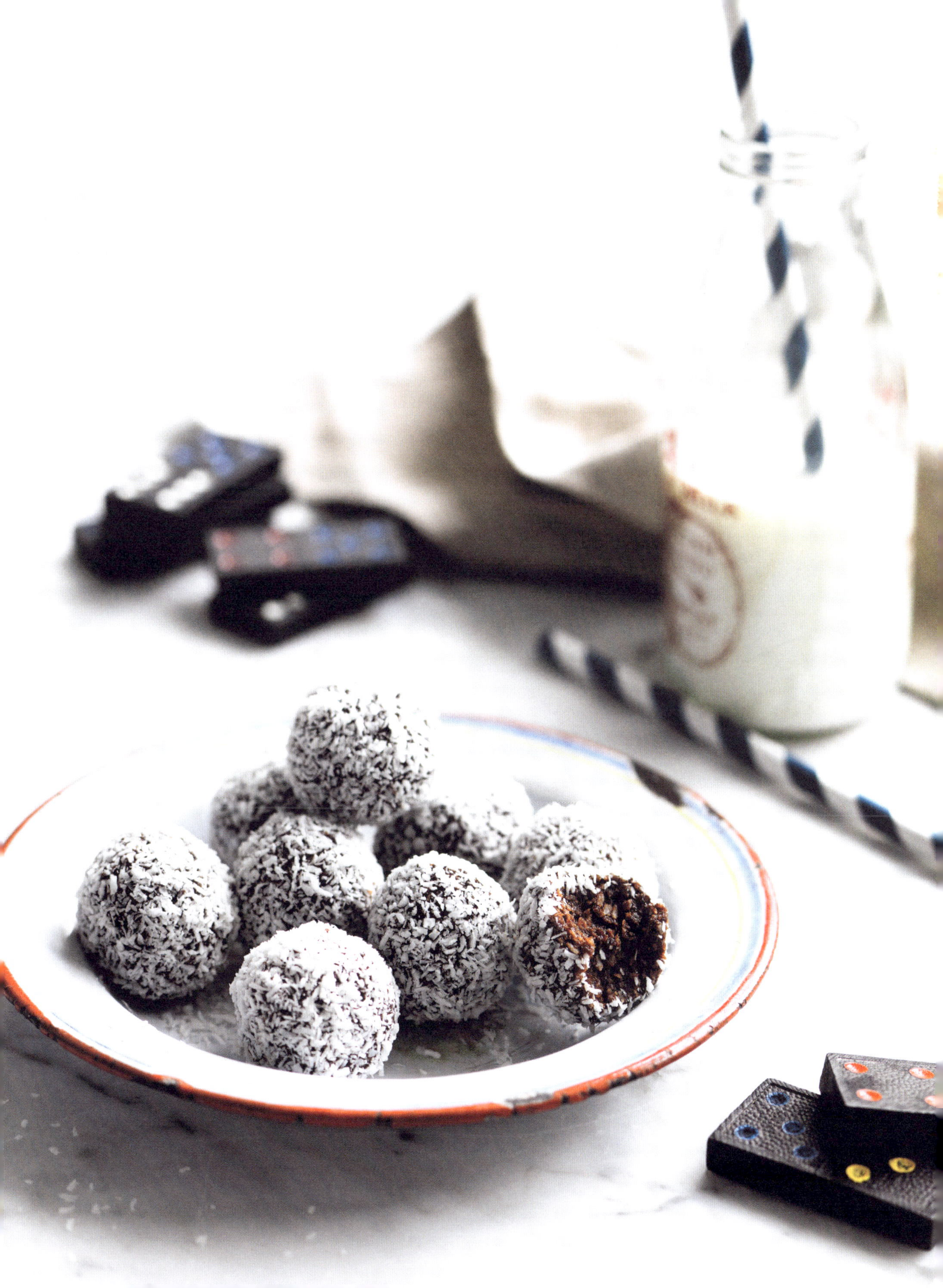

Cheese cut-out biscuits

Makes about 30–40 (depending on size of cutters)

These biscuits (cookies) are totally delicious and if you have a food processor or Thermomix, they couldn't be easier to make. Your child will love helping you with the cutting out. At Easter time, I make them with bunny cutters and use sultanas (golden raisins) for eyes. They are also sophisticated enough to be perfect for a grown-up gathering as a nibble with a glass of wine.

175 g (6 oz) plain (all-purpose) flour
50 g (1¾ oz/½ cup) grated parmesan cheese
50 g (1¾ oz/½ cup loosely packed) grated cheddar cheese
½ teaspoon paprika
125 g (4½ oz) butter, cubed
1 tablespoon cold water
sesame seeds and poppy seeds (optional), for decorating

Baby's serve: for a **younger baby**, wait until your baby is confident with finger foods (which may not happen until 8–9 months or older) before offering her one of these biscuits, broken up if needed. For an **older baby**, serve as is, broken up if needed.

Toddler's serve: serve as is.

Place the flour, cheeses and paprika in the bowl of a food processor and pulse for a few seconds until just combined. Add the butter and water and pulse until the mixture starts to ball around the blade. Turn the dough out onto a floured surface and knead very lightly. Divide the dough in half, form each half into a disc shape and wrap in plastic wrap (cling film). Refrigerate for 1 hour. (You can keep the dough in the refrigerator for up to 1 week before baking, or in the freezer for 2 months before thawing and baking.)

When ready to bake, preheat the oven to 180°C (350°F). Line two baking trays with baking paper. Roll the dough out to 5 mm (¼ inch) thickness all over. Use a pastry cutter to cut out the biscuits, arranging on the prepared trays. Lightly re-roll and cut any leftovers.

Sprinkle the sesame and poppy seeds over the biscuits, if liked. Bake in the oven for about 8 minutes, or until light golden and crisp.

Remove from the oven and transfer to a wire rack to cool. The biscuits can be stored in an airtight container.

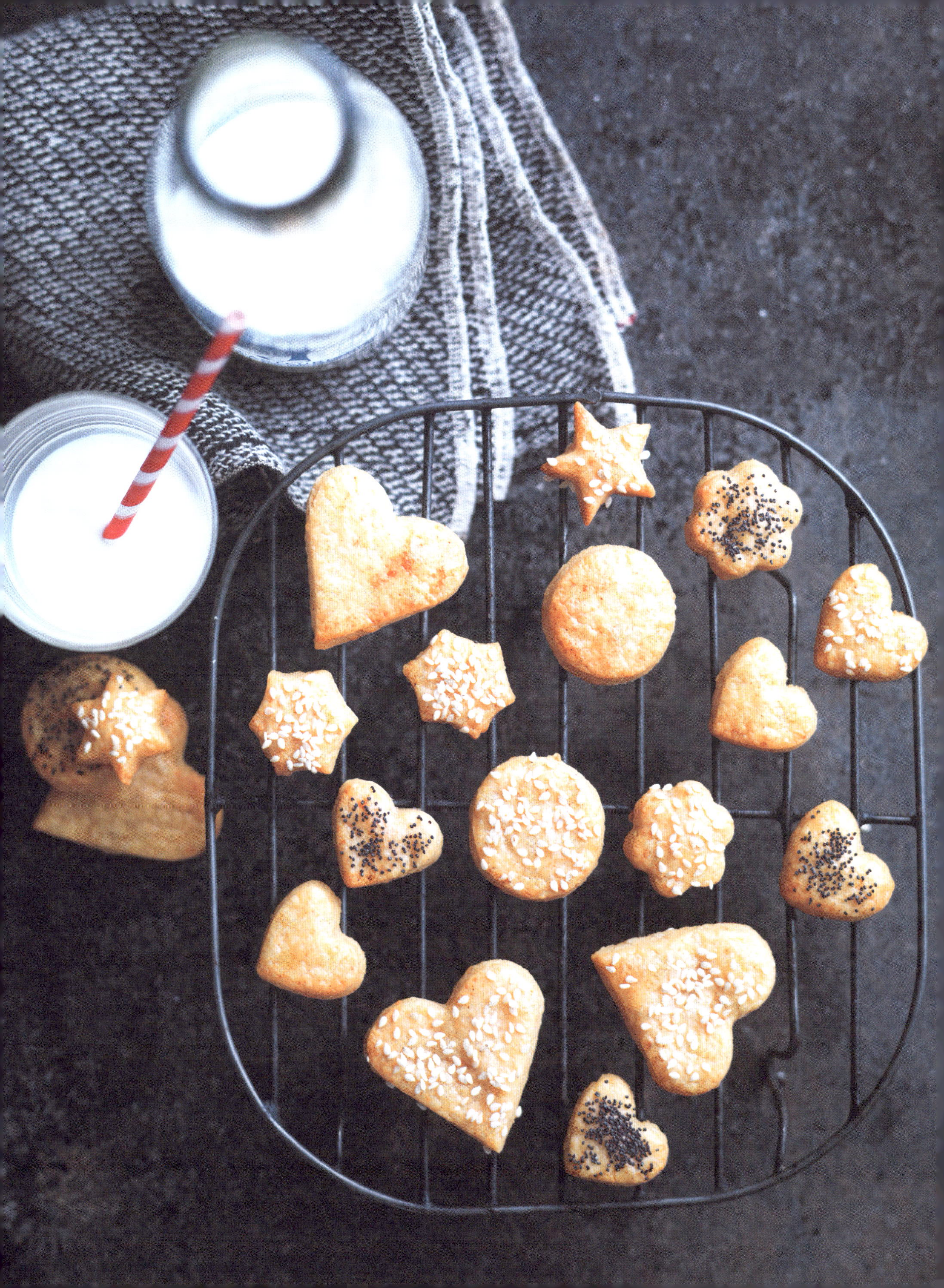

Oat and raisin biscuits

Makes about 28

These tasty biscuits (cookies) are a reliable favourite in my house. They're a bit like an ANZAC biscuit, but with extra protein from the eggs. Because they're nut-free, they're great for lunchboxes.

If you like, you can freeze the dough in balls so they're ready to bake when you need them.

125 g (4½ oz) butter
125 g (4½ oz/⅔ cup lightly packed) brown or rapadura sugar (see note, page 190)
2 tablespoons milk
2 eggs
150 g (5½ oz/1 cup) wholemeal (whole-wheat) self-raising flour
¼ teaspoon ground cinnamon
150 g (5½ oz/1½ cups) rolled oats
85 g (3 oz/⅔ cup) raisins or sultanas (golden raisins)

Using an electric mixer, cream the butter until soft. Beat in the sugar until light and fluffy. Add the milk and eggs and beat thoroughly until well combined. Add the flour and cinnamon and lightly mix through until just combined.

Remove the bowl from the mixer and stir through the oats and raisins. Refrigerate for 2 hours until the dough is firm (this is not crucial, but it does make the dough easier to work with).

Preheat the oven to 180°C (350°F). Lightly grease two baking trays. Take 1 heaped tablespoonful of the dough at a time and roll into balls. Arrange on the prepared trays, leaving 5 cm (2 inches) between each to allow for spreading. Using your hands, press down gently on each ball to flatten slightly.

Bake in the oven for about 15 minutes, or until golden. Remove from the oven, transfer to a wire rack and cool. Store the biscuits in an airtight container.

Baby's serve: because these biscuits do have some added sugar, you should ideally wait until your baby is over 12 months before offering some to her.

Toddler's serve: serve as is, breaking up if needed.

Desserts and baking

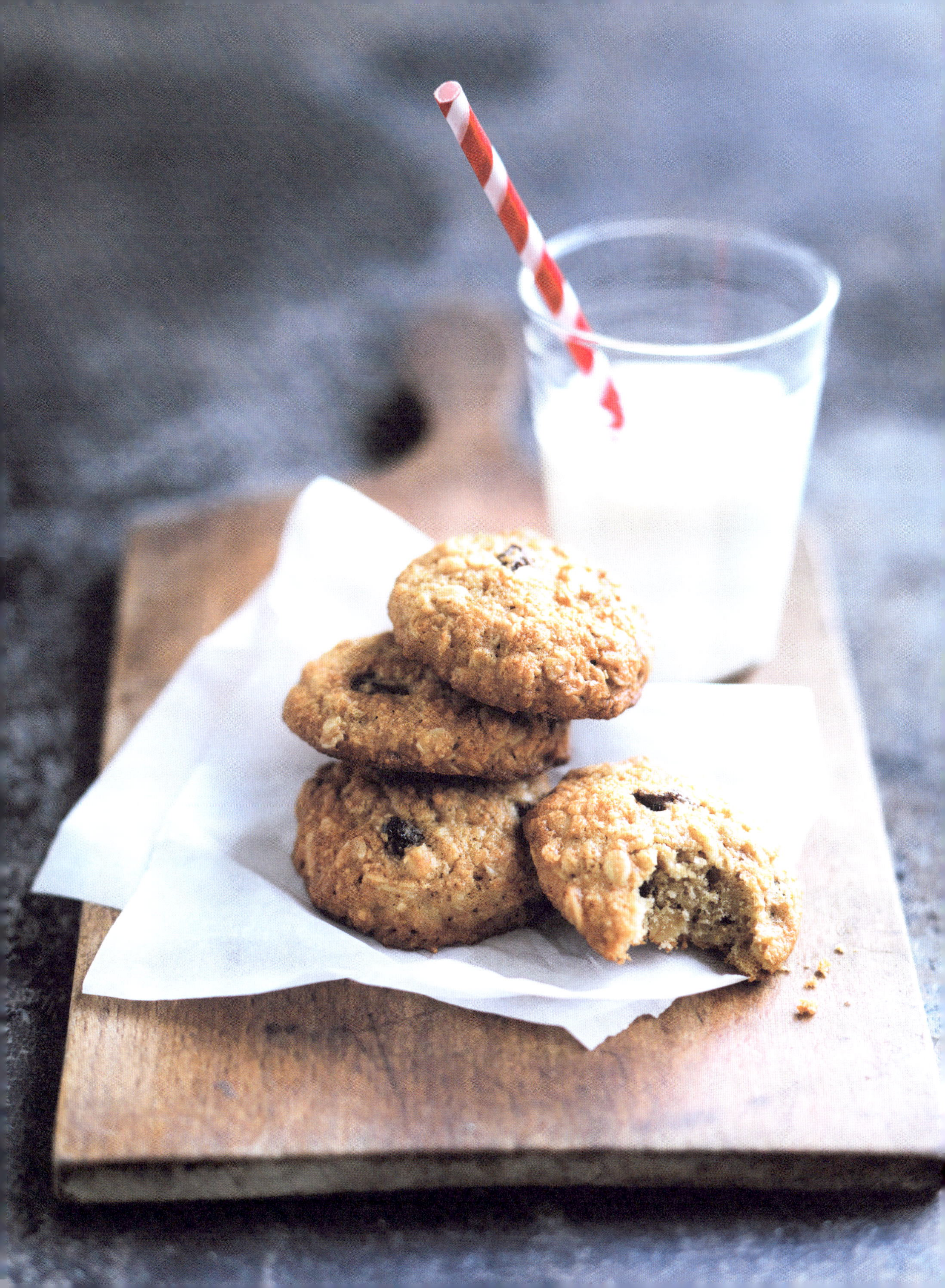

Your homemade cooking will almost certainly be more nourishing and tastier than anything you can buy. What's more, it teaches your children that cooking from scratch is the best way to live – and that's a lesson with lifelong health benefits.

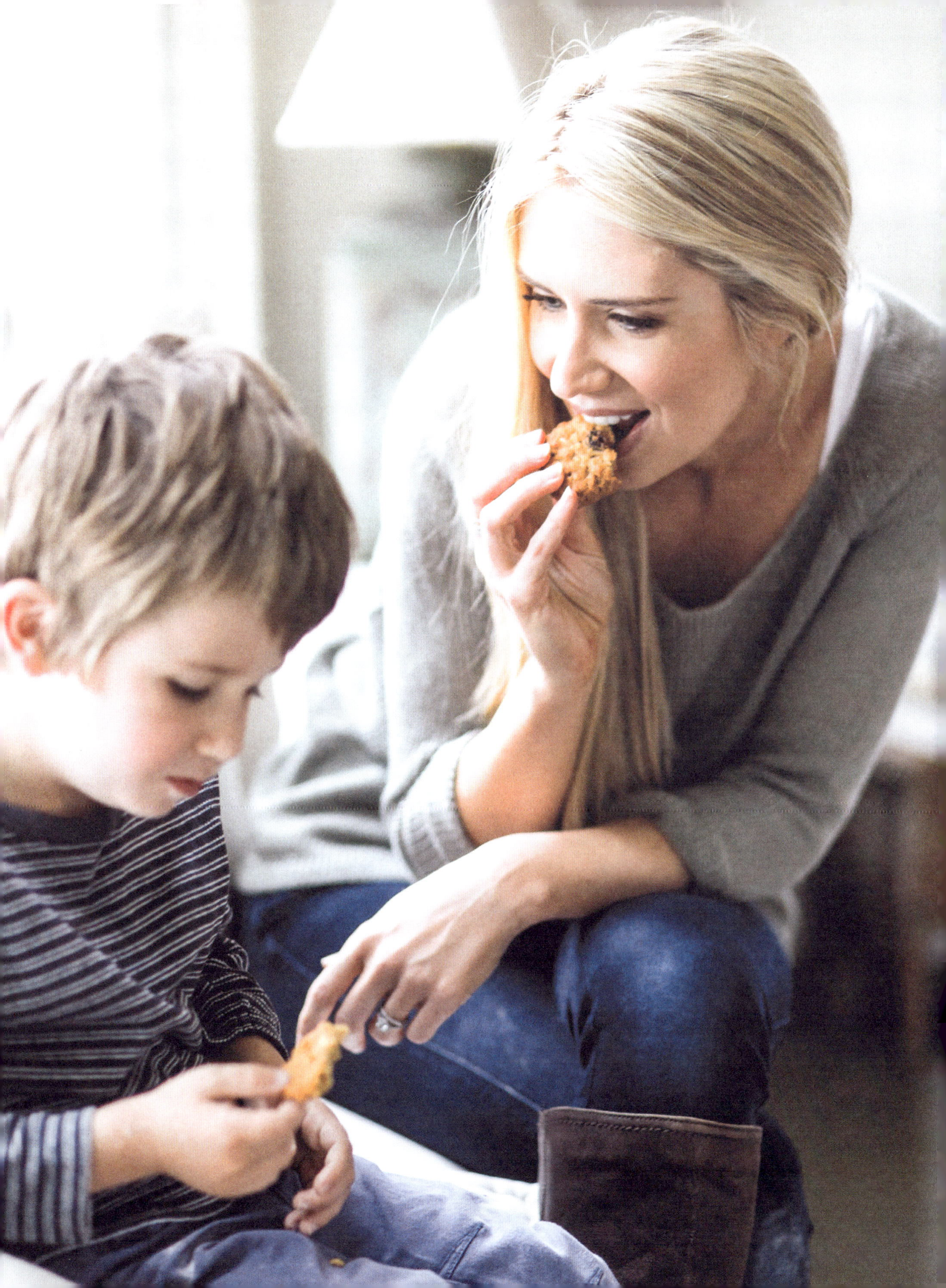

Carrot almond cake with lemon cream cheese icing

Makes 1 cake

Being on the healthier end of the cake spectrum, this cake is perfect for a children's birthday party. The batter can also be baked as muffins, which are moist and totally delicious – just skip the icing if you wish. If you don't have wholemeal flour on hand, that's fine, just use regular self-raising flour.

4 eggs
125 ml (4 fl oz/½ cup) milk
185 g (6½ oz/1 cup lightly packed) brown or rapadura sugar (see note, page 190)
250 ml (8½ fl oz/1 cup) olive oil
310 g (11 oz/2 cups firmly packed) grated carrot
100 g (3½ oz/1 cup) ground almonds
300 g (10½ oz/2 cups) wholemeal (whole-wheat) self-raising flour
1 teaspoon ground cinnamon

LEMON CREAM CHEESE ICING (FROSTING)
375 g (13 oz/1½ cups) cream cheese, softened
125 g (4 oz/1 cup) icing (confectioners') sugar, sifted
60 ml (2 fl oz/¼ cup) fresh lemon juice
finely grated zest of 1 lemon, plus extra to sprinkle on top (optional)

Baby's serve: because this cake does have some added sugar, you should ideally wait until your baby is over 12 months before offering it to her. If you do wish to give her a little taste, you can minimise the sugar by skipping the icing.

Toddler's serve: cut up as needed, skipping the icing for a low-sugar option.

Preheat the oven to 160°C (320°F). Grease and line two 20 cm (8 inch) round cake tins with baking paper.

Whisk together the eggs, milk, sugar and oil in a mixing bowl. Stir in the carrot and ground almonds. Add the flour and cinnamon, and stir until just combined.

Divide the mixture between the two cake tins and bake for about 30 minutes, or until a skewer inserted into the centre of the cakes comes out clean. Leave in the tins for 10 minutes, before transferring to a wire rack to cool.

To make the icing, use an electric mixer to beat together the cream cheese, icing sugar, lemon juice and lemon zest (if using), until well combined and smooth.

To assemble the cake, trim the domed top off one of the cakes once cooled. Place the trimmed cake on a cake stand, trimmed side up, and spread some of the icing on top. Top with the second cake, dome side up, and spread the remaining icing over the top. Scatter over some extra lemon zest, if liked.

Tip: For a nut-free version you can replace the almonds with a ground seed mix (see tip on page 68).

Desserts and baking

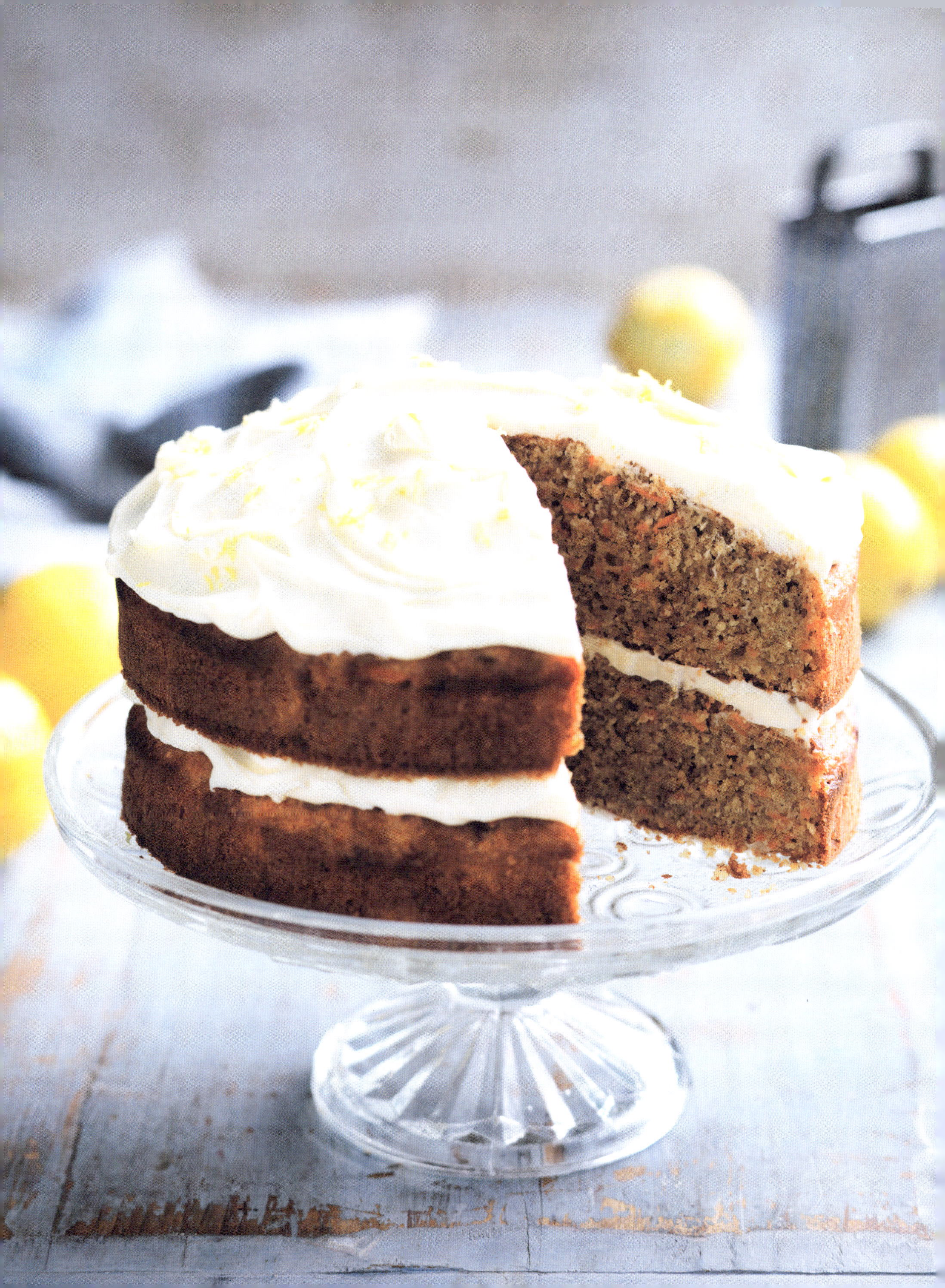

INDEX

Entries beginning with a capital letter are recipes; lower case entries refer to general topics.

A

academic performance 15
alcohol abuse 16
allergies 17, 19
  main causes 19
amount of food 26
asparagus: Boiled eggs with two green dippers 56
avocado
  Avocado salsa 54
  Baby beetroot salad with orange, avocado and walnuts 118
  Guacamole 112
avoidance of certain food/drinks 17–19, 28

B

babies
  and family meals 15, 16–17, 21, 22
  nutrition 23
  sun exposure 23
Baby beetroot salad with orange, avocado and walnuts 118
baby-led weaning 19, 24
Banana date puddings 200
Banana, hazelnut and honey bread 210
Banana oat breakfast muffins 74
barley: Lamb and barley soup 130
beans
  Broad bean dip 56
  Broad bean yoghurt sauce 106
  Chicken with cherry tomatoes and butter beans 170
  dried beans 52
  Edamame yoghurt purée 80
  Homemade baked beans 52
  Osso bucco with white bean purée 180
  Straight-up edamame 80
beef
  Beef meatballs with roasted eggplant dip 86
  Beef and vegetable pie 178
  Mini burgers with guacamole 112
  Slow-cooked beef ragu with penne 152
beetroot
  Baby beetroot salad with orange, avocado and walnuts 118
  Chocolate beetroot cupcakes 214
Best pumpkin soup 128
biscuits
  Cheese cut-out biscuits 220
  Jam thumbprint biscuits 216
  Oat and raisin biscuits 222
Black coconut rice 198
blenders 21
Boiled eggs with two green dippers 56
bread, Banana, hazelnut and honey 210
breakfast 33, 37
breastmilk 17, 19, 22
  amount 23
Broad bean dip 56

C

Calamari with tartare sauce 100
calcium 29, 33
calcium deficiency 32
Cardamom rosemary baked custards 194
carrots
  Carrot almond cake with lemon cream cheese icing 226
  Carrot quinoa muffins 208
  Chicken schnitzel with mushy peas and purple carrots 164
cauliflower
  Cauliflower macaroni cheese 150
  Herb crusted lamb racks with roast pumpkin and cauliflower purée 174
  Pumpkin cauliflower dal 154
cheese
  Cauliflower macaroni cheese 150
  Cheese cut-out biscuits 220
  Chocolate cream cheese icing 214
  Lemon cream cheese icing 226
  Orange cream cheese icing 212
  Ricotta gnocchi with cherry tomato sauce 144
  soft cheeses 38
  Sweet potato rösti with herbed ricotta and poached egg 58
  Tomato and bocconcini wholemeal pizza 110
  Zucchini, pea and ricotta frittata 114
chewing 17, 19
chicken
  Chicken with cherry tomatoes and butter beans 170
  Chicken ginger wontons 108
  Chicken, mushroom and leek pot pies 168
  Chicken sausage rolls 84
  Chicken schnitzel with mushy peas and purple carrots 164
  Chicken and soba noodle soup 132
  Crunchy chicken bites 96
  Fried brown rice with chicken and snow peas 138
  Quinoa chicken rissoles 92
  Red quinoa and chicken salad 134
  Thai green chicken curry with eggplant 162
Chocolate beetroot cupcakes 214
Chocolate coconut balls 218
Chocolate cream cheese icing 214
choking 19, 21, 24, 28
coconut
  Black coconut rice 198
  Chocolate coconut balls 218
  coconut chips 46
  Strawberry coconut porridge 46
cookies *see* biscuits
Cooking For Your Baby and Toddler 16, 24
couscous: Seafood and pearl couscous stew 158
cow's milk 17, 18, 19, 21
Crêpes with warm maple oranges 66
Crunchy chicken bites 96
Cucumber dipping sauce 98
cupcakes

Index

Chocolate beetroot cupcakes 214
Pumpkin and walnut cupcakes 212

D
dal, Pumpkin cauliflower 154
desserts
   Banana date puddings 200
   Black coconut rice 198
   Cardamom rosemary baked custards 194
   Peach almond crumble 190
   Poached pears with whole-egg custard 188
   Roasted rhubarb and strawberry 186
   Strawberry jellies 204
   Yoghurt panna cotta with mango 196
dinner 123
dips
   Guacamole 112
   Roasted eggplant dip 86
dressings *see* sauces/dressings
drinks to avoid 17–19
drug use 16

E
eating disorders 16, 32
Edamame yoghurt purée 80
eggplant
   Roasted eggplant dip 86
   Thai green chicken curry with eggplant 162
eggs 17, 18, 19, 32
   Boiled eggs with two green dippers 56
   Cardamom rosemary baked custards 194
   French toast with raspberry apple purée 72
   Mediterranean baked eggs 60
   Picnic eggs 94
   Poached pears with whole-egg custard 188
   Sweet potato rösti with herbed ricotta and poached egg 58

F
familiarity of food 22, 26
family cohesion 16
family meals
   and babies 15, 16–24
   benefits 14–16
   and teenagers 15, 16
   and toddlers 24–30
fats 23
Fig bircher muesli 44
finger food 19, 21, 24, 28
fish
   Flathead fillets with pepita pesto 156
   Salmon with roasted fennel purée and crispy smashed potatoes 160
   Sesame-crunch fish fingers with broad bean yoghurt sauce 106
   Sweetcorn fritters with smoked salmon 54
   Thai fish cakes 98
   Tuna and sweet potato logs 88
   see also seafood
Five-vegetable pasta 142
Flathead fillets with pepita pesto 156
fluoride 21
food fussiness *see* fussy eaters
food neophobia 22, 24
food poisoning 22, 38
food refusal *see* fussy eaters
food rewards 27
food to avoid 17–19, 28
French toast with raspberry apple purée 72
Fresh fruit with cinnamon ricotta yoghurt 38
Fried brown rice with chicken and snow peas 138
frittata, Zucchini, pea and ricotta 114
frosting *see* icing
fruit
   French toast with raspberry apple purée 72
   Fresh fruit with cinnamon ricotta yoghurt 38
   Hazelnut oat pancakes with crushed berry sauce 68
   Raspberry and pear quinoa porridge 40
   Roasted rhubarb and strawberry 186
   Spiced fruit compote 50
   Stone fruit almond tarts 202
   Three-grain blueberry and apricot porridge 42
   Wholemeal almond berry pikelets 62
   Wholemeal blueberry scones 70
fruit skins 50
fussy eaters 15, 24–8, 29, 30

G
growth of child 26
Guacamole 112

H
Hazelnut dressing 134
Hazelnut oat pancakes with crushed berry sauce 68
Herb-crusted lamb racks with roast pumpkin and cauliflower purée 174
Herb yoghurt sauce 84
high-fibre foods 23
Homemade baked beans 52
hunger 26

I
ices, Pink grapefruit raspberry 206
icing
   Chocolate cream cheese 214
   Lemon cream cheese 226
   Orange cream cheese 212
iron 17
   baby 23, 24
   daily intake 30
   and milk 29
   teens 33
   toddlers 29

J
Jam thumbprint biscuits 216
juice 23, 29

L
lamb
   Herb-crusted lamb racks with roast pumpkin and cauliflower purée 174
   Lamb and barley soup 130
   Lamb souvlaki with tzatziki 116
   Oven-braised lamb shanks with creamy polenta 176
   Shepherd's pie with parsnip and pumpkin topping 172
Lemon cream cheese icing 226
LSA 44

M

Mediterranean baked eggs 60
menstruation 33
mental health 15
milk
   daily intake 33
   and iron 29
   see also breastmilk; cow's milk
Mini burgers with guacamole 112
muffins
   Banana oat breakfast muffins 74
   Carrot quinoa muffins 208
   Vegetable muffins 82
mushrooms
   Chicken, mushroom and leek pot pies 168
   Mushroom and spinach lasagne 148
Mussel fritters 102

N

noodles: Chicken and soba noodle soup 132
nut oils 62
nutrients destroyed by heat 23
nutrition 14, 30
   babies 23
   school-age children 33
   toddlers 29
nuts 18, 19

O

oats
   Banana oat breakfast muffins 74
   Fig bircher muesli 44
   Hazelnut oat pancakes with crushed berry sauce 68
   Oat and raisin biscuits 222
   Three-grain blueberry and apricot porridge 42
omega 3 fats 32
oranges
   Baby beetroot salad with orange, avocado and walnuts 118
   Crêpes with warm maple oranges 66
   Orange cream cheese icing 212
Osso bucco with white bean purée 180
Oven-braised lamb shanks with creamy polenta 176

P

pasta
   Cauliflower macaroni cheese 150
   Five-vegetable pasta 142
   Mushroom and spinach lasagne 148
   Slow-cooked beef ragu with penne 152
Peach almond crumble 190
peak bone mass 33
pears
   Poached pears with whole-egg custard 188
   Raspberry and pear quinoa porridge 40
peas
   Chicken schnitzel with mushy peas and purple carrots 164
   Fried brown rice with chicken and snow peas 138
   Pea and prawn risotto 140
   Zucchini, pea and mint soup 124
   Zucchini, pea and ricotta frittata 114
performance anxiety 28
picky eaters *see* fussy eaters
Picnic eggs 94
pies
   Beef and vegetable pie 178
   Chicken, mushroom and leek pot pies 168
Pink grapefruit raspberry ices 206
pizza, Tomato and bocconcini wholemeal 110
Poached pears with whole-egg custard 188
polenta: Oven-braised lamb shanks with creamy polenta 176
porridge
   Raspberry and pear quinoa porridge 40
   Strawberry coconut porridge 46
   Three-grain blueberry and apricot porridge 42
positive mealtimes 28
potatoes, Salmon with roasted fennel purée and crispy smashed 160
protein 32
pumpkin
   Best pumpkin soup 128
   Herb-crusted lamb racks with roast pumpkin and cauliflower purée 174
   Pumpkin cauliflower dal 154
   Pumpkin and walnut cupcakes 212
   Shepherd's pie with parsnip and pumpkin topping 172
purées 21
   consistency 19, 22
   preparing 21–2
   storing 22, 72

Q

quinoa
   Carrot quinoa muffins 208
   Quinoa chicken rissoles 92
   Raspberry and pear quinoa porridge 40
   Red quinoa and chicken salad 134

R

rapadura sugar 190
Raspberry and pear quinoa porridge 40
Red quinoa and chicken salad 134
restriction of food 27–8
rice
   Black coconut rice 198
   Fried brown rice with chicken and snow peas 138
   Pea and prawn risotto 140
Ricotta gnocchi with cherry tomato sauce 144
Roasted rhubarb and strawberry 186
role models 27
rusks 21

S

salads
   Baby beetroot salad with orange, avocado and walnuts 118
   Red quinoa and chicken salad 134
   Tzatziki 116

Wild rice, prawn and mango salad 136
Salmon with roasted fennel purée and crispy smashed potatoes 160
salt 124
sauces/dressings
　Broad bean yoghurt sauce 106
　Cherry tomato sauce 144
　Crushed berry sauce 68
　Cucumber dipping sauce 98
　Hazelnut dressing 134
　Herb yoghurt sauce 84
　Lemon parsley sauce 174
　Sesame dressing 136
　Tartare sauce 100
　Tofu mayonnaise 94
school-age children 30–3
　nutrition 33
scones, Wholemeal blueberry 70
seafood
　Calamari with tartare sauce 100
　Mussel fritters 102
　Pea and prawn risotto 140
　Seafood chowder 126
　Seafood and pearl couscous stew 158
　Wild rice, prawn and mango salad 136
　see also fish
self-feeding 28, 30
Sesame-crunch fish fingers with broad bean yoghurt sauce 106
Sesame dressing 136
Shepherd's pie with parsnip and pumpkin topping 172
Slow-cooked beef ragu with penne 152
snacks 29, 33, 79
soft drinks 33
solid foods
　best age for 17
　introducing 15, 16
　timing of 17
　see also purées
soup 22
　Best pumpkin soup 128
　Chicken and soba noodle soup 132
　Lamb and barley soup 130
　Seafood chowder 126
　Zucchini, pea and mint soup 124
sparkling water 21
Spiced fruit compote 50
Spinach and mushroom lasagne 148
Stone fruit almond tarts 202
Straight-up edamame 80
Strawberry coconut porridge 46
Strawberry jellies 204
sugar 18, 29
sulphites 42
sun exposure 23
sweet potato
　Sweet potato rösti with herbed ricotta and poached egg 58
　Tuna and sweet potato logs 88
Sweetcorn fritters with smoked salmon 54

T
tarts, Stone fruit almond 202
taste preferences 14–15, 22, 24
teenagers
　and family meals 15, 16
　food choices 30, 33
temperature danger zone 22
texture of food 19, 25, 28
Thai fish cakes 98
Thai green chicken curry with eggplant 162
Three-grain blueberry and apricot porridge 42
toddlers
　and family meals 24–30
　nutrition 29
Tofu mayonnaise 94
tomatoes
　Cherry tomato sauce 144
　Chicken with cherry tomatoes and butter beans 170
　Tomato and bocconcini wholemeal pizza 110
Tuna and sweet potato logs 88
Tzatziki 116

U
unhealthy food 27, 33

V
variety 29
vegan diet 32
vegetables
　Five-vegetable pasta 142
　Vegetable muffins 82
vegetarian diet 30, 32
vitamin B12 32
vitamin D 23, 32
vitamin supplements 29

W
waste of food 25
water 21, 23
wholegrains 23
Wholemeal almond berry pikelets 62
Wholemeal blueberry scones 70
Wild rice, prawn and mango salad 136

Y
yoghurt 21
　Edamame yoghurt purée 80
　Fresh fruit with cinnamon ricotta yoghurt 38
　Herb yoghurt sauce 84
　Yoghurt panna cotta with mango 196

Z
zinc 32
Zucchini, pea and mint soup 124
Zucchini, pea and ricotta frittata 114

Published in 2014 by Hardie Grant Books

Hardie Grant Books (Australia)
Ground Floor, Building 1
658 Church Street
Richmond, Victoria 3121
www.hardiegrant.com.au

Hardie Grant Books (UK)
Dudley House, North Suite
34–35 Southampton Street
London WC2E 7HF
www.hardiegrant.co.uk

All rights reserved. No part of this publication may be reproduced, stored in a retrieval system or transmitted in any form by any means, electronic, mechanical, photocopying, recording or otherwise, without the prior written permission of the publishers and copyright holders.

The moral rights of the author have been asserted.

Copyright text © Louise Fulton Keats
Copyright photography © Ben Dearnley
Copyright design © Hardie Grant Books 2014

A Cataloguing-in-Publication entry is available from the catalogue of the National Library of Australia at www.nla.gov.au

Something for Everyone

978 1 74270 719 8

Publishing Director: Paul McNally
Managing Editor: Lucy Heaver
Editor: Jacqui Blanchard
Designer: Arielle Gamble
Photographer: Ben Dearnley
Stylist: Michelle Noeriento
Production Manager: Todd Rechner

Colour reproduction by Splitting Image Colour Studio
Printed in China by 1010 Printing International Limited

Find this book on **Cooked.**

cooked.com.au
cooked.co.uk

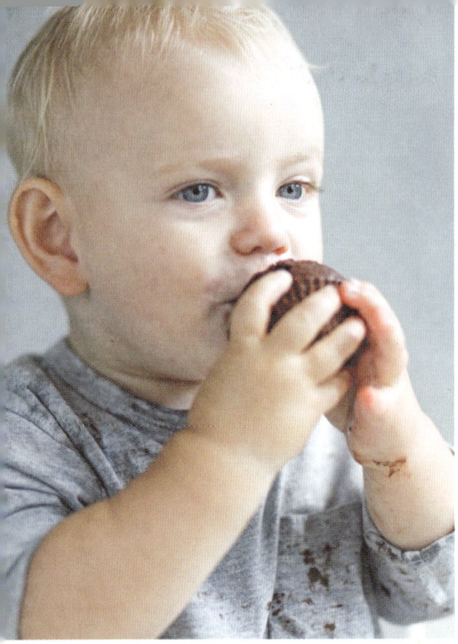
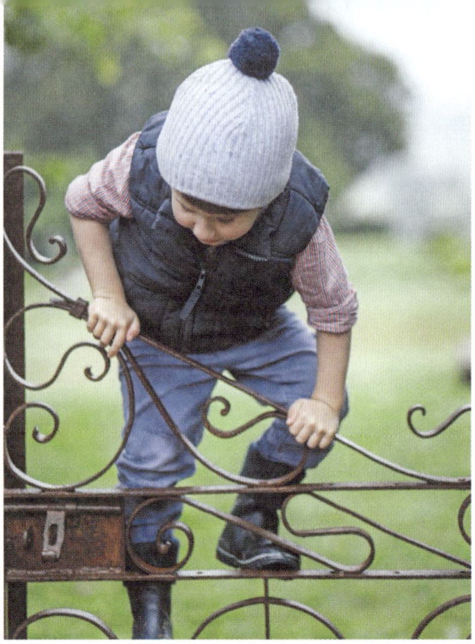
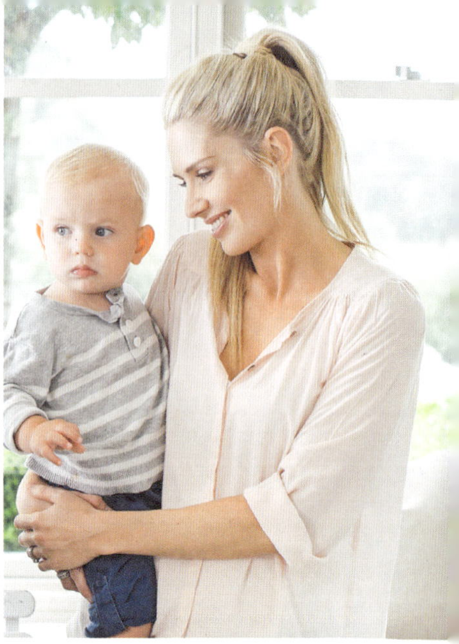
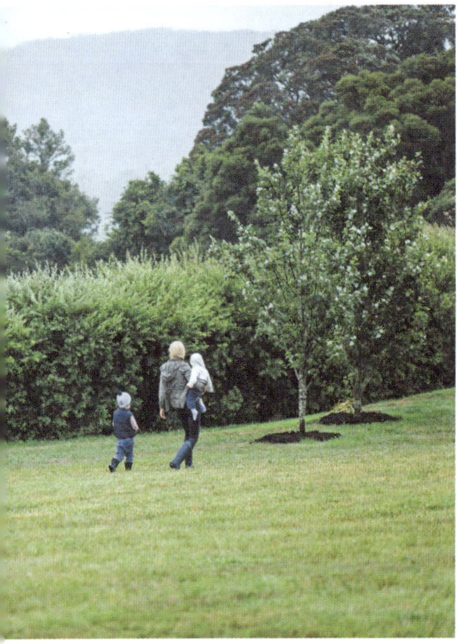
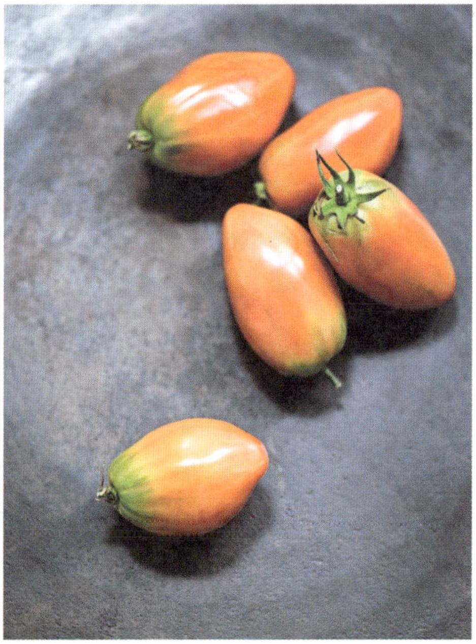
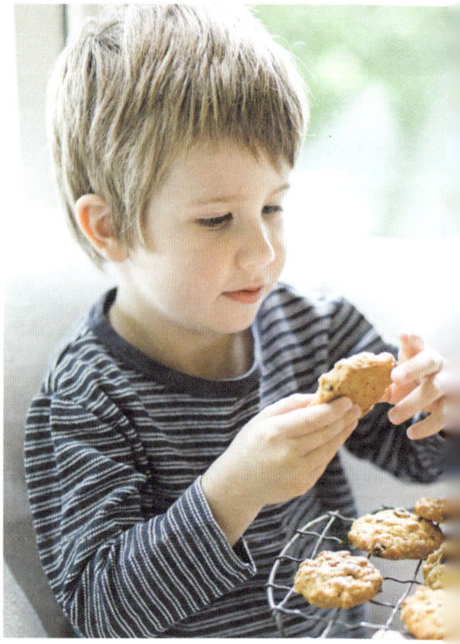
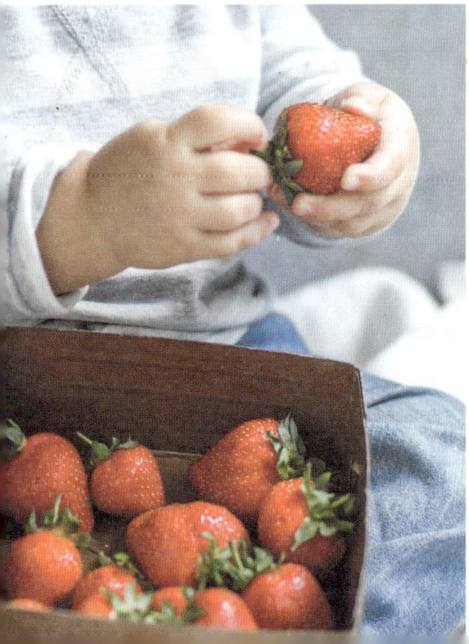
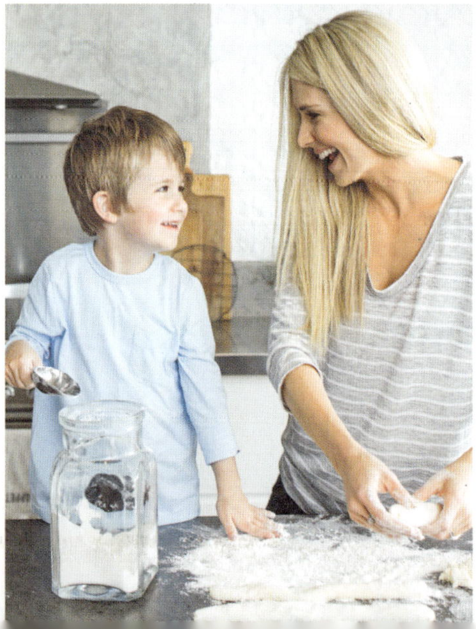
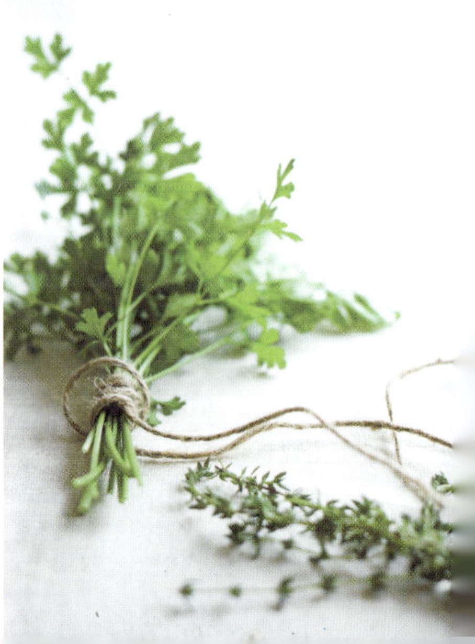